Dear Valued Customer,

We realize you're a busy professional with deadlines to hit. Whether your goal is to learn a new technology or solve a critical problem, we want to be there to lend you a hand. Our primary objective is to provide you with the insight and knowledge you need to stay atop the highly competitive and ever-changing technology industry.

Wiley Publishing, Inc., offers books on a wide variety of technical categories, including security, data warehousing, software development tools, and networking — everything you need to reach your peak. Regardless of your level of expertise, the Wiley family of books has you covered.

- For Dummies® – The *fun* and *easy* way™ to learn
- The Weekend Crash Course® –The *fastest* way to learn a new tool or technology
- Visual – For those who prefer to learn a new topic *visually*
- The Bible – The *100% comprehensive* tutorial and reference
- The Wiley Professional list – *Practical* and *reliable* resources for IT professionals

The book you hold now, *Complete Flash Remoting MX*, is the expert guide to this exciting new Macromedia® Flash™ technology. Inside, Flash programming expert Joey Lott skillfully explains the theory necessary to understand this amazing technology, and then guides you through Flash Remoting with ColdFusion®, J2EE™, and .NET. Packed with hands-on instructions and plenty of complete example applications, this book is everything you need to master the power of Flash Remoting MX to quickly and easily integrate server-side services into your Flash MX applications.

Our commitment to you does not end at the last page of this book. We'd want to open a dialog with you to see what other solutions we can provide. Please be sure to visit us at www.wiley.com/compbooks to review our complete title list and explore the other resources we offer. If you have a comment, suggestion, or any other inquiry, please locate the "contact us" link at www.wiley.com.

Finally, we encourage you to review the following page for a list of Wiley titles on related topics. Thank you for your support and we look forward to hearing from you and serving your needs again in the future.

Sincerely,

Richard K. Swadley

Richard K. Swadley
Vice President & Executive Group Publisher
Wiley Technology Publishing

Visual

Bible

DUMMIES

WILEY
Wiley Publishing, Inc.

*more information
on related titles*

The Next Level of Flash MX Books
Available from Wiley Technology Publishing

Flash MX Design for TV and Video
0-7645-3681-8

Your guide to broadcast-quality Flash animations

Macromedia Flash MX ActionScript Bible
0-7645-3614-1

Discover how to architect interactive Flash MX projects

Flash MX Bible
0-7645-3656-7

Take your projects to the next level with tips and techniques from over 30 Flash experts

50 Fast Macromedia Flash MX Techniques
0-7645-3692-3

Your easy guide to Flash MX tricks and techniques

INTERMEDIATE/ADVANCED

BEGINNER

Complete Flash™ Remoting MX

Complete Flash™ Remoting MX

Joey Lott

WILEY

Wiley Publishing, Inc.

Complete Flash™ Remoting MX

Published by
Wiley Publishing, Inc.
10475 Crosspoint Boulevard
Indianapolis, IN 46256
www.wiley.com

Copyright © 2003 by Wiley Publishing, Inc., Indianapolis, Indiana

Published simultaneously in Canada

LOC: 2002114846

ISBN: 0-7645-2586-7

Manufactured in the United States of America

10 9 8 7 6 5 4 3 2 1

1B/SU/QS/QT/IN

WILEY is a trademark of Wiley Publishing, Inc.

About the Author

Joey Lott currently resides in Los Angeles, California. He has taught ActionScript and Flash Remoting classes and is the co-author of *Macromedia® Flash™ MX ActionScript Bible* (Wiley, 2002). Joey enjoys hearing from readers and welcomes any inquiries at joey@person13.com.

Credits

Executive Editor
Chris Webb

Project Editor
Eric Newman

Technical Editors
Jen and Peter deHaan
Michael Angelo Libio
Niko Alejandre

Copy Editor
Luann Rouff

Editorial Manager
Mary Beth Wakefield

Vice President & Executive Group Publisher
Richard Swadley

Vice President and Executive Publisher
Bob Ipsen

Executive Editorial Director
Mary Bednarek

Project Coordinator
Dale White

Graphics and Production Specialists
Jennifer Click
Carrie Foster
Kristin McMullan
Heather Pope
Jeremey Unger

Quality Control Technicians
Laura Albert
Dave Faust
Andy Hollandbeck
Carl Pierce

Proofreading and Indexing
TECHBOOKS Production Services

This book is dedicated to That which we all are.

Preface

Macromedia Flash has established itself as one of the premier Web technologies. Early on, Flash took its place as an alternative to the comparatively flat and lackluster "brochure" Web sites of the late 1990s. Since then, Flash has certainly evolved in leaps and bounds. ActionScript, the scripting language of Flash, has undergone the most dramatic transformation of any of the application's elements, and yet up until recently, developers have struggled with finding viable solutions for using Flash as a user interface to applications that rely heavily on dynamic data.

Gone are the days of static Web content. Today, successful Web sites offer users experiences rich in content, and services ranging from the sale of products to the provision of a wide array of resources. It is commonplace today to purchase items, to do banking and bill paying, and to conduct all kinds of research online. However, although the available content is rich, the presentation is often anything but. Flash Remoting, a new technology from Macromedia, enables Flash movies to efficiently and effectively interact with back-end logic on the server. This technology reinvents the way in which Web applications are built and utilized by enabling you, the developer, to create rich-media, dynamic, data-driven applications with Flash user interfaces.

In *Complete Flash™ Remoting MX*, you learn about this powerful new technology — what it can do, and how you can use it. Flash Remoting is a specific technology that enables you to create interactions between your Flash movies and server-side applications built in ColdFusion, Java, or .NET. Flash Remoting is not a standalone technology — it does not provide much functionality on its own. Rather, it helps you to bring together otherwise disparate pieces to form a whole, integrated application. For this reason, a complete discussion of the subject requires looking at a wide range of technologies, including ActionScript, databases and SQL, ColdFusion MX, Java and J2EE application servers, and the .NET Framework. In this book, you can learn how each of these technologies fits together with Flash Remoting. Volumes have been written about each of these technologies separately, and so while every attempt is made to provide you with as much essential information as possible in each area, I necessarily assume that you have some background in Flash and at least one of the server technologies (ColdFusion MX, J2EE, or .NET).

Who Should Read This Book

If you are interested in building new and exciting, data-driven applications using Flash as the user interface, then this book is for you. Successful Flash Remoting applications comprise at least two parts: the Flash user interface and the server-side application portion. Therefore, in order to get the most from this book, you will benefit from some prior knowledge of Flash and ActionScript, as well as of one of the server-side technologies with which Flash Remoting works (ColdFusion MX, J2EE, or .NET). I have done my best to structure this book so that it is accessible to both Flash/ActionScript developers with even just the tiniest bit of server-side development experience as well as those who are experienced in server-side development with minimal Flash/ActionScript knowledge.

Necessarily, I assume that you already have some background in Flash, but extensive knowledge is not essential. If you have only minimal experience with Flash and ActionScript, you can still gain much from this book. For those of you who need a little refresher on using ActionScript, Chapter 2 provides just such a crash course. While it is certainly not meant to offer complete coverage of ActionScript, it does cover the essentials necessary to get started working with Flash Remoting. If you want a more in-depth coverage of ActionScript, I recommend *Macromedia® Flash™ MX ActionScript Bible* (Wiley, 2002), which I co-wrote with Robert Reinhardt.

To get started, I recommend you use the server-side technology with which you are already most familiar. This book includes parts for ColdFusion MX, J2EE, and .NET. I do not attempt to offer basic information for working with Java or .NET but assume that if you choose to work with one of these technologies, you are already familiar with the language syntax and structure. If you are an ActionScript developer who is just getting started with server-side development, and if you are using this book as your only reference, then I highly recommend you choose ColdFusion MX as your server-side technology. For any such readers, I provide rather extensive introductory material for getting started with ColdFusion MX.

This book is mainly intended for readers with adventurous spirits. Flash has always been for those who want to learn something new and forge new pathways. Flash Remoting is no different. I hope this book finds its way to you and assists you in your own personal adventures, and I look forward to seeing you share your gifts with us all.

How This Book Is Organized

This book is organized into five parts.

Part I: Introducing Flash Remoting

The first four chapters of this book cover the essentials for getting started with Flash Remoting. You learn what Flash Remoting is and how it works. In addition, you can refresh yourself about ActionScript fundamentals and then apply that knowledge as you learn the new ActionScript that is specific to Flash Remoting. Because databases are likely to be an important part of many Flash Remoting applications, this part of the book includes information about databases and how Flash Remoting interacts with them, including extensive coverage of the new RecordSet ActionScript class. Additionally, Part I discusses Web services — what they are and how to use them with Flash Remoting.

Part II: Flash Remoting with ColdFusion

Part II offers extensive coverage of using ColdFusion MX with Flash Remoting. In the chapters in this part of the book, you learn about getting started with ColdFusion MX and working with ColdFusion pages and Components with Flash Remoting. Part II also includes extensive coverage of ColdFusion's Web services, special ways in which ColdFusion can interact with databases, and a special feature of Flash Remoting that enables you to develop server-side functionality using ActionScript.

Part III: Flash Remoting with J2EE Application Servers

Part III discusses working with Flash Remoting for J2EE. In these chapters, you can learn about setting up and configuring your application server to work with Flash Remoting — including special configuration instructions if you are working with JRun 4. Also covered are servlets and JavaServer Pages, Enterprise JavaBeans, and JRun-only topics.

Part IV: Flash Remoting with .NET

In the fourth part of the book, you learn about using Microsoft's .NET Framework with Flash Remoting. You learn about setting up and configuring a Web application, as well as how to write ASP.NET pages and assembly libraries (DLLs) to work with Flash Remoting. In addition, you can learn about using Web services with .NET.

Part V: Building Remoting Applications

The chapters in the final part of the book take you through the process of building complete applications using Flash Remoting. The three programs you build are an e-commerce application, a messageboard system, and an e-mail client.

How to Approach This Book

All readers should read the chapters in Part I in order to understand the basics of Flash Remoting and Flash Remoting–specific ActionScript. The only exception to this is that if you are already quite familiar with Flash MX ActionScript, you might not need to read Chapter 2 in depth. However, if you are familiar with ActionScript from previous versions of Flash, but you are not familiar with the changes since the advent of Flash MX, you should read Chapter 2. Used throughout the book are conventions and coding practices that are specific to Flash MX ActionScript.

Once you have completed Part I, you should decide which server technology platform you intend to use and then jump to the corresponding section of the book. Although you are certainly welcome to browse through and read all the sections, I recommend that initially you stick to one platform. Additionally, each section for each server-side technology platform includes chapters on various topics within the scope of that platform. You may not necessarily be interested in implementing all of the topics. For example, you will likely use ColdFusion pages *or* ColdFusion Components, but not both.

After you have read the chapters of interest to you in Parts II, III, or IV, consider looking at Part V and building the example applications. This will give you working experience building complete Flash Remoting applications.

Conventions Used in This Book

Each chapter in this book begins with a list of the topics covered so you can easily locate the information you want to know. Additionally, each chapter ends with a summary of the its highlights.

In each chapter, keep an eye out for icons that draw attention to special information that may be of interest to you:

Cross-References show you where you can find additional, related information in another part of the book.

Notes provide additional details related to the current topic.

The On the Web icon indicates that there is a resource available on the companion Web site that relates to the topic being discussed.

Tips are short, useful pieces of information that can help you gain a deeper understanding of a particular subject.

Additionally, this book uses the following typographical conventions:

✦ Code examples appear in a `fixed width font`.

✦ Other code elements, such as variable names and class names, appear in `fixed width`.

✦ Filenames and World Wide Web addresses (URLs) also appear in `fixed width`.

✦ The first occurrence of an important term in a chapter is highlighted with *italic* text. *Italic* is also used for placeholders — for example, *remoteProcedureName*, where *remoteProcedureName* is the name of the function residing on the server.

✦ A menu command is indicated in hierarchical order, with each menu command separated by an arrow. For example, File⇨Open means to click the File command on the menu bar, and then select Open from the menu that appears.

✦ Keyboard shortcuts are indicated with the following syntax: Ctrl+C.

What Is a Sidebar?

Sidebars, which appear at various points throughout the book, offer additional, in-depth coverage of topics related to the subject at hand. Sidebars provide supplemental information that you may find useful or interesting, but that is not absolutely essential to understanding the material.

Complete Flash Remoting MX Web Site

You can find additional resources related to Flash Remoting and this book on the companion Web site found at the following URL:

`www.wiley.com/compbooks/lott`

Contacting the Author

I always welcome and appreciate any comments and feedback. I want to know what has been helpful to you and what might need more clarification. Please feel free to e-mail me at:

`joey@person13.com`

Acknowledgments

Only one name goes on the cover, but so many people have come together to create this book. I am deeply grateful to all the beautiful and kind souls who have made this possibility a reality. I have many people at John Wiley & Sons to acknowledge. I thank Eric Newman, my project editor, for his dedication and commitment, his humor, his insights, and his unrivaled brilliance. Many thanks go to Luann Rouff, my copy editor, for the ways in which she kindly and lovingly transformed my words into sheer elegance and clarity. I am grateful to Chris Webb, my acquisitions editor, for his faith and belief in me and for tirelessly working to support me in every way he can. Many, many other people at Wiley have given of their infinite wisdom, creativity, and unique talents to make this book all that it is.

I acknowledge my literary agent, David Fugate at Waterside Productions. David has come through for me in so many ways throughout the writing of this book. His faith in me and his kindness have done more than he can possibly know.

Robert Reinhardt, my dear friend, has helped to open many a door for me. Robert is a truly wonderful and generous person (not to mention a fantastic teacher and author) for whom I am very grateful.

Many thanks go to all the technical editors who have ensured that some of these crazy ideas actually work! I am truly grateful for all that Jen and Peter deHaan, Niko Alejandre, and Michael Angelo Libio have done. Their comments and suggestions shine through the pages of this book.

I also thank very much the people at Macromedia who have been so helpful through the writing of this book. Dave Gruber has been so kind with his words and support. Jeremy Allaire has taken time from his undoubtedly busy schedule to answer questions and reply to my e-mails. Thanks go to Heather Hollaender for all her help in directing me to the proper resources. Additionally, I acknowledge Peter Farland for his help in sorting out various questions. I am also thankful for all the people who have provided help behind the scenes.

I am so grateful to all of you, the kind readers who have come across this book. It is wonderful to have this work received so well. I thank all of you who have asked me questions and given me the gift of being of service.

I thank everyone who has supported me in so many other ways that have made it possible to write this book. Thank you to all those who show me kindness, love, friendship, and acceptance. I love you all.

And, most of all, I am deeply and truly grateful to That which no words can begin to describe.

Contents at a Glance

· ·

Contents

Part II: Flash Remoting with ColdFusion   143

Introducing Flash Remoting

Getting Started with Flash Remoting

Flash Remoting is an exciting technology that has already revolutionized how Flash can be used in Web development. In fact, in the near future, Flash Remoting promises to be an integral part of not only all Flash development, but also most Web development in general. In order to understand what Flash Remoting does, it is useful to understand the circumstances in which its development came about.

Looking at the Evolution of Flash

The evolution of Flash has mirrored the evolution of the Web in many respects. When Flash entered the market, it was primarily used as an animation tool. At the time, the Web was used largely as a medium for advertising and sharing information. It was a time of popularity for what have been termed "brochure Web sites" (sites offering information, but no services). However, user demands of the Web have evolved. Today, the emphasis is much less on simply advertising, but much more on providing users with complete services such as online shopping, auctions, banking, stock trading, and e-mailing, just to name a few. Offering these services required that technologies for creating dynamic content draw upon resources such as databases. As a result, technologies such as ASP (now .NET), ColdFusion, and Java applications (JSP, JavaBeans, EJBs) became increasingly important in Web development.

Flash has responded to this evolution with significant advances in ActionScript. For example, at one point, it was possible to load data into a Flash movie from an external source only by way of the `loadVariables()` command (global function). Flash 5 then introduced the `XML` object, making it possible for Flash movies to load and send XML data to external sources. Flash MX has improved the `XML` object and introduced the `LoadVars` object to replace and improve on the functionality of the `MovieClip` object's `loadVariables()` method. Flash Remoting is the next step in this evolution. Indeed, it is a giant step—one that radically changes the ways in which Flash can be used.

What Flash Remoting Does

Prior to Flash Remoting, Flash movies could connect to external sources of data only in very limited ways. Creating Flash movies that served as the client interface for highly dynamic Web applications was possible, but tedious. There was a serious bottleneck in the process of sending and receiving data because Flash's only interfaces were `loadVariables()`, `LoadVars`, and `XML` objects. Although each of these objects and methods serves a purpose, they are completely inadequate to meet all the demands that fell upon them by default.

Flash Remoting serves to do the following with regard to this process:

✦ **Simplify:** In order to work with more complex data types between a Flash movie and a server-side application, developers used to have to implement their own serialization and deserialization techniques. Although this worked, it was rather complicated, because it meant that data had to be manually serialized and deserialized both in the Flash movie and in the server-side script/program. Flash Remoting offers support for passing complex data types of many kinds between client and server.

✦ **Empower:** Whereas non–Flash Remoting movies could communicate with text documents and static and dynamic Web pages, there was no direct way to interact with a Web application's business logic. With Flash Remoting, however, it is possible (and often advisable) for your Flash movies to make calls to functions and/or methods within ColdFusion Components, JavaBeans/Java classes, EJBs, and .NET DLLs. Not only is this a better model for an application, but it also means that in most cases, existing business logic (meaning the functions and methods defined within the CFCs, Java classes, and DLLs) can be utilized by a Flash movie without any modification. Furthermore, with Web services as an emerging new force, it is important that Flash Remoting for ColdFusion and .NET enable a Flash movie to directly consume a Web service (the word "consume" is used in this context to describe the use of services by an application).

✦ **Expand:** Flash Remoting also introduces new classes for handling the types of data that can be returned from the server. `RecordSet` objects are available in ActionScript with Flash Remoting, which means that database information returned from the server can be effectively utilized within Flash movies without additional processing.

Table 1-1 provides an idea of the advantages of Flash Remoting, comparing a few examples of calling remote services without Flash Remoting with calling the same kinds of remote services with Flash Remoting.

Table 1-1: Comparing processes with and without Flash Remoting

Type of Remote Procedure	Without Flash Remoting	With Flash Remoting
ColdFusion page, .NET page	Can be called directly using a `LoadVars` object, but can only return values as name-value pairs. Additionally, only string values can be passed as parameters to the pages (numbers and Booleans are converted to strings).	Can be called directly, and can be passed and return values of all kinds already typed, such as number, string, Boolean, `Array`, and `Object`.

Type of Remote Procedure	Without Flash Remoting	With Flash Remoting
JavaBean methods	Cannot be called from Flash. In order to call JavaBean methods, an intermediary page or script (ColdFusion, JSP, etc.) must be written and called (via `LoadVars` or another available object), which calls the JavaBean method. All the restrictions that apply to ColdFusion and .NET then apply as well.	The methods of JavaBeans can be called directly from within Flash. When you use Flash Remoting to invoke a method of a JavaBean, you can pass it parameters and have it return values of many different data types.
Web services	Cannot be called from Flash. Web services can be consumed first by a ColdFusion or .NET page (or other such script), and the results can be returned to Flash through this intermediary process.	Web services can be directly consumed from Flash.

Essentially, Flash Remoting enables a Flash movie to make calls to remote service functions as though they were actually within the Flash movie. Remote service functions in Flash Remoting can include any of the following:

✦ ColdFusion page

✦ ColdFusion component function

✦ ASP.NET page

✦ .NET DLL

✦ Servlet or JSP

✦ Java class public method

✦ JavaBean public method

✦ Enterprise JavaBean method

✦ MBean method

✦ Web services

Benefiting from Flash Remoting

Flash Remoting offers many benefits over developing applications in Flash MX without the addition of Flash Remoting. Obviously, the primary benefit of Flash Remoting, as described in the previous section, is that it enables Flash movies to access remote services directly. This obviates the need to create proprietary systems for passing data to and from Flash movies. Not only is working with Flash Remoting a much simpler process in this regard, it is also much more efficient.

You should also be aware of several other key features. Following are some additional bene-fits offered by Flash Remoting:

✦ Automatic conversions between ActionScript and server-side (ColdFusion, Java, or .NET) data types

✦ Well-designed n-tier applications (meaning applications with multiple layers of pro-gramming) with Flash presentation

✦ Complete, end-to-end debugging with the NetConnection debugger

✦ Easy record set (values from a database) handling within Flash movies

✦ The `DataGlue` class for enabling easy and powerful ways to populate Flash UI Components

What You Can Do with Flash Remoting

While Flash Remoting may open up all kinds of exciting new possibilities, the bottom line for most companies and developers is "What can it do for me?" Quite simply, Flash Remoting enables you to quickly and efficiently integrate Flash movies with business logic. The busi-ness logic (meaning the back-end programming that makes everything "go") can be devel-oped using ColdFusion, .NET, or Java. This is important because it enables developers to work with the language and platform that they prefer. Furthermore, in many cases, no special, additional, server-side programming may be necessary to perform this integration. Finally, Flash Remoting for ColdFusion MX and .NET enables Flash movies to consume Web services without any server-side programming.

Cross-Reference   Web services are covered in detail in Chapter 5.

The possibilities with Flash Remoting are virtually limitless, projecting Flash into an exciting new arena. Following is only a partial list of what Flash Remoting makes possible:

✦ Interaction with databases

✦ File operations

✦ Use of system information and resources

✦ The sending and receiving of e-mail

✦ The consumption of Web services

✦ Interaction with the application server itself

Looking at the Bigger Picture

The Internet as a whole is evolving into a service-based platform. If you are not already famil-iar with the exciting horizons of Web services, you can read more about them in Chapter 5. For now, suffice it to say that applications on the Internet are becoming more *distributed* — meaning that many companies and individuals are examining ways to create applications from building blocks that can be consumed from various locations. These various locations can be on different legacy systems within the same company, or on different servers from various companies around the world. Flash Remoting begins to guide Flash into this arena, whereby Flash movies can consume all kinds of services.

Setting Up Flash Remoting

Flash Remoting consists of two main parts:

✦ Flash Remoting Components: This is the free download from Macromedia (`http://www.macromedia.com/software/flashremoting/downloads/components/`) that installs the necessary ActionScript classes for developing the Flash movies. To install the Flash Remoting Components, download the installation file and run it. When you have done this successfully, open Flash. You should now see a Remoting folder in the Actions Toolbox (see Figure 1-1).

✦ Flash Remoting gateway: The gateway is a server-side part of Flash Remoting that enables the movies to communicate with services. JRun 4 and ColdFusion MX both come with the gateway already included, and it is installed and configured by default. The gateway for .NET and for other J2EE application servers is available to try and to buy from Macromedia. In the case of .NET, the gateway consists of a DLL; for J2EE servers, the gateway is a JAR file.

Cross-Reference

Installing and configuring these gateways are covered in Chapters 12 and 17, respectively.

Figure 1-1: The Remoting folder installed by the Flash Remoting Components

How Flash Remoting Works

Using Flash Remoting, data is sent to and from the service (such as a ColdFusion Component, JavaBean, or .NET DLL) over HTTP using AMF (Action Message Format). AMF is a messaging format that has been developed for use with Flash Remoting. It is modeled on SOAP (Simple Object Access Protocol) and is used in many Web services (see Chapter 5). Using AMF, requests and responses (and all the data contained within them) are serialized and deserialized automatically. This means that Flash Remoting does all of the "dirty work" for you transparently.

Summary

Flash Remoting offers any company or individual an array of benefits. In this chapter, you learned about many of these benefits as well as the necessary steps in getting started with Flash Remoting. Important points to remember include the following:

✦ Flash Remoting provides a way for efficient integration of Flash presentation logic and business logic developed using ColdFusion, .NET, and Java.

✦ Using Flash Remoting, you can pass complex data types between the Flash client and the server.

✦ To use Flash Remoting, you need to install the Flash Remoting Components (a free download from Macromedia) for authoring, and you need to have a server-side Flash Remoting gateway for your application server.

✦ Flash Remoting communicates between the Flash movie and the server using AMF (Action Message Format), and it automatically serializes and deserializes the data on both the client and server ends.

✦   ✦   ✦

ActionScript Fundamentals

There are two basic pieces to consider in a broad overview of Flash Remoting—the Flash movie client and the Flash Remoting server. Each has its own language in which you can instruct it to do what you want it to do. ActionScript is the language of Flash, so it is essential that you understand the fundamentals and the terminology used.

Many people seem to have an aversion to the words *basic* and *fundamental*. Perhaps this is because they equate these words with *unimportant*. However, nothing could be further from the truth! Consider, if you will, the creation of a building. Before the walls can be built, a foundation must be created. If there is no foundation, then no matter how much care is put into the walls, the building is sure to fail. Therefore, please don't think that *basic* and *fundamental* mean *unimportant*. These words should actually signal to you that what is being discussed is the *most* important thing.

The importance of a foundation applies almost universally to creating and learning. Therefore, it should come as no surprise that this is true of programming languages such as ActionScript as well. Therefore, because ActionScript is essential for success with Flash Remoting, a solid foundation in ActionScript is key to success with Flash Remoting.

This chapter is not intended to provide comprehensive or in-depth coverage of ActionScript; rather, it serves as a refresher for some basic concepts and some of the new features added to ActionScript in Flash MX. If you are new to ActionScript, however, this chapter can provide you with enough of a foundation to work with Flash Remoting. The rest of this book necessarily assumes that you have a working understanding of ActionScript. The code throughout many of the examples in later chapters will assume you are familiar with many types of objects (Color, Date, XML, etc.), or that you at least have a reference available (such as *Macromedia® Flash™ MX ActionScript Bible* [Wiley, 2002]).

This is going to be an easy chapter, so don't feel overwhelmed as we get started.

Determining Where to Place ActionScript

Before you even look at *what* ActionScript is, you first have to know *where* ActionScript goes. The answer to this question is pretty simple. Obviously, because ActionScript is understood only by Macromedia Flash MX, ActionScript code must be placed within Flash files in order to be of value to a Flash application. That is the broadest answer to the question. Slightly more specifically, it is also true that ActionScript code written within Flash is added by means of the Actions panel.

Note   Although the preceding paragraph states that ActionScript code must be placed within Flash files, this may be a little misleading or confusing. ActionScript can be also be saved in external files and still be utilized by Flash movies by using the #include statement. However, when the Flash movie is exported, the contents of the external file are included in the SWF or other exported format. Therefore, for simplicity's sake, we can say that ActionScript code must be placed within Flash files, meaning that the code, whether written in the Flash authoring environment directly or included from an external file, must be part of the exported Flash file.

The Actions panel can be accessed from the Flash menus by selecting Window➪Actions or by pressing F9. In the default panel layout in Flash, the Actions panel is visible but collapsed, located just above the Properties panel, as shown in Figure 2-1. You can also display the Actions panel by clicking once on the panel title (i.e., Actions - Frame) on the panel title bar.

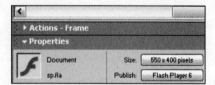

Figure 2-1: The collapsed Actions panel

In Figure 2-2, you can see the Actions panel as it appears when opened. The Actions panel comprises several parts. At the top is a jump menu that enables you to select from the various objects or frames onto which actions can be placed. We will look at this a little more closely in just a moment. The left portion of the panel is the Actions Toolbox—a menu of folders containing ActionScript items that can be double-clicked or dragged and dropped in order to add them to your code. On the right is the Actions pane—the location where all your code is actually added and displayed.

The Actions panel has two different modes—normal and expert. I recommend you use expert mode exclusively, as it is the only way to actually type in code and not have to select code snippets from menus. You can choose expert mode from the Actions panel menu in the upper right-hand corner, as shown in Figure 2-3.

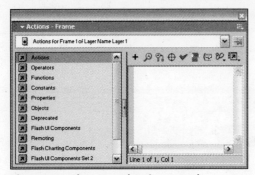

Figure 2-2: The opened Actions panel

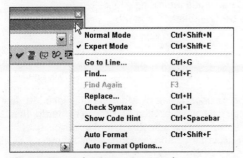

Figure 2-3: Selecting expert mode

Although all ActionScript within Flash documents is authored using the Actions panel, there are options as to which object or frame to which the code should be applied. In Flash MX, you can apply code to frames of timelines, MovieClip instances, and Button instances that have been created on the stage. However, with the advent of the event handler methods described later in this chapter, there is no longer any reason why code should be applied to MovieClip or Button instances. Therefore, I suggest you apply code exclusively to frames. The exercises throughout this book direct you to apply code to frames. You can do this by selecting the frame in the timeline with your mouse (see Figure 2-4) while the Actions panel is open, or by selecting the frame from the Actions panel jump menu (see Figure 2-5). Either way you do this, however, you must make sure the frame is selected *before* you add code to the Script pane. You can ensure that the code is applied to a frame (and not to a MovieClip or a Button instance) by making sure that the title of the Actions panel reads Actions - Frame (see Figure 2-6).

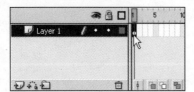

Figure 2-4: Selecting a frame to which code should be applied

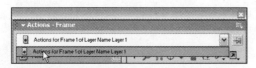

Figure 2-5: Selecting a frame from the jump menu

Figure 2-6: Actions panel title indicating that the actions are being applied to a frame

Getting Started with ActionScript

ActionScript is a programming language that is understood by Macromedia Flash MX. Just like a spoken language, a programming language can be broken down into its component parts. For example, spoken languages use nouns, verbs, adjectives, and other parts of speech. Likewise, ActionScript comprises parts that can be categorized as follows:

✦ Data (data types)

✦ Variables

✦ Expressions and operators

✦ Statements

✦ Conditional and looping statements

✦ Arrays

✦ Functions

✦ Objects

The following sections examine these components of ActionScript and how they work together to create a Flash application.

Adding Comments

Comments are parts of code that are not interpreted by ActionScript (this is true of languages other than ActionScript as well). You can place them in your code as notes to remind yourself (and others) about how the code is functioning and what you were trying to do. In addition, because commented code is not interpreted, comments are often used temporarily around existing code for the purposes of debugging — for example, to identify where a problem might be occurring.

There are two styles of comments in ActionScript — single-line and multiline.

Single-line comments are preceded by two forward slashes (//). For example:

```
// this is a single-line comment
```

Multiline comments must be both opened and closed. They are opened with a forward slash and an asterisk (/*), and closed with an asterisk and a forward slash (*/). Here is an example:

```
/* this is an example
   of a multiline
   comment.*/
```

Outputting Test for Testing

A special statement in ActionScript that is extremely useful for both debugging and for learning purposes is the `trace()` statement. Many of the following sections show examples using `trace()`, which you can use to see the results of certain code for yourself. Therefore, I want to introduce you to this statement first.

The `trace()` statement takes a value and writes it to the Output window when you test your movie (Control⇨Test Movie) within Flash. The value that is placed between the parentheses is interpreted by ActionScript and then displayed in the Output window. For example, the following `trace()` statement would display 5 in the Output window:

```
trace(5);
```

Notice that the line ends with a semicolon. This is like ending a sentence with a period. You will examine this more within this chapter in the section "Understanding Statements." For now, just be aware of the semicolon and be sure to put it at the end of each `trace()` statement you use if you are going to try any of the example code.

If you want to use the example code to test some of the concepts discussed throughout this chapter, you should place the example code as given onto the first frame of a new Flash document and then test the movie (Control⇨Test Movie).

Understanding Data

The word *data* is so commonplace today, you likely already have a good understanding of what it means. Basically, data is just information or values. In the context of ActionScript (or any programming language), data is information that ActionScript can interpret. For ActionScript to interpret your data, it must fit into one of the basic data type categories:

- ✦ string
- ✦ number
- ✦ Boolean
- ✦ object

The first three data types — string, number, and Boolean — are called *primitive* data types. This does not mean they are less important. In fact, they are, in a sense, the most important because they are the building blocks for the more complex data types (objects). This section examines the primitive data types; you will look at objects in a later section.

Strings

Strings are any data that you enclose in quotation marks. For example, the following are string values:

```
"this is a string"
'this is a string'
```

You can use the following to test this with the `trace()` statement to see for yourself that Flash will correctly understand these strings:

```
trace("this is a string");  // outputs: this is a string
trace('this is a string');  // outputs: this is a string
```

The ActionScript interpreter can understand a string value only if the beginning and ending quotation marks match. Therefore, if a single quotation mark is used to begin the string value, then the ending quotation mark must also be a single quotation mark. The following would not be understood as strings by ActionScript:

```
"this is not a string
"neither is this'
```

If you test this out with the following, you will notice that it generates an error:

```
trace("this is not a string);  // this causes an error
trace("neither is this');      // so does this
```

Be careful if you want to include quotation marks inside a string value. If you are not careful, the quotation marks can be misinterpreted by ActionScript as being the ending quotation marks for the string value. For example, the following strings would not be understood properly by the ActionScript interpreter. In the first string, the double quote before "Hello" matches up with the opening double quote, and it is interpreted as the end of the string (even though it is not). The second string has the same problem, only with single quotes. Because a single quote is used to open the string, the single quote before "chirp" is understood by the ActionScript interpreter to be the end of the string.

```
"Fritz said, "Hello," but Susan was not there."
'The bird sang 'chirp, chirp' in the morning.'
```

There are a few ways to overcome this obstacle. One way is simply to make sure that the starting and ending quotation marks of the string value are not the same type as used within the string. For instance, the previous example could be rewritten as follows and be properly understood by ActionScript:

```
'Fritz said, "Hello," but Susan was not there.'
"The bird sang 'chirp, chirp' in the morning."
```

Another approach is to use the backslash prior to the quotes that are used within the string value. The backslash (\) signals the ActionScript interpreter that the character it precedes is to be interpreted literally and not with any special meaning that it might have otherwise (see list of special characters in next paragraph). Using the backslash, the preceding example could be rewritten as follows:

```
"Fritz said, \"Hello,\" but Susan was not there."
'The bird sang \'chirp, chirp\' in the morning.'
```

Other special values within strings can be escaped (meaning they are interpreted literally) using the backward slash:

- ✦ \b: backspace
- ✦ \t: tab
- ✦ \n: newline
- ✦ \r: carriage return
- ✦ \f: formfeed

These values would normally be interpreted with their special meanings by the ActionScript interpreter. However, if you wanted a string value to actually contain the value of \b, for instance, you would type the following:

```
"\\b"
```

Try it out with the following code to see the difference:

```
trace("this is a special value: \b");   // this is a special value: €
trace("this is a special value: \\b");  // this is a special value: \b
```

Because the backslash character itself has a special meaning (escaping other special values within a string), if you want the backslash to appear within a string value, be sure to precede it with another backslash. For example:

```
"\\"
```

Numbers

Numbers are just what you think they are. All of the following are examples of numbers:

- ✦ 13
- ✦ 12.34
- ✦ 0x0000FF

The section "Expressions and Operators" later in this chapter examines operators, but in the meantime everyone should understand the basic meaning of the + operator. When used with number values, the + operator simply adds the values together. For example:

```
29 + 1.4
```

In this example, the result would be 30.4. You can test this with the following trace() statement:

```
trace(29 + 1.4);
```

The reason I am bringing this up is to show you the difference between data as a number and data as a string. There is a difference between the values 5 and "5". The first is a number and the second is a string. Now, in many cases, ActionScript is smart enough to actually convert "5" to a number (5) for you. However, in many other cases it will not. For example, see what happens with the following trace() statement:

```
trace(5 + "5");
```

You might have expected that this operation would provide the result 10. However, instead it resulted in a string value of "55". This is because the + operator (as you will see a bit later on) concatenates string values. Therefore, in this example, ActionScript actually converted the first value (5) to a string instead of converting the second value ("5") to a number. The purpose of this example is to simply point out the importance of making sure you use the correct data type in your code.

Although we have not yet discussed functions, a few functions that relate to numbers are worth mentioning here. Their use is relatively straightforward, so you don't yet need to know the theory behind functions in order to understand how to use these particular functions.

The parseInt(), parseFloat(), and Number() functions all convert other data types to number values. This conversion can be useful for making sure that the values you are working with are actually numbers, in order to avoid problems such as those we saw in the previous example. You might wonder why you would need to do this when you can simply make sure you type in a number value instead of a string value, for instance. With Flash Remoting, you will be pulling data from lots of external sources. This data will be dynamic, and so you will not always have the same kind of control you would have if you were typing the values into the Actions panel yourself.

The parseInt() function enables you to convert a string value to a number by placing that string value between the parentheses. For example, the following would convert the string value "5" to the number value 5:

```
parseInt("5");
```

With parseInt(), you can also convert string values into numbers even if the string value does not represent a base-10 number. In the following example, 0000FF is a string representation of a hexadecimal value. You can convert this to a number with the following:

```
parseInt("0000FF", 16);
```

Note   If you try to use parseInt() with a string representation of a hexadecimal number in ActionScript format (e.g., 0x0000FF vs. 0000FF), you should not specify the optional, second parameter.

Because hexadecimal numbers are base-16, you simply specify this base for conversion within the parentheses. The base for conversion (called the *radix*) should be specified following the string value and a comma, as shown above. The following example converts a binary string representation and writes it to the Output window using trace():

```
trace(parseInt("10101", 2)); // outputs: 21
```

Note   Most numbers that humans work with are base-10, or decimal. This means that there are ten possible digits (0–9). A base-16 number (hexadecimal) has 16 possible digits (0–F). Therefore, the decimal value 11, for example, is represented by the hexadecimal B. ActionScript can convert strings into numbers using radices from 2 (binary) to 35 (using digits 0–Z).

The parseFloat() function also converts a string value to a number, but it will also convert any decimal places, whereas parseInt() will not. You can test this out for yourself with the following code:

```
trace(parseInt("5.5"));    // outputs: 5
trace(parseFloat("5.5")); // outputs: 5.5
```

Finally, the Number() function will try to convert any value to a number. This includes not only string values, but also Boolean values (see the next section). For example, the following would convert "13" to 13:

```
Number("13");
```

Boolean

Boolean data can have only one of two values — true or false. Booleans are most often the result of conditional expressions, as we will see later in the section "Conditional and Looping Statements." However, Booleans are also sometimes used when you want to store a value for something that is only either true or false, such as whether a person has green eyes or not or whether today is a Sunday.

Working with Variables

Variables are very important in any programming language. A variable serves as a named container for data. You might think of data as being like a liquid. Without the proper container, it can be difficult to handle. Imagine trying to carry around water in your hands. With liquids, therefore, we use containers such as cups. Variables serve as cups for data. We can pour the data into the variable cup and then just work with the variable, instead of with the data itself. Moreover, because we are always instructing the Flash movie to do something with our ActionScript code, we need a convenient way to refer to these variables. Therefore, we give them names. In addition, note that when you have a cup you can pour different liquids into and out of it. The same cup can contain different liquids at different times. Likewise, the same variable can contain different data at different times.

Obviously, this is just a metaphor to help illustrate the concept; there are no cups or liquids inside a Flash movie. In short, variables are quite simple.

In order to work with variables, all you need to do is create a variable name and assign a value to it. Here are some examples:

```
name = "Ima Goodie";
isMarried = true;
yearsAtFactory = 56;
```

Although each variable assignment above uses a different data type, the assignment is exactly the same. The variable assignment uses the equals sign (assignment operator) to give a value to a variable. On the left side of the assignment operator is the name for the variable, which describes the kind of value it will hold. On the right side of the assignment operator is the value that gets assigned to the variable.

Once the variable has been created and assigned a value in this way, the variable can be used in place of the actual value. For example:

```
name = "Ima Goodie";
trace(name);          // outputs: Ima Goodie
```

If you try this, notice that the value written to the Output Window is the value that has been assigned to the variable.

Naming variables

ActionScript has some important naming rules. They are as follows:

✦ Variable names can begin only with an underscore (_), the dollar sign ($), or a letter. Do not begin variable names with a number.

✦ Allowable characters for the rest of a variable name include underscores (_), the dollar sign ($), letters, and numbers.

✦ There can be no spaces in variable names.

✦ Variable names cannot be the same as ActionScript reserved words (such as `this`, `var`, `Color`, etc.).

In order to have descriptive variable names, you will often want to use multiple words. However, because you cannot use spaces, it can get kind of indecipherable. (Consider the name `yearsatfactory`, for example, which is a little difficult to read at first.) Therefore, two conventions have arisen to address this problem. One is to use underscores between words, as in `years_at_factory`. The other is to capitalize the first letter of each word after the first, as in `yearsAtFactory`. Throughout this book, I generally prefer to use the second technique. Feel free to use whatever seems best to you, so long as you don't use spaces.

One last word about naming your variables. Although there is no rule about capitalization, there are some conventions. By convention, variable names begin with lowercase letters. This format is used to distinguish variable names from object class names, as you will learn about later in this chapter in the section titled "Looking at Object-Oriented ActionScript." You are not obligated to adhere to this convention. Be aware, however, that generally the name `yearsAtFactory` is preferred over `YearsAtFactory`.

Using global variables

Variables have what is known as *scope*. A variable's scope is the boundary within which it is defined. Therefore, variables that are created on timelines are defined only within that timeline. While it is possible to access variables on other timelines, doing so is not always the most desirable solution because it tends to lead to poorly structured code. The exception to this is to target variables on the _root timeline in which _root is used as a centralized location for storing variables. However, since the release of Flash MX you can also choose to use a global variable instead.

Global variables are those which have scope within all timelines. You can create a global variable simply by prepending the _global identifier to the name of the variable, separated by a dot. Here are a few examples of assigning values to global variables:

```
_global.myString = "some val";
_global.myNumber = 6;
_global.myBoolean = true;
```

Once a global variable has been defined, it can be accessed from anywhere within a Flash movie for reading the value, without the need for the _global identifier. This can be beneficial because it obviates the need to know the absolute or relative location of a variable. For example, the global variables declared in the preceding example could be used in the following way on any timeline in a movie:

```
trace(myString);
trace(myNumber);
trace(myBoolean);
```

However, any time you want to assign a new value to the variable, you must use the _global identifier. It is optional only when reading the value.

Using Expressions and Operators

So far, you have learned what data *is*. However, mostly you will want to *do* something with that data. For example, you might want to add number values. When you do this, you create an *expression*. An expression is anything that represents a single value. Therefore, 5 + 7 is an example of an expression.

All expressions are composed of two types of elements: *operators* and *operands*. An operator is that which signifies the type of action that takes place. For example, in the expression 5 + 7, the operator is +. An operand is that upon which the operator performs its action. Therefore, in the same expression (5 + 7), the 5 and the 7 are the operands. The operands are always the data.

ActionScript has eight main groups of operators:

✦ assignment

✦ mathematical

✦ string

✦ equality

✦ logical

✦ bitwise

✦ conditional

✦ typeof

Table 2-1 lists all the operators in ActionScript. Many of these operators will be familiar to you. We will examine in more detail a few with which you might not yet be well acquainted.

Table 2-1: Operators

Assignment Operators

Operator	Name	Example	What It Means
=	Equals (assignment)	x = y	x = y
+=	Add by value	x += y	x = x + y
+=	Join by value	x += "y"	x = x + "y"
-=	Subtract by value	x -= y	x = x - y
*=	Multiply by value	x *= y	x = x * y
/=	Divide by value	x /= y	x = x / y
%=	Modulo by value	x %= y	x = x % y
<<=	Left shift by value	x <<= y	x = x << y

Continued

Table 2-1: *(continued)*

Assignment Operators

Operator	Name	Example	What It Means
>>=	Right shift by value	x >>= y	x = x >> y
>>>=	Right shift zero fill by value	x >>>= y	x = x >>> y
&=	Bitwise AND by value	x &= y	x = x & y
|=	Bitwise OR by value	x |= y	x = x | y
^=	Bitwise XOR by value	x ^= y	x = x ^ y

Mathematical Operators

Operator	Name	Example	Result
+	Plus	x + y	x + y
-	Minus	x − y	x − y
*	Multiply	x * y	x * y
/	Divide	x / y	x / y
%	Modulo	x % y	remainder of x / y
++	Increment	x++	x + 1
--	Decrement	x--	x - 1
-	Unary Negation	- x	-1 * x

String Operators

Operator	Name	Example	Result
+	Join	"x" + "y"	"xy"

Equality Operators

Operator	Name	Example	Result
==	Equals	5 == 6	false
!=	Not equals	5 != 6	true
>	Greater than	5 > 6	false
<	Less than	5 < 6	true
>=	Greater than or equal	5 >= 6	false
<=	Less than or equal	5 <= 6	true
===	Strict equality	5 === "5"	false
!==	Strict inequality	5 !== "5"	true

Logical Operators

Operator	Name
&&	And
||	Or
!	Not

Bitwise Operators

Operator	Name
&	Bitwise And
|	Bitwise Or
^	Bitwise Xor (exclusive or)
<<	Bitwise Left Shift
>>	Bitwise Right Shift
>>>	Bitwise Unsigned Right Shift
~	Bitwise Not

Conditional Operator

Operator	Name	Example	Result
?:	Conditional	true?6:5	6

TypeOf Operator

Operator	Name
typeOf	TypeOf

Shortcut operators

Some of the operators that you see listed I like to call *shortcut operators*. You might also think of them as *compound operators*. These operators perform operations that can be done with other operators, but they do them with less code.

The majority of these shortcut operators are under the assignment operator category. Although you can find a lot of operators in that category, all of them are actually variations of a theme, so to speak. The primary assignment operator is the equals sign (=). This operator is used to assign a value to a variable, such as the following:

```
myVariable = "some value";
```

The rest of the operators are shortcuts. For example, the += operator is a shortcut such that the following two lines of code are equivalent:

```
price = price + 10;
price += 10;
```

The rest of the shortcut assignment operators work in the same general way. For example, the following lines of code are equivalent:

```
myVariable = myVariable << 2;
myVariable <<= 2;
```

Although you might not yet know what the << operator does (we'll get to it in a few sections), you can see the pattern with these shortcut operators.

Two other shortcut operators are the increment (++) and decrement (- -) operators under the mathematical operator grouping. These are special shortcut operators that are common in programming languages. For example, the following three lines of code are equivalent:

```
myVariable--;
myVariable = myVariable - 1;
myVariable -= 1;
```

Undoubtedly, you have already inferred that the following lines of code are also equivalent:

```
myVariable++;
myVariable = myVariable + 1;
myVariable += 1;
```

There is one point I would like to make you aware of, however. If the increment or decrement operator occurs *after* the operand, then the operation takes place after everything else. However, if it is *before* the operand, then the operation takes place first. This is most easily illustrated with the following example, which you can test for yourself:

```
myVariable = 5;
trace(myVariable++);
trace(myVariable);
myVariable = 5;
trace(++myVariable);
```

In this example, the Output window would display the following:

```
5
6
6
```

Because the first trace() statement outputs the value of myVariable++, the value is 5 because the trace() statement outputs the value of myVariable before it is incremented. The value is still incremented, however, because in the next trace() statement the incremented value is displayed. However, in the third trace() statement, the value that is displayed is the incremented value because the operator appears before the operand.

Tip

Do not add spaces between the operand and the operator when using the increment and decrement operators:

```
myVariable ++; // this will not work because of the space
```

The last shortcut operator is the conditional operator (? :). This operator is the only ternary operator in ActionScript. That means that the conditional operator operates on three operands, instead of two like all the rest of the (binary) operators. The first operand that it operates on should be an expression that resolves to a Boolean value. The other two operands are the possible result of the operation—one is the result if the Boolean operand is true, and the other is the result if the Boolean operand is false. Here is an example of the conditional operator being used in actual code:

```
today = "Sunday";
message = (today == "Friday") ? "it is Friday" : "it is not Friday";
```

This is a rather simplistic example, but to see how much of a shortcut this operator provides, look at the code that would be required to perform this same sort of operation otherwise:

```
today = "Sunday";
if(today == "Friday"){
  message = "it is Friday";
}else{
  message = "it is not Friday";
}
```

Cross-Reference See the discussion of if/else statements later in the chapter in the section titled "Conditional and Looping Statements."

Strict equality operators

Under the grouping of equality operators, you will find the strict equality (===) and strict inequality (!==) operators. These might not be entirely intuitive, so they are worth a little explanation.

The normal equality operator (==) and inequality operator (!=) will do data type conversions before comparing the values. Therefore, in a normal equality operation, the number 5 and the string "5" will be seen as equal. Likewise, in a normal inequality operation, the number 5 and the string "5" will be seen as equal, so the operation will result in false. However, in the strict equality and inequality operations, no data type conversion is done. Table 2-2 shows a few comparisons between normal and strict equality operations.

Table 2-2: Strict Equality Operation Comparsion

Normal	Normal Result	Strict	Strict Result
5==5	true	5===5	true
5!=5	false	5!==5	false
5=="5"	true	5==="5"	false
5!="5"	false	5!=="5"	true

Binary operators

Despite their simplicity, binary operations can be a relatively large topic, and a detailed explanation is beyond the scope of this book. However, it would be good for you to understand a few common binary operations.

First, you should know that binary operations are performed on binary values. Binary values are simply numbers that are base-2. This means that only 0 and 1 are used. Binary numbers are usually thought of in chunks called *bytes*. A byte is simply 8 columns, or bits. Table 2-3 shows you a few examples of bytes and their decimal (base-10) equivalents.

Table 2-3: Binary Numbers

Decimal equivalent	Byte
0	00000000
1	00000001
2	00000010
3	00000011
4	00000100
5	00000101
255	11111111

One of the most common uses of binary operations is with color. Color values are often thought of in terms of 24 bits (hence the expression 24-bit color). 24 bits is the same as 3 bytes. The bytes represent the red, green, and blue components of the color. For example, black is represented in binary format when all the bits are 0. The color white is represented when all the bits are 1. All the colors in between are some combination of 1s and 0s. However, in order to be able to successfully work with color values in binary, you need to understand the basic bitshift left (<<) and binary or (|) operations.

The bitshift left operator (<<) simply takes all the bits of the first operand and shifts them over to the left by the number of bits specified by the second operand. For example:

```
5 << 1
```

This operation takes the binary representation of 5 (101) and shifts the bits to the left by 1 (1010), which results in the decimal value of 10.

The bitshift or operator (|) takes two binary representations and combines them such that in each bit where either of the values has a 1, the resultant value has a 1 in that bit as well. For example:

```
4 | 3
```

This operation takes the binary representations of 4 (100) and 3 (011) and results in 7 (111).

You can easily apply both of these operations to colors in the following way:

```
blue = 255;
green = 255 << 8;
red = 255 << 16;
purple = blue | green;
```

Notice that the value for green is shifted over to the left by 8 bits, which is 1 byte, and red is shifted 16 bits, which is 2 bytes.

Understanding Statements

Statements are simply instructions to the Flash movie. They are the complete sentences of ActionScript grammar. You have already seen some examples of statements, such as the following:

```
trace("this is a string");
today = "Sunday";
```

In contrast, other examples we have looked at have not been statements. Expressions such as

```
1 + 2
today == "Friday"
5 << 1
```

are not statements because they do not really *do* anything by themselves. However, they can be included as parts of statements such as the following:

```
myVariable = 1 + 2;
message = (today == "Friday")?"it is Friday":"it is not Friday";
binOpVal = 5 << 1;
```

Notice that in each statement we have looked at, the statement ends with a semicolon (;). The semicolon is like the period at the end of a sentence. It lets the ActionScript interpreter know that it has reached the end of a statement. Because ActionScript is highly flexible and forgiving, the semicolon is not strictly required. Nonetheless, it is best to get into the habit of using it because under some circumstances, you could run into problems if you omit it.

Introducing Conditional and Looping Statements

Some statements that control the flow of ActionScript are what I call control structures. Normally, the code is executed one line after the other. But with the use of statements such as if, for, while, and switch, the flow of the code in the movie can be made such that it is not necessarily completely linear. Each of these statements groups together a code block (a group of lines of code) between curly braces, and that code executes if certain conditions are met. How these conditions are specified differs for each of these control structures.

The if statement

The if statement is a conditional statement. It groups together a block of code and executes it only if a condition is met. For example, maybe you want to create a Flash application that performs particular tasks only if a user is logged in. Using an if statement would be perfect for this situation.

The syntax of an if statement looks like this:

```
if(condition){
  // code block goes here
}
```

Here is a simple example of an if statement you can test yourself:

```
myBoolean = true;
if(myBoolean){
  trace("myBoolean must be true");
}
```

If you use the same example but change the value of myBoolean to false, then the trace()
statement will not execute. If the condition does not evaluate to true (if it is false) in an if
statement, then the whole code block is skipped.

In some instances, you might want to determine whether one of several conditions is met and
perform different tasks depending on which condition is true (if any). You can then use the
if/else if structure. This is a variation on the basic if statement, and the basic syntax is
as follows:

```
if(condition 1){
   // code block goes here
}
else if (condition 2){
   // code block goes here
}
```

Here is an example of an if/else if statement you can try:

```
today = "Monday";
if(today == "Sunday"){
   trace("today is named for the Sun.");
}
else if (today == "Monday"){
   trace("today is named for the Moon.");
}
else if (today == "Tuesday"){
   trace("today is named for Mars!");
}
```

Finally, there is the if/else variation, which functions as a sort of catch-all for situations in
which a condition or conditions are not met. Here are a few examples:

```
testNumber = 5;
if (testNumber == 1){
   trace("the value is 1");
}
else{
   trace("the value is not 1");
}

testName = "Alan";
if (name == "Mark"){
   trace("hey, it's Mark!");
}
else if (name == "Joseph"){
   trace("wow, it's Joseph");
}
else{
   trace("it could be anyone other than Mark or Joseph!");
}
```

Note If the code block in an `if` statement is only 1 line, you can omit the curly braces. This is the only circumstance under which you should do this, however.

The for statement

The `for` statement is a looping statement. It enables you to easily loop through a block of code multiple times. The `for` statement is structured similarly to the `if` statement except that in place of the simple condition that the `if` statement has, the `for` statement has a three-part condition.

The three-part condition is composed of three expressions: the initializing expression, the terminating expression, and the incrementing expression. The initializing expression assigns an initial value to a variable. The terminating expression specifies a condition for the variable under which the looping should terminate. The incrementing expression increments (or decrements) the value of the variable. Semicolons separate the expressions.

Here is an example of a simple `for` statement:

```
for (i = 0; i < 10; i++){
   trace(i);
}
```

When the `for` loop is first encountered, the initializing expression is executed. In the preceding example, the variable `i` is set to the value of 0. Then, the `for` loop checks to make sure the terminating condition has not been met. If it has, then the code in the `for` loop is never executed. If the condition has not yet been met, the code inside the `for` loop is executed one time. At the end of the `for` loop, the initializing expression is executed, and the terminating expression is checked once again. This process continues until the terminating condition is met. Therefore, in the preceding example, the Output window would display the numbers 0 through 9 on their own lines. Once the value has been incremented to 10, the terminating condition has been met and the `for` loop ends.

The while statement

The `while` statement is another looping statement. It is simpler than the `for` statement, however. It has a simple condition just as an `if` statement does. As long as the condition is true, the code block within the `while` statement will continue to be executed. However, once the condition is no longer true, the `while` loop exits. Here is a simple example:

```
aNumber = 0;
while(aNumber < 10){
   trace(aNumber);
   aNumber++
}
/* outputs:
   0
   1
   2
   3
   4
   5
```

```
      6
      7
      8
      9
*/
```

There is a variation on the while statement called the do/while statement. It is possible that if a while statement's condition is not met at all, the code within it will never be executed. For example:

```
aNumber = 0;
while(aNumber > 1){
  // this code will never execute
  trace(aNumber);
  aNumber++;
}
```

A do/while statement assures you that the code block will always be executed at least once. Here is what it looks like:

```
aNumber = 0;
do{
  // this code will execute once no matter what
  trace(aNumber);
  aNumber++;
}while(aNumber > 1)
```

The break and continue statements

With looping statements, there is always the possibility that you will want to either stop the loop or skip over a certain iteration. This is where the break and continue statements come in handy.

The break statement can break out of a for or while loop. This might be useful in many cases. For example, you might be looping through a list of usernames that the Flash movie has retrieved from a database. If you are looking for only one username, then once that name has been found there is no point in going through the rest of the list. The break statement can do this. Here is an example:

```
usernames = ["Patanjali", "BIyengar", "JFriend"];
for(i = 0; i < usernames.length; i++){
  // check to see if the name in the array (usernames) is
  // the one you are looking for
  if(usernames[i] == "BIyengar"){
    break;
  }
}
```

The continue statement will simply skip the current iteration through a looping statement and continue to the next. The classic example of this is in avoiding the use of 0 as a divisor (which is an illegal operation):

```
for (i = -20; i < 20; i++){
  if(i == 0)
    continue;
  trace(100/i);
}
```

The switch statement

The `switch` statement is similar in functionality to an `if` statement with `else if` and `else` clauses. With a `switch` statement, you specify an expression and what actions should be performed depending on different values to which the expression could resolve. Each of the different possible values is called a *case*. The cases are enclosed within the `switch` statement's code block. Each case is indicated by the `case` keyword, followed by the possible value and a colon. The code to execute for that case should follow. You can also specify a default case with the keyword `default`. The default case is true if the expression does not resolve to any of the other cases. Here is an example:

```
num = 1;
switch(num){
  case 1:
    trace("is 1");
  case 2:
    trace("is 2");
  default:
    trace("is not 1 or 2");
}
```

If you were to test this `switch` statement, then the following would display in the Output window:

```
is 1
is 2
is not 1 or 2
```

If `num` has a value of 2 (instead of 1 as in the example), then the output is as follows:

```
is 2
is not 1 or 2
```

And if `num` has a value of anything other than 1 or 2, then the following is simply output:

```
is not 1 or 2
```

Notice that the case that is true is executed along with all the other code that follows. If you want *only* the code for each case to execute, you need to add a `break` statement at the end of the case block as follows:

```
switch(num){
  case 1:
    trace("is 1");
    break;
  case 2:
    trace("is 2");
    break;
  default:
    trace("is not 1 or 2");
}
```

Note   You don't need to add a `break` statement to the last case (or `default`) within a `switch` statement because there are no more cases afterward.

Keeping Track of Data with Arrays

Arrays are a great way to keep track of related data in your programs. I like to think of an array as a CD tower—an ordered structure with slots for each piece of data. Each slot can be referenced by an index (a number), making it easy to retrieve the data if you know the index. Moreover, just as a CD tower enables you to keep all your CDs in one place where you can easily find them, an array makes it easy to keep all your related data in one place. For example, if you create a Flash application that functions as a scheduler for the user, the user might create different categories for reminders such as kids, pets, work, cars, and sister. Rather than create all kinds of variables to keep track of these values, you can store them all in a single array as follows:

```
remindersCategories = ["kids", "pets", "work", "cars", "sister"];
```

This way of creating an array is called creating an array literal. You can also create an array using the Array object constructor:

```
remindersCategories = new Array("kids", "pets", "work", "cars",
"sister");
```

Either way is just fine. Once you have created an array, you can access the elements by their index. Arrays in ActionScript begin with the index 0. Therefore, the first element of the array will have an index of 0. Here is an example of how to access elements of an array by index:

```
trace(remindersCategories[0]);
trace(remindersCategories[3]);
```

This would output the following:

```
kids
cars
```

You can also write to an element of an array in much the same way:

```
remindersCategories[2] = "parents";
```

When you access the elements of an array, you work with them just as you did with variables. Therefore, you can reassign values to the same element of an array as many times as you want.

You do not have to create an array already populated with values. You can create an empty array and then assign values to the elements one at a time. To create an empty array, you can choose between the array literal:

```
remindersCategories = [];
```

or the Array object constructor:

```
remindersCategories = new Array();
```

In either case, once the array has been created, you can populate it in the same way:

```
remindersCategories[0] = "kids";
remindersCategories[1] = "pets";
remindersCategories[2] = "work";
remindersCategories[3] = "cars";
remindersCategories[4] = "sister";
```

Arrays are often used in conjunction with `for` loops. For example, if you wanted to output all the values of an array, you could loop through them using a `for` loop. All arrays have a special property that tells you how many elements are in the array. The property is called `length`, and it can be accessed in the following way:

```
trace(remindersCategories.length);
```

Therefore, it is quite simple to loop through all the elements of an array as follows:

```
for(i = 0; i < remindersCategories.length; i++){
    trace(remindersCategories[i]);
}
```

Making Reusable Code with Functions

Functions are a way of breaking up ActionScript code into smaller procedures. These procedures can then be invoked or called within the Flash movie to perform the actions they contain. Functions are a great way of making application development more manageable. Breaking up the code of a Flash application into smaller subroutines with functions provides at least two advantages:

✦ Well-written functions can be reused. If they are written in a generalized way, you can call them several times if you need to, rather than having to write the same (or similar) code several times.

✦ Placing related code into functions can make reading the ActionScript in a Flash application easier to understand when you or someone else revisits the code. Rather than having one giant main routine of code to decipher, you can group related parts into functions with names that make it easy to understand. Reading function calls with names like `initializeValues`, `login`, `makeForm`, and `processForm` (along with well-documented code) can make the program quite easy to understand.

Beginning Custom Functions

Creating a custom function is a quite simple process once you get the hang of it. Keep a few key points in mind throughout:

✦ Functions should be, as much as possible, self-contained. Of course, it is not always possible or even desirable that the function be completely self-contained. However, you should always try to make functions as independent as possible. This means try to reduce or avoid references to variables, objects, and any other code outside of the function itself.

✦ Functions can be passed parameters (also called arguments) when they are called. Parameters are simply values that can be sent to a function when it is invoked. Before you write a custom function, you should consider how the function will be used and what kinds of parameters, if any, will be passed to it. Passing parameters to a function is a very good way to ensure that the function remains independent and self-contained.

✦ Functions can also return values (or not). This is important because it means that functions can act not only as subroutines, but that they can also be used as values within expressions. When defining a function, keep in mind whether or not it should return a value when it is called. For example, a function that calculates the area of a circle (when passed the value of the radius as a parameter) would likely return a value — the area. On the other hand, a function that formats data and sends it to a server might not need to return a value.

Defining Functions

You can define two kinds of functions: *named* and *anonymous*. Fortunately, they are almost exactly the same. First, let's look at the way to create a named function.

A named function is, as its description implies, a function that is given a name in the definition. All named function definitions begin with the `function` keyword, followed by the function name, function operator (`()`) and optional parameters, and the function body (defined within curly braces [`{}`]). Here is an example of the simplest case function definition:

```
function writeMessage(){
  trace("hey there");
}
```

In this case, the function name is `writeMessage`. This function can be called now in the following manner:

```
writeMessage();
```

When this is done, the Output window will display the following:

```
hey there
```

An anonymous function (also sometimes referred to as an *inline function*), as its description implies, does *not* have a name assigned to it in its definition. Here is an example of how the previous function would be written as an anonymous function:

```
function(){
  trace("hey there");
}
```

Of course, if the function is not named it becomes difficult to do anything with it. Therefore, in order to do anything with the function (such as invoke it), a reference to the function must be assigned to a variable. For example:

```
writeMessage = function(){
  trace("hey there");
}
```

Now the function can be called just as it was before:

```
writeMessage();
```

The purpose of anonymous functions might not be immediately clear. They are most often used with objects, as you will see a little later in this chapter in the section titled "Looking at Object-Oriented Programming."

Passing parameters to a function

The previous functions passed no parameters. If you want to pass parameters to the function, you have two choices. One option (and usually the preferred technique) is to define variables (separated by commas) for each parameter within the function operator. For example, the previous function is pretty much a waste of time to us because all it does is call the `trace()` statement with a static message. However, we could define a function that allows a name to be passed to the function as a parameter, thus personalizing the output message:

```
function writePersonalizedMessage(username){
  trace("hey there, " + username);
}
```

Although this is still a trivial function, you can begin to see how the parameter enables the function to be more generalized. Now the same function can be called as follows:

```
writePersonalizedMessage("Joey");
writePersonalizedMessage("Tania");
```

Now the Output window will display the following:

```
hey there, Joey
hey there, Tania
```

Every function also has available to it an array of the parameters passed to it, called arguments. This is the second way in which you can use parameters within a function. Here is an example of a function that will output all the parameter values passed to it:

```
function displayParameters(){
  for(i = 0; i < arguments.length; i++){
    trace(arguments[i]);
  }
}
```

If this function is called in the following way:

```
displayParameters("Carolyn", "Jerry", "Joey", "Laura");
```

then the Output window will display the following:

```
Carolyn
Jerry
Joey
Laura
```

It is also worth pointing out that when variables containing primitive values (strings, numbers, and Booleans) are passed to a function as parameters, the values themselves, not the variables, are passed. This means that even if the value is altered within the function, the variable outside the function will still contain the same value. For example:

```
function addToNumber(startNum){
  startNum++;
}
myNumber = 5;
addToNumber(myNumber);
trace(myNumber);
```

In this case, the Output window will display 5 because the value of myNumber remains unchanged. Only the number of startNum (within the function) is changed.

On the other hand, reference data types (meaning objects) are passed by reference. This means that when these types of variables are passed to a function, any alterations made to the parameter value will affect the object outside the function as well.

```
function myFunction(myObject){
  myObject.property = 24;
}

obj = new Object();
```

```
obj.property = 21;
trace(obj.property);   // outputs: 21
myFunction(obj);
trace(obj.property);   // outputs: 24
```

Returning a value

Functions can also return values. If a function returns a value, it is done with the `return` keyword. When `return` is encountered in a function, the function subroutine is ended and the specified value is returned to the point from which the function was invoked. Here is an example of a function that returns a value:

```
function rectangleArea(length, height){
   return length * height;
}
```

When this function is called, it returns a value and so the function call can be treated much like reading a variable. For example:

```
len = 5;
hgt = 10;
area = rectangleArea(len, hgt);
trace(area);
```

The preceding code would display the following in the Output window:

```
50
```

Using Local Variables

By default, variables declared inside of a function have scope within the entire timeline in which the function is defined. Here is an example that shows this:

```
function testLocal(){
   myVariable = "inside function";
}

myVariable = "outside function";
testLocal();
trace(myVariable);
```

In this example, the value that will appear in the Output window will be `"inside function"` because `myVariable` is defined inside the function *after* it is defined outside the function (because the function is called after the variable value is assigned outside the function). This is seldom a desired result. Because you want to make functions as self-contained as possible, it is best to avoid naming conflicts with variables inside the function and outside the function.

You can avoid this whole problem quite easily by using *local* variables inside the function. To create a local variable, you simply use the keyword `var` before the variable is first defined inside a function. Here is the same example with a local variable instead of a timeline variable as before:

```
function testLocal(){
   var myVariable = "inside function";
}

myVariable = "outside function";
```

```
testLocal();
trace(myVariable);
```

This time, the value displayed in the Output window is `"outside function"` because the variable inside `testLocal()` no longer has scope outside of the function. In addition, note that all parameters are treated as local variables automatically.

Looking at Object-Oriented ActionScript

Whether you are aware of it or not, you deal with abstractions all the time. Rarely do you walk up to someone and start talking about sentient bipedal entities with hair who are warm-blooded and have opposable digits on the ends of two extremities. Usually, you just start talk-ing about people, but the concept of "people" is an abstraction. Abstractions are mechanisms for grouping things with similar characteristics.

In language, abstractions are essential. Imagine if you had to describe all the characteristics of something each time you wanted to talk about it with someone. It could take you all day just to get across a seemingly simple concept like vegetable or car. Perhaps in the earliest stages of language development, abstractions were not necessary. After all, there might not have been very many things about which to communicate. However, as language evolved, it quickly became necessary to be able to use abstractions. Likewise, when computer languages were in their earlier stages of development, there was not so much complexity. A computer program might have to do only a few very basic tasks. But as programming languages have evolved to be able to handle increasingly complex tasks, the same need for abstractions has come about.

When we talk about abstractions with relation to ActionScript, be aware of two fundamental concepts: classes and instances, or objects:

- ✦ A class is the collection of characteristics of a group of things. For example, the class people is defined by sentient bipedal entities with hair who are warm-blooded and have opposable digits on the ends of two extremities. These characteristics more or less describe all people and help to distinguish them from things that do not fit into the cat-egory of people, such as rocks, snakes, and air.

- ✦ Objects are the specific instances of a class. John or Betty may be examples of instances of the people class. All people have hair, but John has no hair on his head, while Betty has long, red hair on her head. Obviously, they both fit the criteria to be people, but they are individualized, unique expressions within the category. Where a class is generalized, an object is specific.

Creating Objects from Predefined Classes

ActionScript comes with an entire library of predefined classes. It is well beyond the scope of this book to examine most of these objects in detail. However, it is essential that you under-stand how to create instances from classes in ActionScript.

Although not all objects in ActionScript are created the same way, the majority are. The pre-dominant way in which objects are created is through *constructors*. A constructor is a special function with the same name as the class that is used together in a statement with the `new` keyword. You've already seen an example of this in the discussion of arrays. In fact, all arrays are actually `Array` objects. `Array` objects are created using the `Array` constructor as follows:

```
myArray = new Array();
```

Notice that when you create an object, you want to assign that object's value to a variable. In this example, the `Array` object is created and assigned to the variable named `myArray`.

As I said, not all objects are created in this way. For all of the classes that are introduced specifically for working with Flash Remoting, I will explain exactly how to create the objects and work with the objects once created.

Tip   For most of the standard Flash classes, you may want to consult *Macromedia® Flash™ MX ActionScript Bible* (Wiley, 2002) for more information on how to use them.

Working with Object Properties and Methods

If you consider the people class once again, you will notice that there are two defining aspects of the class: characteristics and actions. People have characteristics such as hair and warm-bloodedness, and people can take actions such as walk and talk. Classes in ActionScript are also defined by characteristics and actions. The characteristics are called *properties,* and the actions are called *methods*.

You are already familiar with at least one property because you learned about it in the "Keeping Track of Data with Arrays" section of this chapter. The `length` property of an Array object tells you how many elements are in the object. If you want to access the property of an object, you do so by first specifying the object name (the variable to which the object has been assigned) and the dot operator (`.`) followed by the name of the property. For example:

```
trace(myArray.length);
```

Obviously, although the types of properties of an object are often shared among all other objects in the same class, the values for the properties for each object can be different. One array might have a length of 5 while another's might be 5000.

Methods are the actions that an object can take. For example, array objects can sort themselves so that all the elements are in order from least to greatest. This method is called `sort()`. Methods are accessed from an object just as properties are by using the dot operator between the object name and the method. Here is how to call the `sort()` method of an Array object:

```
myArray.sort();
```

Again, although objects in the same class may have the same types of methods, the actions that the methods perform are performed on only the object from which the method is called. If you sort one array, only that array is sorted.

Defining Custom Classes

In addition to using the predefined classes, you can create your own custom classes within ActionScript. This can be beneficial if you want to work with a lot of things in your movie that have common traits. For example, if you make a Flash application for working with e-mail, it might be very useful to have a class that defines the characteristics and actions that are held in common by all e-mail messages.

The first thing to do when creating a custom class is to define the constructor. The constructor is simply a named function. A simple constructor for a class called `EmailMessage` could be as follows:

```
function EmailMessage(){}
```

Once the constructor has been created, you can create a new `EmailMessage` object simply by calling it. For example:

```
newMessage = new EmailMessage();
```

Note You may notice that `EmailMessage` is capitalized in the example. By convention, class names are capitalized, whereas object names (variable names) are not.

Understanding the prototype property

Every object in ActionScript has what is called a `prototype` property (which is an object itself). The `prototype` property defines everything that will be inherited by instances of that object. Therefore, classes in ActionScript are actually objects themselves. However, they are special objects with a prototype property defined such that instances of the object will inherit common characteristics and actions.

Adding properties and methods

With the `EmailMessage` class, you might want to define properties such as `smtpServer`, `toAddress`, `fromAddress`, and `subject` that will be shared by all instances, perhaps with default values. You can do this simply by defining the properties for the constructor's prototype object as follows:

```
EmailMessage.prototype.smtpServer = "smtp.myserver.com";
EmailMessage.prototype.toAddress = null;
EmailMessage.prototype.fromAddress = null;
EmailMessage.prototype.subject = "A new email message for you";
```

Note The assignment of the `null` value to the `toAddress` and `fromAddress` properties is not explicitly necessary. The purpose of the assignment is to be very clear in defining values and to practice good form so that it is easy for another developer to read your class code and determine the properties of the class.

Similarly, you can define methods for the class by assigning functions to the prototype object. For example, you might want to create `send()` and `spellCheck()` methods for all `EmailMessage` objects:

```
EmailMessage.prototype.send = function(){
  if(this.toAddress != null){
    // code to send email
  }
}
EmailMessage.prototype.spellCheck = function(){
  // check the spelling and return true or false
}
```

Notice that within the `send()` function, the `toAddress` property is used in an expression and that it is preceded by the word `this` and the dot operator. The keyword `this` is a special word that enables an object to refer to itself. Therefore, when the `send()` method is called, it ensures that the `toAddress` property of the object from which the method is called is not equal to `null`.

Understanding the Event Handler Methods

Now that you have learned about functions and have examined some advanced application of functions in the creation of custom methods, understanding Flash MX's event handler methods should be a snap. I include the discussion of the event handler methods in this chapter because we will be using them extensively throughout the examples and exercises in the book. Therefore, you should become familiar with them beforehand. They are new to Flash MX, so even if you are a Flash 5 ActionScript pro, you may not yet be familiar with how the event handler methods work.

The event handler methods in Flash MX largely replace the `on` and `onClipEvent` event handler constructs from Flash 5. In Flash 5, code was placed on instances of buttons and `MovieClip` objects within these constructs. For example, you might have placed code on a `MovieClip` instance to handle the `enterFrame` event (which occurs at the frame rate of the movie):

```
onClipEvent(enterFrame){
  trace("this gets called a LOT!");
}
```

However, because the code was placed on instances, it was scattered throughout the Flash document and was sometimes difficult to track down. The solution to this problem was obviously to centralize the code (to place it all on one frame as much as possible), and this is exactly what the event handler methods do. The event handler methods enable you to handle the events for individual `MovieClip` and `Button` objects while keeping all the code on *frames*. This means that you never have to hunt for code on instances again. For example, assuming that the preceding code was placed on a `MovieClip` object named `myMc` on the Main Timeline (`_root`), it could be replaced by the following code placed on a frame of the Main Timeline:

```
myMc.onEnterFrame = function(){
  trace("this gets called a LOT!");
}
```

Table 2-4 shows all the event handler methods available, along with the Flash 5 event handler construct equivalent. The table also lists which methods can be used with `MovieClip` objects and which methods can be used with `Button` objects.

Table 2-4: Event Handler Methods

Method	Flash 5 Equivalent	Use with MovieClip?	Use with Button?
onPress	on(press)	yes	yes
onRelease	on(release)	yes	yes
OnReleaseOutside	on(releaseOutside)	yes	yes

Method	Flash 5 Equivalent	Use with MovieClip?	Use with Button?
onRollOver	on(rollOver)	yes	yes
onRollOut	on(rollOut)	yes	yes
onDragOver	on(dragOver)	yes	yes
onDragOut	on(dragOut)	yes	yes
onKeyDown	on(keyPress)/ onClipEvent(load)	yes	yes
onKeyUp	onClipEvent(load)	yes	yes
onSetFocus	None	yes	no
onKillFocus	None	yes	no
onLoad	onClipEvent(load)	yes	no
onUnload	onClipEvent(unload)	yes	no
onEnterFrame	onClipEvent(enterFrame)	yes	no
onMouseDown	onClipEvent(mouseDown)	yes	no
onMouseUp	onClipEvent(mouseUp)	yes	no
onMouseMove	onClipEvent(mouseMove)	yes	no

Summary

In this chapter, you learned about or reviewed the fundamentals of ActionScript. Because ActionScript is a big topic that cannot be easily summarized in one chapter, this chapter covered the main points that you will want to know for use in your Flash Remoting client movies. If later in the book you encounter some ActionScript structure or concept that is unfamiliar to you, come back to this chapter, which discusses the following points:

✦ There are three primitive data types in ActionScript — string, number, and Boolean.

✦ Storing data in variables enables you to easily work with your data. Variables should have descriptive names that adhere to the rules of naming in ActionScript.

✦ Multiple pieces of data can be combined into an expression that resolves to a single value. The pieces of data are combined using operators, to describe the way in which they are related, such as by addition, subtraction, concatenation, or assignment.

✦ Commands in ActionScript are called statements. These statements can be simple, such as simply telling a timeline to stop or play. They can also be more complex, as in the case of conditional and looping statements, which control the flow of code in a movie.

✦ Using arrays is a great way to keep track of related data all in a single structure.

✦ Functions are a way of creating reusable code that can be written once and called many times. They also serve as a great way to break up a program into more manageable pieces.

✦ Object-oriented programming is essential to meeting the demands of larger-scale development such as Flash Remoting applications. Classes describe prototypes for their many instances, which are called objects. Each object is unique and individual, but inherits similar characteristics and functionality from the class.

✦ Flash MX introduced the event handler methods, which can replace the use of Flash 5 event handlers, which were placed on `MovieClip` and `Button` instances. The event handler methods enable all of a Flash document's code to be centralized, rather than scattered throughout instances.

✦   ✦   ✦

Flash Remoting ActionScript Basics

In Chapter 2 you learned about the fundamentals of the ActionScript language. In this chapter I introduce you to the parts of ActionScript that are specific to Flash Remoting. Most of the code and descriptions in this chapter require that you have successfully installed the Flash Remoting Components as described in Chapter 1. The Flash Remoting Components include new ActionScript files such as NetServices.as and NetDebug.as that you learn to utilize throughout this chapter.

Including the NetServices Class

All the Flash Remoting capabilities within ActionScript are based upon a predefined class called NetConnection. I will discuss this class in more detail in just a little bit for those hardcore programmers who want to know how it all works. However, Macromedia has provided a whole set of custom classes that make working with NetConnection objects much easier and more robust than working with the NetConnection class directly. Therefore, the preferred technique is to use these custom classes and not worry about the NetConnection class directly. All these classes are included in the Flash Remoting Components that you installed in Chapter 1.

To connect to the server running Flash Remoting, make sure you add the NetServices class in your Flash document. You can do this with the following line of code:

```
#include "NetServices.as"
```

Tip　Remember that the #include statement should appear on its own line and should not end with a semicolon.

As long as you have added the NetServices class, you can take advantage of the additional functionality this class provides. Therefore, the first line of code you should have in any Flash Remoting Flash document is the #include directive followed by NetServices.as.

Connecting to the Server

All Flash Remoting applications have a client (the Flash movie) and the server (ColdFusion, JRun, .NET, etc.). Without either component, Flash Remoting cannot take place. Therefore, the primary step in developing any Flash Remoting client movie is to create a connection to the server.

Flash movies cannot arbitrarily connect to just any server. It is important to understand that only a server running Flash Remoting will be found when trying to connect from a Flash movie. As you know, ColdFusion MX and JRun 4 come with Flash Remoting already installed. If you wish to work with .NET or Java server other than JRun, you can do that as long as you have installed Flash Remoting successfully for that server. In this chapter, the exercises assume you already have a server running Flash Remoting to which you will be able to connect. If you are using a server other than ColdFusion MX, then you may want to pause here and briefly skip ahead to the chapter that explains how to install Flash Remoting for the server you are using.

Cross-Reference   Chapter 12 discusses how to install and configure Flash Remoting for J2EE application servers (including special instructions for JRun 4 users). Chapter 18 covers installing and configuring Flash Remoting for .NET.

Creating the Connection Object

Once you ensure that you have included the `NetServices` class, you will want to create the connection object. To create this object, you do not use a constructor, but call a static method (one that is called directly from the class, not from an instance of the class) of the `NetServices` class. This method, `createGatewayConnection()`, takes a single parameter — a string value of the URL to which you wish to connect, and returns the connection object (which is actually a `NetConnection` object). Here is an example of the `createGatewayConnection()` method as it might be used in a typical Flash Remoting client file (the FLA):

```
connectionString = "http://localhost/flashservices/gateway";
conn = NetServices.createGatewayConnection(connectionString);
```

Note   The `createGatewayConnection()` method does not create the connection to the server at the time it is called. It waits until the remote procedure is called before attempting to connect.

As an alternative to passing the URL parameter to the `createGatewayConnection()` method, you can first call the static method named `setDefaultGatewayURL()`. When a default URL has been defined in this way, the parameter does not need to be specified in the `createGatewayConnection()` method call. For example:

```
NetServices.setDefaultGatewayURL("http://localhost/flashservices/gateway");
conn = NetServices.createGatewayConnection();
```

Additionally, you can even pass a value to the Flash movie through the `OBJECT` and `EMBED` tags when the movie is embedded in HTML. This is a particularly advantageous technique because it enables your Flash Remoting movies to be as portable as possible. Simply include the `flashParams` parameter for both the `OBJECT` and `EMBED` tags as shown below (in bold) and pass it a name-value pair called `gatewayUrl`:

```
<OBJECT
  classid="clsid:D27CDB6E-AE6D-11cf-96B8-444553540000"
  codebase="http://download.macromedia.com/pub/shockwave/
cabs/flash/swflash.cab#version=6,0,0,0"
  WIDTH="100%"
  HEIGHT="100%"
  id="myMovieName">
<PARAM
  NAME=flashvars
  VALUE="gatewayUrl=http://localhost/flashservices/gateway">
<PARAM NAME=movie VALUE="myMovie.swf">
<PARAM NAME=quality VALUE=high>
<PARAM NAME=bgcolor VALUE=#FFFFFF>
<EMBED src="myMovie.swf"
  FLASHVARS="gatewayUrl=http://localhost/flashservices/gateway"
    quality=high
  bgcolor=#FFFFFF
  WIDTH="100%"
  HEIGHT="100%"
  NAME="myMovieName"
  TYPE="application/x-shockwave-flash"
  PLUGINSPAGE="http://www.macromedia.com/go/getflashplayer">
</EMBED>
</OBJECT>
```

Note

The `gatewayUrl` parameter is picked up by the Flash movie only if the movie is being viewed via HTTP. What this means is that if the HTML page in which the movie is being played is viewed in a Web browser as a local file (i.e., `file://`), then the `gatewayUrl` parameter will not be used. The HTML page must be viewed by way of HTTP (i.e., `http://`) for this functionality to work.

Macromedia recommends (and I see no reason to contradict this recommendation) that you always specify the default gateway URL using the `setDefaultGatewayURL()` method — even if you are planning to pass the `gatewayUrl` parameter through the `OBJECT` and `EMBED` tags. If a `gatewayUrl` parameter is passed to the Flash movie from the HTML page, then that always takes precedence over any other URL that is specified within the ActionScript itself by way of `setDefaultGatewayURL()`. Here is the order in which Flash looks for the gateway URL:

1. If a parameter specifying the URL has been passed to the `createGatewayConnection()` method, then that URL is *always* used to create the connection.

2. The Flash movie will always check whether a `gatewayUrl` parameter has been passed to it via the HTML page. If so, this value takes precedence over the value specified in the `setDefaultGatewayURL()` method, but not over the value specified in the `createGatewayConnection()` method.

3. If no other value is specified (by way of `createGatewayConnection()` or from the `gatewayUrl` parameter passed from the HTML page), then Flash will try to use the URL set using `setDefaultGatewayURL()`.

Choosing the Right Gateway

As you have learned, three types of application servers are compatible with Flash Remoting. The Flash Remoting services can be installed (and already are installed in several cases) for ColdFusion MX, for J2EE application servers (JRun, WebSphere, JBoss, etc.), and for .NET. Once the Flash Remoting services are installed for an application server, the Flash Remoting gateway can be accessed from Flash applications. However, you have to know the proper URL to use in order to gain access to the gateway.

When you use ColdFusion MX with Flash Remoting, you always use the same gateway URL of `http://`*`serverNameOrIP`*`:`*`portNumber`*`/flashservices/gateway/`. For example, if you are running ColdFusion MX in standalone mode (through port 8500) on your local computer, then the gateway URL you'll use within a Flash application is likely to be either `http://localhost:8500/flashservices/gateway/` or `http://127.0.0.1:8500/flashservices/gateway/`.

Flash Remoting for J2EE applications servers requires that you configure the gateway as a servlet in the Web application's web.xml file. You should follow the instructions in Chapter 12 for setting up Flash Remoting for J2EE. Even though Flash Remoting comes preinstalled for JRun, you need to configure that installation in order for it to work properly. When you have properly installed and configured Flash Remoting for J2EE as outlined in Chapter 12, then the correct gateway URL is in the format `http://serverNameOrIP:`*`portNumber`*`/`*`webApplicationContext`*`/gateway`.

The Flash Remoting services installed for .NET use an ASPX file. You should follow the installation instructions in Chapter 18 for setting up your .NET Web application. The ASPX file you use to connect to the gateway needs to be in the root directory of the Web application. It does not need to contain any code whatsoever. Chapter 18 contains instructions for creating this ASPX file. I recommend you always name the file flashgateway.aspx. Therefore, the gateway URL when using Flash Remoting for .NET is in the format `http://serverNameOrIP:`*`portNumber`*`/`*`webApplicationContext`*`/flashgateway.aspx`.

Tip   As you will see, the connection to the gateway (Flash Remoting application server) is not actually made when `createGatewayConnection()` is called. The attempt to connect is not made until a remote procedure is called. This means that you will not receive an error message if the gateway URL is invalid until the remote procedure is called.

Understanding the Gateway Connection

As you now know, creating the gateway connection object is the first step in working with Flash Remoting from the client side. You have seen the three primary ways in which a gateway URL can be specified during this process:

✦ The URL can be passed to the `createGatewayConnection()` method as a parameter.

✦ The URL can be passed to the `setDefaultGatewayURL()` method as a parameter.

✦ The URL can be passed to the Flash movie from the HTML page in which it is embedded using the parameter name of `gatewayUrl`.

You also now know that Flash movies use a precedence in order to determine which of these URL values to use when creating the connection object. The order is as follows:

1. The value specified in `createGatewayConnection()` is always used if defined.

2. The value `gatewayUrl` parameter passed from the HTML page is used if defined.

3. The value specified in `setDefaultGatewayURL()` is used if no other value is found.

The following exercise illustrates these various techniques, and demonstrates the precedence outlined above. This exercise uses an undocumented property of the `NetConnection` class called `uri`. All `NetConnection` objects have this property, and it contains the value of the gateway URL that it will use to make the connection to the server. Here, you will use this property to display the URL for `NetConnection` objects created under each of the possible combinations (value specified in `createGatewayConnection()`, `setDefaultGatewayURL()`, or as the `gatewayUrl` parameter passed from the HTML page).

 Note
You don't need to use working gateway URLs in this exercise. Use the gateway URLs in the example code even if they are not the correct URLs for your system. In this case no connections are actually being made. The purpose is just so that you can see the difference between setting a gateway URL using the `setDefaultGatewayURL()` method and specifying the value during the `createGatewayConnection()` method call. In subsequent exercises throughout this book, however, you will need to be sure to use the correct gateway URL.

1. Make sure that you have installed the Flash Remoting Components and restarted Flash.

2. Open a new Flash document and save it to your hard drive as `gatewayURLTest.fla`.

3. Rename the default layer to `buttons`.

4. Create a new layer and name it `actions`.

5. On the buttons layer, create (drag) two `PushButton` component instances in the lower portion of the stage, as shown in Figure 3-1. Name these instances `defaultBtn` and `specifiedBtn`.

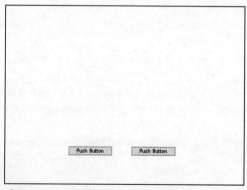

Figure 3-1: Position the buttons on the stage as shown here.

6. Next, open the Actions panel and place the following code on frame 1 of the actions layer:

```
// first things first: include the NetServices class
#include "NetServices.as"

// this function will create the connection object and output the uri
// property of that NetConnection object to a TextField on the stage.
function createConnection(gwUrl){
  conn = NetServices.createGatewayConnection(gwUrl);
  _root.gateway.text = conn.uri;
}

// set up the TextField that will display the value of the URL
x = Stage.width/2 - 150;
y = Stage.height/2;
_root.createTextField("gateway", 0, x, y, 300, 20);
gateway.border = true;

// set the default gateway URL
NetServices.setDefaultGatewayURL("http://localhost/flashservices/
gateway/");

// the defaultBtn will create a NetConnection object with no
// gateway URL specified in the createGatewayConnection() method.
// Therefore, the created object will use the default gateway URL.
defaultBtn.setLabel("use default URL");
defaultBtn.onRelease = function(){
  _root.createConnection();
}

// the specifiedBtn will create a NetConnection object with a
// gateway URL value that is passed to the
// createGatewayConnection() method.
specifiedBtn.setLabel("specify a URL");
specifiedBtn.onRelease = function(){
  _root.createConnection("http://127.0.0.1/flashservices/gateway/");
}
```

7. Publish the SWF and the HTML page with the default publishing settings.

8. These files will need to be viewed by way of a Web server. If the files are not already in a Web server–accessible directory, move these two files to a directory that is accessible from the Web server running on your computer. I recommend you just move them to the Web root.

9. Open the HTML file from your Web browser. You should see something similar to what is shown in Figure 3-2.

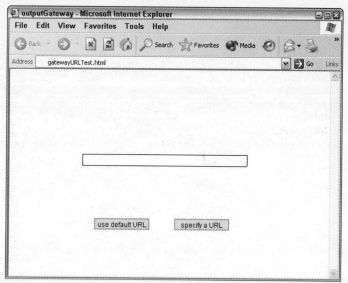

Figure 3-2: A view of the movie after completing steps 1 through 9

10. If you click on the button labeled use default URL, then the value `http://localhost/flashservices/gateway/` should appear in the `TextField` because the default URL is being used in the connection. If you click on the button labeled specify a URL, then you should see the value `http://127.0.0.1/flashservices/gateway/` because the URL is being specified in the `createGatewayConnection()` method and therefore overrides the default URL.

11. Open the `gatewayURLtest.html` file in a text editor or HTML editor such as Dreamweaver. Change the `OBJECT` and `EMBED` tags by adding a `FlashVars` parameter named `gatewayUrl` with a value of `http://localhost:80/flashservices/gateway/`. The HTML should look similar to the following when you have made the changes indicated (modifications are in bold):

```
<HTML>
<HEAD>
<meta http-equiv=Content-Type content="text/html; charset=ISO-
8859-1">
<TITLE>outputGateway</TITLE>
</HEAD>
<BODY bgcolor="#FFFFFF">
<!-- URL's used in the movie-->
<!-- text used in the movie-->
<OBJECT
classid="clsid:D27CDB6E-AE6D-11cf-96B8-444553540000"
codebase="http://download.macromedia.com/pub/shockwave/cabs/flash/swf
lash.cab#version=6,0,0,0"
WIDTH="550"
HEIGHT="400"
```

```
id="outputGateway"
ALIGN="">
<PARAM
  NAME=flashvars
  VALUE="gatewayUrl=http://localhost:80/flashservices/gateway">
<PARAM NAME=movie VALUE="gatewayURLtest.swf">
<PARAM NAME=quality VALUE=high>
<PARAM NAME=bgcolor VALUE=#FFFFFF>
<EMBED
src="gatewayURLtest.swf"
FLASHVARS="gatewayUrl=http://localhost:80/flashservices/gateway"
quality=high
bgcolor=#FFFFFF
WIDTH="550"
HEIGHT="400"
NAME="outputGateway"
ALIGN=""
TYPE="application/x-shockwave-flash"
PLUGINSPAGE="http://www.macromedia.com/go/getflashplayer">
</EMBED>
</OBJECT>
</BODY>
</HTML>
```

 12. Save the HTML file and view it in the browser again. This time, when you click on the
     button labeled specify a URL, the same value should appear as previously
     (http://127.0.0.1/flashservices/gateway/). However, clicking on the button
     labeled use default URL will display http://localhost:80/flashservices/gateway/,
     as the value passed from the HTML page will override the value set by
     setDefaultGatewayURL().

Choosing a Service

Once you have established the gateway URL and created a NetConnection object, the next
step is to choose a service. A service in the context of Flash Remoting refers to the container
for the remote procedure that will be called. For example, if you want to call a JavaBean
method, then the service is the JavaBean — the container for the method. If you want to call a
ColdFusion function, then the service is the ColdFusion Component that contains the function. Table 3-1 shows the service that corresponds to each kind of remote procedure.

Table 3-1: Services Corresponding to Remote Procedure Types

Remote Procedure	Service
ColdFusion	
ColdFusion page	Directory structure (from the web root) containing ColdFusion page
ColdFusion function	Path (from the web root) and name (without file extension) of ColdFusion Component
ColdFusion web services method	Web service namespace

Remote Procedure	Service
Java	
JavaBean (or other Java class) public method	Fully qualified Java class name (including packages)
EJB method	JNDI name for the home interface
MBean method	MBean object name
.NET	
ASP.NET page	Directory structure (from the web root) containing ASP.NET page
DLL method	Fully qualified DLL name (without file extension)
.NET web services method	Web service namespace

When you create a service object, you specify the service that will be used. The service object is actually an instance of the NetServiceProxy class, and it is created by way of the getService() method of the connection (NetConnection) object. Once you have created a connection object, you can call the getService() method from that object. The getService() method returns a NetServiceProxy object (the service object), so you will likely want to assign that returned value to a variable. The getService() method requires that it be passed a string value indicating the service to be used (refer to Table 3-1). Here is an example of a service object being created (using a connection object named conn, as was created in the previous stage):

```
srv = conn.getService("flashPages");
```

This example most likely (based on the name of the service) would be indicating the directory under the web root where either ColdFusion or ASP.NET pages could be found. If the desired page (which will be the remote procedure) is actually located in a subdirectory of the flashPages directory, then the directory names would be separated by a dot (.), with the parent directory coming first. For example, if the ColdFusion page to be used as a remote procedure by Flash is located in the subdirectory of flashPages named databaseCalls, then the service object creation would look like this:

```
srv = conn.getService("flashPages.databaseCalls");
```

In the previous examples, I suggested that the services indicated were most likely directories. Obviously, a directory name has no file extension. Therefore, the value passed to the getService() method will have no extension either. However, many of the other types of services that can be used by Flash Remoting *do* have file extensions. For example, JavaBeans (.class), DLLs (.dll), and ColdFusion Components (.cfc) all have file extensions. However, when indicating the service name, you *should not* include the file extension. For example, to create a service object using a JavaBean class named FlashBean.class, you would indicate that service in the following way when creating the service object:

```
srv = conn.getService("FlashBean");
```

If there are packages or namespaces that need to be indicated to make the name fully qualified, then these paths or packages should be separated by a dot (.) as well. For example, if FlashBean is a part of the package flash, then the service object creation code would look like this:

```
srv = conn.getService("flash.FlashBean");
```

Calling a Remote Procedure

When you have created both the connection object and the service object, you can then make calls to the remote procedures available from the selected service. For example, if you created a service object that maps to a Java class, then you can call all the public methods of that class directly from the service object within the Flash application. Or, if you created a service object that maps to a directory containing ASP.NET or ColdFusion pages, you can then invoke those pages from the service object within Flash.

Invoking the Remote Procedure from the Service Object

Assuming that you have a service object named `srv` mapped to a service on the Flash Remoting server (such as a JavaBean or a directory containing a ColdFusion page), and that the service has a procedure named `someProcedure`, you can call that procedure using the following code:

```
srv.someProcedure();
```

This code will then make a connection to the server (based on the gateway URL contained in the connection object), locate the service (specified in the service object), and invoke `someProcedure`. Based on the type of service that is being used, the Flash Remoting server will automatically search for the appropriate procedure type. For instance, if the service is a `JavaBean` class, then the Flash Remoting server will attempt to locate a public method with the name `someProcedure`. On the other hand, if the service is a directory containing ColdFusion pages, then the Flash Remoting server will automatically search for a ColdFusion page named `someProcedure.cfm`. Notice that no remote procedure call should include any file extensions, even for ASP.NET and ColdFusion page calls. Table 3-2 shows how to determine the remote procedure name to use in ActionScript.

Table 3-2: Determining the Remote Procedure Name to Use in ActionScript

Remote Procedure	Service
ColdFusion	
ColdFusion page	ColdFusion page name without file extension
ColdFusion function	ColdFusion function name
ColdFusion web services method	Web services method name exposed through WSDL
Java	
JavaBean (or other Java class) public method	Public method name
EJB method	Method name
MBean method	Method name
.NET	
ASP.NET page	ASP.NET page name without file extension
DLL method	Public method name
.NET web services method	Web services method name exposed through WSDL

Here are a few different examples of remote procedures being called:

```
// include the NetServices.as file
#include "NetServices.as"
// ----------- ColdFusion examples ------------ //

// create the connection object to the ColdFusion gateway
cfGwUrl = "http://localhost:8500/flashservices/gateway/";
cfConn = NetServices.createGatewayConnection(cfGwUrl);

// create service object for CF pages directory service where
// directory is called flashCFPages and resides under the
// CF web root
cfDirSrv = cfConn.getService("flashCFPages");

// call CF pages in the flashCFPages directory named getTime.cfm
// and getUsers.cfm
cfDirSrv.getTime();
cfDirSrv.getUsers();

// create a service object for a CF Component named dbFunctions.cfc
// that is in a directory named flashCFCs under the CF web root
cfcSrv = cfConn.getService("flashCFCs.dbFunctions");

// call a function defined inside dbFunctions.cfc named
// incrementVisitCounter()
cfcSrv.incrementVisitCounter();

// ----------- Java examples ------------ //

// create the connection object to the gateway. In this example
// we will pretend that we are using the JRun 4 samples server
// running on port 8200
jrunGwUrl = "http://localhost:8200/flashservices/gateway/";
jrunConn = NetServices.createGatewayConnection(jrunGwUrl);

// create a service object for a JavaBean using a class named//
FlashBean (file named FlashBean.class). FlashBean is in the flash
// package in this example.
jBeanSrv = jrunConn.getService("flash.FlashBean");

// now call a public method of the bean called logout();
jBeanSrv.logout();

// ----------- .NET examples ------------ //

// create the connection object to the gateway
netGwUrl = "http://localhost/flashservices/gateway.aspx";
netConn = NetServices.createGatewayConnection(netGwUrl);

// create a service object for ASP.NET pages directory service
// where directory is called flashASPages and resides under the
// .NET web root
aspNetSrv = netConn.getService("flashASPages");
```

```
// call the ASP.NET page named getAccountInfo.aspx that is in the
// flashASPages directory
aspNetSrv.getAccountInfo();
```

Passing Parameters to Remote Procedures

Thus far, you have learned how to call remote procedures that do not require any parameters. However, as you likely know, you will often want to be able to pass parameters to a remote procedure. For example, if you want to call a function or method that retrieves account information, you likely would want to pass that function parameters, such as a user identification number to specify the account for which you want information. Fortunately, passing parameters to a remote procedure works much like it would if the procedure were being called in any other context. After all, the purpose of Flash Remoting is to enable remote procedures to be accessed in much the same manner as if they were defined within the Flash application itself.

In order to pass parameters to a remote procedure, you can simply add them as a comma-delimited list between the function call operators (( )), as you would with any other function call in Flash. For example, suppose that you have created a service object named srv that maps to a JavaBean. This bean has a public method called getAccountInfo(). The method expects a parameter as a number (account ID) specifying the account for which you wish to retrieve the information. You could then call this method in the following manner:

```
srv.getAccountInfo(12345);
```

If the method instead expected two parameters — a username and a password — then you could call it with the following code:

```
srv.getAccountInfo("johnDoe", "IPass");
```

One of the major advantages that Flash Remoting offers over non–Flash Remoting application development is that you can pass parameters to remote methods from Flash with all kinds of data types, and not just as string values. This includes passing string, number, Boolean, Array, and Object data types, just to name a few. These data types are converted by the gateway to native data types for each platform (Java, C#, etc.); these data type conversions are covered in greater detail in their corresponding chapters later in the book.

Cross-Reference Chapter 6 contains more information on converting between ColdFusion and ActionScript data types. Chapter 12 covers the conversions between Java and ActionScript data types, and Chapter 18 discusses conversions between .NET (C# and VB) and ActionScript data types.

Handling Results

You should now know how to make remote procedure calls using Flash Remoting. What we have not yet covered is how to process any results or returned values. Obviously, this is a very important part of making calls to any procedures. Many procedures will return a value. For example, a function named getAccountInfo() (used as an example in the previous section) implies that it will return an object containing information about a user account such as name, contact information, and account activity. Therefore, handling this returned data is an important part of working with such a procedure. However, even if a procedure does not return a value (such as a function that simply inserts a value into a database), you still will likely want to be able to handle any possible errors. For example, if the gateway is down or the provided URL is invalid, then an error will be returned. Handling this error (and any errors) is a good idea so that the application user can be alerted as to what has happened.

Remote procedure calls in Flash are asynchronous, meaning that the ActionScript interpreter does not wait for a response from the server before continuing to the next line of ActionScript code after the remote procedure call. For example, with the following code:

```
#include "NetServices.as"
gwUrl = "http://localhost:8500/flashservices/gateway/";
conn = NetServices.createGatewayConnection(gwUrl);
srv = conn.getService("someService");
srv.someProcedure();
trace("this will write to the Output window");
```

the `trace()` action will likely be executed before any results are returned from the server from the preceding line of code (the remote procedure call). If a function defined within a Flash application returns a value, then the function call is normally assigned to a variable or used in an expression. For example:

```
function returnVal(){
  return "someVal";
}


outputMessage = returnVal();
trace(outputMessage);
```

However, because you cannot rely on the remote procedure's returning a value quickly enough, you need another way of working with the results of a remote procedure call. In fact, there is another way. There are essentially two ways for handling results with remote procedure calls:

✦ Named response/callback functions

✦ Response object

Regardless of which technique is used, you can handle two types of responses — results (returned value) and status (generally an error of some kind).

Working with Named Response Functions

Named response functions are one way of handling responses from remote procedure calls. These custom functions (meaning you define them) must be named as *remoteProcedure Name*_Result and *remoteProcedureName*_Status. For example, if the remote procedure being called is named `getTime`, then there should be a pair of named response functions called `getTime_Result` and `getTime_Status`.

When you use the named response function technique, you need to pass a second parameter to the `getService()` method. The second parameter should specify the location of the named response functions. Generally, the value of this parameter will simply be `this`, but it is possible for the value to be any other object (`Object` object or `MovieClip` object, for instance) in which the named response functions are defined.

You can also specify the location of the named response functions for each remote procedure call, as you will do with response objects (see the next section). Although this approach works (and there is technically nothing wrong with it), it simply makes more sense to use a response object instead in most cases.

The named response functions are each automatically passed parameters. The result function is passed a single parameter that contains the returned value, and the status function is passed a parameter that contains information about the type of error that occurred.

Listing 3-1 is an example of a remote procedure call, complete with results and status handling via named response functions.

Listing 3-1: **Using Named Response Functions**

```
#include "NetServices.as"
gwUrl = "http://localhost:8500/flashservices/gateway/";
conn = NetServices.createGatewayConnection(gwUrl);

// define the named response functions for the getTime procedure
function getTime_Result(result){
  trace("the following was the result: " + result);
}

function getTime_Status(status){
  trace("a status change occurred. Here is some information:");
  trace(status.description);
}

// creates a service object mapped to the CF web root
// and specifies that the named response functions
// are defined in this
srv = conn.getService("", this);

// call a CF page called getTime.cfm
srv.getTime();
```

Notice that the status parameter is an object with a property named description. The parameter passed to the status function is always an object with the following properties:

✦ level: This property currently always has the value of "Error".

✦ description: This property provides a description of the error that occurred. For example, if a ColdFusion page of the specified name were not found, the value of this property would be "Service threw an exception during method invocation: null".

✦ type: This property indicates the type of error that occurred.

✦ code: This property currently always has the value of "SERVER.PROCESSING".

✦ `details`: This property contains the stack trace of the error that occurred.

✦ `rootcause`: If the error is `java.ServletException`, then this property is included and contains additional information about the error.

There is one major shortcoming in working with named response functions, however. If you make several calls to the same remote procedure and want to handle each result individually, then the named response functions can be potentially problematic. Fortunately, you have another technique for working with responses to remote procedures.

Working with Response Objects

Response objects are my preferred technique for handling responses from remote procedure calls. For this reason, I use this technique throughout the rest of the book. Response objects are not necessarily better than working with named response functions. However, I prefer them for the following reasons:

✦ Response objects allow for multiple calls to a single remote procedure, with each response being handled by a different object (with each object being an instance of the same class).

✦ Organizationally, response objects are neater and simpler to use.

The response object can be any object for which an `onResult()` (and optionally an `onStatue()`) method is defined. Generally, you can define these objects in one of two ways:

✦ Create a new `Object` object and define an `onResult()` and `onStatus()` method for it.

✦ Create a definition for a class of objects for which the an `onResult()` (and optionally an `onStatus()`) method is also defined. Then create an instance of this class to be used as the response object. (You can see an example of this in the section "Creating a class of response objects.")

In either case, the `onResult()` and `onStatus()` methods are automatically passed parameters when invoked. This is exactly the same as when the named response functions are used. When the `onResult()` method is called, it is automatically passed a parameter with the value returned by the remote procedure., The `onStatus()` method is automatically passed a parameter with the properties indicated in the previous section.

Note   The ActionScript interpreter requires only that an `onResult()` method be defined if an object is to be considered a response object. But the `onResult()` method must always be defined — even if you wish to only handle errors with `onStatus()`. An object with an `onStatus()` method but without an `onResult()` method will not be understood to be a response object.

Creating a Single Response Object

First let's look at creating a response object using an `Object` constructor. This technique differs from the named response function technique only slightly. Rather than having numerous named response functions to contend with, this technique groups the function pairs into a single object. For example:

```
// first create the object itself
res = new Object();
// next, define the onResult() and onStatus() methods
```

```
res.onResult = function (result){
  trace("the following was the result: " + result);
}
res.onStatus = function (status){
  trace("a status change occurred. Here is some information:");
  trace(status.description);
}
```

Once a response object has been created in this way, you can then simply specify that this object should be used to handle the responses for the remote procedures. One way of doing this mirrors what you did with the named response functions. You can specify a default response object to handle all the responses for a particular service by passing a reference to the object as the second parameter of the getService() method call:

```
srv = conn.getService("someService", res);
```

Listing 3-2 rewrites Listing 3-1 by using a response object created with the Object constructor (changes are indicated in bold).

Listing 3-2: **Using an Object Response Object**

```
#include "NetServices.as"
gwUrl = "http://localhost:8500/flashservices/gateway/";
conn = NetServices.createGatewayConnection(gwUrl);

// define the response object
res = new Object();
res.onResult = function (result){
  trace("the following was the result: " + result);
}
res.onStatus = function (status){
  trace("a status change occurred. Here is some information:");
  trace(status.description);
}

// creates a service object mapped to the CF web root
// and specifies that the response object named res
// should be used for all procedures invoked from this
// service
srv = conn.getService("", res);

// call a CF page called getTime.cfm
srv.getTime();
```

I still prefer the aesthetics of using a response object in this manner, rather than using a named response function, but it is true that there is little functional advantage in this example. The next section describes how to create a custom class of response objects, and the advantages that this technique offers.

Creating a class of response objects

Creating a class of response object can allow for increased flexibility and power in handling responses in some cases. For instance, in the previous examples, if multiple calls were made to the same remote procedure, there would be no way to effectively distinguish between the results—to know which result matched which procedure call. If, however, each procedure call is assigned its own response object based on the same class, then the possibility exists.

Therefore, the first thing you need to learn is how to specify a unique response object for each remote procedure call. Thus far, you have seen only how to assign a default response object for all procedures called from a given service. This is done by passing a reference to the object as a second parameter to the getService() method. However, you can also specify a unique response object for each remote procedure call by specifying a reference to the response object as the first (in some cases, the only) parameter in the remote procedure call. For example:

```
// assuming a connection object named conn already exists
srv = conn.getService("someService");

res = new Object();
res.onResult = function (result){
  trace("the following was the result: " + result);
}
res.onStatus = function (status){
  trace("a status change occurred. Here is some information:");
  trace(status.description);
}


// call the remote procedure and pass it a parameter specifying
// that the response for this call should be handled by
// the res object
srv.someProcedure(res);
```

In this example, the remote procedure (someProcedure()) does not require any parameters. Because the parameter passed to it is a response object (an object with onResult() and onStatus() defined), the ActionScript interpreter automatically knows to interpret the parameter as the response object and not to send it to the remote procedure. If you are going to pass parameters to the remote procedure, then you should simply add the response object reference just before the rest of the parameters. If the remote procedure named someProcedure() from the previous example required three parameters, for instance, then it could be called in the following way to specify the response object at the same time:

```
srv.someProcedure(res, "one", "two", "three");
```

Listing 3-3 shows how the code from Listing 3-2 could be rewritten (changes in bold) by specifying the response object in the procedure call and not as a default response object for the service.

Listing 3-3: Specifying the Response Object in the Procedure Call

```
#include "NetServices.as"
gwUrl = "http://localhost:8500/flashservices/gateway/";
conn = NetServices.createGatewayConnection(gwUrl);

// define the response object
res = new Object();
res.onResult = function (result){
  trace("the following was the result: " + result);
}
res.onStatus = function (status){
  trace("a status change occurred. Here is some information:");
  trace(status.description);
}

// creates a service object mapped to the CF web root
srv = conn.getService("");

// call a CF page called getTime.cfm and specify
// that the res object should handle the response
srv.getTime(res);
```

Caution   Do not specify a response object both in the getService() method and in the remote procedure call. Doing so will cause the response object specified in the remote procedure call to
be passed to the remote procedure, instead of interpreted as a response object. This can
(and likely will) cause errors.

Now that you know how to specify a response object for each procedure call, let's examine
how to use this in conjunction with a custom class for response objects to produce a more
sophisticated and powerful model for handling remote procedure responses.

The first thing to do when creating a custom class of response objects is to create a constructor function. Here is an example of a generic constructor function for a class of response
objects:

```
function Responder(){}
```

With a constructor function defined, the next step is to define an onResult() and
onStatus() method for the class's prototype. Here is an example of both an onResult() and
an onStatus() method defined for the Responder class's prototype:

```
Responder.prototype.onResult = function (result){
  trace("the following was the result: " + result);
}
Responder.prototype.onStatus = function (status){
  trace("a status change occurred. Here is some information:");
  trace(status.description);
}
```

Now that you have defined a class of response objects, you can specify instances of this class to be used to handle responses from remote procedure calls. For example, Listing 3-3 could be rewritten as shown in Listing 3-4 (with the changes shown in bold).

Listing 3-4: Using a Response Object Class Instance

```
#include "NetServices.as"
gwUrl = "http://localhost:8500/flashservices/gateway/";
conn = NetServices.createGatewayConnection(gwUrl);

// define the response object class
function Responder(){}
Responder.prototype.onResult = function (result){
  trace("the following was the result: " + result);
}
Responder.prototype.onStatus = function (status){
  trace("a status change occurred. Here is some information:");
  trace(status.description);
}


// creates a service object mapped to the CF web root
srv = conn.getService("");

// call a CF page called getTime.cfm and create a new
// instance of the Responder class to handle the response
srv.getTime(new Responder());
```

The example code shown in Listing 3-4 does not yet really illustrate the power of creating a custom class of response objects. To really see this, you will want to call the remote procedure several times and use different instances of the `Responder` class to handle the responses. For example:

```
srv.getTime(new Responder());
srv.getTime(new Responder());
srv.getTime(new Responder());
```

In this example, each remote procedure call's response will be handled by a different object. As this example stands thus far, each response is handled identically. However, you can add additional logic to the `Responder` class, enabling each response to be handled more intelligently. As I have suggested previously, there is no inherent way to know which response is from which procedure call. However, if some additional functionality is built into the class of response objects, then this becomes relatively easy to track. You can take several different approaches to this task. The one that seems most straightforward to me is simply to give each response object an ID when it is created. Then it is easy to know which response is from which procedure call. Listing 3-5 rewrites the code from Listing 3-4 (with changes in bold) such that each response object is given an ID when it is created so that you can easily tell which response goes with which procedure call.

Listing 3-5: Assigning IDs to Each Response Object

```
#include "NetServices.as"
gwUrl = "http://localhost:8500/flashservices/gateway/";
conn = NetServices.createGatewayConnection(gwUrl);

// define the response object class
function Responder (id){
  this.id = id;
}
Responder.prototype.onResult = function (result){
  trace("there was a response from " + this.id);
  trace("the following was the result: " + result);
}
Responder.prototype.onStatus = function (status){
  trace("there was a response from " + this.id);
  trace("a status change occurred. Here is some information:");
  trace(status.description);
}

// creates a service object mapped to the CF web root
srv = conn.getService("");

// call a CF page called getTime.cfm three times and create a new
// instance of the Responder class with a id to handle the response
// for each
srv.getTime(new Responder(0));
srv.getTime(new Responder(1));
srv.getTime(new Responder(2));
```

It is hoped that this gives you an idea of how classes of response objects can be utilized. There are so many possibilities that I couldn't possibly cover them all in this section. Now that you are familiar with how response objects work, and particularly with how classes of response objects work, you should be ready to start using response objects throughout the examples in the rest of the book.

Understanding Precedence with Response Handlers

There exists a precedence by which responses are handled. First of all (and fairly obviously), if a response object is specified in the procedure call, then that response object is used to handle the response and takes precedence over any other response objects or named response functions otherwise specified.

Otherwise, the precedence for how responses are handled is as follows:

1. If the specified response object contains a method (a function) named *procedureName*_Result(), that method is used to handle the results. If the specified response object contains a method (a function) named *procedureName*_Status(), that method is used to handle any errors.

2. If no methods (functions) follow the named response function naming format, then ActionScript will next look for methods named `onResult()` and `onStatus()` to handle the result and any error, respectively.

3. If the response object contains no method (function) following the named response function naming format *and* no `onStatus()` method, then in the event of an error response, ActionScript will last look to see if there is an `onStatus()` method defined for `_root`. If so, this method will be used to handle the response.

Working Directly with NetConnection

The `NetConnection` class is a native class in Flash MX (meaning that it is part of the standard installation along with `MovieClip`, `Date`, `XML`, etc.). In the previous sections of this chapter, you learned how to make calls to remote procedures using additional functionality provided by `NetServices` and other classes that are installed as part of the Flash Remoting Components installation. These classes are all written in ActionScript and simply serve to make the use of the `NetConnection` class a little more friendly. As such, I see every reason to use these additional classes when writing Flash Remoting applications. However, for those who wish to know more about the low-level functionality of the `NetConnection` class, I am including this section.

There are essentially three steps to making a remote procedure call using only a `NetConnection` object:

1. Create the `NetConnection` object using the constructor function.

2. Make the connection to the Flash Remoting gateway using the `connect()` method.

3. Call the remote procedure using the `call()` method.

Creating the NetConnection Object

The first step in working directly with the `NetConnection` class is to instantiate an object. Doing this is as simple as calling the constructor function:

```
conn = new NetConnection();
```

Making the Connection to the Server

The next step in working directly with the low-level `NetConnection` class is to create the connection to the server. To do this, you need only to call the `connect()` method of the newly created `NetConnection` object. The `connect()` method takes a single parameter — the gateway URL. Here is an example of how the `connect()` method might be used to create a connection to the Flash Remoting gateway running on the standalone ColdFusion MX server running on the local computer:

```
conn.connect("http://localhost:8500/flashservices/gateway/");
```

Incidentally, when you use the `connect()` method, you have the option of omitting the `http://` or `https://` portion of the URL. For example, the following would be perfectly acceptable:

```
conn.connect("localhost:8500/flashservices/gateway/");
```

However, be aware that this applies *only* to the `connect()` method. This will *not* work when using the `setDefaultGatewayURL()` or `createGatewayConnection()` methods.

Calling the Remote Procedure

When you include the `NetServices` class, it adds a few methods to the `NetConnection` class, such as the `getService()` method you used in previous sections. However, the service and procedure names are all lumped into one step when you work directly with a `NetConnection` object. The final step in calling a remote procedure with a `NetConnection` object (used directly) is using the `call()` method. The `call()` method requires two parameters — a string value representing the service and procedure names and a reference to a response object to handle the results. Any parameters that are to be passed on to the remote procedure can be included as well.

Following is an example of the `call()` method being invoked to call a remote procedure named *someProcedure* that exists for a service named *someService*. The response from this procedure is passed to a response object named `res`.

```
conn.call("someService.someProcedure", res);
```

If the procedure expects some parameters to be passed to it, those parameters can be specified after the response object. For example:

```
conn.call("someService.someProcedure", res, "one", "two", "three");
```

Note   The `call()` method allows for only response objects with `onResult()` and `onStatus()` methods defined to be used. The named response functions feature is something that is added by the additional classes installed as part of the Flash Remoting Components.

Putting Remoting into Action

Now that you have learned the fundamentals of Flash Remoting ActionScript, it is time for you to put it to use. In this exercise, you will apply most of the principles that you learned in this chapter in order to do the following:

✦ Specify a gateway URL to use for making the connection to the Flash Remoting gateway.

✦ Set a default gateway URL in case none is selected.

✦ Choose the service to be used.

✦ Make a call to a remote procedure both with and without parameters.

✦ Handle responses.

On this book's companion Web site, ColdFusion, Java, and .NET samples have been provided for you for this exercise. Therefore, you don't yet have to worry about how to write the server-side code. For now, the focus is on the ActionScript, client-side part of Flash Remoting. I will provide you with instructions on what to do with these files. Then we will create the Flash application.

The Flash application will provide the user with the opportunity to select the gateway. Once a gateway is selected, the user can then log in. Once logged in, the user can retrieve account information such as name, address, city, and job description. Of course, this is all just a tutorial at this point. The data is all hardcoded into the server-side scripts/classes/pages. However, by working through this exercise, you should gain enough hands-on knowledge to feel comfortable working with Flash Remoting ActionScript.

Setting Up the Server Side

The first step in this exercise is to make sure that you have the server-side part set up. The server-side part comprises the ColdFusion Component, JavaBean class, and the ASP.NET DLL provided for you on the Web site. You are certainly not obligated to use all three versions. They all do the same thing. In fact, I am assuming that most of you will be using only one platform. However, if you happen to be using two or even three platforms, feel free to set up all three versions and try them out.

Setting up the Coldfusion component

If you are working with ColdFusion MX, then you will find on the Web site a ColdFusion Component named `User.cfc`. This file contains both of the functions that your Flash movie will call. Therefore, all you need to do is to move this file. Because the service that will be called by the Flash movie is named `Wiley.chapter3.User`, make sure that you place `User.cfc` in a directory named `Wiley\chapter3` (where `chapter3` is a subdirectory of the `Wiley` directory). These directories should be created inside the ColdFusion MX web root (see Figures 3-3 and 3-4). In a typical Windows installation of ColdFusion, the Web root is located in `C:\CFusionMX\wwwroot\`.

Figure 3-3: Creating the Wiley directory inside the ColdFusion Web root

Setting up the JavaBean

In this book, I primarily assume that if you are on a Java platform, you are either using JRun or you are sufficiently adept with your chosen application server (WebSphere, JBoss, etc.) that you do not need to be instructed in detail about where to place files such as JavaBean classes so that they will be picked up by the application server. If you are on a Java platform, then you will want to locate the `User.class` file found on the Web site and download this file to the location in which it will be picked up by the application server. In addition, note that the `User` class is in the `wiley.chapter3` package (to correspond to the `wiley.chapter3.User` service called by the Flash movie). This means that you need to ensure that the class file is copied into a folder named `wiley\chapter3`.

Figure 3-4: Creating the chapter3 subdirectory within Wiley

In most exercises throughout this book I recommend you create a new Web application and manually configure the Flash Remoting gateway following the steps outlined in Chapter 12. If you are using a non-JRun application server, you need to complete those steps before proceeding. Once you have completed those steps, you should create a `wiley\chapter3` directory within the application's `WEB-INF\classes` directory and copy `User.class` to it.

If you are using JRun 4 you do not need to burden yourself with setting up a Web application and configuring the application server. I suggest you use the samples server running on port 8200 for this exercise. The samples server (in the default JRun 4 installation) can be located in the Windows file system under `C:\JRun4\servers\samples`. To have the JavaBean be picked up by this server, create a directory named `wiley` in the `SERVER-INF\classes` subdirectory (see Figures 3-5 and 3-6) of the samples server installation, and within that directory create a subdirectory named chapter3. Then copy the `User` class file to that new directory.

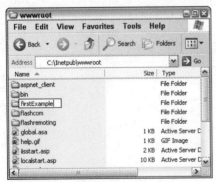

Figure 3-5: Creating the Wiley directory for the JRun samples server

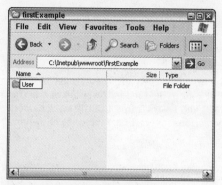

Figure 3-6: Creating the chapter3
directory within Wiley

Setting up the ASP.NET pages

If you are using .NET, then you will want to use the DLL file found on the Web site named
User.dll. In later exercises throughout this book you will be instructed how to set up a custom Web application. However, for the purposes of this exercise you should use the default
application that is set up when you installed Flash Remoting. If you have a standard installation,
then the Web root will be C:\Inetput\wwwroot\, and within this directory you should find the
flashremoting directory (the root of the default Flash Remoting application). Copy the
User.dll file from the Web site to the bin directory of the default Flash Remoting application.

Writing the Flash Remoting Client

Now that you have successfully set up the server-side part of this exercise, the next step is to
create the Flash application that will make the calls to the server-side procedures.

1. On the Web site, you will find a file named firstExample_starter.fla. Open this file
   and save it to your local hard disk as firstExample.fla.

2. Name all the TextField instances:

   a. The large, multiline, dynamic TextField instance in the center of the stage
      should be named output. This instance will display the output to the user during
      use of the application, such as the gateway URL being used, the login status, and
      user information.

   b. At the bottom left are two input TextField instances. The top one should be
      named username and the bottom one should be named password. These will be
      used for enabling the user to log in.

3. Name the ComboBox component instance. This instance, located in the upper part of
   the stage (labeled "select a gateway") should be given a name of gateway.

4. Name the PushButton component instances:

   a. The PushButton instance located at the top of the stage next to the gateway
      ComboBox should be named selectGatewayBt.

    b. The `PushButton` instance located in the bottom left of the stage nearest the `username` and `password` `TextField` instances should be named `loginBt`.

    c. The `PushButton` instance located in the bottom right of the stage (the only remaining one) should be named `getUserInfoBt`.

5. Everything should now be named, so the final step is to add the ActionScript code. All of the code is provided here; you can find a more detailed explanation of it in the next section. Open the Actions panel (press F9) and select frame 1 of the layer named actions (which I generally refer to as the actions layer). Place the code shown in Listing 3-6 on this frame:

Listing 3-6: The ActionScript code in firstExample.fla

```
// make sure to always include NetServices.as if you plan
// to use any of its functionality!
#include "NetServices.as"

// this is a function that will be used to ensure that the
// contents of the output TextField are always scrolled
// all the way to the bottom
function scrollDown(){
  _root.output.scroll = _root.output.maxscroll;
}

// define the response object for the login procedure call
loginRes = new Object();
loginRes.onResult = function(result){
  // the result should be either true or false...display that
  // result in the output TextField
  _root.output.text += "login status: " + result + newline;
  // make sure the output is scrolled down
  _root.scrollDown();
  // once the user has logged in, enable the button to
  // get the user information
  _root.getUserInfoBt.enabled = result;
}
loginRes.onStatus = function(status){
  // if an error occurs make sure to output that
  _root.output.text += "an error occurred..." + newline;
  _root.output.text += status.description + newline;
  // make sure the output is scrolled down
  _root.scrollDown();
}

// define the response object for the getUserInfo procedure call
infoRes = new Object();
infoRes.onResult = function(result){
  // display the result properties in the output TextField
```

```
  _root.output.text += "name: " + result.name + newline;
  _root.output.text += "address: " + result.address + newline;
  _root.output.text += "city: " + result.city + newline;
  _root.output.text += "job: " + result.job + newline;
  // make sure the output is scrolled down
  _root.scrollDown();
}
infoRes.onStatus = function(status){
  // if an error occurs make sure to output that
  _root.output.text += "an error occured..." + newline;
  _root.output.text += status.description + newline;
  // make sure the output is scrolled down
  _root.scrollDown();
}


// define the action for when the selectGatewayBt is released
selectGatewayBt.onRelease = function(){
  // first set the gateway connection URL and create the
  // connection object
  _root.conn =
NetServices.createGatewayConnection(_root.gateway.getValue());
  // then create the service object
  _root.userSrv = conn.getService("wiley.chapter3.User");
  // display the connection information in the output TextField
  _root.output.text += "using gateway: " + _root.gateway.getValue() +
newline;
  // make sure the output is scrolled down
  _root.scrollDown();
}


loginBt.onRelease = function(){
  // check to see if no gateway URL was selected
  if(_root.conn == undefined){
    // use default gateway URL and create connectio object
    _root.conn = NetServices.createGatewayConnection();
  // create the service object
    _root.userSrv = conn.getService("wiley.chapter3.User");
  // tell the user that the default gateway URL is being used
  _root.output.text += "using default gateway URL" + newline;
  // make sure the output is scrolled down
    _root.scrollDown();
  }
  // call the login procedure, specify that the loginRes object
  // should be used to handle the response, and pass the procedure
  // the username and password the user entered into the form
  _root.userSrv.login(_root.loginRes, _root.username.text,
_root.password.text);
}
```

Continued

```
getUserInfoBt.onRelease = function(){
  // call the getUserInfo procedure and specify that the
  // infoRes object should be used to handle the response
  _root.userSrv.getUserInfo(_root.infoRes);
}

// the init() function will be called to initialize the movie
function init(){
  // when the movie first starts make sure that the getUserInfoBt
  // button is not enabled
  getUserInfoBt.enabled = false;

  // set the labels on the PushButton objects
  selectGatewayBt.setLabel("Use Selected");
  loginBt.setLabel("Login");
  getUserInfoBt.setLabel("Get User Info");

  // add the items to the gateway ComboBox
  // the values defined here are the standard values, but if
  // you have a non-standard installation of your application
  // server make sure to modify the values accordingly
  gateway.addItem("ColdFusion",
"http://localhost:8500/flashservices/gateway/");
  gateway.addItem("JRun",
"http://localhost:8200/flashservices/gateway/");
  gateway.addItem("Non-JRun J2EE",
"http://localhost:8880/Wiley/gateway");
  gateway.addItem(".NET",
"http://localhost/flashremoting/gateway.aspx");

  // set the default gateway URL in case no other URL is selected

NetServices.setDefaultGatewayURL("http://localhost:8500/flashservices/g
ateway/");
}

// call the init() function
init();
```

6. Now you are ready to test it. Either export the SWF and run it or test the movie (Control⇨Test Movie):

    a. Select the correct gateway from the ComboBox menu (see Figure 3-7) and click the Use Selected button. Alternatively, if the default gateway you specified using setDefaultGatewayURL() is the one you want, you can skip this step and proceed to b.

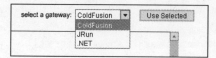

Figure 3-7: Selecting the correct gateway from the menu

b. Enter the login information and click the Login button. The correct username is `igoodie` and the correct password is `12345` (see Figure 3-8). You may want to first try a wrong combination to verify that it returns `false`.

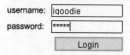

Figure 3-8: Enter the username and password and click the Login button.

c. Once you have entered and submitted the correct username and password, the remote procedure should return `true`. This enables the Get User Info button. Click this button and you should see the information for Ima Goodie displayed in the `output` TextField (see Figure 3-9).

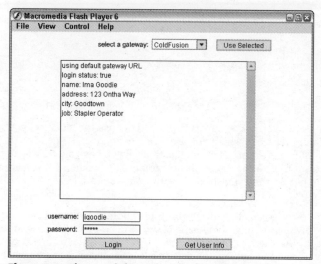

Figure 3-9: The user information displayed in the output TextField

Tracking Down Errors

It is hoped that everything worked just fine for you in this exercise. However, in case you encountered a problem or an error, let's examine a few possible common problems and their sources.

✦ When you run the movie and press the Login button, you get one of the following messages in your `output TestField`:

- `Service threw an exception during method invocation: null.`

- `Service threw an exception during method invocation: No service named wiley.chapter3.User is known to Flash Remoting.`

- `No Such Service wiley.chapter3.User with function login (or getUserInfo).`

Any of these errors means that the Flash Remoting gateway could not find any service and remote procedure as specified. Make sure that you do not have any typos either in your ActionScript code or in any of the directory names and filenames you created and copied in the server-side part of this exercise. In addition, make sure that you have the correct directory structure in each case. For example, if you forgot to create the directory for the ColdFusion Component (Wiley.chapter3) or the JavaBean (wiley.chapter3), then the Flash Remoting service won't be able to locate the service you are requesting in the Flash movie.

✦ When you run the movie and press the Login button, you get an error in the Output window (this will occur only if you are using Test Movie) that looks something like the following:

```
Error opening URL "http://localhost:8500/flashservices/gateway/"
```

or

```
Error opening URL "http://localhost:8200/flashservices/gateway/"
```

or

```
Error opening URL "http://localhost/flashremoting/gateway.aspx"
```

To troubleshoot these errors, ensure that you did not use the incorrect gateway URL for the application server to which you are trying to connect. Remember that I am giving you the URLs for the standard installations. If you have another installation, then you will want to make adjustments accordingly. For example, if you are running ColdFusion on port 80, then you should use the gateway URL `http://localhost/flashservices/gateway/`.

Otherwise, this error means that either the application server is not running (most likely the case if you are using ColdFusion MX or JRun 4) or the Flash Remoting service was not correctly installed for the application server. If it is the former problem, then you need only to start the application server. If it is the latter, then you will need to consult the appropriate chapters in this book to make sure you can get the Flash Remoting services correctly installed for your application server.

Cross-Reference

You can read about setting up Flash Remoting for J2EE application servers in Chapter 12. Chapter 18 discusses setting up Flash Remoting for .NET.

✦ Chances are good that if you received any other errors, they are due to typos in your code. Please double-check for any inconsistencies. If you still cannot sort it out, then test the completed Flash movie that is included on the Web site.

Looking at the Code in Detail

Now that you have created your movie and tested it (and hopefully gotten it working), let's briefly look at the code that was added in step 5 of the exercise (comments have been removed). Mostly, there should not have been anything new or surprising in it. And, as always, keep in mind that I chose **one** of the **many** ways of going about doing this. Many variations could also work. Once you have gotten this code working, feel free to make modifications to it as you see fit in order to suit your own style.

At the very beginning of the code is the following line:

```
#include "NetServices.as"
```

Of course, this is always the first bit of code you want to add to any Flash Remoting project you do (unless, of course, you decide for some reason to use the NetConnection object directly). This line adds the NetService and accompanying classes to the Flash application.

Next comes the scrollDown() function:

```
function scrollDown(){
    _root.output.scroll = _root.output.maxscroll;
}
```

There should be nothing mysterious about this function. It simply assigns the maxscroll property value to the scroll property. Of course, this function is not very reusable. You could make it much more generic by passing it a reference to the TextField object instead of hardcoding the specific object. Even better, you could make it a method of the TextField class as follows:

```
TextField.prototype.scrollDown = function(){
    this.scroll = this.maxscroll;
}
```

Then you could call the scrollDown() method from the TextField you want to scroll.

Next comes the creation of the response object that will be used for the login procedure:

```
loginRes = new Object();
loginRes.onResult = function(result){
    _root.output.text += "login status: " + result + newline;
    _root.scrollDown();
    _root.getUserInfoBt.enabled = result;
}
loginRes.onStatus = function(status){
    _root.output.text += "an error occured..." + newline;
    _root.output.text += status.description + newline;
    _root.scrollDown();
}
```

The loginRes object has both an onResult() and an onStatus() method. The onResult() method handles the returned value from the remote procedure, which in this case is a Boolean value (the login was either successful or not). In this case, the result is displayed in the output TextField, the output TextField is scrolled down, and if the login was successful, then the getUserInfoBt button is enabled. On the other hand, if an error occurs, the onStatus() method alerts the user, indicating what the error was.

Next, we create the response object for the procedure that gets the user information:

```
infoRes = new Object();
infoRes.onResult = function(result){
  _root.output.text += "name: " + result.name + newline;
  _root.output.text += "address: " + result.address + newline;
  _root.output.text += "city: " + result.city + newline;
  _root.output.text += "job: " + result.job + newline;
  _root.scrollDown();
}
infoRes.onStatus = function(status){
  _root.output.text += "an error occured..." + newline;
  _root.output.text += status.description + newline;
  _root.scrollDown();
}
```

The `infoRes` object also has both an `onResult()` and an `onStatus()` method. The `onResult()` method handles the returned value from the remote procedure. In this case, the returned data is an object that contains four properties—`name`, `address`, `city`, and `job`. The method then displays these values in the `output` `TextField` and scrolls that `TextField` down all the way if necessary.

Now we want to define the actions to take place for each of the buttons:

```
selectGatewayBt.onRelease = function(){
  _root.conn =
NetServices.createGatewayConnection(_root.gateway.getValue());
  _root.userSrv = conn.getService("wiley.chapter3.User");
  _root.output.text += "using gateway: " + _root.gateway.getValue() +
newline;
  _root.scrollDown();
}

loginBt.onRelease = function(){
  if(_root.conn == undefined){
    _root.conn = NetServices.createGatewayConnection();
    _root.userSrv = conn.getService("wiley.chapter3.User");
  _root.output.text += "using default gateway URL" + newline;
    _root.scrollDown();
  }
  _root.userSrv.login(_root.loginRes, _root.username.text,
_root.password.text);
}

getUserInfoBt.onRelease = function(){
  _root.userSrv.getUserInfo(_root.infoRes);
}
```

The `selectGatewayBt` button should create the connection and service objects based on the selected gateway when released. The `createGatewayConnection()` method is called with the parameter indicating the gateway URL selected from the `ComboBox`. Then the service object is created. This is always going to be the same service, so that parameter is hard-coded. Then, of course, display for the user what gateway is being used and scroll the `TextField` object.

Next, the `loginBt` button will attempt to call the `login()` procedure. If the connection object has already been created then it is used. However, we check to see if the `NetConnection` object has been defined. If not, then we need to define it (and the service object) using the default gateway URL. Then, once you are sure that the connection object and the service object exist, you can call the `login()` procedure, specify the `loginRes` response object, and pass it the username and password parameters using the values that the user has entered.

Once the user has logged in successfully, the `getUserInfoBt` button becomes enabled. You already can be assured, therefore, that if the `release` event is triggered for this button, the connection and service objects already exist (because they were required for the login). Therefore, all that needs to happen for this event is that the `getUserInfo()` procedure needs to be called and the `infoRes` object needs to be specified as the response object.

Next, we define a function that will initialize the movie:

```
function init(){
  getUserInfoBt.enabled = false;
  selectGatewayBt.setLabel("Use Selected");
  loginBt.setLabel("Login");
  getUserInfoBt.setLabel("Get User Info");
  gateway.addItem("ColdFusion",
"http://localhost:8500/flashservices/gateway/");
  gateway.addItem("JRun",
"http://localhost:8200/flashservices/gateway/");
  gateway.addItem(".NET",
"http://localhost/flashremoting/gateway.aspx");

  NetServices.setDefaultGatewayURL("http://localhost:8500/flashservices/
gateway/");
}
```

The `init()` function just takes care of a few initialization issues. For example, it sets the `getUserInfoBt` button so that it is disabled until it is enabled upon successful login. The buttons need to be labeled, which is done here with the `setLabel()` methods. The `ComboBox` items are added using the `addItem()` method. Next, you set the default gateway URL.

Finally, you need only to ensure that the `init()` function is called from the main routine of the movie. Otherwise, though it may be defined, the actions will not execute:

```
init();
```

Debugging Flash Remoting

You can use the NetConnection Debugger to help get information about and resolve problems with Flash Remoting movies when you are testing them from the authoring environment (using test movie). This can be an extremely useful way of getting information about the Flash Remoting application. The NetConnection Debugger can display information about each request and response, including both the client-side and the server-side information.

Introducing the NetConnection Debugger

The NetConnection Debugger is a window within the Flash authoring application from which you can view all the debugging information related to Flash Remoting.

Opening and initializing the NetConnection Debugger

The NetConnection Debugger does not automatically open when you test your movie. Instead, before you test your movie you must manually open the window by choosing Window➪NetConnection Debugger.

Additionally, in order for your Flash player to know to send data to the NetConnection Debugger, you must add the `NetDebug` class to your Flash document with the following line of ActionScript placed at the beginning of your code:

```
#include "NetDebug.as"
```

This line of code does two things. First of all, it automatically configures the movie to send debugging information to the NetConnection Debugger. Second, it adds the methods of the `NetDebug` class to your Flash document so that you can use them (as discussed in the section "Using Debug Methods").

Exploring the NetConnection Debugger

Figure 3-10 shows the NetConnection Debugger running in default view. You can see the Events pane on the left side. This pane lists the Flash Remoting events as they occur. In the example in the figure there are two events listed — a connection and trace.

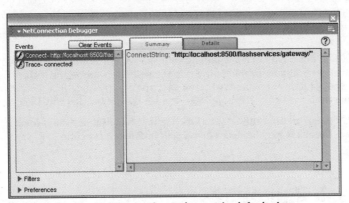

Figure 3-10: The NetConnection Debugger in default view

When you select an event from the Events pane, you can see a summary of that event in the Summary pane as shown in Figure 3-10, or you can select the Details pane tab as shown in Figure 3-11. The Details pane displays the entire AMF header information, and this can be useful when you want more information than the Summary pane displays.

At the bottom of the NetConnection Debugger you can expand the Filters (Figure 3-12) and Preferences (Figure 3-13) menus by clicking the menu names. These menus allow you to configure what kinds of messages are displayed in the Debugger as well as how much is displayed and how. You can collapse the menus when you are done with them by clicking the menu names again.

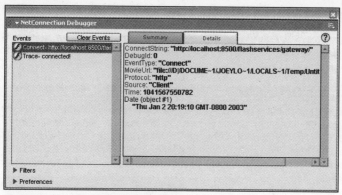

Figure 3-11: The Display pane view

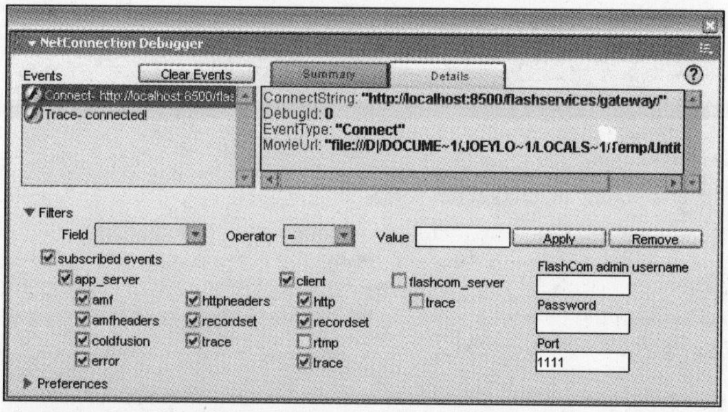

Figure 3-12: The Filters menu

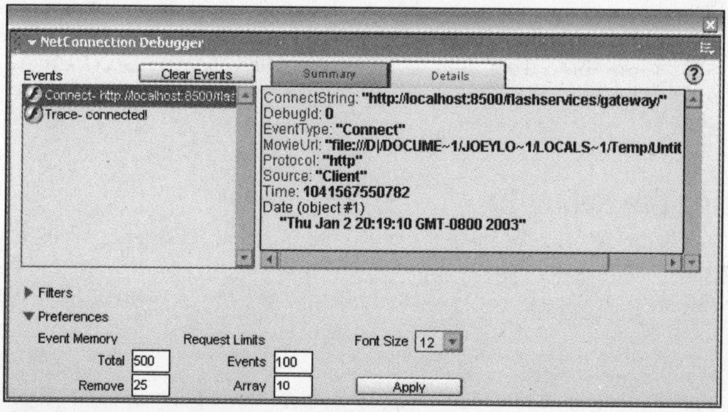

Figure 3-13: The Preferences menu

Using Debug Methods

Once you have included the `NetDebug` class in your Flash document, you can also use the special debug methods. You can use these methods to write and control the output to the NetConnection Debugger.

Writing output to the Debugger

The `trace()` method works similarly to the `trace()` global function in that it writes output to a window. The difference is that the `trace()` method is invoked from a connection object and it writes output to the NetConnection Debugger instead of to the Output window. This is useful because it enables you to keep all your output to a single window instead of two windows (the NetConnection Debugger and the Output window). Here is an example of how to use the `trace()` method:

```
#include "NetServices.as"
#include "NetDebug.as"

gwURL = "http://localhost:8500/flashservices/gateway/";
NetServices.setDefaultGatewayURL(gwURL);
conn = NetServices.createGatewayConnection();

conn.trace("this outputs to the NetConnection Debugger");
```

Getting and setting debug configurations

You can turn debugging on and off individually for each connection object. If you have two connection objects, for example, you could turn off debugging for one of them while leaving it on for the other. When you add the `NetDebug` class to your Flash document, every connection object automatically has a `NetDebugConfig` object property that you can access using the `getDebugConfig()` method. For example:

```
debugConfig = conn.getDebugConfig();
```

`NetDebugConfig()` objects have two methods — `getDebug()` and `setDebug()`. The `getDebug()` method returns either true or false depending on whether or not the connection object has debugging turned on. All connection objects default to debugging turned on. The `setDebug()` method allows you to turn debugging on or off for a connection object. If you pass true to the `setDebug()` method, then debugging is turned on. If you pass the method a value of false, then debugging is turned off.

```
debugConfig.setDebug(false);  // turn off debugging
```

Getting and setting the debug ID

Every connection object is automatically assigned a unique numeric ID starting at 0. In other words, the first connection object you create automatically has an ID of 0, the second connection object has an ID of 1, and so on. You can retrieve the debug ID for a connection object using the `getDebugID()` method.

```
id = conn.getDebugID();
```

You can also set the debug ID for a connection object using the `setDebugID()` method. While the IDs are automatically set to numbers by Flash, they can be of any data type. Therefore, you can set the debug ID to a more descriptive value such as:

```
conn.setDebugID("Inventory Server Connection");
```

The debug ID shows up in the NetConnection Debugger under Details for each event associated with that connection.

Summary

In this chapter, you learned about ActionScript for use with Flash Remoting applications. At this point, you should be familiar with the following concepts:

✦ Add the `NetServices` and related classes to your Flash document using an `#include` directive.

✦ Create a connection object using the `createGatewayConnection()` method.

✦ Specify the gateway URL either as a default URL, in the `createGatewayConnection()` method, or through the `OBJECT` and `EMBED` tags of an HTML page.

✦ Create a service object.

✦ Call a remote procedure from a service object.

✦ Pass parameters to a remote procedure.

✦ Handle the response from a remote procedure either as named response functions or as a response object.

✦   ✦   ✦

Using Databases and Record Sets

## CHAPTER 4

In This Chapter

Getting started with databases and SQL

Using MySQL

Learning about record sets and the RecordSet class

Integrating RecordSet objects with UI components in Flash

In this chapter you will read about databases and record sets—both of which are important to many, if not most, Flash Remoting applications.

Understanding Databases

Although you may not be aware of it, databases are operating in the background of your daily life all the time. The details of your bank account are kept in a database, your utility and phone usage records are all stored in databases, and your e-mail messages and contacts on your computer are stored in a database, to name just a few. Not that many years ago, databases were mostly discussed in the context of episodes of "Star Trek." However, now that every service imaginable is on the Web, there are databases buzzing around the globe for everything—from personalized tissue dispenser orders to e-mail lists to online bill paying. In fact, many organizations today rely heavily on databases—including corporations, wholesalers, retailers, libraries, universities, and most governments.

What Is a Database?

So we know there are databases everywhere. And we know that the IT specialist certainly complains about the database enough. But what exactly *is* a database? In the simplest terms, a database is merely a collection of related information. Therefore, technically speaking, when you make a grocery list, you are putting together a sort of rudimentary database. Of course, generally when we refer to a database, we are talking about something a little more sophisticated than grocery items scribbled on a scrap of paper. In the context of computer applications, and specifically Web applications, a database is usually a storage system for related information that can be inserted, manipulated, and retrieved.

When a database is used on a computer, the means for interfacing with that database (which is basically just a giant repository for information) is referred to as a database management system (DBMS). Many database management systems are available. Some of the main points that differentiate one from another include the following:

✦ The amount of data the database can hold efficiently

✦ Sophistication of security and permissions (e.g., who has access to the database and who is permitted to modify it)

✦ Number of simultaneous connections (users)

✦ Speed of operation (how long the queries take)

✦ Cost

You are probably familiar with some of the *many* available DBMSs out there:

✦ Microsoft Access

✦ Microsoft SQL Server

✦ Oracle

✦ FileMaker

✦ MySQL

If you use the Windows operating system and have Office installed, you already have Access on your computer. Several exercises throughout the book require that you use a database. You are welcome to use any database server you want—whatever you are most familiar with. However, the exercises presented here use MySQL. Later in this chapter, in the section titled "Introducing MySQL," I explain why I prefer MySQL, and show you how to set it up on your computer.

Examining the Structure of a Database

Not all databases are structured in the same way. However, in most applications today, when a database is used it is a **relational** database. That means that all the data is organized into various groupings called **tables**. These tables have relationships with one another that make accessing the data as efficient as possible. In a nonrelational database, all the data is simply lumped together in one giant mass.

Before discussing the relationships between tables, however, you should first understand the elements of a single table. Each table in a database looks similar to a spreadsheet or a chart, with both rows and columns (see Figure 4-1).

USER_ID	USERNAME	PASSWORD	NAME	ADDRESS	CITY	JOB
1	igoodie	12345	Ima Goodie	123 Ontha Way	Goodtown	Stapler Operator
2	rshaw	abcde	Rick Shaw	555 Somewhere Lane	Heresville	Crime Fighter
3	nlee	ipass	Norma Lee	6 Eezee St.	Abracadabra	Pencil Maker

Figure 4-1: A database table looks similar to a spreadsheet.

Each table has a name and is defined by the specific columns that it contains. In addition, each column has rules governing the type of data that can be inserted into it. For example, a column in a table can be defined such that only numbers up to 10 digits can be inserted into it, or so that only strings up to 50 characters long can be inserted. Furthermore, it is a good practice for each table to have what is known as a *primary key*. A primary key is a column in which all the values are unique. In the table view shown in Figure 4-1 the USER_ID column is the primary key. That means that there cannot be more than one row in the table with the same primary key value. This ensures that each row can be uniquely identified.

When multiple tables have been created, relationships can be defined between them. These relationships usually involve the primary key of one of the tables. When the primary key of one table is referenced in a second table, it is known in the second table as the *foreign key*. In Figure 4-2, you can see a relationship defined between two tables in which the USER_ID primary key in the USER table is a foreign key in the ACCESS table. These tables and their relationship might be a way of keeping track of how often and when particular users access their accounts. By having two different tables, you can avoid a lot of redundancy. With this setup, you can keep track of account information (such as name, address, city, etc.) in the USER table with only one row (or record) per account. At the same time, however, you can write to the ACCESS table each time a user accesses his or her account—without needing redundant data in each record.

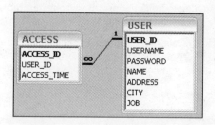

Figure 4-2: The relationship between two database tables. USER_ID is the primary key in USER table and the foreign key in the ACCESS table.

Talking to Databases

Although there are many different DBMSs available from which to choose, most of them speak a common language: Structured Query Language, which is usually written simply as SQL. Some people read (and pronounce) "SQL" as "sequel," while others say "es-cue-ell." Either pronunciation is acceptable.

Note

My preferred pronunciation is "sequel," so that's what I've used in this book. Hence, you may see the wording "a SQL" where you expect to see "an SQL."

SQL is a language that has evolved over the years and for which a standard has been agreed upon such that almost all DBMSs will understand it. Each DBMS tends to have its own specialized additions to the language, and these may not adhere to the standard. However, the core language is understood by most every DBMS.

With SQL, you can create, modify, and delete databases, tables, and columns, as well as add, modify, and delete data within a database. It is well beyond the scope of this book to examine SQL in detail. Entire books have been written on the subject. However, this chapter provides some of the basics for working with SQL so that you will be able to understand the examples and exercises used throughout the book.

Tip

A good book on the subject is *A Visual Introduction to SQL, Second Edition,* by David Chappell and J. Harvey Trimble Jr. (Wiley, 2001).

Selecting data

Assuming that data already exists in a table, you can retrieve that data by using a SQL SELECT statement. Here is an example of a SELECT statement in its simplest form:

```
SELECT *
FROM USER
```

This SQL statement will retrieve all the data from the table named USER in the current database. The * is a wildcard character in this context. It means that *every* column should be selected (as opposed to only selected columns, as you can read about in the following paragraph). The FROM keyword is required and is followed by the name of the table (or tables) from which the data should be retrieved. If you think about it, this is a relatively intuitive syntax so far, as it reads pretty much like a human language: "Select everything from (the table named) USER."

Perhaps, however, you do not want to retrieve data from all the columns in the table. In this case, in place of the *, you can indicate the columns from which the data should be retrieved. If you wanted only a list of the usernames in the table, you could use the following SELECT statement:

```
SELECT USERNAME
FROM USER
```

Note   The spelling of the column name used in a SQL statement, such as the preceding SELECT statement, must exactly match the spelling of the column name as it is stored in the database.

Similarly, if you wanted to retrieve only the name, address, city, and job from the table, you could use the following SELECT statement, in which the column names are separated by commas:

```
SELECT NAME, ADDRESS, CITY, JOB
FROM USER
```

Thus far, of course, the data for the specified columns has been selected for *all* records (rows) in the table. What if you want to select data from only some records? For example, what if you wanted to select the name, address, city, and job from the record in which the USER_ID is 1? This can be easily accomplished with the addition of a WHERE clause to the SELECT statement.

The WHERE clause enables you to specify a condition to be met. For example, to select the name, address, city, and job from the record in which USER_ID is 1, you can use the following SELECT statement with the added WHERE clause:

```
SELECT NAME, ADDRESS, CITY, JOB
FROM USER
WHERE USER_ID = 1
```

Of course, the conditional can be compound—joining multiple conditions to create a more complex condition. You can do this with the AND and OR operators. For example, if you want to select the name, address, city, and job from the records in which the username is igoodie and the password is 12345, the SELECT statement would look like this:

```
SELECT NAME, ADDRESS, CITY, JOB
```

```
FROM USER
WHERE USERNAME = 'igoodie' AND PASSWORD = '12345'
```

Note   The SQL equality comparison operator is a single equals sign (=). That's different from the ActionScript equality comparison operator, which is *two* equals signs (==).

Note   In the preceding code example the username `igoodie` is in quotation marks. All string values must appear in quotation marks in a SQL statement.

Inserting data

Inserting data using SQL always creates an entirely new record. Even if you insert data for only a single column, an entire record is created. How you insert a new record depends on whether or not you have data for each column of the new record (the new row). Assuming you do have data for every column, you can use the first, simpler variation of the SQL `INSERT` statement. The basic syntax for this first variation is as follows:

```
INSERT INTO table_name
VALUES (comma_delimited_list_of_values)
```

For example, if you want to insert a new record into the USER table, you could use the following SQL:

```
INSERT INTO USER
VALUES (4, 'Sam Aroton', 'wund3rbar', 'Sam Aroton', '23 Livehere
Place', 'Nice City', 'Investigator')
```

However, it is also possible that you want to insert a new user record, complete with the user ID, the username, and the password, but you do not yet know the address, city, or job description. In this case, you can use the second variation of the INSERT statement, whose basic syntax is as follows:

```
INSERT INTO table_name(comma_delimited_list_of_column_names)
VALUES (comma_delimited_list_of_values)
```

Here is a specific example:

```
INSERT INTO USER(USER_ID, USERNAME, PASSWORD)
VALUES (4, 'Sam Aroton', 'wund3rbar')
```

Updating data

Aside from just inserting new data, you will often want to modify data for existing records. For example, if the user Sam Aroton is added to the table without values in all the columns, then it would seem reasonable that at some point *after* the record was inserted you would want the capability to provide values for those columns. You can do this using the UPDATE statement in SQL.

The basic syntax for an UPDATE statement is as follows:

```
UPDATE table_name
SET column_name1 = value1[,
    column_name2 = value2...]
```

Notice, however, that this basic syntax does not specify which rows should be updated. Therefore, be very careful with UPDATE statements, because in their basic form, *all* rows will be updated. However, UPDATE statements usually include a WHERE clause. The following example updates the name, address, city, and job description columns of the record with a user ID of 4:

```
UPDATE USER
SET NAME = 'Sam Aroton',
    ADDRESS = '23 Livehere Place',
    CITY = 'Nice City',
    JOB = 'Investigator'
WHERE USER_ID = 4
```

Deleting data

Finally, of course, you need the capability to delete data from a database. The DELETE statement takes care of this in SQL. A DELETE statement removes an entire record at a time, just as the INSERT statement adds an entire record at a time. The basic syntax for a DELETE statement is as follows:

```
DELETE FROM table_name
```

Again, be aware that, as with the UPDATE statement, using a DELETE statement without a WHERE clause can have disastrous consequences — all the records in a table will be deleted.

Here is an example that deletes just one record from a table:

```
DELETE FROM USER
WHERE USER_ID = 4
```

Here is another example that deletes *all* records from a table:

```
DELETE FROM USER
```

Introducing MySQL

If you already work with a DBMS with which you are comfortable, then by all means continue to use that DBMS. One of the challenges in a book like this one is to provide a reference that is as universal and accessible as possible. With that goal in mind, here are a few of the trade-offs involved in choosing a DBMS:

✦ Because Flash Remoting can work on Windows, Mac OS X, and various Unix flavors (including Linux), I've sought to provide examples, exercises, and suggestions that are as cross-platform as possible. Many DBMSs are designed for only a single platform. For example, Access and SQL Server work only on Windows operating systems.

✦ Cost is a big issue as well. Part of accessibility is financial accessibility. Many DBMSs are very costly.

✦ Another aspect of accessibility is disk space and file size. Some DBMSs require a great deal of disk space to install. In addition, if you are going to download the installation, it needs to be a manageable download. Believe it or not, the installation file for some DBMSs can be larger than 500MB (which is mostly of concern if you are trying to download it).

✦ Performance is an important factor to consider when selecting a DBMS. Some DBMSs are able to handle more simultaneous users and hold more records than others. If you foresee your application having heftier requirements in this regard, whether now or in the near future, you should select your DBMS carefully based on performance.

Considering all these issues, there are probably many fine options. However, for the sake of uniformity and simplicity, I recommend MySQL. Here's why:

✦ MySQL is available for many different operating systems, including Windows, Mac OS X, Linux, and many other various Unix flavors.

✦ When used on a web server, MySQL is absolutely free. If this is a completely new idea to you, then you might want to look at an excellent book, *Open Source: The Unauthorized White Papers* by Donald K. Rosenberg (Wiley, 2000).

✦ The installation of MySQL is well under 30MB. The download size varies depending on platform, but ranges from under 5MB to no more than 12.5MB.

✦ MySQL consistently rivals commercial DBMSs such as Oracle and MS SQL Server in performance. MySQL consistently outperforms many other commercial databases in benchmark tests.

Note Nearly any DBMS can be used successfully in conjunction with Flash Remoting. For simplicity, only one is used for the examples in this book. The Flash Remoting ActionScript will not vary whatsoever based on your selection of a DBMS (or the operating system on which you run it). Neither will the ways in which the remote procedure code interacts with Flash Remoting be affected. The only differences are reflected by how the application server connects to the database. In the case of ColdFusion, this is only a matter of selecting the correct database type for the data source. In .NET and Java, it is a matter of having the correct connection string. These relatively small variations are pointed out in the examples.

Installing MySQL

If you plan to use MySQL as your DBMS, obviously the first step is to install the MySQL application itself. The process is simple:

1. Download the installation files. You can download these from the MySQL web site (www.mysql.com) under the downloads/MySQL database section. Make sure you download the latest (stable) version of MySQL for your platform.

2. Once you have downloaded the installation files, simply open them up and follow the instructions for installation.

Of course, read the installation instructions in the MySQL manual (included as HTML documents in the installation), as well as any instructions that come with the download. Each platform may have its own nuances.

Once the MySQL application is installed, you will also need to get the server running. You should find instructions for this in the provided documentation.

Configuring MySQL to work with application servers

Once you have installed MySQL itself, the next step is to make sure that your application servers (and other applications in general) can find the MySQL server. This requires some kind of bridge, which is generally supplied in the form of drivers. There are three main drivers in which you might be interested:

✦ ODBC: Open Database Connectivity is used for communicating with DBMSs on Microsoft operating systems.

✦ OLE DB: Object Linking and Embedding Database is also used for communicating with DBMSs on Microsoft operating systems.

✦ JDBC: Java Database Connectivity is used for communicating with DBMSs from Java applications.

You can likely find several different drivers of each specification for MySQL. Table 4-1 lists the drivers I recommend, who should use them, and where you can download them. All of these drivers are free to download and use.

Table 4-1: MySQL Drivers

Driver Name	Download	Description
MyODBC	http://www.mysql.com/downloads	This is a MySQL ODBC driver. This is a useful driver to have since it is required by many third-party applications (such as graphical user interfaces for MySQL).
MyOLEDB	http://old.sw.com.sg/products/myoledb/	This is a MySQL OLE DB driver. If you use .NET, then I recommend you download and install this driver.
MySQL Connector/J	http://www.mysql.com/downloads	This is a MySQL JDBC driver. If you want to use Java to connect to a MySQL database, you should install this driver.

Note   ColdFusion MX does not require you to install any drivers if you use MySQL. It comes with the necessary drivers already configured.

Both the MyODBC and MyOLEDB driver installations should be completely intuitive. All that is required is that you run an installation executable (*.exe file) and you will be taken through the process by a wizard. Installing the MySQL Connector/J driver is slightly more complicated, but not much more.

If you are using MySQL Connector/J (or any other MySQL JDBC-compliant driver), then you should follow the installation instructions that come with the download. MySQL Connector/J enables several alternative installation options. If you are installing the JDBC driver on your computer, then I recommend you simply copy the JAR file to your $JAVA_HOME\jre\lib\ext/ directory, or copy the JAR file to another location and include it in your classpath.

Creating your first MySQL database

In this exercise, you will create a MySQL database containing data about books.

1. Create a new text file and save it to your hard disk root (e.g., C:\) as createChapter4SQL.txt.

2. Add the following to the file and save it:

```
# create database WileyFlashRemoting
CREATE DATABASE WileyFlashRemoting;

# open the database
USE WileyFlashRemoting;

# create a table named books with columns named BOOK_ID,
# TITLE, AUTHOR_LAST, AUTHOR_FIRST, and PUBLICATION_DATE
# setting the primary key to BOOK_ID
CREATE TABLE books (

  BOOK_ID int(10) unsigned NOT NULL  auto_increment,  TITLE
varchar(50)   ,
  AUTHOR_LAST varchar(50)   ,
  AUTHOR_FIRST varchar(50)   ,
  PUBLICATION_DATE date NOT NULL  DEFAULT '0000-00-00'  ,
  PRIMARY KEY (BOOK_ID)
);


# insert the new values
INSERT INTO books VALUES(1,"Complete Flash Remoting
MX","Lott","Joey","2003-03-01");

INSERT INTO books VALUES(2,"Dreamweaver MX
Bible","Lowery","Joseph","2002-08-01");

INSERT INTO books VALUES(3,"XML Web Services with
ASP.NET","Evjen","Bill","2002-05-01");

INSERT INTO books VALUES(4,"Building Great Flash MX
Games","David","Matthew","2002-11-01");

INSERT INTO books VALUES(5,"JMX
Programming","Janowski","Mike","2002-07-01");
```

Note   If this book is your first introduction to SQL, then the CREATE and USE statements will be unfamiliar to you. Creating new databases and tables is not a common practice within Flash Remoting applications. If you want to learn more about these statements, you can find more about them in the MySQL manual, as well as in *A Visual Introduction to SQL*.

3. Open a command prompt on your computer. On a Windows computer, you can do this by selecting Start⇨Run... on the Windows taskbar, typing cmd, and clicking OK. On Mac OS X, open the Terminal application, which is found in *boot disk*/Applications/ Utilities/Terminal/.

4. Unless you have added the MySQL `bin` directory to your path, you need to change to the directory where `mysql.exe` or `mysql.sh` is saved. On a Windows machine, this is generally in C:\mysql\bin (so you would type cd \mysql\bin).

5. Type `mysql -h localhost` and press Enter to connect to the MySQL terminal.

6. You should now be at the `mysql>` prompt. Now you are ready to call the SQL text file from steps 1 and 2. This will create and populate a new database called `WileyFlashRemoting`. You can do this with the MySQL `source` command. This command should be followed by the path and name of the file to use. For example, on a Windows computer, you might type `source C:\createChapter4SQL.txt` and press Enter. This should create the database and output the following:

```
Query OK, 1 row affected (0.00 sec)

Database changed
Query OK, 0 rows affected (0.00 sec)

Query OK, 1 row affected (0.01 sec)

Query OK, 1 row affected (0.00 sec)

Query OK, 1 row affected (0.00 sec)

Query OK, 1 row affected (0.00 sec)

Query OK, 1 row affected (0.00 sec)
```

7. Now type the following `SELECT` statement to display the contents of the `books` table:

```
SELECT * FROM books;
```

Be sure to add the semicolon at the end of the statement, and press Enter. (The semicolon at the end of commands is specific to the MySQL terminal and is not required as part of standard SQL.) You should see the results displayed as shown here:

```
| BOOK_ID | TITLE | AUTHOR_LAST | AUTHOR_FIRST | PUBLICATION_DATE |
+---+--------------------------------+----------+---------+------------+
| 1 | Complete Flash Remoting MX     | Lott     | Joey    | 2003-03-01 |
| 2 | Dreamweaver MX Bible           | Lowery   | Joseph  | 2002-08-01 |
| 3 | XML Web Services with ASP.NET  | Evjen    | Bill    | 2002-05-01 |
| 4 | Building Great Flash MX Games  | David    | Matthew | 2002-11-01 |
| 5 | JMX Programming                | Janowski | Mike    | 2002-07-01 |
+---+--------------------------------+----------+---------+------------+
5 rows in set (0.00 sec)
```

Understanding Record Sets

Now that you understand database fundamentals, you may be wondering exactly what they to do with Flash. After all, this is a book about Flash Remoting. Stay with me: I have not led you astray. In fact, databases are fundamental to Flash Remoting in the following manner: As you have already learned, databases are at the core of a vast array of computing technologies and services. In fact, it is a rare application that does ***not*** rely heavily on a database for some portion of its functionality. This holds true for Web applications as much as any other, if not more so. Therefore, as Flash becomes a viable option for the presentation logic of Web applications through the use of Flash Remoting, databases become highly important and relevant to Flash, so much so that Flash Remoting introduces a new class of objects just for working with database results—the RecordSet class.

What Is a Record Set?

Through the use of Flash Remoting and remote procedure calls, Flash movies can now interact with databases by directing SQL statements to them for adding, modifying, and retrieving data. As you learned earlier in this chapter, some SQL statements do not need to return any sort of values. For example, when performing an INSERT or DELETE statement in SQL, you are instructing the database to do something, but not expecting any answer in return. On the other hand, when *querying* the database with a SELECT statement in SQL, you necessarily *do* expect an answer. The answer that you expect comes in the form of a record set.

A record set is exactly that—a set of records, or rows. For example, if you perform a SELECT statement on a database such as

```
SELECT NAME, ADDRESS, CITY, JOB
FROM USER
```

you would expect a response containing the name, address, city, and job description column values to be returned for every record in the table. If there were three records (or rows) in the table, then the resulting value would have three records as well. If you represented the returned value in a chart or grid, it might look something like Table 4-2.

Table 4-2: Representation of a Record Set

NAME	ADDRESS	CITY	JOB
Ima Goodie	123 Ontha Way	Goodtown	Stapler Operator
Rick Shaw	555 Somewhere Lane	Heresville	Crime Fighter
Norma Lee	6 Eezee St.	Abracadabra	Pencil Maker

Each programming language has its own construct for working with record sets. When working with Flash Remoting, we are primarily concerned with three server-side languages: ColdFusion Markup Language (CFML), Java, and C#. These languages each have a data type specifically for working with record sets. They are as follows:

✦ **CFML:** Query

✦ **Java:** java.sql.ResultSet

✦ **C#:** System.Data.DataTable

When an object of one of these types is returned to a Flash movie from a remote procedure, it is automatically converted to a RecordSet object in ActionScript. This conversion (known as data marshaling) works both ways. Therefore, an ActionScript RecordSet object passed to a remote procedure is automatically converted to the appropriate data type on that end as well.

Introducing the RecordSet Class

Now you know what a record set is, and you know that record sets passed to a Flash movie by way of Flash Remoting are converted to `RecordSet` objects. Now you'll learn what objects of the `RecordSet` class are and what they can do.

The `RecordSet` class is actually a custom ActionScript class that is built using the `XML` object. It is installed in the Flash MX installation's `Configuration\Include` directory as part of the Flash Remoting Components. The file itself is named `RecordSet.as`, and you can add it directly into a Flash application with the following `#include` statement:

```
#include "RecordSet.as"
```

However, as the `RecordSet` class is of little use within Flash unless used in conjunction with Flash Remoting, and because the class is automatically loaded when you add the `NetServices.as` file, it is doubtful you will often need to add it directly as above. Instead, the same `#include` statement that you already use will add the `RecordSet` class automatically:

```
#include "NetServices.as"
```

Creating a New Recordset Object

More often than not, your Flash movies will likely be ***receiving*** `RecordSet` objects from the server, not creating them within the Flash movie itself. `RecordSet` objects are far more likely to be the result of a database query than anything else. However, you might encounter a situation in which you want to create a `RecordSet` object and use it for the purpose of populating a UI component, for example. Therefore, and because it is a much easier starting point for learning about `RecordSet` objects than setting up a database and an entire Flash Remoting application just to have a remote procedure return a `RecordSet` object to the Flash movie, let's first examine how to create a new `RecordSet` object with ActionScript.

 Note   You cannot send `RecordSet` objects to remote procedures as parameters. The Flash Remoting gateway does not know how to convert the data type *from* ActionScript.

Actually, creating a new `RecordSet` object requires nothing fancy whatsoever. It is done using the constructor method, just as you might have anticipated. The constructor method takes a single parameter—an array indicating the names of the columns for the new object. The following example creates a `RecordSet` object with four columns: `NAME`, `ADDRESS`, `CITY`, and `JOB`:

```
clmnNames = new Array("NAME", "ADDRESS", "CITY", "JOB");
rs = new RecordSet(clmnNames);
```

The same code could be rewritten using an array literal instead:

```
rs = new RecordSet(["NAME", "ADDRESS", "CITY", "JOB"]);
```

Using ActionScript, you can add new records, replace records, modify records, delete records, and read records. Every record in a `RecordSet` object is given an index. The index indicates the order of the records, starting with 0. This should be a familiar concept, as it is essentially the same thing as an array in this respect.

Writing to a RecordSet Object

Once you have an existing RecordSet object, you can add and modify records using an assortment of predefined methods. These methods fall generally into three categories:

✦ Inserting new records

✦ Modifying records

✦ Replacing records

Inserting new records

When you insert new records, you must insert the entire record at one time (as opposed to only select columns within the record). This is the same as using the SQL INSERT statement you learned about previously in this chapter. Although you must insert an entire record at a time, you can later modify individual columns in each record (using the setField() method), as you will see in just a bit. Therefore, both of the insertion methods for RecordSet objects require that an entire record be defined. A record is defined by an ActionScript object (an Object object) with property names corresponding to the column names of the RecordSet object. For example, if you define a RecordSet object with four columns — NAME, ADDRESS, CITY, and JOB — as follows:

```
rs = new RecordSet(["NAME", "ADDRESS", "CITY", "JOB"]);
```

then any record added to it must be an object with the corresponding properties. For example:

```
aRecord = {NAME: "Ima Goodie", ADDRESS: "123 Ontha Way", CITY:
"Goodtown", JOB: "Stapler Operator"};
```

Of course, you can define this same object in other ways and it will still be valid. For example:

```
aRecord = new Object();
aRecord.NAME = "Ima Goodie";
aRecord.ADDRESS = "123 Ontha Way";
aRecord.CITY = "Goodtown";
aRecord.JOB = "Stapler Operator";
```

A record can be added to a RecordSet object by one of two methods:

✦ addItem(): This method appends the record to the end of the RecordSet object.

✦ addItemAt(): This method inserts the new record into the RecordSet object at a specific index. If a record already exists at that index, then it and all records that follow are shifted by 1.

First, let's look at an example using the addItem() method. This method takes only one parameter — the record object to be appended to the RecordSet object. In this example, a record is added to a new RecordSet object:

```
rs = new RecordSet(["NAME", "ADDRESS", "CITY", "JOB"]);
rs.addItem({NAME: "Ima Goodie", ADDRESS: "123 Ontha Way", CITY:
"Goodtown", JOB: "Stapler Operator"});
```

Again, there is no reason why the record object has to be defined within the method call. It could just as well be defined outside the method call, and a reference could be passed to the method instead, as shown in the following example:

```
rs = new RecordSet(["NAME", "ADDRESS", "CITY", "JOB"]);
aRecord = new Object();
aRecord.NAME = "Ima Goodie";
aRecord.ADDRESS = "123 Ontha Way";
aRecord.CITY = "Goodtown";
aRecord.JOB = "Stapler Operator";
rs.addItem(aRecord);
```

In both examples, a new record is added to the newly created `rs` RecordSet object. At this point, the RecordSet object might be represented visually by Table 4-3.

Table 4-3: rs RecordSet Object After addItem() Call

NAME	ADDRESS	CITY	JOB
Ima Goodie	123 Ontha Way	Goodtown	Stapler Operator

The `addItemAt()` method is similar to the `addItem()` method in that it inserts a new record into the RecordSet object. It too takes a parameter with a value of an object representing the record to be inserted. The difference, however, is that the `addItemAt()` method *also* takes another parameter before that — an integer (a whole number) — which indicates at what index the new record should be inserted. For example, if you wanted to add another record to the `rs` object created in the previous example but you wanted to insert that record *before* the Ima Goodie record, using `addItemAt()` would be a good choice. The following example does exactly that:

```
rs.addItemAt(0, {NAME: "Rick Shaw", ADDRESS: "555 Somewhere Lane",
CITY: "Heresville", JOB: "Crime Figher"});
```

This method call will insert the Rick Shaw record at index 0 (as indicated by the first parameter value), thus displacing the record already occupying that slot and all subsequent records by 1. Table 4-4 shows what the `rs` object will look like after this record has been added.

Table 4-4: rs RecordSet Object After addItemAt() Call

NAME	ADDRESS	CITY	JOB
Rick Shaw	555 Somewhere Lane	Heresville	Crime Fighter
Ima Goodie	123 Ontha Way	Goodtown	Stapler Operator

If you inserted yet another record at index 0, then both existing records would be displaced by 1 index. For example:

```
rs.addItemAt(0, {NAMF: "Norma Lee", ADDRESS: "6 Eezee St.", CITY:
"Abracadabra", JOB: "Pencil Maker"});
```

Now the RecordSet object could be represented as shown in Table 4-5.

Table 4-5: rs RecordSet Object After addItemAt() Call

NAME	ADDRESS	CITY	JOB
Norma Lee	6 Eezee St.	Abracadabra	Pencil Maker
Rick Shaw	555 Somewhere Lane	Heresville	Crime Fighter
Ima Goodie	123 Ontha Way	Goodtown	Stapler Operator

Modifying records

Once you have existing records in a RecordSet object, you might want to make modifications to them. For example, you may decide that Norma Lee's job as Pencil Maker is something a little more than that. Norma's job, you decide, is more aptly described as Pencil Maker *Extraordinaire*. You can make this change to just the JOB column of Norma's record with the setField() method.

The setField() method modifies the value of a single column of a single row. Therefore, the method takes three parameters: the index of the record, the name of the column, and the new value for that record's column. The following example uses the setField() method to change Norma's job description:

```
rs.setField(0, "JOB", "Pencil Maker Extraordinaire");
```

In this example, the first parameter is given a value of 0 because Norma's record is the first record in the RecordSet object. The second parameter is given a value of "JOB" because that is the column in which we wish to make the change. Finally, the last parameter is given a value of "Pencil Maker Extraordinaire" because that is the new value we want to assign to the column for that record.

Replacing records

When working with record sets, you may want to replace a record with another. For example, you may have added a record to a RecordSet object, such as the rs object containing user information, but then later that user may be replaced by another. You can swap these records with the replaceItemAt() method. The replaceItemAt() method's syntax is the same as the addItemAt() method's syntax, but whereas the addItemAt() method displaces any existing record at that index, the replaceItemAt() method replaces that record completely.

Assuming that the rs RecordSet object contains three records (as shown in Table 4-5), then an addItem() method would append a new record to the object with an index of 3. For example:

```
rs.addItem({NAME: "Justin Teim", ADDRESS: "11 Aowr Ave.", CITY:
"Franklinville", JOB: "Model Train Collector"});
```

Now the record set would look something like Table 4-6.

Table 4-6: rs RecordSet Object After Adding Justin Teim

NAME	ADDRESS	CITY	JOB
Norma Lee	6 Eezee St.	Abracadabra	Pencil Maker Extraordinaire
Rick Shaw	555 Somewhere Lane	Heresville	Crime Fighter
Ima Goodie	123 Ontha Way	Goodtown	Stapler Operator
Justin Teim	11 Aowr Ave.	Franklinville	Model Train Collector

However, if Justin Teim's slot in the record set were replaced by Sam Aroton's, you could use the replaceItemAt() method as follows:

```
rs.replaceItemAt(3, {NAME: "Sam Aroton", ADDRESS: "23 Livehere Place",
CITY: "Nice City", JOB: "Investigator"});
```

Now that the replaceItemAt() method has been called, the record set looks something like what you see in Table 4-7.

Table 4-7: rs RecordSet Object After replaceItemAt() Call

NAME	ADDRESS	CITY	JOB
Norma Lee	6 Eezee St.	Abracadabra	Pencil Maker Extraordinaire
Rick Shaw	555 Somewhere Lane	Heresville	Crime Fighter
Ima Goodie	123 Ontha Way	Goodtown	Stapler Operator
Sam Aroton	23 Livehere Place	Nice City	Investigator

Reading from a RecordSet Object

Now that you know how to add records to a RecordSet object, naturally you will want to be able to read the data back *from* the object as well. Reading the data from a RecordSet object falls into two main categories:

✦ Retrieving information about the entire RecordSet object

✦ Retrieving individual records

Getting information about an object

You will generally want to know two important pieces of information about any RecordSet object you are using:

✦ The names of the columns

✦ The number of records

The names of the columns of a `RecordSet` object can be retrieved using the `getColumnNames()` method. This method returns an array of the column names of the given `RecordSet` object. For example, using the `rs` object from the previous examples, the `getColumnNames()` method would return an array with four column name values: `NAME`, `ADDRESS`, `CITY`, and `JOB`:

```
cn = rs.getColumnNames();
for(i = 0; i < cn.length; i++){
  trace(cn[i]);
}
/*
Output window displays:
NAME
ADDRESS
CITY
JOB
*/
```

You can retrieve the number of records in a `RecordSet` object using the `getLength()` method. This method returns an integer value indicating how many records are in the object. For example, if the `getLength()` method of the `rs` `RecordSet` object (as it was represented in Table 4-7) is called, it will return 4.

```
trace(rs.getLength()); // Outputs 4
```

Reading individual records

The `getItemAt()` method of `RecordSet` objects enables you to read a record given the index of that record within the object. The method requires one parameter—an integer indicating the index of the requested record—and it returns a record object representing that record. For example, using the `rs` object as it was represented in Table 4-7, you could retrieve Norma Lee's record with the following code:

```
NormaRecord = rs.getItemAt(0);
```

The `NormaRecord` object returned will have four properties corresponding to the columns of the `RecordSet` object. Here is an example of how the resulting record object could be used in code:

```
trace(NormaRecord.NAME); // Outputs Norma Lee
trace(NormaRecord.JOB); // Outputs Pencil Maker Extraordinaire
```

If you want to iterate (loop) through all the records of a `RecordSet` object, you can use the `getColumnNames()` and `getLength()` methods in conjunction with the `getItemAt()` method. For example:

```
cn = rs.getColumnNames();
len = rs.getLength();
for(i = 0; i < len; i++){
  record = rs.getItemAt(i);
  for (c in cn){
    output += record[cn[c]] + ", ";
  }
  trace(output);
  output = "";
}
```

This example would display the following in the Output window:

```
Pencil Maker Extraordinaire, Abracadabra, 6 Eezee St., Norma Lee,
Crime Fighter, Heresville, 555 Somwhere Lane, Rick Shaw,
Stapler Operator, Goodtown, 123 Ontha Way, Ima Goodie,
Investigator, Nice City, 23 Livehere Place, Sam Aroton,
```

In addition to having an index, every record in a RecordSet object is also assigned a unique ID automatically. At first glance, this might seem completely redundant. After all, if the index values are already unique, why also give each record an ID? However, the index value is dependent upon the position of the record within the RecordSet object. Thus, if a record is moved from one position to another, its index also changes. The ID, on the other hand, never changes. Moreover, once an ID has been assigned to a record within a given RecordSet object, even if the record is removed, the ID will not be assigned to another record in the same RecordSet object. You can obtain the ID for a record by using the getItemID() method. This method requires one parameter—the index of the record for which you wish to know the ID. For example:

```
trace(rs.getItemID(0));
```

If you iterate through the records of the rs RecordSet object we have been working with thus far and output the IDs for the records, you will notice that the IDs are assigned in the order that the records were added:

```
len = rs.getLength();
for(i = 0; i < len; i++){
  trace(rs.getItemID(i));
}
```

The preceding example code would display the following in the Output window:

```
2
1
0
3
```

You might also notice that displaying the IDs in this way reveals an interesting fact about the replaceItemAt() method. If you recall, we use the replaceItemAt() method to replace the record at index 3 with another record. Because the ID for that index is still 3 and not 4, you can infer that replacing a record substitutes the data in the record slot without assigning a new ID.

Removing Records

When you want to remove records from a RecordSet object, you have two methods to choose from: removeAll() and removeItemAt(). Both methods are named in an intuitive manner, so their functionality should come as no surprise.

The removeAll() method removes all records from a RecordSet object. The method requires no parameters. You can call the method with the following syntax

```
someRecordSetObject.removeAll();
```

On the other hand, the removeItemAt() method removes a single record from a RecordSet object. This method requires one parameter—an integer indicating the index of the record to remove. When you remove a record, all subsequent records are shifted up by one index to fill the slot that had been previously filled by the record just removed. Here is an example that removes the Rick Shaw record from the `rs` object:

```
rs.removeItemAt(1);
```

Once a record has been removed, that record's ID will still not be assigned to a newly inserted record. This is true even if the new record is inserted into the same index slot and contains the same data. For example, after having deleted the Rick Shaw record, you might re-insert it using the `addItemAt()` method as follows:

```
rs.addItemAt(1, {NAME: "Rick Shaw", ADDRESS: "555 Somwhere Lane", CITY:
"Heresville", JOB: "Crime Fighter"});
```

This code inserts the same record data back into the same index slot. However, the ID for this new record will be different than the old record. You can test this out by displaying the IDs for the records:

```
cn = rs.getColumnNames();
len = rs.getLength();
for(i = 0; i < len; i++){
  trace(rs.getItemID(i));
}
```

The preceding example code would display the following in the Output window:

```
2
4
0
3
```

Notice that whereas the Rick Shaw record previously had an ID of 1, it now has an ID of 4. This is because the Rick Shaw record is a new record, even if it contains the same data.

Sorting Records

When working with `RecordSet` objects, it is highly conceivable that you would want to re-order the records according to various criteria. For example, you may want to sort the records alphabetically according to a column indicating the username, or you may want to sort the records in descending order according to a birthday or a column that indicates how many years an employee has worked for the company. There are all kinds of reasons why, and ways in which, you might want to order the records in a record set, and `RecordSet` objects give you two methods for doing just that — `sortItemsBy()` and `sort()`.

Let's first look at the `sortItemsBy()` method because it is a little simpler to use. This method requires at least one parameter — a value indicating the column name on which to sort — and allows for a second, optional parameter to indicate the order in which the records should be sorted (either ascending or descending). If only the first parameter is passed to the method, then it automatically sorts the records in an ascending fashion. The code in the following example will sort the `rs` `RecordSet` object in ascending order according to the values in the NAME column:

```
rs.sortItemsBy("NAME");
```

Table 4-8 shows how the records would now be sorted.

Table 4-8: rs RecordSet Object Sorted By Name

NAME	ADDRESS	CITY	JOB
Ima Goodie	123 Ontha Way	Goodtown	Stapler Operator
Norma Lee	6 Eezee St.	Abracadabra	Pencil Maker Extraordinaire
Rick Shaw	555 Somewhere Lane	Heresville	Crime Fighter
Sam Aroton	23 Livehere Place	Nice City	Investigator

If you want to sort the records in *descending* order, you can specify the string value DESC as a second parameter to the method. The code in the following example will sort the rs object in descending order according to the CITY column:

```
rs.sortItemsBy("CITY", "DESC");
```

Table 4-9 shows how the records would now be sorted.

Table 4-9: rs RecordSet Object Sorted By City in Descending Order

NAME	ADDRESS	CITY	JOB
Sam Aroton	23 Livehere Place	Nice City	Investigator
Rick Shaw	555 Somewhere Lane	Heresville	Crime Fighter
Ima Goodie	123 Ontha Way	Goodtown	Stapler Operator
Norma Lee	6 Eezee St.	Abracadabra	Pencil Maker

As you can see, sorting a RecordSet object using the sortItemsBy() method is simple and straightforward. However, it does have certain limitations. For example, it does not allow you to sort based on multiple column values, which might be something you want to do (if, for example, the RecordSet object had a column for both first name and last name and you wished to sort the records alphabetically by name. Listing 4-1 creates such a RecordSet object, and Table 4-10 illustrates what the records would look like.

Listing 4-1: **Creating the employees RecordSet Object**

```
#include "NetServices.as"
employees = new RecordSet(["FIRST_NAME", "LAST_NAME"]);
employees.addItem({FIRST_NAME: "Roberta", LAST_NAME: "Johnson"});
employees.addItem({FIRST_NAME: "Alexis", LAST_NAME: "Smith"});
employees.addItem({FIRST_NAME: "Bob", LAST_NAME: "Johnson"});
employees.addItem({FIRST_NAME: "Alex", LAST_NAME: "Smith"});
```

Table 4-10: The employees RecordSet Object

FIRST_NAME	LAST_NAME
Roberta	Johnson
Alexis	Smith
Bob	Johnson
Alex	Smith

If you simply call the sortItemsBy() method, it will not accurately sort the records according to *both* the FIRST_NAME and LAST_NAME columns, only to the one that you specify. For example:

```
employees.sortItemsBy("LAST_NAME");
```

This would result in the records being ordered as shown in Table 4-11.

Table 4-11: The employees RecordSet Object Sorted By LAST_NAME

FIRST_NAME	LAST_NAME
Roberta	Johnson
Bob	Johnson
Alex	Smith
Alexis	Smith

It *does* sort according to last name just fine. However, we want it to sort on the first name as well. Fortunately, though the sortItemsBy() method cannot do this for us, the sort() method can. However, the sort() method is a little more complicated. It takes a single parameter — a reference to a custom function that will be used to determine the sort order. Therefore, the additional effort required to use the sort() method is defining the custom function.

The function that is passed as a reference to the sort() method is expected to follow these basic guidelines:

✦ The function will be automatically passed two parameters (call these a and b) each time it is called. The two parameters are the two records being compared.

✦ The function should return either -1, 1, or 0. -1 means that a should be sorted before b. 1 means that a should be sorted after b. And 0 means that both a and b are equal.

The following example illustrates a custom sorting function definition and the sort() method call using that function. This example uses the same employee RecordSet object from Listing 4-1.

```
function sorter(a, b){
  // first just set up some local variables
  // to save typing later on
  var aFN = a.FIRST_NAME;
  var aLN = a.LAST_NAME;
  var bFN = b.FIRST_NAME;
  var bLN = b.LAST_NAME;

  // now start comparing the values
  if(aLN < bLN){
    // if the a last name comes before the b last name
    // alphabetically, then return -1
    return -1;
  }
  else if(aLN > bLN){
    // if the a last name comes after the b last name
    // alphabetically, then return 1
    return 1;
  }
  else{
    // otherwise the last names are the same...so start comparing
    // the first names
    if(aFN < bFN){
      // if the a first name comes before the b first name
      // alphabetically, then return -1
      return -1;
    }
    else if(aFN > bFN){
      // if the a first name comes after the b first name
      // alphabetically, then return 1
      return 1;
    }
    else{
      // otherwise the first and last names are both the same...
      // so the function should return 0
      return 0;
    }
  }
}

// call the sort() method and pass it a reference to the custom
function
employees.sort(sorter);
```

When sorted using this code, the `employee RecordSet` object will be ordered as shown in Table 4-12.

**Table 4-12: The employees RecordSet Object
Sorted By LAST_NAME, FIRST_NAME**

FIRST_NAME	LAST_NAME
Bob	Johnson
Roberta	Johnson
Alex	Smith
Alexis	Smith

Filtering Records

You will sometimes want to create subsets of RecordSet objects, subsets that contain only some of the records from the original object. For instance, you may have a RecordSet object that contains records of users with columns for both username and species. You may want to keep this original object intact, but be able to filter it into multiple RecordSet objects based on the species value. Using the filter() method you can do exactly that.

The filter() method requires one parameter — a reference to a custom function. This custom function, the filter function, is automatically passed each record (one at a time) as a parameter. Within the function body, write the code that determines whether the record should be added to the new RecordSet object. If it should be added, then the function should return true. Otherwise, it should return false. The filter() method filters each of the records through the custom filter function and returns a *new* RecordSet object. This is an important point: the filter() method does *not* affect the original object.

The example shown in Listing 4-2 filters a RecordSet object to create a new RecordSet object containing only those records in which the SPECIES column value is Human.

Listing 4-2: Filtering a RecordSet Object

```
// make sure to include the NetServices.as file (or at least the
// RecordSet.as file)
#include "NetServices.as"

// create the new RecordSet object with two columns - USERNAME and
// SPECIES
// the populate it with records
users = new RecordSet(["USERNAME", "SPECIES"]);
users.addItem({USERNAME: "JJ Someguy", SPECIES: "Flaz"});
users.addItem({USERNAME: "Spacelady", SPECIES: "Dinarpian"});
users.addItem({USERNAME: "Gretel Gal", SPECIES: "Human"});
users.addItem({USERNAME: "Donald Smarts", SPECIES: "Dreman"});
users.addItem({USERNAME: "Pat Yat", SPECIES: "Human"});
users.addItem({USERNAME: "Freefall Jim", SPECIES: "Dreman"});
users.addItem({USERNAME: "Susy Duzy", SPECIES: "Human"});
```

Continued

Listing 4-2: *(continued)*

```
users.addItem({USERNAME: "Willis Wow", SPECIES: "Elaphiardin"});
users.addItem({USERNAME: "Cheery Chaz", SPECIES: "Elaphiardin"});

// define the filter function...notice that the function
// is going to be automatically passed a parameter - a record object
function filterSpecies(record){
  // return true is SPECIES is Human, false otherwise
  return (record.SPECIES == "Human");
}

// call the filter() method, pass it a reference to the filter
// function, and assign the result (a new RecordSet object) to a new
// variable
humans = users.filter(filterSpecies);

// output the usernames of all the records in the new RecordSet
// object
len = humans.getLength();
for(i = 0; i < len; i++){
  trace(humans.getItemAt(i).USERNAME);
}
/*
OUTPUT:
Gretel Gal
Pat Yat
Susy Duzy
*/
```

Although this example works perfectly in this one case, it could be improved slightly by making the filter function a little more abstract. Right now, the filter function can only filter out records where the species is Human. It would be much better if the function could be passed a second parameter to indicate how to filter the records. Fortunately, the filter() method enables you to do just that with a second, optional parameter. In general, if you pass a second parameter to the filter() method, that value is then passed as a second parameter to the filter function. In the example shown in Listing 4-3, the users object from Listing 4-2 is filtered again. This time, however, it is filtered using a filter function that gets passed a second parameter.

Listing 4-3: **Filtering a RecordSet By Passing a Second Parameter to the Filter Function**

```
// redefine the filter function so that it expects
// a second parameter
function filterSpecies(record, species){
  return (record.SPECIES == species);
```

```
}

// call the filter() method...and pass it a second parameter
// value specifying the species name value for which to filter
humans = users.filter(filterSpecies, "Human");
// now that the filter function is more generic, you can
// also filter for other species as well
elaphiardins = users.filter(filterSpecies, "Elaphiardin");
dremans = users.filter(filterSpecies, "Dreman");

// now output all the new RecordSet objects' records
// to make sure it works
len = humans.getLength();
trace("--- HUMANS ---");
for(i = 0; i < len; i++){
  trace(humans.getItemAt(i).USERNAME);
}
len = elaphiardins.getLength();
trace("--- ELAPHIARDINS ---");
for(i = 0; i < len; i++){
  trace(elaphiardins.getItemAt(i).USERNAME);
}
len = dremans.getLength();
trace("--- DREMANS ---");
for(i = 0; i < len; i++){
  trace(dremans.getItemAt(i).USERNAME);
}

/*
OUTPUT:
--- HUMANS ---
Gretel Gal
Pat Yat
Susy Duzy
--- ELAPHIARDINS ---
Willis Wow
Cheery Chaz
--- DREMANS ---
Donald Smarts
Freefall Jim
*/
```

Using RecordSet Objects with Components

One of the great advantages of RecordSet objects is that you can easily use them to populate UI (and other) components such as ListBox or ComboBox components. There are two ways to populate such components with data from a RecordSet object:

✦ Use the component's `setDataProvider()` method

✦ Use the `DataGlue` class

Using RecordSet objects as data providers

Just when you thought you had it down, I am going to throw you a curve ball. I told you that `RecordSet` objects were `RecordSet` objects, and they are. However, they are also `RsDataProviderClass` objects (that is, `RecordSet` is a subclass of `RsDataProviderClass`). And `RsDataProviderClass` objects are the same as `DataProviderClass` objects (for simplicity, I will henceforward refer to both types simply as data provider objects) used by components such as `ListBox` and `ComboBox`. These components have `setDataProvider()` methods that enable you to specify a data provider object to be used in order to populate the menus.

So what exactly is a data provider object? Well, you have already seen it. They are essentially arrays of objects. In the case of the `RecordSet` class of objects, we refer to the elements of the array as record objects. Data provider objects have the same set of methods, such as `addItem()` and `addItemAt()`.

What this means is that `RecordSet` objects can be used in any place where a data provider object is expected. For instance, a reference to a `RecordSet` object can be passed to a `ListBox` component's `setDataProvider()` method. The example shown in Listing 4-4 uses a `ListBox` component named `myMenu`.

Listing 4-4: **Using a RecordSet Object as a Data Provider for a ListBox Component**

```
#include "NetServices.as"

movies = new RecordSet(["TITLE", "RANK", "YEAR"]);
movies.addItem({TITLE: "Citizen Abel", RANK: 1, YEAR: 1941});
movies.addItem({TITLE: "Casarojo", RANK: 2, YEAR: 1942});
movies.addItem({TITLE: "The Godmother", RANK: 3, YEAR: 1972});
movies.addItem({TITLE: "Gone With the Breeze", RANK: 4, YEAR: 1939});
movies.addItem({TITLE: "Florence of Arabia", RANK: 5, YEAR: 1962});


myMenu.setDataProvider(movies);
```

This code would produce a result similar to what is shown in Figure 4-3.

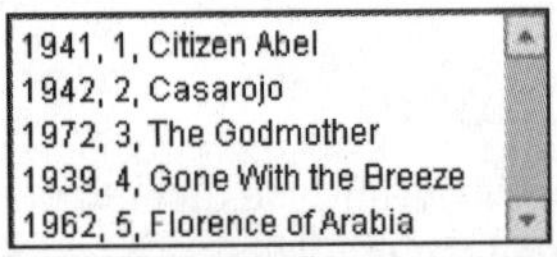

```
1941, 1, Citizen Abel
1942, 2, Casarojo
1972, 3, The Godmother
1939, 4, Gone With the Breeze
1962, 5, Florence of Arabia
```

Figure 4-3: An example of a ListBox component populated by a RecordSet object

Notice, however, the seemingly random way in which the columns are displayed. This is where the `DataGlue` class comes in handy.

Introducing the DataGlue class

In order to take full advantage of using `RecordSet` objects with components, you need to learn about a small, simple class called `DataGlue`.

The first thing to learn about `DataGlue` is that it is a part of the Flash Remoting Components installation. This means that you must use an `#include` statement to add the `DataGlue` class in your Flash application before you can take advantage of its functionality. You can add the `DataGlue` class with the following line of code:

```
#include "DataGlue.as"
```

Once you have included the class, you can begin using its two static methods:

✦ `bindFormatStrings()`

✦ `bindFormatFunction()`

The `bindFormatStrings()` method is the simplest of the two. This method takes four parameters—the component instance, the `RecordSet` object, a string indicating how to generate the label values (we'll call this the label parameter), and a string indicating how to generate the data values (we'll call this the data parameter). Of the four parameters, the first two are relatively straightforward; the second two parameters warrant some additional discussion.

Components that use data provider objects are called *data consumers*. Data consumers generally have both labels and the data associated with those labels. For instance, `ListBox` components have labels that are displayed to the user in the menu as well as data that is associated with each of the labels. This makes sense, because you often want the labels to be more verbose (something like `Citizen Abel (1941)`) than the associated data, which is more concise and technical (such as simply ranking the movie as 1). Therefore, the `bindFormatStrings()` method accommodates this distinction with the second two parameters, which specify the label and data values, respectively.

There is another consideration with these parameters. You need a way to make the values specified in the label and data parameters dynamic. This is accomplished by using pound signs (#) around the `RecordSet` object column names. These column names enclosed by pound signs are then treated as variables, and the values from the appropriate columns are substituted in their place. An example will likely clarify this. This example uses the `myMenu` component and the `movies` RecordSet object created in the previous example. In place of the `setDataProvider()` method call, however, you can use the following code:

```
DataGlue.bindFormatStrings(myMenu, movies, "#TITLE# (#YEAR#)",
"#RANK#");
```

This now produces the result shown in Figure 4-4.

You can see that the label parameter is what is displayed in the menu. The `RecordSet` object column names that were placed between pound signs in the label parameter were substituted for the actual values from the records. What you cannot see is that the data associated with each of the menu elements is the ranking of the movie (as retrieved from the `RecordSet` object).

However, even the `bindFormatStrings()` method has some limitations. One such limitation is that you cannot alter how individual column values are used by the data consumer. For instance, in the example with the movie titles, you cannot, using `bindFormatStrings()`, rearrange the formatting of the movie titles (such as moving articles like "The," "A," and "An" to the end of the title). However, using the `bindFormatFunction()` method you can.

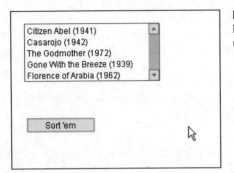

Figure 4-4: An example of a ListBox component populated using bindFormatStrings()

Like `bindFormatStrings()`, the `bindFormatFunction()` method requires parameters specifying the data consumer and the data provider. However, instead of label and data parameters, it requires a reference to a custom function that determines the label and data values (we'll call this the formatting function).

The formatting function is passed each record, one at a time, as a parameter. The `bindFormatFunction()` method then expects the formatting function to return an object with `label` and `data` properties. Again, a good example will probably do a much better job of explaining this concept than words. The code in Listing 4-5 includes both the formatting function definition and the `bindFormatFunction()` call. This example uses the same `ListBox` component and `movies RecordSet` object created previously.

Listing 4-5: **Using a Custom Formatting Function**

```
#include "NetServices.as"

function formatter(record){
  // make variables to save typing
  var title = record.TITLE;
  var year = record.YEAR;
  var rank = record.RANK;

  // now check to see if the first word of the title
  // is an article. If so, rearrange the title.
  // i.e. - The Godmother --> Godmother, The
  if (title.substring(0, 4).toLowerCase() == "the "){
    title = title.substring(4) + ", The";
  }
  else if (title.substring(0, 3).toLowerCase() == "an "){
    title = title.substring(3) + ", An";
  }
  else if (title.substring(0,2).toLowerCase() == "a "){
    title = title.substring(2) + ", A";
  }
```

```
// now create the object that will be returned
o = new Object();
o.label = title + " (" + year + ")";
o.data = rank;

// and don't forget to return the object!
return o;
}

movies = new RecordSet(["TITLE", "RANK", "YEAR"]);
movies.addItem({TITLE: "Citizen Abel", RANK: 1, YEAR: 1941});
movies.addItem({TITLE: "Casarojo", RANK: 2, YEAR: 1942});
movies.addItem({TITLE: "The Godmother", RANK: 3, YEAR: 1972});
movies.addItem({TITLE: "Gone With the Breeze", RANK: 4, YEAR: 1939});
movies.addItem({TITLE: "Florence of Arabia", RANK: 5, YEAR: 1962});

DataGlue.bindFormatFunction(myMenu, movies, formatter);
```

This example code will result in something similar to what is shown in Figure 4-5.

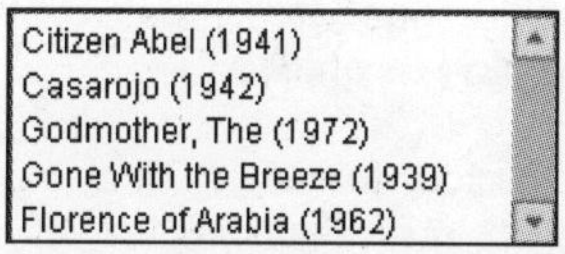

Citizen Abel (1941)
Casarojo (1942)
Godmother, The (1972)
Gone With the Breeze (1939)
Florence of Arabia (1962)

Figure 4-5: A ListBox component populated using the bindFormatFunction()

Listening for Changes to Record Sets

If a RecordSet object has been used as a data provider, then the data consumer should be alerted to any updates or changes to the RecordSet object. In fact, most data consumers already do this automatically. For example, the code in Listing 4-4 created a RecordSet object (movies) and set that object to be used as the data provider for a ListBox component named myMenu. If the RecordSet object is modified by any activity, such as being sorted, then the data consumer is automatically alerted to this fact and takes appropriate action. Listing 4-6 adds some code to the code from Listings 4-4 and 4-5. The new code simply calls the sort() method of the movies object when a button named sortButton is released.

Listing 4-6: sort() Method Called When sortButton Is Released

```
// sortButton is a PushButton instance on the stage
sortButton.onRelease = function(){
  _root.movies.sortItemsBy("TITLE");
}
```

Figure 4-6 shows the results before the button is pressed, and Figure 4-7 shows the results after the button has been released.

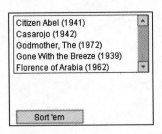

Figure 4-6: Before the button is pressed

Figure 4-7: After the button is released

Although the button actions do not directly affect the ListBox, the update is made to the component indirectly because it is the data consumer for the movies object.

Note   Although *The Godmother* is displayed (by means of the custom formatting function) as *Godmother, The*, the value of the column in the RecordSet object remains unchanged. Therefore, when sorted, it is placed after *Florence of Arabia* (because *The Godmother* comes alphabetically afterward).

Although all of this is done apparently seamlessly, it actually takes advantage of the addView() method of the RecordSet class (more accurately, the addView() method of the RsDataProviderClass class). The addView() method enables other objects to be alerted every time a change is made to a RecordSet object. Although you don't need to worry about it when using RecordSet objects as data providers for predefined components such as ListBox and ComboBox components, you *can* use it for other types of objects and for creating your own UI components.

The addView() method can be called from any RecordSet object and passed a reference to another object that you wish to have alerted when changes are made to the RecordSet object. Table 4-13 describes the different types of changes (called events) that can be detected.

Table 4-13: Events for RecordSet Objects

Event	Description
Sort	Occurs any time the sort() or sortItemsBy() method has been called
UpdateAll	Occurs when the whole object has been affected in some way, such as when the addView() method has been called
AddRows	Occurs when the addItem() or addItemAt() method has been called

Event	Description
UpdateRows	Occurs when the `setField()` or `replaceItemAt()` method has been called
DeleteRows	Occurs when the `removeAll()` or `removeItemAt()` method has been called
allRows and fetchRows	Occur in relation to ColdFusion-specific functionality (discussed in Chapter 6)

The object that is to be alerted when events occur with the `RecordSet` object must have a method named `modelChanged()`. This method is then automatically called when the events occur. Additionally, it is passed a parameter in the form of an object containing information about the event that has occurred. For all events, this object has an `event` property with a string value equal to one of the events in Table 4-13. For a few of the events, two other properties are included in the object, as you will learn in just a moment. First, let's look at an example of the `addView()` method in action. Listing 4-7 shows the `addView()` method being called for a `RecordSet` object as well as the definition of the object that is alerted when events occur.

Listing 4-7: **Using addView()**

```
#include "NetServices.as"

// create the object that will be alerted when events occur
obj = new Object();
// define the modelChanged() method
obj.modelChanged = function(info){
  // the method is automatically passed an object value
  // here just trace() the event property of that object
  trace(info.event);
}

// define a custom sorting function that is used later on
function sorter(a, b){
  // return 0, so nothing is really sorted
  // this function is just to demonstrate that
  // the sort event occurs when the sort() method is called
  return 0;
}

// create the new RecordSet object
rs = new RecordSet(["ITEM", "PRICE"]);

// call addView() and pass it a reference to the object
// with modelChanged() defined
rs.addView(obj);

// now just call all the assorted methods
// of the RecordSet object that will produce
// events that will be sent to obj
```

Continued

Listing 4-7: *(continued)*

```
rs.addItem({ITEM: "widget", PRICE: "$99.99"});
rs.addItemAt(0, {ITEM: "sprocket", PRICE: "$66.66"});
rs.setField(1, "PRICE", "$9.99");
rs.replaceItemAt(0, {ITEM: "sprocket v2", PRICE: "$6.99"});
rs.sortItemsBy("PRICE");
rs.sort(sorter);
rs.removeItemAt(0);
rs.removeAll();

/*
OUTPUT:
updateAll
addRows
addRows
updateRows
updateRows
sort
sort
deleteRows
deleteRows
*/
```

The `addRows`, `updateRows`, and `deleteRows` events also send along additional properties to the `modelChanged()` method in the parameter object. Along with the `event` property, the parameter object for these events also has both a `firstRow` property and a `lastRow` property, indicating which rows have been affected. Listing 4-8 shows how the `modelChanged()` method from Listing 4-7 might be modified to also take into account these additional properties, as well as the resulting output.

Listing 4-8: Outputting the firstRow and lastRow Properties

```
obj.modelChanged = function(info){
  // create a local variable just to save typing
  var ev = info.event;
  trace(ev);
  // if the event has the firstRow or lastRow property, output
  // those values as well
  if(ev == "addRows" || ev == "updateRows" || ev == "deleteRows"){
    trace("  affected rows: " + info.firstRow + " - " + info.lastRow);
  }
}

/*
OUTPUT:
updateAll
addRows
  affected rows: 0 - 0
addRows
```

```
    affected rows: 0 - 0
updateRows
    affected rows: 1 - 1
updateRows
    affected rows: 0 - 0
sort
sort
deleteRows
    affected rows: 0 - 0
deleteRows
    affected rows: 0 - -1
*/
```

Displaying Records in a Table

In this exercise, you will use much of the RecordSet functionality that you have learned in order to do the following:

✦ Create a new RecordSet object and populate it with values

✦ Read the RecordSet object's information, including the number of records and the column names

✦ Sort the records by column

✦ Work with a RecordSet object in a meaningful way to display the results in a table

Perform the following steps in order to complete this exercise:

1. Open a new Flash document and save it as tableMaker.fla.

2. Rename the default layer to form.

3. Create two new layers and name them actions and Table.

4. On the form layer, create a PushButton component instance and a ComboBox component instance. Name these instances sortButton and sortMenu, respectively. These should be placed in the lower portion of the stage, as shown in Figure 4-8.

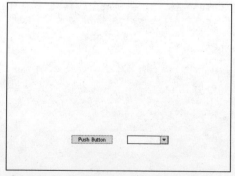

Figure 4-8: The layout on the form layer

5. Create a `Table` class that will be responsible for displaying the records. This class should be something that can be re-used for any `RecordSet` object (or any type of data provider object). Open the Actions panel and place the following code on the first frame of the `Table` layer:

```
/* define the Table constructor
    it should take two parameters - a reference to the
    MovieClip object that will be the "parent" of the
    Table and a Boolean value indicating whether or not
    the Table should have a border.
*/
function Table(mcRef, border){
  // create the tbl MC...the equivalent to the HTML <table>
  mcRef.createEmptyMovieClip("tbl", 0);

  // set up some properties for the new object
  this.table = mcRef.tbl;
  this.y = 0;
  this.row = 0;
  this.col = 0;
  this.colWidth = new Array();
  this.border = border;
}

// this method adds a new row - equivalent to HTML <tr>
Table.prototype.addTR = function(){
  // increment the row property
  this.row++;
  // create a row MC inside the main table MC
  this.table.createEmptyMovieClip("tr" + this.row, this.row);
  // increment the y property if not first row
  if(this.row > 1)
    this.y += this.table["tr" + (this.row - 1)]._height + 5;
  // reset the col property to 0 for a new row
  this.col = 0;
  // set the row's _y property
  this.table["tr" + this.row]._y = this.y;
}

// this method adds a new column to a row - equivalent to HTML <td>
// it takes a parameter indicating the value that should
// appear in the column
Table.prototype.addTD = function(val){
  // local var to save typing
  var row = this.table["tr" + this.row];
  // increment the col property
  this.col++;
  // create the new column MC and set up a local var
  // to save typing
  row.createEmptyMovieClip("td" + this.col, this.col);
  var col = row["td" + this.col];
```

```
    // create the new TF object inside the td MC and set
    // its text property equal to the value passed the method
    col.createTextField("val", this.col, 0, 0, 0, 0);
    var tf = col.val;
    tf.text = val;
    tf.autoSize = true;
    // if the new TF's width is the greatest in the whole
    // column thus far, set that width value to be the width
    // for the whole column (all rows) to make sure everything
    // is aligned properly
    if(tf._width > this.colWidth[this.col - 1]){
      this.colWidth[this.col - 1] = tf._width;
    }
}

// this method closes up the table and formats everything
Table.prototype.endTable = function(){
  // x keeps track of the x position of a column
  var x = 0;
  // loop through all the rows
  for(var i = 0; i < this.row; i++){
    // loop through all the columns of a row
    for(var j = 0; j < this.colWidth.length; j++){
      // c is a reference to the current column
      var c = this.table["tr" + (i + 1)]["td" + (j + 1)];
      // set the column's _x to the max width for the whole
      // column (all rows)
      c._x = x + this.colWidth[j-1] + 5;
      x = c._x;
      var w = this.colWidth[j];
      var h = c._height;
      // if the border property is true, draw the border
      // around all the cells of the table
      if(this.border){
        c.createEmptyMovieClip("border", -1);
        c.lineStyle(1, 0, 100);
        c.lineTo(w, 0);
        c.lineTo(w, h);
        c.lineTo(0, h);
        c.lineTo(0, 0);
      }
    }
    x = 0;
  }
}

// this method allows a table to be created based on the
// data provider object
Table.prototype.setDataProvider = function(dp){
  // if the data provider property is not yet defined
  // set it to be a reference to the dp value and call the
```

```
      // addView() method so that the table will be automatically
      // notified when any changes occur to the data provider.
      if(this.dp == undefined){
        this.dp = dp;
        dp.addView(this);
      }
      // this section simply populates the table
      // with the data from the data provider
      var len = dp.getLength();
      var cn = dp.getColumnNames();
      this.addTR();
      for (var i = 0; i < cn.length; i++){
        this.addTD(cn[i]);
      }
      for (i = 0; i < len; i++){
        this.addTR();
        for (var j = 0; j < cn.length; j++){
          this.addTD(dp.getItemAt(i)[cn[j]]);
        }
      }
      this.endTable();
    }


    // returns the data provider object
    Table.prototype.getDataProvider = function(){
      return this.dp;
    }


    // the clear() method should just clear the table data
    Table.prototype.clear = function(){
      for(var i = 0; i < this.row; i++){
        this.table["tr" + (i + 1)].removeMovieClip();
      }
      this.row = 0;
      this.y = 0;
    }


    // the modelChanged() method is called automatically when
    // the data provider is changed
    Table.prototype.modelChanged = function(info){
      // as long as the event is not updateAll
      // clear the table and repopulate it with the
      // new info from the data provider
      if(info.event != "updateAll"){
        this.clear();
        this.setDataProvider(this.dp);
      }
    }
```

6. On frame 1 of the `actions` layer, add the following code to set up the `RecordSet` object, initialize the form, and create the table:

```
// make sure to include the NetServices.as file
#include "NetServices.as"

// create the RecordSet object
movies = new RecordSet(["TITLE", "RANK", "YEAR"]);
movies.addItem({TITLE: "Citizen Abel", RANK: 1, YEAR: 1941});
movies.addItem({TITLE: "Casarojo", RANK: 2, YEAR: 1942});
movies.addItem({TITLE: "The Godmother", RANK: 3, YEAR: 1972});
movies.addItem({TITLE: "Gone With the Breeze", RANK: 4, YEAR: 1939});
movies.addItem({TITLE: "Florence of Arabia", RANK: 5, YEAR: 1962});

// populate the sortMenu with the column names
cn = movies.getColumnNames();
sortMenu.setDataProvider(cn);

// create the table and align it on the stage
_root.createEmptyMovieClip("resultsTable", 0);
t = new Table(resultsTable, true);
t.setDataProvider(movies);
resultsTable._x = Stage.width/2 - resultsTable._width/2;
resultsTable._y = Stage.height/2 - resultsTable._height/2;

// when the sortButton is released, sort the movies RS
// by the selected column
sortButton.setLabel("Sort!");
sortButton.onRelease = function(){
  var sb = _root.sortMenu.getValue();
  // sort the data provider object (the RecordSet object)
  _root.t.getDataProvider().sortItemsBy(sb);
}
```

7. Test the movie. It should display the values from the RecordSet object in a table, as shown in Figure 4-9. When you select a column from the menu and sort by the column (by clicking on the button), the table should automatically update to reflect the change.

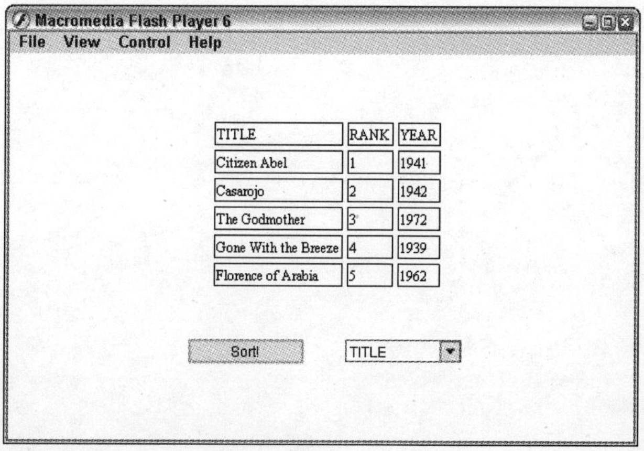

Figure 4-9: The resulting movie

Getting Remote Record Sets

In this exercise, you will modify the `tableMaker.fla` Flash document you made in the previous exercise so that the `RecordSet` object is loaded from a remote procedure. This exercise requires that you have a database set up, as outlined in this chapter, "Creating Your First MySQL Database."

1. Make sure that you have the provided CFC\JavaBean\DLL properly in place.

   a. If you are using ColdFusion MX, create a directory named `chapter4` under the `Wiley` directory within the ColdFusion web root. In this folder, place the `Database.cfc` file.

   b. If you are using a J2EE application server, create a `chapter4` directory under the Wiley directory within the server's `WEB-INF/classes` or `SERVER-INF/classes` directory (for JRun, just use the sample server for now). In this folder, place the `Database.class` file.

   c. If you are using .NET, copy `Database.dll` into the web root's `flashremoting/bin` directory.

2. Open `tableMaker.fla` and save it as `tableMaker_v2.fla`.

3. The code on the `Table` layer should remain the same. On the `actions` layer, replace the existing code with the following:

```
// make sure to include the NetServices.as file
#include "NetServices.as"

function displayResult(result){
    // we don't want to display all the columns, so instead
    // let's make a new RecordSet object with just TITLE, AUTHOR,
    // and PUBLICATION_DATE columns and populate it with
    // data formatted how we want it to appear
    _root.rs = new RecordSet(["TITLE", "AUTHOR", "PUBLICATION_DATE"]);
    // local variables to be used
    var r, t, a, pd;
    // loop through all the resulting RS object's records
    for(var i = 0; i < result.getLength(); i++){
        // assign values to the local vars to save typing
        r = result.getItemAt(i);
        t = r.TITLE;
        a = r.AUTHOR_FIRST + " " + r.AUTHOR_LAST;
        pd = r.PUBLICATION_DATE.getMonth() + "/" +
r.PUBLICATION_DATE.getFullYear();
        // add the new record to the new RecordSet object
        _root.rs.addItem({TITLE: t, AUTHOR: a, PUBLICATION_DATE: pd});
    }

    // populate the sortMenu with the column names
    var cn = _root.rs.getColumnNames();
    _root.sortMenu.setDataProvider(cn);

    // set the table's data provider to the new RS object
    _root.t.setDataProvider(_root.rs);
```

```
    // position the table in the center of the stage
    // (Windows users might have to test the movie in the
    // standalone player for this part to work properly
    _root.resultsTable._x = Stage.width/2 -
_root.resultsTable._width/2;
    _root.resultsTable._y = Stage.height/2 -
_root.resultsTable._height/2;
}

// first assign the gateway URL to a string.
// shown here are the likely possibilities.
//gwUrl = "http://localhost:8200/flashservices/gateway/";
//gwUrl = "http://localhost:8500/flashservices/gateway/";
gwUrl = "http://localhost/flashremoting/gateway.aspx";

// set the default gateway URL to the string's value
// and create the connection object
NetServices.setDefaultGatewayURL(gwUrl);
conn = NetServices.createGatewayConnection();

// create the service object
srv = conn.getService("chapter4.Database");

// create the response object
rsRes = new Object();
rsRes.onResult = function(result){
  // call the displayResult() function
  _root.displayResult(result);
}
rsRes.onStatus = function(status){
  for(i in status){
    trace(status[i]);
  }
}

// call the remote procedure and pass it the database name
// and a valid SQL SELECT statement as the parameters
srv.getRS(rsRes, "WileyFlashRemoting", "SELECT * FROM BOOKS");

// create the table and align it on the stage
_root.createEmptyMovieClip("resultsTable", 0);
t = new Table(resultsTable, true);

// when the sortButton is released, sort the movies RS
// by the selected column
sortButton.setLabel("Sort!");
sortButton.onRelease = function(){
  var sb = _root.sortMenu.getValue();
  _root.t.getDataProvider().sortItemsBy(sb);
}
```

4. Make sure your application server is running and test the movie. You should see something similar to what is shown in Figure 4-10.

TITLE	AUTHOR	PUBLICATION_DATE
Complete Flash Remoting	Joey Lott	1/2003
Dreamweaver MX Bible	Joseph Lowery	6/2002
XML Web Services with ASP.NET	Bill Evjen	3/2002
Building Great FlashTM MX Games	Matthew David	9/2002
JMXTM Programming	Mike Janowski	5/2002

Sort!		TITLE ▾

Figure 4-10: The resulting movie

Summary

In this chapter, you looked at many topics related to databases. Although it was a lot of information, it is hoped that you now have a good understanding of the following:

✦ Databases are part of the backbone of countless applications used on a daily basis — even if you are not typically aware of it. This is especially true of Web applications.

✦ Relational databases (the kind we are interested in) store related data in tables, which are basically grids of columns and rows. Storing data in this way helps to make access to data more efficient.

✦ SQL is the common language understood by all kinds of databases. Basic `INSERT`, `SELECT`, `UPDATE`, and `DELETE` statements form a simple toolset for working with data.

✦ Database information returned to Flash Remoting movies is automatically converted into `RecordSet` objects.

✦ You can perform many operations on `RecordSet` objects, including adding, updating, removing, and sorting records.

✦ `RecordSet` objects can be easily integrated with other objects, to be used as data providers and to automatically update those objects when any change occurs.

✦   ✦   ✦

Getting Started with Web Services

Web services are a hot topic these days. Moreover, as with any emerging technology, Web services are not without controversy and drama. This may be especially true of Web services, in fact, with major proponents such as Microsoft and IBM transforming the concept into reality. As a technology positioned to be the next major advance not only for Internet development and software development, but also for computing in general (including entirely new markets made accessible to computers by way of Web services), the prospect of Web services has fostered the development of new protocols, new standards, and new specifications. All this novelty can be overwhelming for a developer who wants to understand Web services. You may have heard the hype — how Web services will revolutionize how business is done and how applications are built. But what exactly *is* a Web service? What does it mean for you, the developer? These are the questions examined in this chapter.

Introducing Web Services

To understand Web services, it helps to understand the impetus for the creation of this technology — the existing environment prior to its development and the growing needs that the environment did not meet very well.

One of the frequently uttered catchphrases regarding the Internet, and particularly the World Wide Web, is that it has globalized business. And it has, to a large extent. Certainly, the Web has enabled businesses to reach worldwide — not only to consumers, but also to other businesses — in ways that were not available before. One of the outcomes of this has been an increasing desire among companies to be able to integrate multiple systems to form feature-rich applications. E-commerce illustrates this quite well. At one time, a company might have displayed its catalog in static Web pages, providing a telephone number or an e-mail address that customers could use to place orders. The orders would then be processed manually by human beings. However, that system did not suffice for long. From a business standpoint, it was inefficient to do all the order and transaction processing manually. By placing the catalog on the Web, a company can potentially reach more consumers. However, a larger volume of orders processed manually means having to hire more people. Furthermore, there was little added incentive to the consumer. Therefore, a new model had to emerge. What emerged was the development of completely automated order and transaction processing. However, new problems arose, including the following:

✦ It was necessary to integrate the automated ordering system with an existing (legacy) inventory system.

✦ It was necessary to integrate the automated ordering system with an existing billing system (legacy system).

✦ It was necessary to integrate the ordering system with a credit-card processing system (legacy system of a third party).

✦ Shipping and handling calculations (legacy system of a third party) needed to be integrated into the ordering system.

Figure 5-1 illustrates the system integration needs of a traditional retailer trying to move into a Web-based model. You can see that the model is inefficient and enables plenty of errors to occur at multiple points.

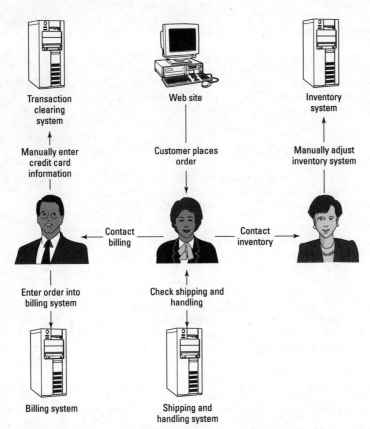

Figure 5-1: A look at pre-systems integration in which each step is handled manually

As you can see, the overall theme of the potential problems is one of communication between systems. Because these systems are likely behind different firewalls, in different physical locations, running on different platforms, using different, possibly incompatible technologies, and even operated by different companies, all sorts of obstacles have to be overcome. These obstacles have been overcome in the past by way of extensive, proprietary development in what has been termed traditional Enterprise Application Integration (EAI). Figure 5-2 shows the process from Figure 5-1 after EAI has been implemented.

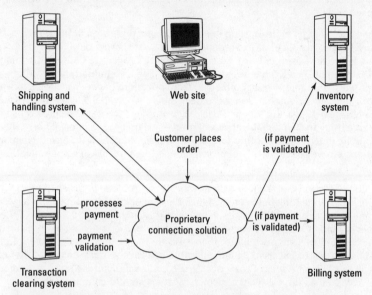

Figure 5-2: A look at a system after EAI in which each part of the process is automated through proprietary integration code

It might be obvious to you that there are many downsides to the traditional EAI model as well. Namely, each time a system needed to be integrated with another, a custom solution has to be developed — costing huge amounts of money, time, and resources to essentially reinvent the wheel each time. Here are a few key points that demonstrate some of the model's shortcomings:

✦ Relatively large investments in initial development for connecting systems

✦ Results in proprietary connectors that do not react well to change and that are not reusable

✦ A monolithic application that does not scale well

✦ Platform-specific solutions

✦ Single points of failure

Over the years, various solutions have been proposed and implemented in an attempt to eliminate the need to reinvent the wheel. Indeed, to a large extent these solutions have provided relief. Java RMI (Remote Method Invocation), DCOM (Distributed Component Object Model), and DSOM (Distributed System Object Model) are examples of these solutions. Even good, old CGI (Common Gateway Interface, a specification for sending data from a Web server and a program) provides a workable solution. However, each of these models also has its shortcomings in that they are tied to particular platforms and/or protocols. For example, DCOM works only in an all-Microsoft integration, and CGI is a viable solution only when the protocol being used is HTTP.

The introduction of XML (eXtensible Markup Language) was a huge step in the right direction for EAI. XML provides a platform-independent way of sharing data between applications. This led to new protocols for executing Remote Procedure Calls (RPC), such as WDDX (Web Distributed Data Exchange) and XML-RPC. The idea behind these XML-based protocols is essentially the same—to serialize and transport data between systems in ways that remain platform independent. In other words, although two systems might be written using different languages—Java and Visual Basic, for example—the data structures used are essentially the same thing from a high-level view. For every data type in one language there is likely a corresponding data type in another language. Therefore, using XML-based languages, all of these solutions strove to create this platform-independent means of communicating between systems.

Many of the resulting solutions worked. But there was still a problem: In order to create a universal solution for communicating between systems, developers had to come to an agreement on a common approach. In other words, if every system implemented XML-RPC, then it would be possible to communicate. However, with so many solutions developed by so many companies, what resulted was simply a battle to see whose technology would be adopted most widely. Ultimately, Microsoft used its considerable leverage to push its own XML-based protocol, called Simple Object Access Protocol (SOAP), and all indications suggest that SOAP has been largely accepted as the protocol by which systems should communicate.

Another element is required to make system communication as extensible and independent of language and platform as possible. There needs to be a way for these exposed services to be described to the system that is going to call them. This description should include the available procedures, the parameters required, and the values returned, as well as information regarding how to locate the actual procedure that should be invoked and the protocol for transporting data (such as SOAP). Web Services Description Language (WSDL) is an XML-based language used exactly for this purpose. (You'll look more closely at WSDL in the next section.)

Web services are the result of this evolution of RPC. Web services have been defined as self-describing (this is what WSDL does), modular, and self-contained applications that can be accessed over Internet protocols (HTTP, SMTP, etc.). More simply put, Web services are a way for any application to communicate with another application in a standardized, universal manner. With Web services, the calling/requesting client (called the *consuming* application) doesn't have to know anything about how the service it is requesting is actually implemented. It doesn't matter whether the *publisher* (the system on which the requested service resides) implements the procedure using Java, .NET, ColdFusion, Perl, PHP, or any other language. Nor does it matter if the publisher is running Unix, Windows, Mac OS X, or any other operating system. Moreover, multiple clients can consume the same Web service running on the publisher without the publishing system's having any information about the consuming system.

Figure 5-3 shows the basic flow of Web service consumption.

As you can see, a lot of steps are involved in the Web service process (most of which are taken care of automatically). This is not necessarily a bad thing. In fact, it is these layers that make Web services such a perfect solution for the EAI today.

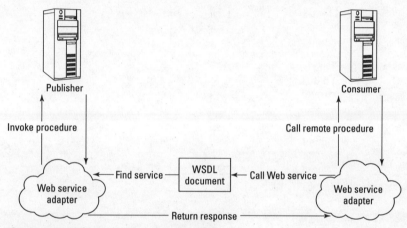

Figure 5-3: Web service consumption flow

Web services create a different model from traditional EAI solutions. Consider again the E-commerce example that we have been looking at throughout this section. With the traditional EAI solution, a proprietary connection was created between each system that needed to communicate. This connection had to know about both the consumer and the publisher. It was coded to enable the two specific systems to share data and functionality in specific ways. However, if anything changed on either end, the connection would likely fail. With Web services, however, the publisher's Web services are self-describing, and the consumer uses the service according to that description. If the Web service changes, then its description changes, and the consumer simply adapts based on the new description. This is a much more flexible and scalable model. Figure 5-4 illustrates how this new model differs from the old one.

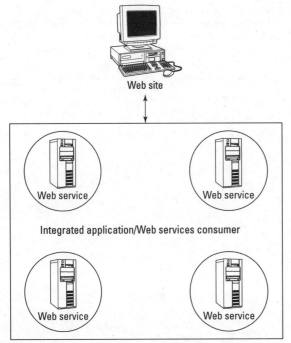

Figure 5-4: An EAI project using Web services

Web Services at a Glance

In the preceding section, you learned a lot about where Web services came from and what you can expect them to do. However, you may still be wondering why they are significant for developers — for *you*. In other words, what can you expect Web services to do for you, and how can they be of benefit to your own application development?

The real goal of Web services is to enable more rapid, standardized, distributed application development. Most every e-commerce application is going to require a credit card processing service as well as a shipping and handling service. Before the advent of Web services, integrating these services into an application was cumbersome at best, and more often than not it was fragile and did not scale well. Web services view all additional systems simply as components that can be readily consumed by any client. It is a way of encapsulating an entire system into a building block, as you saw in Figure 5-4.

This eliminates the time and energy you would have to spend constantly reinventing the wheel. In addition, you can quickly add more features to your application than you could have before. For instance, in the past, if you wished to add a stock quote service, weather or traffic service, or any other kind of feature to your application, you had to locate someone with such a system and then partner up with them to devise a custom service that could be integrated with your systems. With Web services, however, all you need to do is locate a publisher of such a Web service (see the "Locating Web Services" section of this chapter) and add to your application the few lines of code that consume the service — as if you were simply calling a procedure within your own application's system. Web services remove the borders and barriers of systems, enabling truly distributed applications.

Interpreting Web Service Documentation Language

One of the important characteristics of Web services is that they are self-describing. In other words, Web services are able to tell a consumer about their functionality and how to access that functionality. As mentioned previously, this self-description is accomplished with Web Service Documentation Language, or WSDL. You can think of WSDL as the gateway of Web services. Requests come to the WSDL, which makes sure the requests are properly formatted and that they get to the proper location. What this means to you in practical terms is that a Web service is made accessible by way of its WSDL document. Therefore, familiarizing yourself with WSDL is an important first step in working with Web services.

Note You can read more about the WSDL specification at `http://www.w3.org/TR/wsdl`.

Getting Started with WSDL

WSDL is an XML-based language, so it is human-readable. At first, WSDL might seem a bit difficult to decipher. With a little practice, however, you will quickly be able to read any WSDL document and understand how to invoke the Web services it describes. I think the best way to start with WSDL is simply to plunge in. To begin, let's look at a simple WSDL document, as shown in Listing 5-1. The document describes a SOAP Web service with one procedure. The procedure is named myFunction, and it takes an input parameter with two parts, and outputs a single value (see bolded text).

Tip I think that learning technologies and languages at a low level is advantageous to any student. For this reason, I outline how to understand WSDL documents in their "raw" form. I encourage you to read all of this section. However, in a later section titled "Using WSDL Tools," I explain how to use tools to more easily interpret WSDL.

Listing 5-1: **A simple WSDL Document**

```
<?xml version="1.0" encoding="UTF-8"?>
<definitions
    xmlns="http://schemas.xmlsoap.org/wsdl/"
    name="MyService"
    targetNamespace="http://www.myDomain.com/MyService.wsdl"
    xmlns:soap="http://schemas.xmlsoap.org/wsdl/soap/"
    xmlns:tns="http://www.myDomain.com/MyService.wsdl"
    xmlns:xsd="http://www.w3.org/2001/XMLSchema"
    xmlns:xsd1="http://www.myDomain.com/MyService.xsd1">
  <message name="MyMessageResponse">
    <part name="outputValue" type="xsd:string" />
  </message>
  <message name="MyMessageRequest">
    <part name="param1" type="xsd:string" />
    <part name="param2" type="xsd:boolean" />
  </message>
  <portType name="MyServicePortType">
```

Continued

Listing 5-1: *(continued)*

```
    <operation name="myFunction">
      <input message="tns:MyMessageRequest" />
      <output message="tns:MyMessageResponse" />
    </operation>
  </portType>
  <binding name="MyServiceBinding" type="tns:MyServicePortType">
    <soap:binding style="rpc"
transport="http://schemas.xmlsoap.org/soap/http" />
    <operation name="myFunction">
      <soap:operation
soapAction="http://www.myDomain.com/Wiley/chapter5/MyCFC.cfc" />
      <input>
        <soap:body
          encodingStyle="http://schemas.xmlsoap.org/soap/encoding/"
          namespace="http://www.myDomain.com/MyService/binding"
          use="encoded" />
      </input>
      <output>
        <soap:body
          encodingStyle="http://schemas.xmlsoap.org/soap/encoding/"
          namespace="http://www.myDomain.com/MyService/binding"
          use="encoded" />
      </output>
    </operation>
  </binding>
  <service name="MyService">
    <port binding="tns:MyServiceBinding" name="MyServicePort">
      <soap:address
location="http://www.myDomain.com/Wiley/chapter5/MyCFC.cfc" />
    </port>
  </service>
</definitions>
```

The document in Listing 5-1 uses the following standard WSDL tags to describe the Web service:

✦ `<definitions>`: This is the root element of any WSDL document. Using attributes of this element, you can define namespaces that will be used throughout the document. Conventionally, the default namespace is set to `http://schemas.xmlsoap.org/wsdl/` to avoid one's having to add the namespace to each of the WSDL elements.

✦ `<message>`: This element defines the data that is sent to and from the Web service. In the document shown in Listing 5-1, two messages are defined — one representing the input parameters for the procedure and one representing the return value for that procedure.

✦ `<part>`: This element always should be nested within a `<message>` element. It defines the name and data type of the message part. In Listing 5-1, the `<message>` element named `MyMessageRequest` has two parts — a string and a Boolean value.

✦ `<portType>`: This element is a parent element in which operations (procedures) are defined.

✦ `<operation>`: This element defines a procedure for the Web service. The `name` attribute of the `<operation>` tag determines by what name the procedure will be called by the consumer.

✦ `<input>`: This element specifies the input parameters for the procedure. It is always nested within an `<operation>` element. The `<input>` tag within the `<portType>` block determines the input parameter's message type.

✦ `<output>`: This element is the return value counterpart to the `<input>` tag.

✦ `<binding>`: This element is used to describe the protocols by which the Web service may be accessed. In Listing 5-1, SOAP is the only protocol binding defined.

✦ `<service>`: This element groups related `<port>` elements.

✦ `<port>`: This element specifies the service location (address) for each binding.

In addition, some WSDL documents define a `<types>` element. The `<types>` element is used to define additional data types used by operation messages. For example, the Google search WSDL defines complex types, as you can see in Listing 5-2.

Listing 5-2: **The Google WSDL <types> Element**

```
<types>
  <xsd:schema
      targetNamespace="urn:GoogleSearch"
      xmlns="http://www.w3.org/2001/XMLSchema"
      xmlns:xsd="http://www.w3.org/2001/XMLSchema">
  <xsd:complexType name="GoogleSearchResult">
    <xsd:all>
      <xsd:element name="documentFiltering" type="xsd:boolean" />
      <xsd:element name="searchComments" type="xsd:string" />
      <xsd:element name="estimatedTotalResultsCount" type="xsd:int" />
      <xsd:element name="estimateIsExact" type="xsd:boolean" />
      <xsd:element name="resultElements"
type="typens:ResultElementArray" />
      <xsd:element name="searchQuery" type="xsd:string" />
      <xsd:element name="startIndex" type="xsd:int" />
      <xsd:element name="endIndex" type="xsd:int" />
      <xsd:element name="searchTips" type="xsd:string" />
      <xsd:element name="directoryCategories"
type="typens:DirectoryCategoryArray" />
      <xsd:element name="searchTime" type="xsd:double" />
    </xsd:all>
  </xsd:complexType>
  ...
</types>
```

The complex type GoogleSearchResult is composed of 11 simple type elements. You can think of a complex type such as GoogleSearchResult as an associative array.

Any types defined in the <types> section of a WSDL document can be used as a message part. For example, the GoogleSearchResult type is used as a part of a message, as you can see from the following snippet:

```
<message name="doGoogleSearchResponse">
  <part name="return" type="typens:GoogleSearchResult"/>
</message>
```

Note You can see the entire Google WSDL at http://api.google.com/GoogleSearch.wsdl.

Looking at Real-World WSDL

Now that you have had a chance to analyze a sample WSDL document, let's look at a WSDL document that defines a real Web service. Listing 5-3 shows the WSDL document for a Web service that determines whether a domain name is available.

Note You can view the WSDL document in Listing 5-3 using Internet Explorer or another browser capable of parsing XML. The URL is http://services.xmethods.net/soap/urn: xmethods-DomainChecker.wsdl.

Listing 5-3: **The DomainChecker WSDL**

```
<?xml version="1.0" encoding="UTF-8"?>
<definitions
    xmlns:wsdl="http://schemas.xmlsoap.org/wsdl/"
    name="net.xmethods.services.domainchecker.DomainChecker"
targetNamespace="http://www.themindelectric.com/wsdl/net.xmethods.servi
ces.domainchecker.DomainChecker/"
    xmlns="http://schemas.xmlsoap.org/wsdl/"
    xmlns:electric="http://www.themindelectric.com/"
    xmlns:soap="http://schemas.xmlsoap.org/wsdl/soap/"
    xmlns:soapenc="http://schemas.xmlsoap.org/soap/encoding/"
xmlns:tns="http://www.themindelectric.com/wsdl/net.xmethods.services.do
mainchecker.DomainChecker/"
    xmlns:xsd="http://www.w3.org/2001/XMLSchema">
  <message name="checkDomainResponse1">
    <part name="Result" type="xsd:string" />
  </message>
  <message name="checkDomainRequest1">
    <part name="symbol" type="xsd:string" />
  </message>
  <portType
name="net.xmethods.services.domainchecker.DomainCheckerPortType">
```

```
      <operation name="checkDomain" parameterOrder="symbol">
        <input message="tns:checkDomainRequest1" />
        <output message="tns:checkDomainResponse1" />
      </operation>
    </portType>
    <binding
      name="net.xmethods.services.domainchecker.DomainCheckerBinding"
type="tns:net.xmethods.services.domainchecker.DomainCheckerPortType">
      <soap:binding style="rpc"
transport="http://schemas.xmlsoap.org/soap/http" />
      <operation name="checkDomain">
        <soap:operation soapAction="urn:xmethods-
DomainChecker#checkDomain" />
        <input>
          <soap:body
            encodingStyle="http://schemas.xmlsoap.org/soap/encoding/"
            namespace="urn:xmethods-DomainChecker"
            use="encoded" />
        </input>
        <output>
          <soap:body
            encodingStyle="http://schemas.xmlsoap.org/soap/encoding/"
            namespace="urn:xmethods-DomainChecker"
            use="encoded" />
        </output>
      </operation>
    </binding>
    <service
name="net.xmethods.services.domainchecker.DomainCheckerService">
      <documentation>net.xmethods.services.domainchecker.DomainChecker
Web service
      </documentation>
      <port
binding="tns:net.xmethods.services.domainchecker.DomainCheckerBinding"
name="net.xmethods.services.domainchecker.DomainCheckerPort">
        <soap:address location="http://66.28.98.121:9090/soap" />
      </port>
    </service>
</definitions>
```

You need to be concerned with three things when looking at a WSDL document:

✦ What is the name of the procedure in which you are interested?

✦ What are the expected input parameters?

✦ In what format is the value returned, if any?

Look at the WSDL in Listing 5-3 and try to answer these three questions before looking at the answers that follow.

✦ The name of the only procedure is checkDomain. This can be found by looking at the ⟨operation⟩ element. The name attribute specifies the operation name, and you can see this value bolded in the following code:

```
<operation name="checkDomain" parameterOrder="symbol">
  <input message="tns:checkDomainRequest1" />
  <output message="tns:checkDomainResponse1" />
</operation>
```

✦ The input parameter is a single string. This can be found by first looking at the ⟨input⟩ element for the procedure (within the ⟨portType⟩ element) and then finding the corresponding ⟨message⟩ element. In this case, the ⟨message⟩ element is as follows — with only one part, defined as a string type:

```
<message name="checkDomainRequest1">
  <part name="symbol" type="xsd:string" />
</message>
```

✦ The returned value is also a string value. First look at the ⟨output⟩ element for the procedure. Then locate the corresponding ⟨message⟩ element. In this case, the ⟨message⟩ element is as follows:

```
<message name="checkDomainResponse1">
  <part name="Result" type="xsd:string" />
</message>
```

Using WSDL Tools

Now that you have braved the task of learning how to read WSDL code, it is time to learn about the tools available that can make your job a little easier, should you want to use them. At this point, you might find that the convenience of simply viewing WSDL in a Web browser such as Internet Explorer outweighs any need to simplify the analysis of the document. However, if you prefer, the tools described in the following sections can make analyzing the contents of a WSDL document a little easier for you.

Dreamweaver MX

If you have Dreamweaver MX, you can use the following steps to analyze a WSDL document:

1. Open Dreamweaver MX and navigate to the Components window. You can find this by expanding the Application panel group and clicking the Components tab. Or, you can choose Window⇨Components.

2. If you don't already have a file open, open one.

3. The current file needs to belong to a site. If you have not defined a site (see the Dreamweaver documentation for details on what this means if you are not already familiar with defining a site), you must do so.

4. You must choose a document type for the opened document (such as ActionScript, ActionScript Remote, ColdFusion Component, etc.).

5. If there are further prompts in the Components window, follow them.

6. From the Components window drop-down menu, select Web Services (see Figure 5-5).

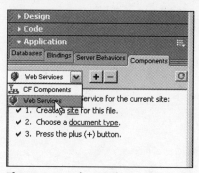

Figure 5-5: Select Web Services from the Components window menu.

7. Click the plus (+) button to add a new Web service.

8. The Add Using WSDL dialog box will appear (see Figure 5-6). Enter a URL to the WSDL document. For an example, use `http://services.xmethods.net/soap/urn: xmethods-DomainChecker.wsdl`. The Proxy Generator menu should already have the correct menu selection chosen. Click OK.

Figure 5-6: Completing the Add Using WSDL dialog box

9. The Web service should now be listed in the Components window. If you expand the menu, you will see that it lists the procedures and their return types. If you expand each procedure menu, you will get a listing of all the input parameters. (see Figure 5-7).

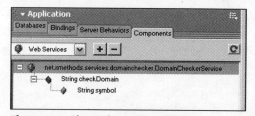

Figure 5-7: The Web service analysis

10. You may want to repeat the same process with the Google WSDL. The URL to use is `http://api.google.com/GoogleSearch.wsdl`. Figure 5-8 shows what the result looks like.

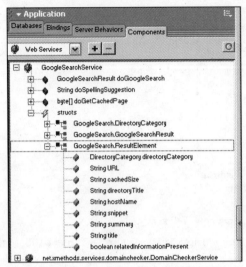

Figure 5-8: The analysis of the Google WSDL

Cape Clear WSDL Editor

Cape Clear Software (www.capeclear.com) is a Web services software company that offers a number of powerful products. Along with some of the pricier applications, you can find the free WSDL Editor program. You can download the program from http://www.capescience .com/downloads/wsdleditor/index.shtml.

Note   The Cape Clear WSDL Editor requires that you have a JRE (Java Runtime Environment) installed. For more information on obtaining and installing a JRE, visit Sun's Java Web site at http://java.sun.com.

The Cape Clear WSDL Editor application is a great graphical tool for creating your own WSDL files. It also enables you to graphically analyze WSDL documents from any URL. Once you have the program installed and running, follow these steps:

1. Choose File➪Load from URL.

2. In the Load WSDL from URL dialog box, enter the URL http://services.xmethods.net/soap/urn:xmethods-DomainChecker.wsdl, and click Open (see Figure 5-9).

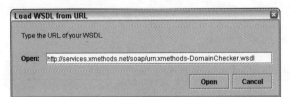

Figure 5-9: Opening the WSDL document from a URL within the Cape Clear WSDL Editor

3. In the Tree pane (on the left), you should now see a graphical representation of the WSDL document, as shown in Figure 5-10.

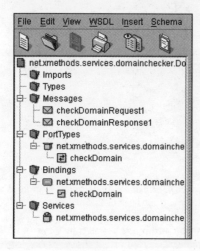

Figure 5-10: The WSDL Editor Tree pane

4. Under `PortTypes`, you can see that a single operation is listed—checkDomain. If you click on the operation name, its description appears in the Editor pane (on the right), as shown in Figure 5-11.

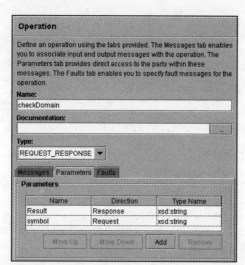

Figure 5-11: The Editor pane display for the checkDomain operation

5. In the Editor pane, you can see that the request (input) parameter is a string, as is the response (output) value. Clicking the Messages tab (see Figure 5-12) reveals the names of the messages in the event that the types are not single, simple types, as in this example.

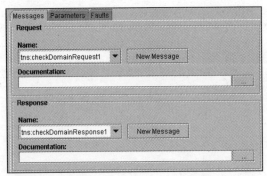

Figure 5-12: Determining the message types used for the operation

6. You might also want to try viewing the WSDL editor analysis of the Google WSDL document. The URL to open is `http://api.google.com/GoogleSearch.wsdl`.

Tip

> You can also view the entire WSDL document in text mode by selecting View⟿Text. To switch back to graphical mode, choose View⟿Graphical.

Locating Web Services

Web services are actually like any other business whose services we wish to utilize. In the "real" world, businesses are useful to us only if we know about them and can locate them. In order to know about businesses and the types of services they offer, we generally learn about them through advertisement or word of mouth, by simply driving or walking by, or by a listing in phone book. The same is true of Web services — they're useful to us only if we can actually locate them. Therefore, as with other businesses, you can discover Web services through similar means.

✦ **Advertisement:** You can count on companies advertising their commercial Web services and building business models around the sale of these services.

✦ **Word of mouth:** This is the tried-and-true method of spreading information about any kind of product or service, and it certainly holds true for Web services.

✦ **Driving or walking by:** Well, you might not physically drive or walk by a Web service, but you could *surf* by.

✦ **Published listing:** This is the method of discovery examined more closely in this section. Two basic categories fall under the "phone book" method of locating Web services:

  • Nonstandardized directories with manual searching/browsing

  • Standardized directories with programmatic discovery

Note

> Of course, a great many Web services are private. For example, a company may want to create a Web service so that the functionality of an existing legacy system can be exposed efficiently and easily to another application. In this case, however, the Web service would really be intended to be consumed by only that one application.

Using Manual Directories

Currently, a handful of Web services directories enable you to search and/or browse through available Web services. These directories are like search engines for Web services. Two prominent examples are www.xmethods.net and www.salcentral.com. Using these directories, you can locate a Web service you wish to use, and gain access to its WSDL.

Introducing UDDI

There is currently a lot of hype about a new specification called Universal Description, Discovery and Integration, or UDDI. UDDI, fueled by companies that include Microsoft and IBM, promises to be a completely programmatic structure for companies that want to publish information about their business and services, discover other businesses with services they wish to use, and integrate with those businesses. Furthermore, it promises all of this through an entirely programmatic interface. In theory, this means that as Web services and distributed application development really take off, it will be possible for applications to be smart enough to figure out how (from a technical standpoint) to do business with other companies.

UDDI is implemented as UDDI registries — both public and private. The public registries are intended to mirror one another. This ensures that one definitive database of business data available is replicated in many locations so that there is no single point of failure. In this respect, it is similar to the way in which DNS is handled. The analogy most commonly used is to a phone book, where information about a company exists in three parts:

✦ **White pages:** Each company listing should include all of the company's basic information, such as name, address (street and e-mail), phone number, etc.

✦ **Yellow pages:** A company can belong to one or more categories based on standard taxonomies.

✦ **Green pages:** A company listing can include information about available services, including references to WSDL documents, URLs, etc.

Using Web Services in Flash

If you use Flash Remoting with ColdFusion MX or .NET, you can call Web services directly from Flash without the need for any additional server-side scripting/programming. The Flash Remoting ActionScript code remains essentially the same when consuming Web services as when calling any other procedure (CFC function, .NET DLL method, etc.). This section outlines how you can determine the values to use for gateway, service, and procedure when calling Web services from Flash movies.

✦ **Gateway URL:** The gateway URL must be to a valid ColdFusion or .NET Flash Remoting gateway. If you are using ColdFusion MX, then use a gateway URL in the form of http://localhost:8500/flashservices/gateway/. If you are using .NET, then the gateway URL is in the form of http://localhost/application/aspxPage.aspx.

✦ **Service name:** The service name should be the URL to the WSDL document. For example, if you want to consume the XMethods Domain Name Checker Web service, use the following code to create the service object:

```
srv =
conn.getService("http://services.xmethods.net/soap/urn:xmethods-
DomainChecker.wsdl");
```

✦ **Procedure name:** The name of the procedure to invoke from Flash should correspond to the operation name defined in the WSDL. For example, to invoke the checkDomain operation from the XMethods Domain Name Checker Web service, you would use the following ActionScript:

```
srv.checkDomain(res, "someDomain.com");
```

If you are using a J2EE application server, note that Flash Remoting does not have a Web services adapter that enables you to directly invoke Web services. However, you can still invoke Web services from a Java class and return the results to a Flash movie. This proxy technique is also required for some Web services, even when using .NET and ColdFusion MX because of the types of results returned. See Chapter 9, "Consuming ColdFusion Web Services," and Chapter 21, "Consuming .NET Web Services, " for more information.

Checking Domain Availability

In this exercise, you put into practice what you have learned about Web services and consuming Web services from Flash movies. This is the first exercise using Web services, so it is a simple one. You will create a Flash movie that enables the user to type in a domain name and check for its availability using the XMethods Domain Name Checker Web service.

1. Pretend that I have not already given you the URL for the WSDL and use either `salcentral.com` or `xmethods.net` to locate the Web service. If you use `salcentral.com`, simply search for `xmethods`, and you will see the Domain Name Checker service in the results.

The `www.salcentral.com` site requires that you register (it is free) in order to view the Web service information.

2. View the WSDL document in your preferred way.

3. Open a new Flash document and save it as domainChecker.fla.

4. Rename the default layer to form, and add a new layer named actions.

5. On the form layer, add an input `TextField` object with border turned on (see Figure 5-13). Name the instance `domainName`.

6. On the form layer, add a `PushButton` component instance (see Figure 5-13). Name the instance `checkBtn`.

7. On the form layer, add a multiline, dynamic `TextField` object with border turned on (see Figure 5-13). Name the instance `output`.

8. Look at the WSDL to determine the name of the operation to invoke as well as the input and output types.

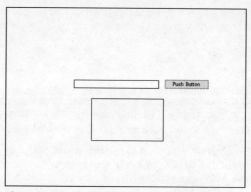

Figure 5-13: The layout of domainChecker.fla

9. Add the following code to the first frame of the actions layer:

```
#include "NetServices.as"

function init(){
  // use the appropriate gateway URL for your server
  var gwUrl = "http://localhost:8500/flashservices/gateway/";
  NetServices.setDefaultGatewayURL(gwUrl);
  var conn = NetServices.createGatewayConnection();
  // this creates the service object for the Web service
  _root.srv =
conn.getService("http://services.xmethods.net/soap/urn:xmethods-
DomainChecker.wsdl");
}

res = new Object();
res.onResult = function(result){
  // the result is either available or unavailable
  _root.output.text = "the domain name is " + result;
}
res.onStatus = function(status){
  trace(status.description);
}

// call the Web service operation when the button is clicked
checkBtn.setLabel("check domain");
checkBtn.onRelease = function(){
  _root.srv.checkDomain(res, _root.domainName.text);
}

// make sure to initialize the movie
init();
```

10. Test your movie. Try checking for the availability of wiley.com. It should come back as unavailable because it is already taken. Then try another domain that is likely not taken. At the time of this writing, the domain rootintootinsteamshovels.com comes back as available, for example.

Tip

When checking domain names, be sure *not* to include the machine name. This means that you should include only the subdomain, such as wiley.com or person13.com, but not the www part, as in www.wiley.com or www.person13.com.

Searching on Google

Google, the popular search engine for the Web, has an available Web service that enables developers to easily incorporate a Google search into their own application. In this exercise, you use this Web service from a Flash movie to create a simple Flash search interface.

Before you can get started with the exercise, you need to register with Google to obtain a developer key. Registration is free, and the developer key is sent to you via e-mail very quickly. To sign up, go to the Google APIs page at http://www.google.com/apis/.

Note

The Google APIs page suggests that you download the developer's kit. You are welcome to do so if you want, and you might find the kit useful. However, you don't need it to complete this exercise.

1. View the Google WSDL document available at http://api.google.com/GoogleSearch.wsdl.

2. Open a new Flash document and save it as googleSearch.fla.

3. Rename the default layer to form and add a new layer named actions.

4. On the form layer, add a PushButton component instance in the lower, right-hand portion of the stage (see Figure 5-14). Name the instance searchBtn.

5. On the form layer, add a single-line input TextField object with border turned on. Name the instance query. Position this object above the PushButton instance, as shown in Figure 5-14.

6. On the form layer, add a multiline, dynamic TextField object with border turned on. Name the instance results, and position it above the query instance, as shown in Figure 5-14.

7. On the form layer, add a ScrollBar component instance, and snap it to the results object. Name the instance sb.

8. On the form layer, add a single-line, dynamic TextField object with border turned off. Name the instance resultsInfo and position it above the results instance.

9. Open the buttons library (Window⇨Common Libraries⇨Buttons), and create an instance of "circle button - next" and "circle button - previous" on the form layer, as shown in Figure 5-14. Name these instances nextBtn and prevBtn, respectively.

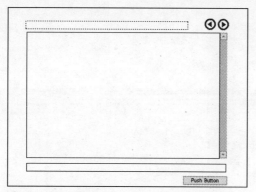

Figure 5-14: The layout of googleSearch.fla

10. On the first frame of the actions layer, add the following code:

```
#include "NetServices.as"

function init(){
  // use the appropriate URL for the gateway on your
  // server
  var gwUrl = "http://localhost:8500/flashservices/gateway/";
  NetServices.setDefaultGatewayURL(gwUrl);
  var conn = NetServices.createGatewayConnection();
  _root.srv =
conn.getService("http://api.google.com/GoogleSearch.wsdl");
}

res = new Object();
res.onResult = function(result){
  var r = _root.results;
  r.html = true;
  r.htmlText = "";
  // resultElements is an array of ResultElement
  // message types (see WSDL)
  var re = result.resultElements;
  // loop through the ResultElement messages
  // and display their information in the results
  // TextField as html. consult WSDL for the names
  // of the parts of ResultElement messages such as
  // url, title, snippet, and summary
  for(var i = 0; i < re.length; i++){
```

```
            // display the title of the result as a link
            r.htmlText += "<a href=\"" + re[i].url +
                        "\">" + re[i].title +
                        "</a>" + "<br>";
            r.htmlText += re[i].snippet + "<br>";
            if(re[i].summary != "")
              r.htmlText += re[i].summary + "<br>";
            r.htmlText += "<br><br>";
          }
          // reset the scroll position to the top
          _root.sb.setScrollPosition(0);
          // refer to WSDL to see that estimatedTotlResultsCount
          // is a part of the GoogleSearchResult message type
          // as is startIndex and endIndex
          var count = result.estimatedTotalResultsCount;
          _root.resultsInfo.text = count + " total records. " +
                              "displaying " + result.startIndex +
                              " - " + result.endIndex;
        }
        res.onStatus = function(status){
          trace(status.description);
        }

        function doSearch(start, query){
          // create the input message to be sent
          // to the operation. the message type should
          // be of type doGoogleSearch as defined in the
          // WSDL
          var params = new Object();
          // make sure to enter your own key here
          params.key = "XXXXXXXXXXXXXXXXXXXXXXXX";
          // query and start are parameters passed to
          // this doSearch() function
          params.q = query;
          params.start = start;
          params.maxResults = 10;
          params.filter = true;
          params.restrict = "";
          params.safeSearch = false;
          params.lr = "";
          params.ie = "";
          params.oe = "";
          // call the operation
          _root.srv.doGoogleSearch(_root.res, params);
        }

        searchBtn.setLabel("search");
        searchBtn.onRelease = function(){
          // always perform a new search using 0
          // as the starting index and the value
```

```
  // entered into query as the query string
  _root.doSearch(0, _root.query.text);
  // set the variables on _root to be accessed
  // by next and previous buttons
  _root.start = 0;
  _root.queryVal = _root.query.text;
}

// get the previous 10 results
prevBtn.onRelease = function(){
  _root.start -= 10;
  if(_root.start < 0)
    _root.start = 0;
  _root.doSearch(_root.start, _root.queryVal);
}

// get the next 10 results
nextBtn.onRelease = function(){
  _root.start += 10;
  _root.doSearch(_root.start, _root.queryVal);
}

// make sure to initialize the movie
init();
```

11. Make sure that you have entered your developer key as the value for `params.key` in the preceding code.

12. Test your movie. Try searching for `ActionScript`. Figure 5-15 shows how it should look. Clicking on the title of a record should open up a new browser window with the corresponding site.

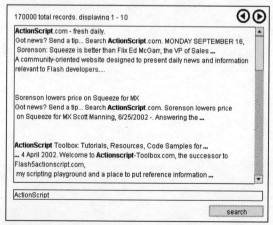

Figure 5-15: Searching Google through a Flash interface

Summary

Web services represent a large shift in application development from a highly centralized environment to a decentralized, distributed environment. Flash Remoting is foresighted in that it incorporates features that make working with Web services as easy as possible. In this chapter, you learned about Web services in general and how to use Web services with Flash movies. Some important highlights from throughout the chapter include the following:

✦ The Web services movement is a departure from an old paradigm in which independent systems relied on fragile, proprietary development to enable communication. Web services encapsulate system functionality, and expose it to remote systems in a platform- and language-independent manner.

✦ A Web service implementation can be written in almost any language and on almost any platform, and yet still be used, or *consumed*, by just about any client application. This is because Web services rely on open standards such as XML, SOAP, and WSDL for communication.

✦ WSDL (Web Services Description Language) is used to create metadata documents for Web services, which makes them self-descriptive. A consumer of a Web service doesn't need to know anything about the service other than the location of its WSDL document.

✦ Once you have understood the basics of a WSDL document, interpreting the language is quite easy. Additionally, many useful tools can graphically represent a WSDL file, making it even easier to retrieve the operation names and the input and output parameters.

✦ Search engines such as www.xmethods.com and www.salcentral.com are currently excellent ways to locate Web services you want to use. In addition, UDDI registries are likely to be a programmatic solution for businesses and their services in the near future.

✦ Flash Remoting enables ColdFusion MX and .NET gateway client movies to access Web services without any server-side scripting — simply using the URL to the WSDL document as the service name.

✦   ✦   ✦

Flash Remoting
with ColdFusion

◆ ◆ ◆ ◆

In This Part

◆ ◆ ◆ ◆

Understanding Flash Remoting for ColdFusion

ColdFusion MX is the latest release of a product dating back to 1995, when ColdFusion 1.0 was released by a company named Allaire. At that time, ColdFusion was the leading (and practically the only) platform for creating dynamic Web content. Since that time, ColdFusion has blossomed into what is now aptly termed a *rapid application development environment* that includes a whole host of fantastic features, making it a great choice for those wanting to develop simple, quick, dynamic content as well as for anyone developing highly scalable, enterprise-level Web applications. Following are just a few of the many features:

✦ Simple database integration

✦ Built-in XML handling

✦ Support for custom tags and JSP tag libraries

✦ Easy-to-use, built-in security features, including sandbox security (Enterprise editions only) and roles-based security

✦ E-mail and FTP server integration for creating Web-based e-mail and FTP clients

✦ Session management

✦ A deployment environment that is easy to manage yet fast and powerful, complete with monitoring tools

✦ Multi-platform availability, including Windows, Linux, and even Mac OS X (though not officially supported)

✦ Easy integration into enterprise systems, with built-in support for LDAP, EJB, COM, and CORBA

From its beginning in 1995, ColdFusion has maintained two features that stand out above and beyond any of its other features — ease of use and a rapid learning curve. With all the power that ColdFusion MX includes, it has not sacrificed its commitment to being easy to use in the least. If anything, the MX release of ColdFusion is *easier* and more flexible.

In 2001, Macromedia and Allaire merged, and so ColdFusion is now a Macromedia product. As such, it should come as no surprise to see a tight integration between ColdFusion MX and Flash MX. This integration has been a prominent marketing point of ColdFusion MX, and Macromedia touts the MX release as enabling the development of Rich Internet Applications. A big part of Rich Internet Applications is the use of Flash Remoting, a built-in feature of ColdFusion MX. Therefore, it is now possible for Flash to harness the power of ColdFusion applications right out of the box.

Getting Started with ColdFusion

When first working with ColdFusion MX for Flash Remoting, you need to address a few matters up front, including the following:

✦ Deciding whether or not ColdFusion is the best choice for you

✦ Installing and configuring ColdFusion MX

✦ Learning the basics of ColdFusion server administration

✦ Setting up data sources

Deciding on ColdFusion

If you are already familiar with and feel comfortable with the ColdFusion environment, then choosing ColdFusion MX as your platform for Flash Remoting seems obvious enough. I also recommend ColdFusion MX as a great selection for those who wish to get started with Flash Remoting but have no prior experience with ColdFusion, Java, or .NET. Of course, choosing a platform is really a matter of preference. One is not inherently better than any other. However, if you are new to application servers and their respective programming languages and environments, ColdFusion MX is probably a great choice for the following reasons:

✦ **Easy to learn:** ColdFusion MX applications are developed using ColdFusion Markup Language (CFML) and CFScript. Both are remarkably easy to learn. CFML shares a similar syntax with HTML, and CFScript shares a similar syntax with JavaScript and ActionScript.

✦ **Easy to use:** ColdFusion makes many common processes easy. For instance, connecting to databases and sending e-mail are both handled through intuitive CFML elements.

✦ **Server-Side ActionScript:** ColdFusion supports this feature, whereas the other platforms do not. With Server-Side ActionScript, you can take advantage of some server-side functionality without even having to learn another programming language.

✦ **Cost:** Of all the options for working with Flash Remoting, ColdFusion MX is the most cost-efficient as well. While it is true that the .NET SDK and several J2EE application servers are free, they do not already include the Flash Remoting services, and you would be required to make a separate purchase.

Installing and Configuring the Server

Once you have decided on ColdFusion MX, the next step is to actually get the ColdFusion application server installed. ColdFusion MX is available for purchase directly from Macromedia's Web site or from many retailers. In addition, a 30-day trial version of ColdFusion MX is available from Macromedia's Web site (http://www.macromedia.com/software/coldfusion/).

ColdFusion MX is available for Windows, Linux, Solaris, and HP-UX. Although there is no official Mac OS X release of ColdFusion MX at the time of this writing, there are reports that with just a small amount of effort it can be done (though it is not supported by Macromedia).

Once you have the ColdFusion MX installation file and a suitable operating system environment, the installation is a snap. You will be walked through a simple wizard that prompts you for only a few items, such as installation directory (it has a default value) and administrator passwords.

Note
ColdFusion MX includes its own Web server and, therefore, can be run as a standalone server running on port 8500. It can also be easily integrated with another Web server — such as IIS — during the installation process, and would then likely be accessed via port 80. Throughout this book, I will assume that you are running ColdFusion MX as a standalone server, thereby assuming port 8500 in all the examples. If you are using a different port number, you will need to make adjustments as necessary throughout.

Once you have completed the installation, no further configuration should be necessary. ColdFusion MX installs with the Flash Remoting services already included and running.

Administration and Data Sources

The next step in getting started with ColdFusion is to log in to the Web-based administration tool. If you have installed ColdFusion MX as a standalone server, then you will be able to access the administration tool in your Web browser at `http://localhost:8500/CFIDE/ administrator/`.

You will then be prompted to enter the administration password that you set during the installation. Figure 6-1 shows you how this page should look.

Figure 6-1: The ColdFusion administration tool login page

Once you have logged in, you will be able to choose from a large selection of ColdFusion administration options, as well as resources. You may want to take some time to read through the documentation to which you will find a link on this screen.

For the most part, ColdFusion should not require any configuration in order to get started. What *will* require some very minor setup on your part are data sources. In ColdFusion, you assign Data Source Names (DSNs) to the databases you wish to use. The ColdFusion server will handle making the connections to these databases and allow you to easily access them from within your ColdFusion applications simply by their DSN.

Follow these steps to add a DSN:

1. Choose the Data Sources option from the links on the left portion of the administration screen (see Figure 6-2).

Figure 6-2: Selecting the Data Sources navigation item

2. In the Add New Data Source form (see Figure 6-3), add a DSN, select the appropriate driver, and click the Add button. The DSN should be a name that describes the database, and need not be the same as the database file or the database as it is identified by the DBMS (though it certainly can be). ColdFusion applications will use the DSN to identify which database to use when making queries. The driver should match the type of database being used. For example, if you wish to set up a DSN for a MySQL database, you should select the MySQL driver from the menu.

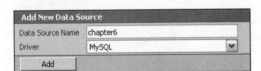

Figure 6-3: Adding a new Data Source

3. The next page requests information specific to the type of database being used. Fill out the form with the necessary information and click Submit. Figure 6-4 shows an example of a MySQL database where both the MySQL database name and the DSN are `chapter6`. No password is required for this database so the fields are left blank.

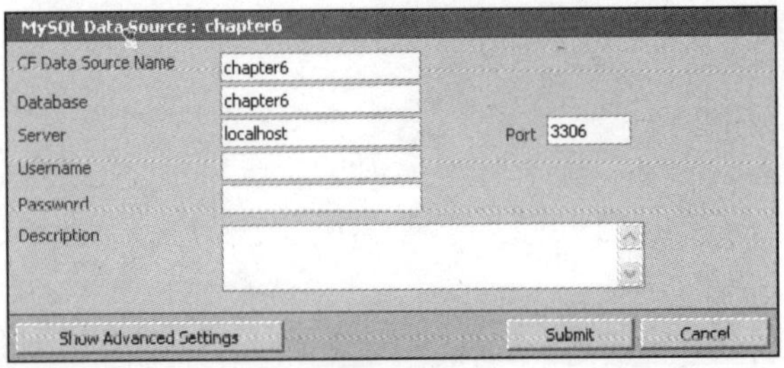

Figure 6-4: Adding a MySQL database as a ColdFusion Data Source

4. Finally, verify that the connection can be made successfully given the information you provided. ColdFusion automatically performs this check for you when you create a new Data Source, so all you have to do is look at the screen and make sure that the status of the new Data Source is ok. See Figure 6-5 for an example of what this looks like.

Figure 6-5: A new Data Source verified as creating a successful connection

ColdFusion Languages

ColdFusion applications have always been built using a language known as ColdFusion Markup Language (CFML), which looks very similar to HTML. CFML is composed of elements including the following:

✦ **Tags:** CFML tags, like tags in HTML and other languages, are derived from XML/SGML, indicated by the < and > characters. In addition, all CFML tag names begin with cf. Examples of common CFML tags are `<cfif>`, `<cfquery>`, and `<cfset>`.

✦ **Variables:** CFML variables, like ActionScript variables, are named containers for information.

✦ **Operators:** CFML operators perform the same sorts of tasks that ActionScript operators perform.

✦ **Functions:** CFML functions perform actions and return a value. Like ActionScript functions, they may or may not take parameters.

✦ **CFScript:** CFScript is a ColdFusion scripting language within CFML that is similar in syntax to ActionScript.

Using Tags

ColdFusion includes a great many tags for many different actions ranging from setting variables, creating conditionally executed code, and outputting variable values to interacting with databases, performing FTP transfers, and even sending and receiving e-mail. Clearly, entire books can be and have been written about ColdFusion and CFML alone. Therefore, it is not my intention to teach you CFML. However, I do want to briefly discuss a few common tags that you will see throughout the examples in Part II.

<cfset>

The `<cfset>` tag is relatively straightforward. This tag is responsible for setting the values of variables. The tag has a single attribute that is the variable name. The value assigned to that attribute is then assigned to the variable:

```
<cfset myVar="some value">
```

In this example, the string value *some value* is assigned to the myVar variable.

You can also assign the value of one variable to another using the `<cfset>` tag. For example:

```
<cfset anotherVar=myVar>
```

\<cfif\>

The \<cfif\> tag is the CFML equivalent to an ActionScript if statement. This tag has both an opening and closing element. The execution of any text or tags appearing between these elements is dependent upon the specified condition being met. The conditional expression is placed inside of the opening \<cfif\> element, as shown in the following:

```
<cfif myVar EQ "some value">
   This text appears only if the value of myVar is "some value"
</cfif>
```

Note The operators used in ColdFusion are not always the same as those used in ActionScript. For instance, the EQ operator is used in ColdFusion to check for equality, whereas the == operator is used in ActionScript. You can learn more about this in the upcoming sections of this chapter.

Just as an ActionScript if statement can include else if and else statements, so too can a \<cfif\> tag include \<cfelseif\> and \<cfelse\> elements. These elements must appear *between* the opening and closing \<cfif\> elements. For example:

```
<cfif myVar EQ "some value">
   This text only appears if the value of myVar is "some value"
<cfelseif myVar EQ "not just some value">
   This text only appears if the value of myVar is "not just some value"
<cfelse>
   Otherwise this text appears
</cfif>
```

\<cfquery\>

The \<cfquery\> tag is used to query databases. Using \<cfquery\> is simple. Once you have defined a data source in the ColdFusion administration tool, you are ready to go. The \<cfquery\> tag has numerous optional attributes. In the simplest form, however, you need to specify values for only two of them—the datasource and name attributes. The datasource attribute should be assigned the value of the data source name, and the name attribute should be assigned a new name for a variable that will hold the results from the database query.

As with the \<cfif\> tag, the \<cfquery\> tag has both beginning and ending elements. Between these elements should be placed the SQL code that you wish to be run on the database. Here is an example in which the entire users table of a data source named chapter6 is assigned to a variable named usersResults:

```
<cfquery datasource="chapter6" name="usersResults">
   SELECT *
   FROM users
</cfquery>
```

Note If you are performing a SQL statement that does not return a result (such as a DELETE or INSERT statement), you do not need to specify a name attribute.

Working with ColdFusion Variables

As you've already seen, ColdFusion variables can be set using the `<cfset>` tag, as well as by being passed to a ColdFusion application by other means, such as a query string or a form submission. Variables belong to a particular scope. Variables from a scope can be referenced by the scope name and the variable name, separated by the dot operator — just as you would access an object's property in ActionScript. The default scope for a variable is the `Variables` scope. This scope is assumed if no other scope is specified. Therefore, the following tags are equivalent:

```
<cfset Variables.myVar = "some value">
<cfset myVar = "some value">
```

In the following example, `myVar` is evaluated within the context of the `<cfset>` tag. That is to say, the value contained by `myVar` (such as `some value`) is assigned to `anotherVar`. Outside the tag, however, `myVar` is not evaluated, and instead the literal string value `myVar` is output, not the value contained by the variable.

```
<cfset anotherVar=myVar>
myVar
```

In the preceding example, the `myVar` in the `<cfset>` tag was automatically evaluated. However, in most other tag contexts, a variable must appear within pound signs in order to be evaluated. For example, in the following `<cfquery>` tag, the `SELECT` statement will look in the `users` table for a record in which the `USERNAME` column has the value of `username` and the `PASSWORD` column has the value of `password`, but not the values `johndoe` and `johnpasses`:

```
<cfset username = "johndoe">
<cfset password = "johnpasses">
<cfquery datasource="chapter6" name="userInfo">
  SELECT *
  FROM users
  WHERE USERNAME = 'username' AND PASSWORD = 'password'
</cfquery>
```

In order for ColdFusion to know that `username` and `password` are variables that should be evaluated, they must be placed inside of pound signs as shown here:

```
<cfset username = "johndoe">
<cfset password = "johnpasses">
<cfquery datasource="chapter6" name="userInfo">
  SELECT *
  FROM users
  WHERE USERNAME = '#username#' AND PASSWORD = '#password#'
</cfquery>
```

This may raise the question as to how one determines when to use pound signs and when not to use pound signs. My answer is simple: When in doubt, use pound signs because using pound signs where they are not necessary will not cause a problem. For instance, although the `<cfset>` tag does not require that variables be enclosed in pound signs in order to be evaluated, it will still evaluate them even if they are in pound signs. The three tags in the following example are equivalent:

```
<cfset anotherVar=myVar>
<cfset anotherVar=#myVar#>
<cfset anotherVar='#myVar#'>
```

While not generally used in conjunction with Flash Remoting, the `<cfoutput>` tag is an important CFML tag in which all variables surrounded by pound signs appearing between the opening and closing `<cfoutput>` elements are evaluated before being output.

Understanding ColdFusion Operators

ColdFusion expressions can be created using ColdFusion operators. The types of operators are similar to the types of operators used in ActionScript, and can be generally categorized as follows:

✦ Mathematical

✦ Boolean/Logical

✦ Comparison

✦ String

Although the types of operations that can be performed are similar, not all the operators themselves are exactly the same. Table 6-1 summarizes the ColdFusion operators that differ from ActionScript and provides their ActionScript equivalents.

Table 6-1: ColdFusion Operators

Operator	Description	ActionScript Equivalent
MOD	Modulus	%
^	Exponentiation	`Math.pow()`
NOT	Boolean not	!
AND	Boolean and	&&
OR	Boolean or	||
EQV	Boolean equivalence — true only if both operands are true or both operands are false	==
IS, EQ, EQUALS	Equality	==
IS NOT, NEQ, NOT EQUALS	Inequality	!=
GT, GREATER THAN	Greater than	>
LT, LESS THAN	Less than	<
GTE, GE, GREATER THAN OR EQUAL TO	Greater than or equal to	>=
LTE, LE, LESS THAN OR EQUAL TO	Less than or equal to	<=
&	String concatenation	+

Note

Table 6-1 is not comprehensive; it includes only the ColdFusion operators that have ActionScript equivalents and differ from those equivalents. In addition, note that some of the operators in ColdFusion have alternates. For example, both GREATER THAN and GT are equivalent.

Using ColdFusion Functions

Predefined ColdFusion functions, like ColdFusion tags, span a huge range of actions, from working with strings and dates to working with XML. Functions are called in ColdFusion in a similar fashion to the way they are called in ActionScript. The name of the function is followed by the function operator (( )). For instance, in the following example, the Now() function is called and the returned value is assigned to a variable named nowDate:

```
<cfset nowDate=Now()>
```

Because predefined functions in ColdFusion always return values, they should be treated like variables when used in expressions. Therefore, they should be enclosed in pound signs whenever they are used in an expression. For example:

```
<cfquery datasource="chapter6" name="schedulesResults">
  SELECT *
  FROM schedules
  WHERE date = #CreateODBCDate(Now())#
</cfquery>
```

If a function requires parameters to be passed to it, the parameters are passed through the function operator — between the parentheses — just as in ActionScript:

```
<cfset total='#DollarFormat(66.9)#'>
```

Note

Pound signs and quotation marks are not necessary in <cfset> tags. They are used in examples throughout the book just for consistency.

Cross-Reference

You can also create custom functions in ColdFusion (called user-defined functions or UDFs). You will learn more about these in Chapter 8 when we look at ColdFusion Components.

Writing CFScript

CFScript is a scripting syntax similar to ActionScript, which, like the rest of CFML, is executed on the server. Because CFScript may be a little more familiar to those who are used to ActionScript, I rely more heavily on CFScript than on the tag-based equivalents throughout the examples in Part II.

All CFScript must appear between the <cfscript> tag's opening and closing elements. For example, the following CFScript simply assigns a value to a variable named myVar:

```
<cfscript>
  myVar = "some value";
</cfscript>
```

Although CFScript has a similar syntax to that of ActionScript, the languages are not exactly the same. CFScript still uses ColdFusion operators, for instance, and not the same operators found in ActionScript. Here is an example that illustrates some differences:

```
<cfscript>

  // the for loop syntax is the same, but there is no ++ operator
  // in ColdFusion, so i++ must be written out as i = i + 1
  for(i = 0; i LT 10; i = i + 1){
    // some actions
  }

  // the if statement syntax is the same, but the ColdFusion EQ
  // operator is used and not the ActionScript == operator
  if(myVar EQ "some value"){
    // some actions
  }

  // ColdFusion allows you to create arrays, but the array
  // constructor is the ColdFusion ArrayNew() function,
  // not the ActionScript new Array() constructor
  myArray = ArrayNew(1);  // creates a 1 dimensional array

</cfscript>
```

Converting Data Types

The Flash Remoting services running on the ColdFusion MX server automatically take care of conversions between ColdFusion data types and ActionScript data types in both directions. Table 6-2 shows the data type conversions from ActionScript data types to ColdFusion data types when sent as parameters; Table 6-3 shows the data type conversions from ColdFusion data types to ActionScript data types when values are returned to ActionScript.

Table 6-2: ActionScript-to-ColdFusion Conversions

ActionScript Data Type	ColdFusion Data Type
Null	undefined
Undefined	undefined
Boolean	Boolean
Number	number
String	string
Date	Date
Array	Array
Object (associative array)	Struct
XML	XML
Typed Object	flashgateway.io.ASObject

Note An ActionScript `Array` object must have only contiguous integer indices in order to be converted to a ColdFusion `Array`. If the indices are not all integers or are not all contiguous, then the Array is viewed as an associative array and is converted to a ColdFusion `Struct`.

Table 6-3: ColdFusion-to-ActionScript Conversions

ColdFusion Data Type	ActionScript Data Type
Boolean	Boolean
number	Number
string	String
Date	Date
Array	Array
Struct	Object (associative array)
Query	RecordSet
XML	XML

ColdFusion Security with Flash Remoting

As mentioned previously in this chapter, ColdFusion includes several security features. Flash Remoting enables Flash movies to be easily integrated with the ColdFusion security features using several techniques. This section explores the following ColdFusion–Flash Remoting security concepts:

✦ ColdFusion `Application.cfm` pages

✦ `<cflogin>` tags

✦ ActionScript `setCredentials()`

Understanding the ColdFusion Application Framework

Simply put, an application is a grouping of related parts that make up a single, cohesive process or program. ColdFusion applications can be made up of ColdFusion pages, ColdFusion components, Java classes, COM components, XML documents, etc. All of these parts should be structured in such a way that makes sense and works. This organization of the parts is generally referred to as the *application framework*. There is no *right* methodology when it comes to setting up a ColdFusion application framework. The important thing is to find a methodology that works for you and your applications.

ColdFusion attempts to group files in the same directories as a single application. As part of this process, whenever a ColdFusion page is requested, the ColdFusion Server automatically tries to include into that page functionality that is shared among all other parts of the application.

It does this by looking for a file named `Application.cfm` and logically including the contents of that file into the beginning of the page being requested. If `Application.cfm` exists in the same directory where the requested page is stored, then that file is used. Otherwise, ColdFusion will move between levels in the directory tree and try to locate a file named `Application.cfm` to include. What this means is that all pages sharing the same `Application.cfm` file also share the common functionality placed inside that file.

Note   Some methodologies rely on the `Application.cfm` file. Others, such as FuseBox (`http://www.fusebox.org`), avoid relying on the `Application.cfm` file—not for reasons of instability, but because of preference.

In various methodologies, different tags and script elements are conventionally placed in the `Application.cfm` file. Among the commonly used elements of the `Application.cfm` file is the `<cflogin>` element discussed in the following sections.

Introducing `<cfloginuser>`

The `<cfloginuser>` tag does just what its name suggests—it logs in a user. The tag requires three attributes:

✦ `name`: The name of the user to log in.

✦ `password`: The password for the user.

✦ `roles`: A comma-delimited list of roles to which the user belongs.

The `<cfloginuser>` tag then lets the ColdFusion Server know that the specified user has been logged in and to which roles the user belongs.

Additionally, the `<cfloginuser>` tag should always appear nested in a `<cflogin>` parent tag. The `<cflogin>` tag acts as a container whose contents are executed only if no user is already logged in. Following is an example of proper syntax for the `<cflogin>` and `<cfloginuser>` tags:

```
<cflogin>
  <cfloginuser name="igoodie" password="12345" roles="Guest">
</cflogin>
```

However, the `<cfloginuser>` tag does not perform any kind of check to confirm that the username and password supplied are valid. You should do this beforehand—checking against a database or LDAP directory. For example, the following code checks to see if a username and password combination is a valid entry in a database and then makes the `<cfloginuser>` tag's execution conditional:

```
<!--username and password are variables whose values are supplied
      by a form -->
<cflogin>
  <cfquery datasource="myDataSource" name="checkUser">
    SELECT *
    FROM users
    WHERE USERNAME = '#FORM.username#' AND PASSWORD = '#FORM.password#'
  </cfquery>
```

```
    <cfif checkUser.RecordCount GTE 1>
      <cfloginuser name="#FORM.username#" password="#FORM.password#"
  roles="#checkUser.ROLES[1]#">
    </cfif>
  </cflogin>
```

Once a user has been logged in using `<cfloginuser>`, you can use the login information to make parts of the application conditional or restricted. The `GetAuthUser()` function returns the name of the user currently logged in, while the `IsUserInRole()` function checks to see if the current user is in the role specified as a parameter, and returns either true or false.

Cross-Reference See Chapter 8 to learn how to restrict access to ColdFusion Component functions based on the role of the current user.

Setting Credentials

If you want a user to be logged in more or less transparently, then Flash Remoting offers a handy way to do this. The `setCredentials()` method of your connection object enables you to pass a username and password along with every remote procedure call in case the user needs to be authenticated by the ColdFusion application. The method takes two parameters — the username and password to be used. Here is an example of how to use `setCredentials()` in your ActionScript code:

```
// assuming conn is a connection object
conn.setCredentials("igoodie", "12345");
```

On the server side, the username and password are passed to the `name` and `password` variables in the `CFLOGIN` scope. Therefore, you can easily adapt your ColdFusion code to use these values, if present. For example:

```
<cflogin>
  <cfif IsDefined("CFLOGIN")>
    <cfloginuser name="#CFLOGIN.name#" password="#CFLOGIN.password#"
  roles="Default Role">
  </cfif>
</cflogin>
```

If you already have login logic in place to use information from a form, you can easily modify that to also use information from Flash. For example:

```
<cflogin>
  <cfscript>
    username = "";
    password = "";
    if(IsDefined("FORM")){
      username = FORM.username;
      password = FORM.password;
    }
    else if(IsDefined("CFLOGIN")){
      username = CFLOGIN.username;
```

```
        password = CFLOGIN.password;
    }
  </cfscript>
  <cfquery datasource="myDataSource" name="checkUser">
    SELECT ROLES
    FROM users
    WHERE USERNAME = '#username#' AND PASSWORD = '#password#'
  </cfquery>
  <cfif checkUser.RecordCount GTE 1>
    <cfloginuser name="#username#" password="#password#"
roles="#checkUser.ROLES[1]#">
  </cfif>
</cflogin>
```

Note   If you want confirmation of a successful login, or to be notified if the login failed, then using `setCredentials()` is probably not the best choice. When you use `setCredentials()`, there is no returned value. Chapters 7 and 8 provide examples of how to return a value that indicates the success of the login attempt.

Summary

This chapter has given you an overview of ColdFusion MX and describes how ColdFusion MX relates to Flash Remoting and the examples and exercises used throughout this part of the book. Highlights from this chapter include the following points:

✦ ColdFusion is a powerful, stable, and easy-to-use application server and rapid application development environment. With Flash Remoting, your Flash movies can leverage ColdFusion's power and functionality.

✦ Installing ColdFusion MX is a relatively quick and simple process that automatically includes the installation and configuration of the Flash Remoting services for ColdFusion.

✦ You can use almost any kind of database with ColdFusion applications, including MySQL databases. You can set up a data source referencing the database in the ColdFusion administration tool.

✦ ColdFusion applications can be developed using components written in Java and many other languages, but the power of rapid ColdFusion application development derives from ColdFusion Markup Language (CFML) and CFScript.

✦ CFML is tag-based, like HTML, whereas CFScript has a syntax similar to ActionScript's.

✦ The Flash Remoting gateway automatically performs data type conversions between ActionScript and ColdFusion data types.

✦ Using a combination of the ColdFusion `<cfloginuser>` tag and the ActionScript `setCredentials()` method, you can quickly and easily take advantage of ColdFusion security with your Flash Remoting applications.

ColdFusion Pages and Flash Remoting

ColdFusion pages have been, since ColdFusion's inception, the means by which data has been submitted, processed, retrieved, and displayed. Therefore, it should come as no surprise that ColdFusion pages can be utilized by Flash Remoting in order to take advantage of the server-side processing and functionality that they make available.

Starting Out with ColdFusion Pages

The purpose of ColdFusion pages has always been intended to enable server-side processes to be easily used by means of a simple markup language (CFML), and to display those results in a Web browser, thus producing dynamic Web pages. This was intended to overcome the inherent limitations of Web servers and Web browsers. It has proven to be a perfect solution.

Because ColdFusion pages are intended to generate output for viewing in a Web browser, they are not exactly the most obvious choice for use with Flash Remoting. After all, Flash Remoting applications are concerned with sending and receiving typed data between Flash movies and services on the application server. On the other hand, it *does* make sense that ColdFusion pages should be accessible to Flash Remoting applications for two reasons:

✦ Many ColdFusion developers are already knowledgeable about how to create and work with ColdFusion pages.

✦ Many applications built using ColdFusion pages already exist. Rather than having to rewrite these applications to allow for a Flash user interface, the pages can instead be slightly modified so that Flash Remoting applications can easily utilize the existing logic.

As you will see in this chapter, most ColdFusion pages can be utilized by Flash Remoting applications with just a few small modifications. Therefore, before we look at the specifics of using ColdFusion pages with Flash Remoting, let's first examine some basic, common ColdFusion page logic. In the next few sections of this chapter, you will create ColdFusion pages to perform various actions. Then, later in the chapter, you will re-use these pages with Flash Remoting movies. This way, you can see the power of being able to leverage existing ColdFusion applications for use with Flash Remoting.

Additional information on the ColdFusion Model can be found on this book's companion Web site (www.wiley.com/compbooks/lott).

Creating a Simple Login Form

A very common functionality that Web developers need to create is the functionality to use and submit forms. Forms show up in all kinds of situations — from feedback forms to forms for adding items to virtual shopping carts and wish lists to forms used for online quizzes. Working with forms is generally a two-part process — the filling out of the form and the submission of the form. In this exercise, you will create a simple login form and the submission logic, all in a ColdFusion page.

1. Create a new directory named `chapter7` in your ColdFusion web root (i.e., `C:\CFusionMX\wwwroot\`).

2. Open a new ColdFusion document in your favorite editor (such as Dreamweaver MX). Save this document to the newly created `chapter7` directory as `login.cfm`.

3. Add the following ColdFusion code to the document:

```
<html>
<head>
<title>Chapter 7 Login</title>

<!-- add some styles to make things prettier :)
      this is optional, of course -->
<style type="text/css">
td {
    font-family: Arial, Helvetica, sans-serif;
    font-size: 14px;
    font-weight: bold;
    font-variant: small-caps;
    color: #003366;
}
h1 {
    font-family: Arial, Helvetica, sans-serif;
    font-size: 18px;
    font-weight: bold;
    font-variant: small-caps;
    color: #999999;
}
body {
    font-family: Arial, Helvetica, sans-serif;
    font-size: 12px;
    font-weight: normal;
    font-variant: small-caps;
    color: #0000CC;
}
</style>
<!-- end of optional code -->
```

```
</head>

<body>

<h1>Welcome to chapter 7</h1>

<!-- the viewForm variable will determine if the form
     should be displayed. the addMessage variable will
     determine whether the "Your username and password
     did not match" message should be displayed -->
<cfset viewForm = true>
<cfset addMessage = false>

<!-- if the form was already filled out and submitted
     then do the following -->
<cfif isDefined("FORM.submitted")>
  <!-- check to see if the username and password entered
       are correct. here I have hardcoded values of "Joey"
and "Pass". you may choose to use your own values. in a
       real-world situation most likely there would be some
       database query to check that the submitted values
       are valid -->
  <cfif FORM.username EQ "Joey" AND FORM.password EQ "IPass">
    <!-- if the u/p are correct then we won't want to display
         the form -->
    <cfset viewForm = false>
  <!-- this is the ColdFusion logic to login a user and
       assign a role -->
  <cflogin>
    <cfloginuser name="#FORM.username#" password="#FORM.password#"
roles="Admin">
  </cflogin>
  <!-- output a welcome message with the logged in username -->
  <cfoutput>
    Thank you for logging in!<br>
  You are logged in as #GetAuthUser()#.
  </cfoutput>
  <cfelse>
    <!-- if the u/p are not correct then the form will still
         be displayed and additionally the message should
         be shown -->
  <cfset addMessage = true>
  </cfif>
</cfif>

<!-- if the form should be viewed, do so -->
<cfif viewForm EQ true>
  <!-- submit to the same page (login.cfm) by post -->
  <form action="login.cfm" method="post">
    <table>
      <tr>
```

```
        <td colspan="2" align="center"><u>please login</u></td>
    </tr>
    <!-- if the user tried to login with the wrong
         username and password, display this message -->
    <cfif addMessage EQ true>
    <tr>
    <td colspan="2" align="center">
    <font color="#FF0000">Your username and password did not
match</font>
    </td>
    </tr>
    </cfif>
    <tr>
    <td>Username:</td>
    <td><input type="text" name="username"></td>
    </tr>
    <tr>
    <td>Password:</td>
    <td><input type="password" name="password"></td>
    </tr>
    <!-- the hidden "submitted" field will let the page
         know when the form has been filled out and submitted -->
    <tr>
    <td><input type="hidden" name="submitted" value="yes"></td>
    <td><input type="submit" value="login"></td>
    </tr>
    </table>
  </form>
</cfif>

</body>
</html>
```

4. Save the document and open your Web browser to `http://localhost:8500/chapter7/login.cfm`. You should see something similar to what is shown in Figure 7-1.

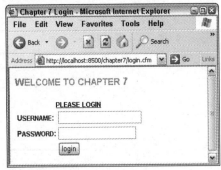

Figure 7-1: The login.cfm form

5. Fill out the username and password fields and click the login button. If you enter an incorrect username or password, then you will be presented with the same form page again, this time with a message alerting you that you have entered the incorrect values (see Figure 7-2). Otherwise, you should be logged in and presented with the welcome message (see Figure 7-3).

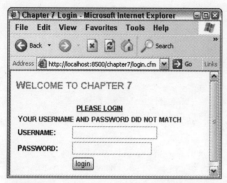

Figure 7-2: login.cfm if the incorrect values were entered

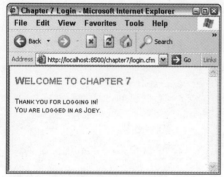

Figure 7-3: login.cfm if the correct values have been entered

Browsing a Computer's Directory Structure

In this exercise, you will use the ColdFusion `<cfdirectory>` tag to browse through the computer's directory structure from a Web browser.

1. Open a new ColdFusion document in your favorite editor. Save this document to the `chapter7` directory (created in the previous exercise) as `dirListing.cfm`.

2. In the document, add the following code:

```
<html>
<head>
<title>Chapter 7 Directory Listing</title>
</head>
<body>

<!-- make sure that this can only be seen from the local
     computer. we don't want to allow the whole world to see
   the files on the computer! CGI.REMOTE_ADDR is a ColdFusion
   variable that contains the IP address of the ColdFusion
   page viewing client -->
<cfif CGI.REMOTE_ADDR EQ "127.0.0.1">
  <cfscript>
    /* this simply initializes the directory to the
      directory in which the dirListing.cfm page is
      stored on the computer
   */
    dir = #GetDirectoryFromPath(GetCurrentTemplatePath())#;
// if a directory value has been passed through the URL
// query string then use that value instead
    if(isDefined("URL.dir")){
      dir = URL.dir;
    }

// use a regular expression to determine the path of
// the parent directory
    oneUp = REReplace(dir, "\\[^\\]*[\\]*$", "");
  </cfscript>

  <!-- output the current directory's absolute path and
      a link that calls this page with the dir value of
      the parent directory -->
  <cfoutput>
    Directory: #dir#<br>
    <a href="dirListing.cfm?dir=#oneUp#">..</a><br>
  </cfoutput>

  <!-- the cfdirectory tag will create a Query object
      named dirListing for the value of dir. it will be
      sorted by type (file or directory) and then by name -->
  <cfdirectory
    directory="#dir#"
    name="dirListing"
    sort="type ASC, name ASC">

  <!-- now output the contents of the directory -->
  <table>
    <cfoutput query="dirListing">
      <tr>
        <td>
        <!-- if the type is directory then make it a link
```

```
         to browse that directory, otherwise just
       output the name -->
     <cfif #type# EQ "Dir">
       <a href="dirListing.cfm?dir=#dir#\#name#">#name#</a>
     <cfelse>
       #name#
     </cfif>
   </td>
   </tr>
   </cfoutput>
 </table>
<cfelse>
  <!-- display a message if someone tries to view this from
     a computer other than the local computer -->
  You must view this page from the local computer
</cfif>

</body>
</html>
```

3. Save the document and use your Web browser to open it using ColdFusion to serve it: `http://localhost:8500/chapter7/dirListing.cfm`. You should see something that looks similar to what is shown in Figure 7-4.

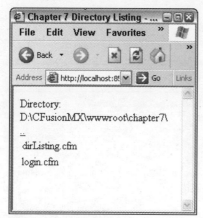

Figure 7-4: dirListing.cfm in the Web browser

4. Test the application you have just created by navigating up and down through the directories on your computer.

Note

If you have a static IP address for your computer, then you can try navigating to the page using that IP address instead of `localhost` or `127.0.0.1`. If you do this, you should find that the page displays the message `You must view this page from the local computer`.

Calling ColdFusion Pages from Flash

Calling a ColdFusion page from a Flash application via Flash Remoting can be divided into three main steps:

1. Invoking a ColdFusion page
2. Passing parameters to the page
3. Returning a value from the page

Invoking a ColdFusion Page

Everything you learn in Chapter 3 about the basics of calling a remote procedure from ActionScript applies to ColdFusion pages. The only thing that you need to be aware of is what is considered the service and what is considered the procedure when it comes to ColdFusion pages.

The service name for a ColdFusion page is determined by the path to the page from the webroot. Each directory name should be separated by a dot. For example, if the ColdFusion page could be accessed from `http://localhost:8500/chapter7/login.cfm`, the service object could be created in ActionScript with the following code:

```
// assuming conn is the connection object
srv = conn.getService("chapter7");
```

Table 7-1 shows some additional examples of URLs and their corresponding service names in ActionScript.

Table 7-1: Example ColdFusion Page Services

URL	ActionScript Service Object Code
http://localhost:8500/ chapter7/examples/ example1.cfm	`srv = conn.getService("chapter7.examples");`
http://localhost:8500/ chapter7/examples/ moreExamples/page.cfm	`srv = conn.getService("chapter7.examples .moreExamples");`
http://localhost:8500/ coolStuff.cfm	`srv = conn.getService("");`

Note   When the ColdFusion page is in the webroot, the service name is simply an empty string.

Because each ColdFusion page is a single routine, a single procedure, that gets executed, the entire page is considered the remote procedure in Flash Remoting. Therefore, the remote procedure name that is used in ActionScript should be the name of the ColdFusion page without the `.cfm` or `.cfml` extension. For example, if the page is named `login.cfm`, then the remote procedure could be called in the following way:

```
// assuming srv is the service object and res is a response object
srv.login(res);
```

Table 7-2 shows some additional examples of ColdFusion page names and how they are called as remote procedures from ActionScript.

Table 7-2: Examples of ColdFusion Pages as ActionScript Procedures

ColdFusion Page Name	ActionScript Procedure Call
example1.cfm	srv.example1(res);
page.cfm	srv.page(res);
coolStuff.cfm	srv.coolStuff(res);

Passing Parameters to a ColdFusion Page

In Table 7-2, none of the ColdFusion pages being called is passed any parameters. In some cases, this may be desirable. Perhaps you want to simply call a ColdFusion page that updates a database that records the IP address of visitors. This would not require that any parameters be passed to the ColdFusion page. However, in plenty of other cases, you will want to send some value or values to the ColdFusion page from the Flash movie.

The way in which parameters are sent from the ActionScript call to the page is nothing new. You see how to do this in Chapter 3. For example, if you wanted to call a ColdFusion page named login.cfm, you would likely want to pass it two parameters—a username and a password. Here is the ActionScript code that does this:

```
srv.login(res, "Joey", "IPass");
```

This should be familiar to you. However, what may not be clear is how to handle those parameters within the ColdFusion page that is called.

You saw how parameters can be passed to ColdFusion pages and are placed into the FORM and URL scopes in the two exercises earlier in this chapter. When you pass parameters to a ColdFusion page with Flash Remoting, all the parameters are automatically placed in the FLASH scope into an array named params. The first parameter passed in the remote procedure call in the Flash movie is the first element of the array. The second parameter is the second element, and so on. Here is a snippet of ColdFusion code that loops through all the parameters passed to it from a Flash movie:

```
<cfscript>
  for(i = 1; i LTE ArrayLen(FLASH.params); i = i + 1){
    // do something with FLASH.params[i]
  }
</cfscript>
```

Note   ColdFusion arrays are 1-based. That means that the first index of a ColdFusion array is 1 and not 0, as in an ActionScript array.

Using an array of integer-indexed values works, but it is not the most user-friendly means by which to process parameters within a ColdFusion page. Therefore, as an alternative, you can choose to pass any and all parameters from ActionScript as named properties of a single object. For example, instead of passing two separate parameters to a login.cfm page as shown previously, you could pass a single object parameter with two properties named username and password. Here is what this might look like:

```
srv.login(res, {username: "Joey", password: "IPass"});
```

Or, if you prefer, you could create the object first, as shown in the following code (which is equivalent to the preceding):

```
params = new Object();
params.username = "Joey";
params.password = "IPass";
srv.login(res, params);
```

This latter approach works better when the object has many properties.

Tip   An ActionScript Object object is automatically converted to a ColdFusion Struct when it is passed to the ColdFusion page as a parameter. Structs in ColdFusion are processed in much the same way as ActionScript objects are.

When a single object parameter is passed to the ColdFusion page, the advantage is that you can then access the Struct's (the parameter's) properties by name. The FLASH.params array will contain just one element—the Struct. Therefore, if you wanted to access a username and password property of that Struct, you could do so as follows in a ColdFusion page:

```
<cfscript>
  un = FLASH.params[1].username;
  pw = FLASH.params[1].password;
</cfscript>
```

Note   Technically, passing a single object parameter to a ColdFusion page does not perform any differently. The single value is still assigned to the first element of the FLASH.params array just as you would expect. The advantage is that you can access the properties of this Struct by name, and you don't need to know the order of the integer-indexed elements of the FLASH.params array.

Returning a Value to Flash

Just as you may sometimes want to pass a value *to* a ColdFusion page, you may sometimes want to pass a value back to Flash *from* the page. Perhaps you want to create a ColdFusion page that returns to Flash the server time. Or, returning to the example of a login page, you might want to return a value that indicates whether the login was successful.

No matter what type of value is returned from a ColdFusion page, the process is the same. If a value is assigned to the result variable in the FLASH scope when the page has completed executing, that value is returned to the Flash movie that called the page. Therefore, if you wanted to return the server time to a Flash movie, you could do so with the following ColdFusion snippet of code:

```
<cfset FLASH.result = Now()>
```

Now, only one value can be returned to the Flash movie. Notice that I said that the value of `FLASH.result` is returned to the Flash movie when the page has completed executing. That means that if the ColdFusion page contains the following:

```
<cfset FLASH.result = "return value 1">
<cfset FLASH.result = "return value 2">
```

only the value `return value 2` will be returned to the Flash movie.

Although you can return only one value, that one value can be a `Struct` or an `Array`. Therefore, you could legally do the following:

```
<cfscript>
  res = StructNew();
  res.value1 = "return value 1";
  res.value2 = "return value 2";
  FLASH.result = res;
</cfscript>
```

Logging In with Flash

In this exercise, you will create a Flash Remoting program that enables you to log in to a ColdFusion application. You will create a new Flash interface that uses the `login.cfm` ColdFusion page you created earlier in this chapter. With only a few slight modifications, the `login.cfm` page can be used by Flash while still functioning as a ColdFusion-only page as well.

1. Open a new Flash document and save it as `login.fla`.

2. Rename the default layer to `form` and create a new layer named `actions`.

   The remaining steps are all performed on the `form` layer.

3. Add two input `TextField` instances. Name these instances `username` and `password`. Place these instances near the center of the stage with the `username` instance higher than the `password` instance.

4. Create two dynamic `TextField` instances. Name these instances `usernameLabel` and `passwordLabel`. Align them parallel to and to the left of `username` and `password`, respectively.

5. Create a dynamic `TextField` instance. Name the instance `errorMessage`. Position this instance above the rest of the instances on the stage.

6. Add a `PushButton` component instance. Name the instance `loginBtn`. Position the instances below the rest of the instances on the stage.

7. Add a static text field. Position this text field above the rest of the items on the stage and enter the text `Welcome to Chapter 7`. You should now have something that looks like what is shown in Figure 7-5.

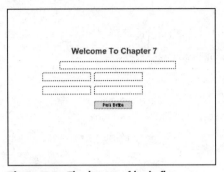

Figure 7-5: The layout of login.fla

8. On the `actions` layer, add the following ActionScript code:

```
#include "NetServices.as"

// first, some TextFormat objects...
labelTF = new TextFormat();
labelTF.font = "Arial, Helvetica, sans-serif";
labelTF.color = 0x003366;
labelTF.size = 14;
labelTF.bold = true;
labelTF.align = "right";
normalTF = new TextFormat();
normalTF.font = "Arial, Helvetica, sans-serif";
normalTF.color = 0x0000CC;
normalTF.size = 14;
normalTF.bold = false;
errorTF = new TextFormat();
errorTF.font = "Arial, Helvetica, sans-serif";
errorTF.color = 0xFF0000;
errorTF.size = 14;
errorTF.bold = true;

// set the values for the TextField instances
usernameLabel.text = "username:";
passwordLabel.text = "password:";
errorMessage.text = "your username and password do not match";

// start with errorMessage invisible
errorMessage._visible = false;

// set the formatting for the objects
usernameLabel.setTextFormat(labelTF);
passwordLabel.setTextFormat(labelTF);
errorMessage.setTextFormat(errorTF);
username.border = true;
password.border = true;
password.password = true;
```

```
// create the connection object
gwUrl = "http://localhost:8500/flashservices/gateway/";
NetServices.setDefaultGatewayURL(gwUrl);
conn = NetServices.createGatewayConnection();

// create the response object
res = new Object();
res.onResult = function(result){
  // success indicates whether or not
  // the login was successful
  var scs = Boolean(result.success);
  if(scs){
    // make the form TextField objects invisible
    for(mc in _root){
      _root[mc]._visible = false;
    }
    // create a new TextField instance to display
    // the login success message
    _root.createTextField("loginMessage", 0, 0, 0, 0, 0);
    with(_root.loginMessage){
      autoSize = true;
      multiline = true;
      text = "Thank you for logging in!\n";
      text += "You are logged in as ";
      text += result.loggedInUser + ".";
      setTextFormat(_root.normalTF);
      _x = Stage.width/2 - _width/2;
      _y = Stage.height/2 - _height/2;
    }
  }
  else{
    // if the login was not successful
    // display the errorMessage and reset
    // the username and password fields
    _root.errorMessage._visible = true;
    _root.username.text = "";
    _root.password.text = "";
  }
}
res.onStatus = function(status){
  trace(status.description);
}

// create the service object
srv = conn.getService("chapter7");

loginBtn.setLabel("login");

// when the button is released, call the
// login.cfm page and pass it the username
// and password entered
```

```
loginBtn.onRelease = function(){
  var params = new Object();
  params.username = _root.username.text;
  params.password = _root.password.text;
  _root.srv.login(res, params);
}
```

9. Save `login.fla` and export the SWF.

10. Open `login.cfm` in the editor you use for ColdFusion pages. Modify the code as shown below. The changes are indicated in bold:

```
<!-- the beginning of the document does not change...use
     what was already here -->

<cfset viewForm = true>
<cfset addMessage = false>

<!-- now we want to check for either FORM.submitted OR
     FLASH.params -->
<cfif isDefined("FORM.submitted") OR isDefined("FLASH.params")>
  <cfscript>
    // this code just sets un and pw to the values
    // passed either from FORM or from FLASH
    if(isDefined("FORM.submitted")){
    un = FORM.username;
    pw = FORM.password;
    }
    else if(isDefined("FLASH.params")){
      un = FLASH.params[1].username;
      pw = FLASH.params[1].password;
    }
    // create a Struct that will be used to return
    // a value to Flash
    fReturn = StructNew();
  </cfscript>
  <!-- check against the values of un and pw -->
  <cfif un EQ "Joey" AND pw EQ "IPass">
    <cfset viewForm = false>
  <cflogin>
    <!-- login using un and pw -->
    <cfloginuser name="#un#" password="#pw#" roles="Admin">
  </cflogin>
  <cfoutput>
    Thank you for logging in!<br>
You are logged in as #GetAuthUser()#.
  </cfoutput>
  <cfscript>
    // return the username of the user who is now
    // logged in and return success as a 1 (for true)
    fReturn.loggedInUser = GetAuthUser();
    fReturn.success = 1;
    FLASH.result = fReturn;
  </cfscript>
  <cfelse>
```

```
     <cfscript>
    // return success is 0 (false) if the username
    // and password did not match
    fReturn.success = 0;
    FLASH.result = fReturn;
      </cfscript>
    <cfset addMessage = true>
    </cfif>
</cfif>

<!-- the end of the document does not change either...
     use what is already here -->
```

11. Save the changes you have made to `login.cfm`.

12. Open the SWF you exported in step 9. Try to log in. Figure 7-6 shows an unsuccessful login, and Figure 7-7 shows a successful login.

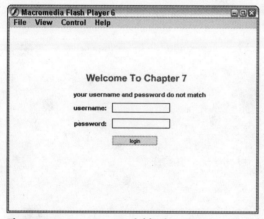

Figure 7-6: An unsuccessful login attempt

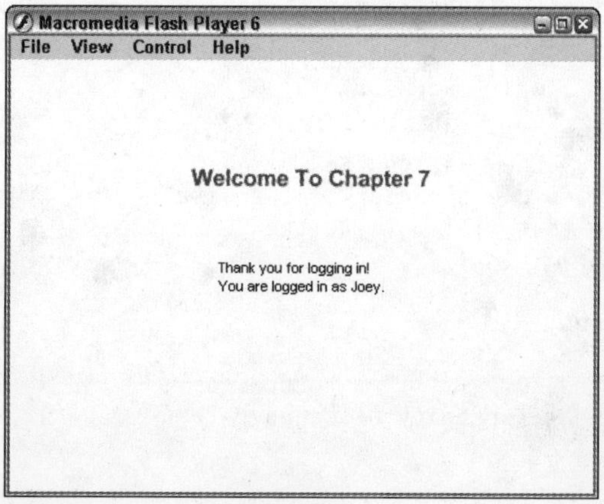

Figure 7-7: A successful login

13. As a final check, open up the ColdFusion page in the Web browser at `http://localhost:8500/chapter7/login.cfm`. You will notice that the page still works in the browser. This is the power of using Flash Remoting with ColdFusion pages. You now have both a ColdFusion interface and a Flash interface using the same ColdFusion page logic.

Listing Your Computer's Directories with Flash

As with the previous exercise, here you will create a Flash interface for an application you completed in a previous exercise. Earlier in this chapter, you used ColdFusion pages to enable you to browse your computer's directories from a Web browser. Now, using Flash Remoting, you will create a Flash movie that also enables you to browse through your computer's directories by utilizing the same ColdFusion page's logic.

1. Open a new Flash document and save it as `dirListing.fla`.

2. Rename the default layer to `listbox`. Create a new layer and name it `actions`.

3. On the listbox layer, create a `ListBox` component instance. Name the instance `directories`.

4. On the first frame of the `actions` layer, add the following code:

```
#include "NetServices.as"
#include "DataGlue.as"

// this is the bind function that adds directories
// to the ListBox
function addDirectories(record){
  // o is the object that gets returned
  // with label and data properties
  o = new Object();
  // the label should be the name of the
  // directory or file
  o.label = record.name;
  // d is an object that will get assigned
  // to the o object's data property, allowing
  // us to store multiple values in the ListBox
  // element's data property
  d = new Object();
  // store the type - "Dir" or "File"
  d.type = record.type;
  // if the value is .. then assign the url
  // value that moves up one directory, otherwise
  // assign the value that will move to the
  // selected directory
  if(record.name == "..")
    d.url = _root.oneUp;
  else
    d.url = _root.currentDir + "\\" + record.name;
    // assign d to the data property of o and return
    // the o object
```

```
  o.data = d;
  return o;
}


// this is the callback function set for the ListBox
// in the init() function later on
function dirChange(lb){
  var v = lb.getValue();
  // only if it is a directory should
  // the page get called again
  if(v.type == "Dir")
    _root.srv.dirListing(res, {dir: v.url});
}


// the sort function is used when a new RecordSet
// object is loaded. sorts by type and then by
// name
function directorySort(a, b){
  var at = a.type;
  var bt = b.type;
  var an = a.name;
  var bn = b.name;
  if(at > bt)
    return 1;
  else if(at == bt){
    if(an.toLowerCase() > bn.toLowerCase())
      return 1;
    else if(an.toLowerCase() < bn.toLowerCase())
      return -1;
    else
      return 0;
  }
  else
    return 0;
}


// the function assigned to the onResult() method
// of the response object
function resResult (res){
  // success should be 1 as long as the SWF is
  // being run on the same computer as CFMX
  if(res.success == 1){
    // assign some values to variables
    // accessible from _root to be used
    // by other functions
    _root.currentDir = res.dir;
    _root.oneUp = res.oneUp;
    _root.rs = res.dirListing;
    // sort the RecordSet
    _root.rs.sort(_root.directorySort);
    // add the .. item to the beginning of the
```

```
                    // RecordSet to be able to navigate up a level
                    _root.rs.addItemAt(0, {name: "..", type: "Dir"});
                    // populate the ListBox with the RecordSet
                    DataGlue.bindFormatFunction(_root.directories, _root.rs,
          _root.addDirectories);
                    /* each time the new directory list is loaded
                        into the ListBox we have to wait until it is
                        fully-populated, then call the setColors() function
                        to color code the directories blue
                    */
                    _root.onEnterFrame = function(){
                       if(this.directories.getLength() == this.rs.getLength()){
                          this.setColors(this.directories, this.dirsTF);
                          // once the colors have been set, don't need
                          // to check anymore
                          this.onEnterFrame = null;
                       }
                    }
                 }
             }
             else{
                trace("must be run on local computer");
             }
          }

          // the function that initializes everything
          function init(){
             // create the connection object
             var gwUrl = "http://localhost:8500/flashservices/gateway/";
             NetServices.setDefaultGatewayURL(gwUrl);
             _root.conn = NetServices.createGatewayConnection();
             // create the service object
             _root.srv = conn.getService("chapter7");
             // create the response object
             _root.res = new Object();
             _root.res.onResult = _root.resResult;
             _root.res.onStatus = function(st){
                trace(st.description);
             }

             // set the size of the ListBox to fill the stage
             _root.directories.setSize(Stage.width, Stage.height);
             // position the ListBox at 0,0
             _root.directories._x = 0;
             _root.directories._y = 0;
             // when an item is selected, call the
             // _root.dirChange() function
             _root.directories.setChangeHandler("dirChange", _root);

             // define the TextFormat object
             _root.dirsTF = new TextFormat();
             _root.dirsTF.color = 0x0000FF;
```

```
      // call the ColdFusion page to get the
      // initial directory listing
      _root.srv.dirListing(res);
   }

   // this function sets the colors of the
   // directories to blue
   function setColors(lb, tf){
      var si = lb.getScrollPosition();
      var item;
      // loop through all the displayed items
      for(var i = 0; i < lb.getRowCount(); i++){
         // get each item one at a time
         item = lb.getItemAt(i + si);
         /* if the item's type is "Dir" then set
            its TextFormat object. this part is a
            little tricky and required poking around
            in the ListBox component for undocumented
            stuff. the container, fListItemN_mc, fLabel_mc,
            and labelField properties are all defined for
            all ListBox instances, so we are just using them
            here
         */
         if(item.data.type == "Dir")

lb.container["fListItem"+i+"_mc"].fLabel_mc.labelField.setTextFormat(
tf);
      }
   }

   /* every time the ListBox is scrolled we
      want to set the colors again (they get lost
      in the scrolling). so this code simply
      checks to see if the ListBox has scrolled at
      all, and if so, calls setColors()
   */
   _root.createEmptyMovieClip("checkScroll", 0);
   checkScroll.onEnterFrame = function(){
      var curScroll = _root.directories.getScrollPosition();
      if(this.prevScroll != curScroll)
         _root.setColors(_root.directories, _root.dirsTF);
      this.prevScroll = curScroll;
   }

   // call the init() function
   init();
```

5. Save the Flash document and export the SWF.

6. Open the dirListing.cfm page you created earlier in this chapter in the editor you use for ColdFusion pages.

7. Make the changes indicated in bold below:

```
<html>
<head>
<title>Chapter 7, Example 1</title>
</head>
<body>

<cfif CGI.REMOTE_ADDR EQ "127.0.0.1">
  <cfscript>
    dir = #GetDirectoryFromPath(GetCurrentTemplatePath())#;
    if(isDefined("URL.dir")){
      dir = URL.dir;
    }
    // if it is being called from Flash use the
    // value passed from Flash
    if(isDefined("FLASH.params")){
      if(NOT ArrayIsEmpty(FLASH.params)){
        dir = FLASH.params[1].dir;
      }
    }
    oneUp = REReplace(dir, "\\[^\\]*[\\]*$", "");
  </cfscript>

  <cfoutput>
    Directory: #dir#<br>
    <a href="dirListing.cfm?dir=#oneUp#">..</a><br>
  </cfoutput>
  <cfdirectory
    directory="#dir#"
    name="dirListing"
    sort="type ASC, name ASC">

  <table>
    <cfoutput query="dirListing">
      <tr>
        <td>
        <cfif #type# EQ "Dir">
          <a href="dirListing.cfm?dir=#dir#\#name#">#name#</a>
        <cfelse>
          #name#
        </cfif>
        </td>
      </tr>
    </cfoutput>
  </table>
```

```
    <cfscript>
      // the return object
      res = StructNew();
      res.success = 1;
      res.dir = dir;
      res.oneUp = oneUp;
      res.dirListing = dirListing;
      FLASH.result = res;
    </cfscript>
  <cfelse>
    You must view this page from the local computer
    <cfscript>
      // the return object
      res = StructNew();
      res.success = 0;
      Flash.result = res;
    </cfscript>
  </cfif>
  </body>
  </html>
```

8. Save the ColdFusion page.

9. Play the SWF you exported in step 5 and test your work (click the .. at the top of the listing to ascend one directory level). You should see something similar to what is shown in Figure 7-8. As with the previous exercise, the ColdFusion page should still function as it did originally when viewed in the Web browser.

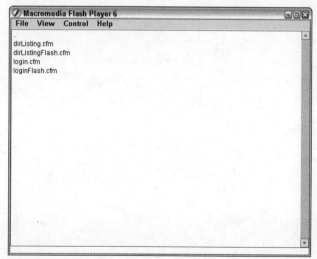

Figure 7-8: An example of what dirListing.swf might look like

Summary

In this chapter, you learned about calling ColdFusion pages from Flash movies using Flash Remoting. Included in this coverage were the following main points:

✦ Typically, ColdFusion pages are intended to be viewed in a Web browser. Using Flash Remoting, however, you can leverage existing ColdFusion logic within a Flash movie.

✦ When ColdFusion pages are accessed using Flash Remoting, the path from the webroot is used as the service name and the filename is the remote procedure name.

✦ Parameters passed to ColdFusion pages are automatically placed into an array named params in the FLASH scope.

✦ To return a value to Flash from a ColdFusion page, simply assign that value to the FLASH.result variable.

✦ Repurposing existing ColdFusion pages to be called from Flash movies is typically a minor task.

✦   ✦   ✦

Interacting with ColdFusion Components

ColdFusion Components, or CFCs, are a new element that Macromedia introduced with ColdFusion MX. Using CFCs is a convenient way to encapsulate code into reusable functions that can be accessed not only from ColdFusion pages, but also from Flash movies; and, as you see in Chapter 9, even remotely as Web services.

The combination of ColdFusion Component functions and Flash Remoting is a perfect match. Using ColdFusion pages, as you do in Chapter 7, makes perfect sense if you want to modify an already existing ColdFusion application for use with Flash Remoting. However, from a purely logical standpoint, it is obvious that ColdFusion pages are intended to be output to a Web browser. ColdFusion Components, on the other hand, are intended to modularize a specific functionality so that it can be called from a client such as a Flash movie.

Using CFCs, you can create reusable functions that can do anything ColdFusion can do. Following are just a few examples of tasks for which CFCs might be useful:

✦ Working with databases — inserting, selecting, deleting, and updating information

✦ Getting server system information such as time and date

✦ Logging in users

✦ Performing file operations

✦ Sending and retrieving e-mail

✦ Creating charts

✦ Adding FTP functionality

The possibilities are almost limitless. By using CFCs to perform these operations, you can create well-organized, effectively encapsulated libraries of reusable functionality — functionality that can be called upon not only by Flash movies, but by other clients as well.

Building ColdFusion Components

ColdFusion Components, from a technical standpoint, are text files with a `.cfc` extension that contain collections of functions. You can think of CFCs as being the CFML equivalent of JavaBeans or ASP.NET DLLs. In fact, CFCs follow many of the same conventions, such as the use of packages and the capability for one CFC to extend the functionality of another CFC.

In showing you how to get started creating your own CFCs, I'll discuss the following:

- ✦ Understanding general CFC structure
- ✦ Creating basic functions
- ✦ Passing parameters to functions
- ✦ Returning values
- ✦ Working with CFC security

All CFCs must adhere to the following basic rules:

- ✦ The filename must end with the `.cfc` extension.
- ✦ The file must be saved in a directory accessible from the Web server, such as the ColdFusion webroot (see the following Note).
- ✦ All contents of the CFC must be enclosed within a `<cfcomponent>` element.

Note   If you are using CFCs for purposes other than being called directly by Flash Remoting, you can save the files in alternative locations. See your ColdFusion documentation for more information regarding this.

Web Resource   Additional information on creating components with Dreamweaver can be found on this book's companion Web site (`www.wiley.com/compbooks/lott`).

Adding Functions to ColdFusion Components

Functions (or methods, as they are sometimes called) are added to CFCs within the `<cfcomponent>` root element and are contained within `<cffunction>` elements. The only attribute of the `<cffunction>` tag that is absolutely required is the `name` attribute—which of course specifies the name of the function as it will be called by a client (be that a Flash movie, another CFC function, a ColdFusion page, etc.). However, in order for your CFC functions to work with Flash Remoting, you must set the `access` attribute to `remote`. Here is an example of an opening `<cffunction>` tag that creates a function named `myFirstFunction` that will be accessible via Flash Remoting (`access` set to `remote`):

```
<cffunction name="myFirstFunction" access="remote">
```

Tip   If you want your function to be accessible to Flash movies, set the `access` attribute of the `<cffunction>` tag to `remote`.

Contained within the `<cffunction>` element is the function body. The function body is composed of any valid CFML (including tags and CFScript). For example, here is a valid CFC with a function named `myFirstFunction`:

```
<cfcomponent>
  <cffunction name="myFirstFunction" access="remote">
    <!-- the function body can contain CFML tags -->
    <cfscript>
      // the function body can also contain CFScript
    </cfscript>
  </cffunction>
</cfcomponent>
```

If you want to add multiple functions to a CFC, simply create additional function definitions with more `<cffunction>` elements. Here is an example of a CFC with two functions:

```
<cfcomponent>
  <cffunction name="myFirstFunction" access="remote">
    <!--this is the first function -->
  </cffunction>
  <cffunction name="mySecondFunction" access="remote">
    <!-- this is the second function -->
  </cffunction>
</cfcomponent>
```

Working with Parameters

As with functions in any language and on any platform, CFC functions are usually of most use if you can pass parameters to them. For example, you might want to create a function to insert data into a database table. Of course, several pieces of information need to be passed along to such a function for it to be of real use. Two pieces of information—the DSN and the SQL `INSERT` statement—are likely candidates for being passed to such a function as parameters.

In order to work with parameters passed to a CFC function, you need only to define them within the function body using `<cfargument>` tags. The `<cfargument>` tag has one required attribute—`name`—which is the variable name for the parameter within the function. Here is an example of a parameter definition for a parameter named `myParam`:

```
<cfargument name="myParam">
```

Tip　It is possible to define parameters without using `<cfargument>` and to access parameters passed to a CFC function simply by using a special array named `arguments`. However, unless you have good reason to do so, I highly recommend you define your parameters using `<cfargument>`. Doing so makes your CFC functions easier for you to understand than accessing the values of the `arguments` array by their indices.

There are three optional attributes you can specify for a `<cfargument>` tag: `type`, `required`, and `default`. I recommend that you define the `type` attribute because it simply ensures that ColdFusion will try to interpret the parameter value properly. The following are acceptable values for the `type` attribute:

✦ any

✦ array

✦ binary

✦ boolean

✦ date

✦ guid

✦ numeric

✦ query

✦ string

✦ struct

✦ uuid

✦ variableName

By default, parameters are not required. However, if you set the required attribute of the `<cfargument>` tag to `true`, the function will throw an error if called without that parameter. On the other hand, if you do not require the parameter, you can set a default value to be used if no value is specified. To do so, simply assign the desired value to the `default` attribute.

Once a parameter has been defined within the function body, it can be used as a variable within the function. For example, if the parameter is assigned the name `myParam` in the `<cfargument>` tag, it can be used in the function as a variable with the name `myParam` (or `arguments.myParam` if you want to fully scope the variable).

Following is an example of a CFC with a function that performs a `<cfquery>` given the DSN and the SQL statement passed to it as parameters. In this example, the SQL statement is required; the DSN parameter is not required but rather has a default value:

```
<cfcomponent>
  <cffunction name="doNonSelect" access="remote">
    <cfargument name="sql" type="string" required="true">
    <cfargument name="dsn" type="string" default="WileyFlashRemoting">
    <cfquery datasource="#dsn#">
      #sql#
    </cfquery>
  </cffunction>
</cfcomponent>
```

Returning Values from Functions

To return a value from a CFC function, you have two options:

✦ Use the `<cfreturn>` tag

✦ Use the `return` statement within a CFScript block

Just as with functions of most languages and on most platforms, a CFC function returns only one value—that in the first `return` statement encountered (whether the `<cfreturn>` tag or the CFScript `return` statement). Once the `return` statement is encountered, the function exits. Therefore, in the function that follows, only the value `returnedVal` is returned, and the `<cfquery>` statement is never executed:

```
<cffunction name="someFunction" access="remote">
  <cfreturn "returnedVal">
  <cfreturn "not returned">
  <cfscript>
    return "also not returned";
  </cfscript>
  <cfquery datasource="MyFavoriteDataSource">
    SELECT * FROM myTable
  </cfquery>
</cffunction>
```

The return type of a CFC function can be of any ColdFusion data type that the gateway can properly cast to a valid ActionScript data type (see Table 6-3 for a list of ColdFusion-to-ActionScript data type conversions). Here is an example of a function that returns a `Query` object:

```
<cffunction name="doSelect" access="remote">
  <cfargument name="sql" type="string" required="true">
  <cfargument name="dsn" type="string" default="WileyFlashRemoting">
  <cfquery datasource="#dsn#" name="myQuery">
    #sql#
  </cfquery>
  <cfreturn #myQuery#>
</cffunction>
```

Adding ColdFusion Security

CFC functions can easily use ColdFusion security in several ways. Two convenient ways of incorporating security are as follows:

✦ Using the `roles` attribute of the `<cffunction>` tag

✦ Adding programmatic security checking within functions

The `roles` attribute of the `<cffunction>` accepts values of comma-delimited lists of role names that should be allowed access to the function. For example, the following `<cffunction>` opening tag specifies that valid roles for the function include both `groupA` and `groupB`:

```
<cffunction name="myFunction" access="remote" roles="groupA, groupB">
```

When you specify a value for the `roles` attribute, ColdFusion will automatically check to see if the requesting user is logged in as a user within a valid role. If the user is in a valid role, the function executes. Otherwise, the function throws an error. Therefore, I recommend using programmatic security checking in place of the `roles` attribute–based security. I think it is a better practice to return a value to the Flash movie via the response object's result method than the status method.

Programmatic security simply means using a `<cfif>` element around the function body in conjunction with the `IsUserInRole()` function. In this way, you can return a specific message to the Flash movie if the user is not logged in as a valid user. For example:

```
<cffunction name="myFunction" access="remote">
  <cfif IsUserInRole("groupA") OR IsUserInRole("groupB")>
    <cfreturn "valid user">
  <cfelse>
    <cfreturn "not logged in to valid role">
  </cfif>
</cffunction>
```

Creating Your First CFC

In this exercise, you create a simple CFC with two functions for making database calls. You'll be using this CFC in several of the other exercises throughout the chapter.

1. Open a new document in your CFC editor. Dreamweaver offers code-hinting as well as additional CFC creation support, but any text editor will do.

2. Save the document to the Wiley\chapter8 directory within the ColdFusion webroot. Name the file Database.cfc.

3. Add the following code to the CFC document:

```
<cfcomponent>
  <cffunction name="doNonSelect" access="remote">
    <cfargument name="sql" type="string" required="true">
    <cfargument name="dsn" type="string"
                default="WileyFlashRemoting"
    >
    <cfquery datasource="#dsn#">
      #sql#
    </cfquery>
  </cffunction>
  <cffunction name="doSelect" access="remote">
    <cfargument name="sql" type="string" required="true">
    <cfargument name="dsn" type="string"
                default="WileyFlashRemoting"
    >
    <cfquery datasource="#dsn#" name="myQuery">
      #sql#
    </cfquery>
    <cfreturn #myQuery#>
  </cffunction>
</cfcomponent>
```

4. Save the document again once you have added the code.

Calling CFC Functions from Flash

Now that you know how to create a CFC, let's look at interacting with the CFC using Flash Remoting. This section describes the following:

✦ Determining the correct service name and procedure name

✦ Passing parameters to functions

✦ Returning a value from a function

Choosing the Service and Procedure Names

Figuring out the proper service and procedure names for CFCs and their functions is very straightforward. The logical path to the Component, including the CFC name, determines the service name. You should replace any slashes with dots in keeping with the ActionScript service name conventions. For example, if the CFC is located at the URL `http://localhost:8500/Wiley/chapter8/Database.cfc`, then the service name would be `Wiley.chapter8.Database`. Table 8-1 shows a few more examples of CFC URLs and the corresponding code used to create the service object in ActionScript.

Table 8-1: Example CFC Services

URL	ActionScript Service Object Code
`http://localhost/Wiley/examples/example.cfc`	`srv = conn.getService ("Wiley.examples.example");`
`http://localhost/Wiley/myCFC.cfc`	`srv = conn.getService ("Wiley.myCFC");`
`http://localhost/someComponent.cfc`	`srv = conn.getService ("someComponent");`

The procedure name to use in ActionScript is simply the CFC function name. For example, if the function is named `myFunction`, you invoke it from ActionScript in the following way:

```
// where srv is the service object and res is a response object
srv.myFunction(res);
```

Passing Parameters to Component Functions

When you pass parameters to CFC functions, you have two options:

✦ Positional parameters

✦ Named parameters

Positional parameters are those that are passed in a comma-delimited list, where the position in the list determines to which parameter variable it will be assigned within the function. This is the standard way in which parameters are passed to most functions. For example, if your CFC function defines three parameters in the following way:

```
<cffunction name="myFunction" access="remote">
  <cfargument name="param1" type="string">
  <cfargument name="param2" type="string">
  <cfargument name="param3" type="string">
  <!-- rest of function body here -->
</cffunction>
```

then you can pass positional parameters to the function by calling it from ActionScript in the following way:

```
srv.myFunction(res, "value 1", "value 2", "value 3");
```

In the preceding example, value 1 is assigned to the parameter variable param1, value 2 is assigned to param2, and value 3 is assigned to param3. This is because their positions correspond. If the order of the parameters passed to the function is switched as follows:

```
srv.myFunction(res, "value 2", "value 1", "value 3");
```

then value 2 is assigned to the parameter variable param1, value 1 is assigned to param2, and value 3 is assigned to param3. As I have stated, this is the standard way of passing parameters to functions of just about any kind, so the concept should be familiar to you already.

However, when you are working with CFC functions, you also have the convenient alternative of using *named* parameters. When you use named parameters, you pass a single object to the function as a parameter. This single object should then have properties with names that correspond to the parameter variable names within the function. For instance, using the same myFunction example from above, you could pass it named parameters from ActionScript as follows:

```
params = new Object();
params.param1 = "value 1";
params.param2 = "value 2";
params.param3 = "value 3";
srv.myFunction(res, params);
```

Note You can also pass an object literal to the function. I chose an example using an object created with a constructor because I find it easier to read.

When you pass named parameters, the order in which the properties are assigned to the parameter object is unimportant. All that matters is that the property names correspond to the parameter variable names within the function.

Returning Values

Returning a value from a CFC function to a Flash movie is not any different from returning a value to any other kind of client. As you learned previously in this chapter, you can return values from CFC functions using either the `<cfreturn>` tag or a `return` statement within a CFScript block. However, there is one data type that can be treated specially when returned to a movie using with Flash Remoting. `Query` objects can be made pageable when returning them to Flash movies. In order to do this, simply set the `pagesize` variable in the `FLASH` scope to the number of records you wish to return in the initial page, *prior* to the return statement or tag. For example:

```
<!-- myQuery is a Query object -->
<cfset FLASH.pagesize = 10>
<cfreturn myQuery>
```

Or, in CFScript:

```
<cfscript>
  FLASH.pagesize = 10;
  Return myQuery;
</cfscript>
```

 Cross-Reference For more information on ColdFusion and record sets, see Chapter 10.

Using a CFC to Insert Values into a Database

In this exercise, you use the Database.cfc file you created previously in this chapter (in the section titled "Creating Your First CFC") to insert new books into the books table of the WileyFlashRemoting database—from a Flash movie.

1. Open a new Flash document and save it as addBook.fla.

2. Rename the default layer to actions and create a new layer named form.

3. On the form layer, add three input TextField objects with borders. Name these objects title, authorFirst, and authorLast, respectively, and position them as shown in Figure 8-1.

4. Create three static text fields with the text title:, author (first name):, and author (last name):, and position them as shown in Figure 8-1.

5. Create an instance of the PushButton component and name it submitBtn. Position it as shown in Figure 8-1.

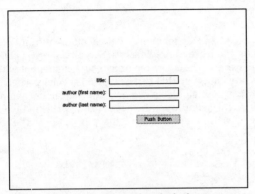

Figure 8-1: The layout of the Flash document

6. On the actions layer, add the following code to the first frame:

```
#include "NetServices.as"

function init(){
  var gwUrl = "http://localhost:8500/flashservices/gateway/";
  NetServices.setDefaultGatewayURL(gwUrl);
  var conn = NetServices.createGatewayConnection();
  _root.srv = conn.getService("Wiley.chapter8.Database");
}

// create the response object. It doesn't
// really need to do much since there will
// not be any result
res = new Object();
res.onResult = function(result){}
res.onStatus = function(status){
  trace(status.details);
}

// set up the button
submitBtn.setLabel("add book");
submitBtn.onRelease = function(){
  // create the SQL statement from the form
  var sql = "INSERT INTO books(TITLE, AUTHOR_FIRST, AUTHOR_LAST)
VALUES(\"" +
            _root.title.text + "\",\"" +
            _root.authorFirst.text + "\",\"" +
            _root.authorLast.text + "\")";
```

```
         // call the CFC function
         _root.srv.doNonSelect(_root.res, sql);
     }

     // make sure to initialize the movie!
     init();
```

7. Test the movie. Type in a title, a first name, and a last name into the form and click the button. Then, you might want to run the tableMaker_v2.swf file from Chapter 4 to see the newly inserted record.

Working with Advanced CFC Operations

So far, you have learned how to create basic CFCs, as well as how to call their functions from Flash movies. This section shows you a few advanced things you can do with CFCs, including the following:

✦ Use metadata

✦ Add inheritance

Viewing CFC Metadata

Once you have created a CFC, you may want to be able to view the metadata without having to edit the file itself. Metadata simply refers to the descriptions of the CFC contents—including function names, parameters, etc. The following sections describe two ways to view and interact with this metadata:

✦ Using a Web browser

✦ Using the Flash Service Browser

Using the cfcexplorer utility

ColdFusion includes a special CFC named cfcexplorer that reads the CFC metadata and displays it in the web browser. ColdFusion is configured such that if you simply enter the desired CFC URL into a Web browser, the cfcexplorer utility is automatically invoked for that Component. For example, if you completed the exercise in the preceding section according to the instructions, then you can view the metadata for Database.cfc by opening the following URL in your Web browser:

```
http://localhost: 8500/Wiley/chapter8/Database.cfc
```

Notice that it automatically redirects to a URL that looks something like the following:

```
http://localhost:8500/CFIDE/componentutils/cfcexplorer.cfc?method=getcf
cinhtml&name=Wiley.chapter8.Database&path=/Wiley/chapter8/Database.cfc
```

You can see that the cfcexplorer utility is actually invoked. Figure 8-2 shows what you should see in your Web browser.

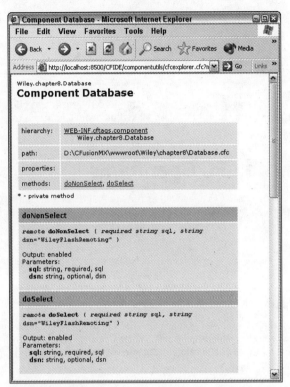

Figure 8-2: Viewing the CFC metadata in the Web browser

You can also add `hint` and `description` attributes to many elements of a CFC document. These values enable you to provide more verbose explanations of the elements, and they are displayed by the cfcexplorer utility. For example, the following code shows how you might modify (in bold) the Database.cfc file by adding these attributes:

```
<cfcomponent
    displayname="Flash Remoting Database CFC"
    hint="Use Database Operations from Flash"
>
  <cffunction name="doNonSelect" access="remote"
            hint="Do INSERT, UPDATE, and DELETE"
    >
    <cfargument name="sql" type="string" required="true"
            hint="The SQL Statement as a String"
    >
    <cfargument name="dsn" type="string"
            default="WileyFlashRemoting"
    >
    <cfquery datasource="#dsn#">
      #sql#
    </cfquery>
  </cffunction>
  <cffunction name="doSelect" access="remote" hint="Do SELECT">
```

```
        <cfargument name="sql" type="string" required="true"
                hint="The SQL Statement as a String"
        >
        <cfargument name="dsn" type="string"
                default="WileyFlashRemoting"
        >
        <cfquery datasource="#dsn#" name="myQuery">
          #sql#
        </cfquery>
        <cfreturn #myQuery#>
    </cffunction>
</cfcomponent>
```

Figure 8-3 shows what the cfcexplorer output in the Web browser looks like after these changes have been made.

Note   Adding `hint` and `description` attributes to CFC elements does not affect their functionality. The purpose is strictly to provide (to developers utilizing the CFC) a more verbose explanation of the use and intent of the component and its functions.

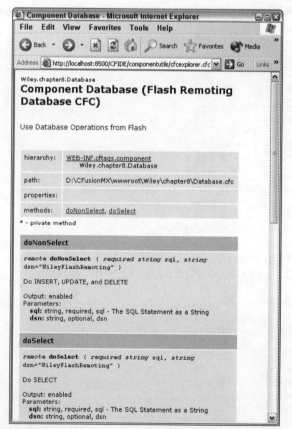

Figure 8-3: The Database.cfc metadata with added hint and description attributes

Using the Service Browser

When you are using CFCs with Flash, you can also use the Flash Service Browser. The Service Browser is likely something you have not yet encountered, simply because it has not (as of this writing) been fully developed. Therefore, its usefulness is rather limited at this time, though I expect it will become more robust in subsequent releases of Flash. It can, however, be a handy tool when working with CFCs. The best way to explain what the Service Browser is and what it can do is to walk you through an example. In this exercise, you use the Service Browser to add a CFC's functions to the Actions Toolbox — having it automatically detect the functions and their parameters.

1. In Flash, open the Service Browser by choosing Window⇨Service Browser.

2. In the Service Browser, click the task button (a blue square with a white arrow in the upper, left-hand corner) and select Add gateway (see Figure 8-4).

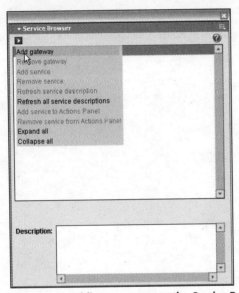

Figure 8-4: Adding a gateway to the Service Browser

3. In the Enter new gateway URL text box, type `http://localhost:8500/flashservices/gateway/` and click the Add Gateway button just above it (see Figure 8-5).

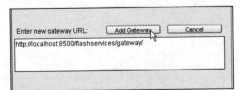

Figure 8-5: Adding the gateway URL

4. You should now see the newly added gateway under the Gateways list. Select the gateway so that it is highlighted (see Figure 8-6), and then select Add service from the task button menu (see Figure 8-7).

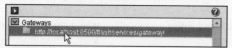

Figure 8-6: Selecting the gateway

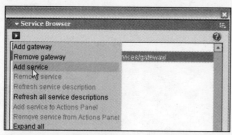

Figure 8-7: Selecting Add service from the task button menu

5. In the Enter new service address type text box, enter `Wiley.chapter8.Database`, and click the Add service button (see Figure 8-8).

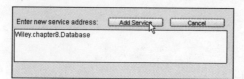

Figure 8-8: Entering the new service

6. Now you should see the Wiley.chapter8.Database service appear under the `http://localhost:8500/flashservices/gateway/` gateway. It should have automatically detected the `doSelect` and `doNonSelect` functions (see Figure 8-9).

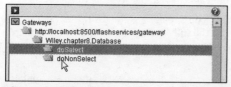

Figure 8-9: The Service Browser automatically detects the functions.

7. Select the `Wiley.chapter8.Database` service so that it is highlighted, and from the task button menu, select Add service to Actions Panel.

8. Your Actions Toolbox should now contain a Services folder. If you expand the Services folder, you will see a folder for the gateway, within which is a folder for the service. Within the service folder (that's a lot of folders!) is a folder called Methods, which contains elements for both the `doSelect` and `doNonSelect` functions (see Figure 8-10).

Figure 8-10: The Actions Toolbox with the added service functions

9. Note that if you add one of the functions to the Actions panel, it provides you with code hints for the parameters expected (see Figure 8-11).

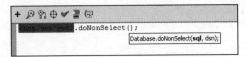

Figure 8-11: Code hinting is provided for service functions.

Extending Components

Another feature of CFCs worth noting, particularly in relation to Flash Remoting, is inheritance. One Component can extend another, meaning that it inherits the (non-private) functions of the parent Component. This is a good idea when you have created a CFC such as Database.cfc that will likely be used by many other, more specific CFC functions from diverse applications. This can also be particularly useful with Flash Remoting because it enables you to combine related functions into a single service.

In order to have one CFC extend another, you specify a value for the `extends` attribute of the <cfcomponent> tag. The value should be the fully qualified CFC name, including its packages (directories). The fully qualified name is the same as the service name used when you are using the CFC with Flash Remoting.

In the following exercise, you create a new CFC that extends Database.cfc, which you created previously.

1. Open a new CFC document and save it as BookManager.cfc to the Wiley\chapter8 directory in the ColdFusion webroot.

2. In the document, add and then save the following code:

```
<cfcomponent extends="Wiley.chapter8.Database">
  <cffunction name="insertBook" access="remote">
    <cfargument name="title" type="string" required="true">
    <cfargument name="authorFirst" type="string" required="true">
    <cfargument name="authorLast" type="string" required="true">
    <cfscript>
      sql = "INSERT INTO books(TITLE, AUTHOR_FIRST," &
            " AUTHOR_LAST) VALUES(""" &
            title  & """,""" &
            authorFirst & """,""" &
            authorLast & """)";
      doNonSelect(sql);
    </cfscript>
  </cffunction>
  <cffunction name="listBooks" access="remote">
    <cfscript>
      sql = "SELECT * FROM books";
      return doSelect(sql);
    </cfscript>
  </cffunction>
</cfcomponent>
```

3. Open addBook.fla and save it as addBook_v2.fla.

4. Modify the code on the actions layer of addBook_v2.fla so that the service it uses is now BookManager. Everything else stays the same. The line of code to change is shown here, with the modification in bold:

```
_root.srv = conn.getService("Wiley.chapter8.BookManager");
```

5. Test the movie. You will notice that although BookManager.cfc does not have a function named doNonSelect, everything still works perfectly. This is because the doNonSelect function is inherited from the parent CFC.

6. Of course, because you have created a new function called insertBook, you might as well use it. Therefore, now modify the ActionScript code a little further, as shown in this snippet (changes in bold):

```
...
submitBtn.setLabel("add book");
submitBtn.onRelease = function(){
  var params = new Object();
  params.title = _root.title.text;
  params.authorFirst = _root.authorFirst.text;
  params.authorLast = _root.authorLast.text;
  _root.srv.insertBook(_root.res, params);
}

init();
```

Note   Within the BookManager.cfc file, the insertBook function calls the doNonSelect function as though it were a local function. It can do this because it extends Database.cfc.

7. Test the movie again, just to confirm that everything works as expected.

8. Though I am not going to walk you through the steps, you might want to challenge yourself and modify tableMaker_v2.fla so that it uses the `listBooks` CFC function.

Charting with Components

In this exercise, you create a Flash movie and a CFC that produce a chart based on user-entered criteria. The chart is created using some native ColdFusion functionality (using <cfchart>), and is saved as an SWF, which can then be loaded into the main Flash movie.

1. Open a new CFC document and save it as Chart.cfc to the Wiley/chapter8 directory of your ColdFusion webroot.

2. Add the following code to the CFC document and then save it:

```
<cfcomponent>
  <cffunction name="makeChart" access="remote">
    <cfargument name="name" type="string" required="true">
    <cfargument name="data" type="array" required="true">
    <cfargument name="type" type="string" required="true">
    <cfchart name="theChart" format="flash" show3d="yes">
      <cfchartseries type="#type#">
        <cfloop from="1" to="#ArrayLen(data)#" index="i">
          <cfchartdata item="#data[i].item#"
                       value="#data[i].value#"
          >
        </cfloop>
      </cfchartseries>
    </cfchart>
    <cfscript>
      path = GetDirectoryFromPath(GetBaseTemplatePath());
      loc = "\charts\" & name;
    </cfscript>
    <cffile action="write"
            file="#path##loc#"
            output="#theChart#"
    >
    <cfreturn loc>
  </cffunction>
</cfcomponent>
```

3. Create a new subdirectory within the Wiley\chapter8 directory. Name the subdirectory charts. This is the directory to which the chart SWFs will be saved by your ColdFusion code.

4. Open a new Flash document and save it as chartMaker.fla.

5. Rename the default layer to form, and add a new layer named actions.

6. On the form layer, add a `ComboBox` component instance near the upper, left-hand corner of the stage (see Figure 8-12). Name the instance `typeMenu`. This instance will be the menu that enables the user to select a type of chart to create (bar, line, pie, etc.).

7. Positioned below `typeMenu`, also on the form layer, add a single-line, input `TextField` object named `numberOfItems` with the border turned on (see Figure 8-12). This will enable the user to choose how many items will be in the chart.

8. Below `numberOfItems`, add a `PushButton` component instance (see Figure 8-12). Name the instance `numberOfItemsBtn`. This button will create the specified number of item input fields.

9. Below `numberOfItemsBtn`, add a `ScrollPane` component instance (see Figure 8-12). Name the instance `itemsSp`. This will be where the item input fields will be viewed once they have been created.

10. Place another `PushButton` component instance below `itemsSp` (see Figure 8-12). Name the instance `makeChartBtn`.

11. Now add some labels using static text fields. In Figure 8-12, you can see how I did this. I use a form heading of SELECT CHART INFO and labels of select a chart type: and number of items:.

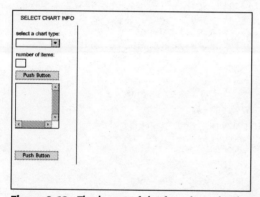

Figure 8-12: The layout of the form in makeChart.fla

12. On the first frame of the actions layer, add the following ActionScript code:

```
#include "NetServices.as"

function init(){
  // create the container for the loaded chart
  _root.createEmptyMovieClip("chartHolder", 0);
  // create the MC that will be replaced by the
  // loaded SWF
  _root.chartHolder.createEmptyMovieClip("holder", 0);
  // make the chartHolder draggable
  _root.chartHolder.onPress = function(){
    this.startDrag();
  }
  _root.chartHolder.onRelease = function(){
    this.stopDrag();
  }
```

```
    // make the scrollpane wide enough to hold
    // the item input fields
    _root.itemsSp.setSize(130, 100);

    // populate the type menu
    var typeAr = new Array("bar",
                           "pie",
                           "line",
                           "pyramid",
                           "area",
                           "cone",
                           "curve",
                           "cylinder",
                           "step",
                           "scatter");
    _root.typeMenu.setDataProvider(typeAr);

    var gwUrl = "http://localhost:8500/flashservices/gateway/";
    NetServices.setDefaultGatewayURL(gwUrl);
    var conn = NetServices.createGatewayConnection();
    _root.srv = conn.getService("Wiley.chapter8.Chart");
}

// the response object
res = new Object();
res.onResult = function(result){
    // load the new chart movie, and position it
    _root.chartHolder.holder.loadMovie(result);
    _root.chartHolder._x = 200;
    _root.chartHolder._y = 100;
}
res.onStatus = function(status){
    trace(status.description);
}

makeChartBtn.setLabel("make chart");
makeChartBtn.onRelease = function(){
    // data is the array of items for the chart
    var data = new Array();
    var item, value;
    // loop through all the items input fields
    for(var i = 0; i < num; i++){
        item = _root.itemsSc["item" + i].text;
        value = _root.itemsSc["value" + i].text;
        // if values have been input, add the item/value
        // pair to the data array
        if(item != "" and value != "")
            data.push({item:item, value:value});
    }
    // params is the named parameter object
    // to be passed to the CFC function
    var params = new Object();
    params.name = "myChart.swf";
    params.type = _root.typeMenu.getValue();
```

```
      params.data = data;
      srv.makeChart(res, params);
  }

  numberOfItemsBtn.setLabel("create items");
  numberOfItemsBtn.onRelease = function(){
      // get the number of items input fields to create
      // and store it on _root to be used by other functions
      // as well
      _root.num = parseInt(_root.numberOfItems.text);
      var item, value;
      // create the scroll content holder MC
      _root.createEmptyMovieClip("itemsSc", 1);
      // placeholder is just an empty TF that is used
      // as a trick for positioning
      _root.itemsSc.createTextField("placeholder", -1, 0, 0, 50, 20);
      // create the item and value column headings
      _root.itemsSc.createTextField("itemLabel", 0, 5, 0, 50, 20);
      _root.itemsSc.createTextField("valueLabel", 1, 60, 0, 50, 20);
      _root.itemsSc.itemLabel.text = "item";
      _root.itemsSc.valueLabel.text = "value";
      // create all the input fields
      for(var i = 0; i < _root.num; i++){
          // create the textfield objects
          _root.itemsSc.createTextField("item" + i, 2 * (i + 1) + 1, 5, 25
* (i + 1), 50, 20);
          _root.itemsSc.createTextField("value" + i, 2 * (i + 1), 60, 25 *
(i + 1), 50, 20);
          item = _root.itemsSc["item" + i];
          value = _root.itemsSc["value" + i];
          // set the border on and make sure they
          // are ready for input
          item.border = true;
          value.border = true;
          item.type = "input";
          value.type = "input"
      }
      // set the scrollpane scroll content to the newly
      // populated holder MC
      _root.itemsSp.setScrollContent(_root.itemsSc);
  }

  // initialize the movie!
  init();
```

13. Test the movie.

   a. Select a chart type from the menu.

   b. Enter a number in the input text field indicating the number of items you want in the chart and click the create items button.

   c. In the item input fields that are created, add item names and values (e.g., Bob/261, Sue/366, Sally/108).

   d. Click the make chart button. (See Figure 8-13 for an example.)

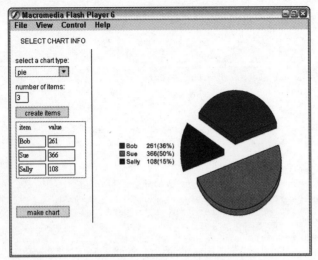

Figure 8-13: A pie chart created using chartMaker.fla

Additional information on `<cfchart>` can be found on this book's companion Web site (`www.wiley.com/compbooks/lott`).

Summary

In this chapter, you learned about ColdFusion Components (CFCs) and how to interact with them using Flash Remoting. Key points covered in this chapter include the following:

✦ ColdFusion Components can do anything that ColdFusion can do, but they provide the functionality in convenient, encapsulated, reusable form.

✦ CFCs can be thought of as ColdFusion classes — they are composed of functions and can even be extended by other CFCs.

✦ The CFC functions can accept parameters and return values. Parameters can be passed to the functions in positional or named formats.

✦ CFC metadata can be read by the cfcexplorer utility in the Web browser and also by the Flash Service Browser. The Service Browser provides a convenient and easy way to add service functions to the Actions Toolbox.

Consuming ColdFusion Web Services

ColdFusion MX was developed with Web services in mind. Whether you are authoring Web services or consuming Web services, ColdFusion provides everything you need to do so quickly, simply, and easily.

Building ColdFusion Web Services

In Chapter 5, you learned what Web services are and how to consume (access the functionality of) those Web services using Flash. This section describes how to develop your own Web services using ColdFusion MX. These Web services enable you to share functionality that can be consumed by both your own clients (Flash, other ColdFusion pages, etc.) and other clients.

Revisiting Components

ColdFusion MX uses ColdFusion Components (CFCs) to create Web services. In Chapter 8, you learned how to create ColdFusion Components, and specifically how to create CFCs that can be called from Flash movies. Because you have already learned that much, learning how to create ColdFusion Web services will be simple.

When you created a CFC function that you wanted to call from Flash Remoting, you had to make sure that you set the `<cffunction>` tag's `access` attribute to `remote`. The same rule applies when you want to create a CFC function that can be called as a Web service. However, you need to observe a few other rules in addition. Following is a complete checklist of guidelines that need to be met in order for a CFC function to be called as a Web service.

✦ Set the `<cffunction>` tag's `access` attribute to `remote`.

✦ Define all the input parameters using `<cfargument>` tags.

✦ Specify a return type by setting the `<cffunction>` tag's `returnType` attribute. The value for `returnType` can be of the name of any ColdFusion data type that Flash Remoting can convert into an ActionScript data type.

Listing 9-1 shows an example of a CFC that can be used as a Web service.

Listing 9-1: A CFC That Can Be Used as a Web Service

```
<cfcomponent>
  <cffunction name="myWSOperation"
              access="remote"
              returnType="string"
  >
    <cfargument name="param1" type="string" required="true">
    <cfreturn "this works">
  </cffunction>
</cfcomponent>
```

Creating a WSDL Document

Once you have created a CFC that can be used as a Web service, you need to create the WSDL document to describe it. With ColdFusion MX, this process is handled completely automatically for you. The WSDL document is created dynamically by simply appending `?wsdl` to the URL of the CFC. For example, if the URL to the CFC is `http://localhost:8500/myWsCFC.cfc`, then the URL to the dynamically created WSDL document is `http://localhost:8500/myWsCFC.cfc?wsdl`. It is truly that easy.

Tip   You might sometimes want to create a static WSDL document for your CFC Web service. For example, you might not be quite satisfied with the ColdFusion-generated version and want to modify it slightly. In this case, you can save a lot of time by viewing the ColdFusion-generated version and copying and pasting that code into the new document.

Making a Poll Web Service

In this exercise, you create a ColdFusion Web service that enables its consumers to create polls (as in surveys) in their client applications. This application has several parts. The first part is the CFC, which is used as the Web service. Next are two consumer Flash movies — a poll administrator movie that enables the creation of new polls, and a poll participant movie that enables users to select a poll and choose an answer for that poll.

Note   The following exercise uses `<cftry>` and `<cfcatch>`. The ColdFusion server attempts to process the code within the `<cftry>` code block. If for some reason that code fails, the code within the `<cfcatch>` block is executed instead.

1. Create polls, poll_answers, and poll_choices tables in your WileyFlashRemoting database. Use the following SQL statements to accomplish this.

```
CREATE TABLE poll_answers (
  POLL_ANSWERS_ID int(11),
  POLL_ID int(11),
  POLL_CHOICE_ID int(11));
```

```
CREATE TABLE poll_choices (
  POLL_CHOICES_ID int(11),
  POLL_ID int(11),
  CHOICE char(255));

CREATE TABLE polls (
  POLLS_ID int(11),
  POLL_NAME char(50),
  POLL_QUESTION char(255));
```

2. Open a new CFC document in your favorite editor (such as Dreamweaver). Save the document as MyPollService.cfc to the Wiley/chapter9 directory within the ColdFusion webroot.

3. Add the following code to the CFC document and then save it:

```
<cfcomponent>
  <!-- add a new poll to the database - requires a poll name and
       a question returns the id of the poll that
       gets inserted -->
  <cffunction name="addPoll"
              access="remote"
              returntype="numeric"
              output="false">
    <cfargument name="pollName" type="string" required="true">
    <cfargument name="pollQuestion" type="string" required="true">
    <cftry>
      <!-- cflock ensures that the enclosed actions will be
           thread-safe - in other words, no one else can insert a
           new value into the database until this process is
           completed. this ensures that the max poll id returned
           corresponds to the record just inserted. -->
      <cflock timeout="10">
        <cfquery datasource="WileyFlashRemoting">
        INSERT INTO POLLS(POLL_NAME, POLL_QUESTION)
        VALUES('#pollName#', '#pollQuestion#')
        </cfquery>
        <cfset id = getMaxPollId()>
      </cflock>
      <cfreturn id>
    <cfcatch type="any">
      <cfreturn 0>
    </cfcatch>
    </cftry>
  </cffunction>

  <!-- add a new choice for the poll to the database - requires a
       poll id and a value to insert for the choice. returns true
       or false -->
  <cffunction name="addChoice"
              access="remote"
              returntype="boolean"
```

```
                         output="false">
    <cfargument name="pollId" type="numeric" required="true">
    <cfargument name="pollChoice" type="string" required="true">
    <cftry>
      <cfquery datasource="WileyFlashRemoting">
      INSERT INTO POLL_CHOICES(POLL_ID, CHOICE)
      VALUES(#pollId#, '#pollChoice#')
      </cfquery>
      <cfreturn true>
    <cfcatch type="any">
      <cfreturn false>
    </cfcatch>
    </cftry>
</cffunction>

<!-- gets the values for all the polls in the database (not
     choices and answers) -->
<cffunction name="getPolls"
            access="remote"
            returntype="query"
            output="false">
    <cfquery datasource="WileyFlashRemoting" name="polls">
    SELECT *
    FROM POLLS
    </cfquery>
    <cfreturn polls>
    </cftry>
</cffunction>

<!-- gets the question and the choices for a poll given the
     poll id -->
<cffunction name="getPoll"
            access="remote"
            returntype="array"
            output="false">
    <cfargument name="pollId" type="numeric" required="true">
    <cftry>
      <cfquery datasource="WileyFlashRemoting" name="poll">
      SELECT *
      FROM POLLS
      WHERE POLLS_ID = #pollId#
      </cfquery>
      <cfquery datasource="WileyFlashRemoting" name="choices">
      SELECT *
      FROM POLL_CHOICES
      WHERE POLL_ID = #pollId#
      </cfquery>
      <cfscript>
        rVal = ArrayNew(1);
        rVal[1] = poll.POLL_QUESTION[1];
        i = 2;
      </cfscript>
      <cfoutput query="choices">
```

```
      <cfscript>
        rVal[i] = choices.POLL_CHOICES_ID & "|" &
                  choices.CHOICE;
        i = i + 1;
      </cfscript>
    </cfoutput>
    <cfreturn rVal>
    <cfcatch type="any">
      <cfscript>
        ar = ArrayNew(1);
        ar[1] = "failed";
        return ar;
      </cfscript>
    </cfcatch>
  </cftry>
</cffunction>

<!-- add an answer for a poll. requires the poll id and the id
     of the selected choice. returns an array of all the
     answered choices for the poll -->
<cffunction name="addAnswer"
            access="remote"
            returntype="array"
            output="false">
  <cfargument name="pollId" type="numeric" required="true">
  <cfargument name="choiceId" type="numeric" required="true">
  <cftry>
    <cfquery datasource="WileyFlashRemoting">
    INSERT INTO
    POLL_ANSWERS(POLL_ID, POLL_CHOICE_ID)
    VALUES(#pollId#, #choiceId#)
    </cfquery>
    <cfquery datasource="WileyFlashRemoting" name="answers">
    SELECT *
    FROM POLL_ANSWERS
    WHERE POLL_ID = #pollId#
    </cfquery>
    <cfscript>
      results = ArrayNew(1);
      for(i = 1; i LTE answers.RecordCount; i = i + 1){
        results[i] = answers.POLL_CHOICE_ID[i];
      }
      return results;
    </cfscript>
    <cfcatch type="any">
      <cfscript>
        ar = ArrayNew(1);
        ar[1] = "failed";
        return ar;
      </cfscript>
    </cfcatch>
  </cftry>
</cffunction>
```

```
<!-- private functions used by other functions
     within the CFC -->

<!-- used to get the max poll id after a poll was inserted -->
<cffunction name="getMaxPollId"
            access="private"
            returntype="numeric">
  <cfquery datasource="WileyFlashRemoting" name="pollId">
  SELECT MAX(POLLS_ID) as lastId
  FROM POLLS
  </cfquery>
  <cfreturn pollId.lastId>
</cffunction>
</cfcomponent>
```

 4. Open a new Flash document and save it as `pollAdmin.fla`.

 5. Rename the default layer to `form` and add a new layer named `actions`.

 6. On the form layer, add a single-line, input `TextField` object with border turned on. Name the instance `name`. Position it near the upper, left-hand corner of the stage (see Figure 9-1).

 7. Below the `name` instance, add a multiline, input `TextField` object with border turned on. Name the instance `question`.

 8. To the right of the `question` instance, add another multiline, input `TextField` object with border turned on. Name the instance `choice`.

 9. Add a `PushButton` component instance below both the `question` and `choice` `TextField` instances (refer to Figure 9-1). Name these instances `addPollBtn` and `addChoiceBtn`, respectively.

10. At the bottom of the stage, add a multiline, dynamic `TextField` object. Name the instance `display`. This will be used simply to display what has been input for the new poll.

11. Add text labels on the stage, as shown in Figure 9-1.

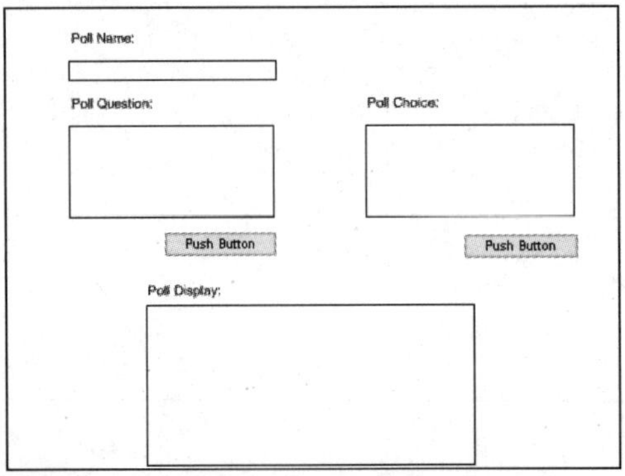

Figure 9-1: The layout of pollAdmin.fla

12. Add the following code to the first frame of the actions layer:

```
#include "NetServices.as"

function init(){

  _root.display.html = true;
  _root.addChoiceBtn.setLabel("add choice");

  // make sure that no choices can be added
  // before a poll has been created
  _root.choice.selectable = false;

  var gwUrl = "http://localhost:8500/flashservices/gateway/";
  NetServices.setDefaultGatewayURL(gwUrl);
  var conn = NetServices.createGatewayConnection();
  _root.srv =
conn.getService("http://localhost:8500/Wiley/chapter9/MyPollService.c
fc?wsdl");
}

// resBase is simply used as the class for the
// response objects so that we don't need to define
// the onStatus method each time
function resBase(){}
resBase.prototype.onStatus = function(status){
  trace(status.details);
}

addPollRes = new resBase();
addPollRes.onResult = function(result){
  if(result != 0){
    // now user can add choices...make TF selectable
    _root.choice.selectable = true;
    // a var on _root to hold the current poll id
    _root.pollId = result;
    // define addChoiceBtn actions now
    _root.addChoiceBtn.onRelease = function(){
      _root.srv.addChoice(_root.addChoiceRes, _root.pollId,
_root.choice.text);
    }
    _root.display.htmlText = "<b>" + _root.name.text + ": " +
                            _root.question.text + "</b><br><br>"
  }
  else{
    _root.display.text = "an error occurred in creating the poll";
  }
}

addChoiceRes = new resBase();
addChoiceRes.onResult = function(result){
```

```
    // display added choice, and clear input TF for
    // next entry
    _root.display.htmlText += _root.choice.text + "<br>";
    _root.choice.text = "";
}

addPollBtn.setLabel("add poll");
addPollBtn.onRelease = function(){
   root.srv.addPoll(_root.addPollRes, _root.name.text,
_root.question.text);
}

// initialize the movie
init();
```

13. Test the movie. Add a new poll, as shown in Figure 9-2. Then add choices, as shown in Figure 9-3.

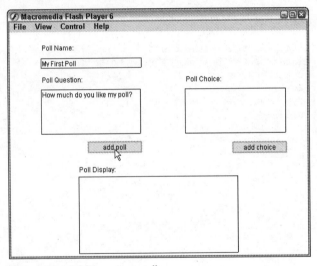

Figure 9-2: Adding a new poll

14. Save the Flash document.

15. Open a new Flash document and save it as `poll.fla`.

16. Rename the default layer to `form` and add a new layer named `actions`.

17. On the `form` layer, create two `ScrollPane` component instances. Name them `pollSp` and `pollsSp`. (The positioning will be taken care of by ActionScript.)

18. Add the `PushButton` and `RadioButton` components to the library. You can drag an instance of each onto the stage and then delete them. They will be retained in the library, however. You will use these programmatically.

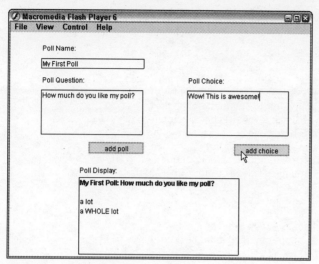

Figure 9-3: Adding choices to the poll

19. Add the following code to the first frame of the actions layer:

```
#include "NetServices.as"

function init(){

  // programmatically size and position
  // the scroll panes
  _root.pollSp.setSize(250, 300);
  _root.pollsSp.setSize(250, 300);
  _root.pollSp._y = 50;
  _root.pollsSp._y = 50;
  _root.pollSp._x = 280;
  _root.pollsSp._x = 10;

  var gwUrl = "http://localhost:8500/flashservices/gateway/";
  NetServices.setDefaultGatewayURL(gwUrl);
  var conn = NetServices.createGatewayConnection();
  _root.srv =
conn.getService("http://localhost:8500/Wiley/chapter9/MyPollService.c
fc?wsdl");

  // when the movie starts, get the current polls
  _root.srv.getPolls(getPollsRes);
}

// used as in pollAdmin.fla
function resBase(){}
resBase.prototype.onStatus = function(status){
  trace(status.details);
}
```

```
getPollsRes = new resBase();
getPollsRes.onResult = function(result){
  var poll, btn;
  // pollsSc is the scroll content for the
  // pollsSp scroll pane
  _root.createEmptyMovieClip("pollsSc", 0);
  // loop through all the returned polls (which
  // is returned as a RecordSet object
  for(var i = 0; i < result.getLength(); i++){
    // get poll record
    poll = result.getItemAt(i);
    // create a PushButton component
    btn = _root.pollsSc.attachMovie("FPushButtonSymbol",
                             "pollBtn" + i, 2 * i);
    // position the button
    btn._y = i * 25;
    btn.setLabel("view poll");
    // set a property for the button that will be
    // used when it is clicked
    btn.id = poll.POLLS_ID;
    btn.onRelease = function(){
      // get the poll info from the Web service
      // for this poll using its id
      _root.srv.getPoll(_root.getPollRes, this.id);
      // set pollId on _root to be used later
      _root.pollId = this.id;
    }
    // a label next to each button
    _root.pollsSc.createTextField("pollName" + i, (2 * i) + 1, 105,
25 * i, 0, 0);
    _root.pollsSc["pollName" + i].text = poll.POLL_NAME;
    _root.pollsSc["pollName" + i].autoSize = true;
  }
  // make sure to set the scroll content of the
  // scroll pane
  _root.pollsSp.setScrollContent(_root.pollsSc);
}

getPollRes = new resBase();
getPollRes.onResult = function(result){
  // pollChoices is used to keep track of the
  // choices for the selected poll for use later
  _root.pollChoices = new Object();
  // pollSc is the scroll content for pollSp
  _root.createEmptyMovieClip("pollSc", 1);
  var mc, choice;
  // question displays the question for the poll
  _root.pollSc.createTextField("question", 0, 0, 0, 0, 0);
  _root.pollSc.question.autoSize = true;
  _root.pollSc.question.text = result[0];
  // loop through the choices
```

```
    for(var i = 1; i< result.length; i++){
      // create a radio button for each choice
      mc = _root.pollSc.attachMovie("FRadioButtonSymbol", "choice" + i,
i);
      // position the radio button
      mc._y = 25 * i;
      // set the size to 200...should accommodate most
      mc.setSize(200);
      // the choice id and choice text are separated
      // by a |. split along this and then set the radio
      // button label and data accordingly
      choice = result[i].split("|");
      mc.setLabel(choice[1]);
      mc.setData(choice[0]);
      // set the group name so that all the radio buttons
      // are in the same group
      mc.setGroupName("choicesGroup");
      // set pollChoices element for retrieval later
      _root.pollChoices[choice[0]] = choice[1];
      // when one of the choices is selected call the
      // onSelectChoice function on _root
      mc.setChangeHandler("onSelectChoice", _root);
    }
    // make sure to set the scroll content of pollSp
    _root.pollSp.setScrollContent(_root.pollSc);
}

answerRes = new resBase();
answerRes.onResult = function(result){
    // replace the poll choices display
    _root.createEmptyMovieClip("pollSc", 1);
    var percents = new Array();
    var choiceCount = 0;
    var i = 0;
    var prcnt;
    // loop through all the poll's choices
    for(var choiceId in _root.pollChoices){
      // loop through all the returned answers
      for(var j = 0; j < result.length; j++){
        // counts the number of answers for each
        // choice
        if (result[j] == choiceId)
          choiceCount++;
      }
      // calculate the percentage for the choice
      prcnt = Math.round(100 * (choiceCount/result.length));
      // store in percents array for display in a moment
      percents[i] = _root.pollChoices[choiceId] + ": " + prcnt + "%";
      // make sure to reset choiceCount each loop
      // and increment the i index
      choiceCount = 0;
```

```
    i++;
  }
  // display the results in a text field in the
  // scroll content mc
  _root.pollSc.createTextField("results", 0, 0, 0, 0, 0);
  _root.pollSc.results.autoSize = true;
  for(var i = 0; i < percents.length; i++){
    _root.pollSc.results.text += percents[i] + newline;
  }
  // set the scroll content for pollSp
  _root.pollSp.setScrollContent(_root.pollSc);
}

// when the radiobutton is selected, add the answer
// via the Web service
function onSelectChoice(rbgroup){
  _root.srv.addAnswer(answerRes, _root.pollId, rbgroup.getValue());
}

// initialize the movie
init();
```

20. Test the movie. An item should show up in the left scroll pane for the poll you created in the administrator movie (see Figure 9-4.) Click the button and the poll choices should show up in the right scroll pane (see Figure 9-5). Select from the choices, and then the current poll results should appear (see Figure 9-6). To vote again, simply click the poll button on the left and repeat the process.

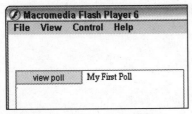

Figure 9-4: The current poll list

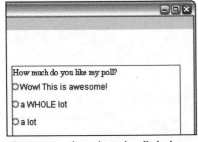

Figure 9-5: The selected poll choices

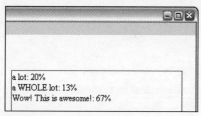

Figure 9-6: The poll results

 Note Obviously, this is a very rudimentary poll application. Much more could be done with it by implementing usernames and passwords, ordering the poll choices in the display, etc. Feel free to make modifications and upgrades as you desire.

Consuming Web Services with ColdFusion

Although you will generally be able to take advantage of the powerful Flash Remoting capabilities that enable your Flash movies to consume Web services without server-side scripting, some Web services can prove to be somewhat resistant to this feature. When you encounter this, you can still use these Web services with your Flash Remoting applications. However, you may have to set up a proxy script to consume the Web service and return the results to the Flash movie. Therefore, I want to briefly describe how you can consume Web services using ColdFusion MX.

ColdFusion MX provides two techniques for consuming Web services:

✦ Using the `<cfinvoke>` tag

✦ Using the `CreateObject()` function within a CFScript code block

Using Web Services with Tags

Using the `<cfinvoke>` tag is a simple way to consume a Web service in ColdFusion if you are comfortable with CFML tags. The tag has several uses other than invoking Web services that are not discussed here. In addition, several variations of usage for `<cfinvoke>` are available when using it to consume Web services. These are not covered here either. The ColdFusion documentation provides excellent coverage on the various uses of `<cfinvoke>` should you want to investigate further.

The use of `<cfinvoke>` that we will look at here should be all you need to consume any Web service. You will want to define values for three of the tag's attributes:

✦ `webService`: The URL that points to the WSDL document

✦ `method`: The name of the Web service operation to invoke

✦ `returnVariable`: The name of the variable that will be used to hold the results of the operation

For instance, if you want to use the `<cfinvoke>` tag to invoke the `addPoll` operation of the `MyPollService` Web service you created in the previous exercise, and store the returned value in a variable named `pollId`, use the following code:

```
<cfinvoke
webService="http://localhost:8500/Wiley/chapter9/MyPollService.cfc?wsdl
      method="addPoll"
      returnVariable="pollId" />
```

If `addPoll` didn't require any parameters, then this would be all that is necessary. However, `addPoll` requires two parameters—the poll name and the question. Therefore, you need to know how to pass parameters to a Web service operation using the `<cfinvoke>` tag.

One way to accomplish this is by using the `<cfinvokeargument>` tag. You can include multiple `<cfinvokeargument>` tags inside of opening and closing `<cfinvoke>` tags. The `<cfinvokeargument>` tag requires that two attributes be set:

✦ name: The name of the parameter

✦ value: The value of the parameter

Here is an example of parameters being passed to the `addPoll` operation using `<cfinvokeargument>` tags:

```
<cfinvoke
webService="http://localhost:8500/Wiley/chapter9/MyPollService.cfc?wsdl
      method="addPoll"
      returnVariable="pollId">
  <cfinvokeargument name="pollName" value="my new poll">
  <cfinvokeargument name="pollQuestion" value="how's things?">
</cfinvoke>
```

Using Web Services with CFScript

If you are more of a CFScript kind of person, you have the option of using the `CreateObject()` function to create a Web service object from which to invoke the operation. This is also a very simple way to invoke Web services.

The `CreateObject()` function takes two parameters:

✦ The string value `webservice`, to indicate that the object being created is a Web service object

✦ The URL that points to the WSDL

Once you have created a Web service object, you can invoke the operation from the object as you would invoke a method of an object in ActionScript. Here is an example using CFScript that invokes the `addPoll` operation of the MyPollService Web service:

```
<cfscript>
  pollWs = CreateObject("webservice",
        "http://locahost:8500/Wiley/chapter9/MyPollService.cfc?wsdl");
  pollId = pollWs.addPoll("my new poll", "how's things?");
</cfscript>
```

Searching Amazon via Proxy

At the time of this writing, the Amazon.com Web service cannot be consumed directly by a Flash movie. In fact, numerous problems seem to be encountered. Using a CFC as a proxy script, however, it is easy enough to use the Amazon.com Web service from a Flash movie after all. In this exercise, you will do just that.

> **Note**   You will need to register with Amazon.com's associates program (free). To do so, go to `http://associates.amazon.com`. Once you have signed up and are logged on, go to their Web services page (`http://associates.amazon.com/exec/panama/associates/ntg/browse/-/1067662/103-5686734-5679061`) and get a developer's token (free), which you will need to complete this exercise.

1. Open a new ColdFusion Component document and save it as AmazonServiceProxy.cfc.

2. In the document, add the following code and then save it:

```
<cfcomponent>
  <cffunction name="doKeywordSearch" access="remote"
returntype="any">
    <cfargument name="devtag" type="string" required="true">
    <cfargument name="keyword" type="string" required="true">
    <cfargument name="mode" type="string" required="true">
    <cfargument name="page" type="string" required="true">
    <cfargument name="tag" type="string" required="true">
    <cfargument name="type" type="string" required="true">
    <cfscript>
      params = StructNew();
      params.devtag = devtag;
      params.keyword = keyword;
      params.mode = mode;
      params.page = page;
      params.tag = tag;
      params.type = type;

    </cfscript>
    <cfinvoke
 webservice="http://soap.amazon.com/schemas2/AmazonWebServices.wsdl"
        method="KeywordSearchRequest"
        returnvariable="results">
      <cfinvokeargument name="KeywordSearchRequest"
value="#params#"/>
    </cfinvoke>
    <cfreturn results>
  </cffunction>
</cfcomponent>
```

3. Open a new Flash document and save it as `amazon.fla`.

4. Rename the default layer to `form`, and create a new layer named `actions`.

5. On the form layer, add a single-line, input `TextField` object near the top of the stage, as shown in Figure 9-7. Name this instance `query`.

6. Beneath `query`, add a `PushButton` component instance (see Figure 9-7). Name this instance `searchBtn`.

7. To the right of the `searchBtn` instance, create back-to-back instances (see Figure 9-7) of the "circle button - previous" and "circle button - next" symbols from the buttons common library (Window⇨Common Libraries⇨buttons). Name these instances `prevBtn` and `nextBtn`, respectively.

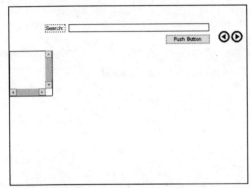

Figure 9-7: The layout of amazon.fla

8. Beneath the rest of the instances, and to the far left of the stage, create a new `ScrollPane` component instance. Name the instance `sp`.

9. Create a new Movie Clip symbol (Ctrl + F8). If the Create New Symbol dialog box is in basic mode, click the Advanced button (see Figure 9-8).

Figure 9-8: Click Advanced if not already in advanced mode

10. Give the symbol a name of `product`, select Export for ActionScript, and give it a linkage Identifier of `Product` (see Figure 9-9).

11. Click OK.

Figure 9-9: Export for ActionScript with an Identifier of Product

12. In the new symbol, rename the default layer to form, and add a new layer named actions.

13. On the form layer, add three single-line, dynamic `TextField` objects, stacking them one over another (see Figure 9-10). Name these instances `productName`, `authors`, and `ourPrice`.

14. Draw a small rectangle about 40 pixels by 50 pixels (the size doesn't really matter) beneath the text fields, as shown in Figure 9-10. Convert this to a Movie Clip symbol. Name the instance `image`. Then convert that instance to a Movie Clip symbol as well, and name the new instance `imageHolder`. You should now have an instance named `imageHolder`, which in turn contains an instance named `image`. This will be used to hold the product image later.

15. Create an instance of the `PushButton` component to the right of `imageHolder`, as shown in Figure 9-10. In the Properties panel for the component, set the label to "buy it" (see Figure 9-11).

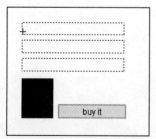

Figure 9-10: Layout of the product symbol

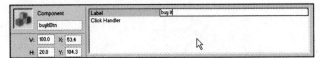

Figure 9-11: Adding the label to the buyItBtn instance

16. On the first frame of the actions layer (of the product symbol), add the following code:

```
// Use the value 0 with #initclip so that this code is the first
// code executed when the movie plays.
#initclip 0

// set Product to inherit from MovieClip
Product.prototype = new MovieClip();

// The Product constructor
function Product(){
  this.productName.html = true;
  this.productName.autoSize = true;
  this.authors.autoSize = true;
  this.ourPrice.autoSize = true;
}

// The set method allows the product instances
// to be easily populated with data
Product.prototype.set = function(url, name, authors, price, img){
  this.productName.htmlText = "<b>" + name + "</b>";
  this.ourPrice.text = price;
  this.authors.text = authors[0];
  for(var i = 1; i < authors.length; i++){
    this.authors.text += ", " + authors[i];
  }
  this.imageHolder.image.loadMovie(img);
  this.url = url;
  this.buyItBtn.onRelease = function(){
    _root.getURL(this._parent.url, "_blank");
  }
}

// register the class so that when
// new Product instance are created using
// attachMovie(), they will automatically
// be typed as Product
Object.registerClass("Product", Product);

#endinitclip
```

17. Return to the Main Timeline and add the following code to the first frame of the actions layer:

```
#include "NetServices.as"

function init(){

  // set the size of the scroll pane
  sp.setSize(550, 300);

  var gwUrl = "http://localhost:8500/flashservices/gateway/";
  //gwUrl = "http://localhost/Wiley/flashgateway.aspx";
  NetServices.setDefaultGatewayURL(gwUrl);
  var conn = NetServices.createGatewayConnection();
  _root.srv = conn.getService("Wiley.chapter9.AmazonServiceProxy");


res = new Object();
res.onResult = function(result){

  // create the scroll content movie
  _root.createEmptyMovieClip("sc", 0);
  // Details is a property of the returned
  // object (see WSDL)
  var itms = result.Details;
  var item, yPos, mc;
  // loop through all the items
  for(var i = 0; i < itms.length; i++){
    item = itms[i];
    prod = _root.sc.attachMovie("product", "product" + i, i);
    // call the set() method of the Product class
    // to populate the instance
    prod.set(item.url,
             item.productName,
             item.authors,
             item.ourPrice,
             item.imageUrlSmall);
    yPos += prod._height + 10;
    prod._y = yPos;
  }
  _root.sp.setScrollContent(_root.sc);
}
res.onStatus = function(status){
  trace(status.description);
}

searchBtn.setLabel("search");
searchBtn.onRelease = function(){
  _root.doSearch(1, _root.query.text);
  _root.queryVal = _root.query.text;
  _root.page = 1;
}
```

```
nextBtn.onRelease = function(){
  _root.page++;
  _root.doSearch(_root.page, _root.queryVal);
}

prevBtn.onRelease = function(){
  _root.page--;
  if(_root.page < 1)
    _root.page = 1;
  _root.doSearch(_root.page, _root.queryVal);
}

function doSearch(page, query){
  params = new Object();
  params.page = "" + page;
  params.keyword = query;
  params.mode = "books";
  params.tag = "webservices-20";
  params.type = "lite";
  // use your developer tag value in the next line of code
  params.devtag = "XXXXXXXXXXXXXX";

  _root.srv.doKeywordSearch(_root.res, params);
}

// initialize movie
init();
```

18. Test the movie. Try searching for ActionScript (see Figure 9-12).

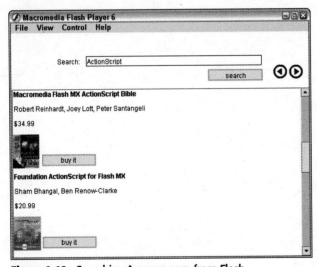

Figure 9-12: Searching Amazon.com from Flash

Note This application is far from production-ready. Many features could and should be imple-mented in order to make it truly useful in a production environment. However, this should give you a good start. Also, note that the images will load only if the movie is running locally. If you wish to run the movie on a Web server, you will need to load the images using a proxy script because of Flash sandbox security.

Summary

In this chapter, you learned about using Web services with ColdFusion. You learned how to create ColdFusion Web services, and how to consume Web services with ColdFusion. Some important points discussed in the chapter include the following:

✦ ColdFusion MX enables you to easily create Web services using ColdFusion Components and set the access of the functions to remote.

✦ ColdFusion Components can generate WSDL documents automatically when you append ?wsdl to the URL.

✦ Some Web services that are problematic when consuming them directly from Flash movies can be instead fed to the Flash movie by way of a ColdFusion proxy.

✦ ColdFusion MX enables you to easily consume Web services using either tag-based syn-tax or CFScript.

✦   ✦   ✦

Working with Pageable Record Sets

Chapter 4 discusses the RecordSet class of objects available in ActionScript for Flash MX. Everything you have learned so far applies to *all* RecordSet objects. This includes objects that have been created in the following ways:

♦ Using the ActionScript RecordSet constructor

♦ Returning a Query object from a ColdFusion page or a CFC function

♦ Returning a ResultSet object from a Java application

♦ Returning a .NET DataTable or DataSet

However, when you are using RecordSet objects returned from ColdFusion, you have available an option that is not available with objects that have been created from the constructor method or that have been returned from Java or .NET applications. ColdFusion Query objects can be returned so that the records are *pageable*. This means that not every record is returned at once; rather, subsets of records are returned as they are used. To understand what this means and why it can be advantageous, let's examine what pageable record sets are and how they operate.

Understanding Pageable Record Sets

You have undoubtedly seen pageable record sets in use, though you may not have known it. Consider a search engine on the Web. In most instances, when you perform a search using any popular search engine service, you get many matching results for your query. The number of results returned can vary greatly depending on the search you are performing—sometimes 100 and sometimes 100,000. More often than not, your search returns more results than you want, and certainly more than you can display on your monitor at one time. Moreover, although certainly the manageability of the display of results is one of the reasons for returning only 10 or 25 results at a time, another very important factor is download time. This is the consideration behind pageable RecordSet objects in Flash Remoting.

On occasion, you may have visited Web sites that consist of one tremendously long page of content. Even if it is all just text, it may seem to take forever to load into the Web browser. This is exactly the kind of situation that you want to avoid when returning a record set to Flash. Sometimes the record set may consist of only a small number of records. In these situations, you will not need any further considerations with regard to load time. Other queries, however, may result in thousands, tens of thousands, or even more records. Trying to return all these records at once to the Flash movie could prove disastrous. Instead, you can first return a reasonable number of records to the Flash client, and then return subsequent records as they are requested. The records that are not yet returned to the Flash client are held on the server until they are requested by the application (such as when a user clicks on a "next results" button). In this way, you avoid having to run many smaller queries (and placing additional processing demands on the server), but you also do not burden the client by trying to load too many records at once.

Creating the Pageable RecordSet Object

By default, RecordSet objects are *not* pageable. You have already seen that this is so. Every RecordSet object you have encountered in this book thus far has been fully loaded into the Flash movie or it has not existed at all. Therefore, in order to make a RecordSet object pageable, you must do a few things. There are two main considerations:

✦ What to do on the ColdFusion side of things

✦ What to do on the Flash side of things

 Additional information on ColdFusion query-building functions can be found on this book's companion Web site (www.wiley.com/compbooks/lott).

Configuring ColdFusion to Return Pageable Results

The ColdFusion code for returning pageable results is short and simple. Moreover, you do the same thing whether you are working with a ColdFusion page or a ColdFusion Component function. In either case, all you need to do is assign a value to the FLASH.pagesize variable to indicate how many records should be initially returned. Listings 10-1 and 10-2 show ColdFusion page and CFC function examples, respectively, of this.

Listing 10-1: ColdFusion Page Returning a Pageable Record Set

```
<cfscript>
  q = QueryNew("col1, col2, col3");
  r1 = QueryAddRow(q, 5);
  for(i = 1; i LTE 5; i = i + 1){
    QuerySetCell(q, "col1", "Column 1 value " & i, i);
    QuerySetCell(q, "col2", "Column 2 value " & i, i);
    QuerySetCell(q, "col3", "Column 3 value " & i, i);
  }
  FLASH.pagesize = 1;
  FLASH.result = q;
</cfscript>
```

Listing 10-2: CFC Function Returning a Pageable Record Set

```
<cfcomponent>
  <cffunction name="getPageableRS" access="remote" returntype="query">
    <cfscript>
    q = QueryNew("col1, col2, col3");
    r1 = QueryAddRow(q, 5);
    for(i = 1; i LTE 5; i = i + 1){
      QuerySetCell(q, "col1", "Column 1 value " & i, i);
      QuerySetCell(q, "col2", "Column 2 value " & i, i);
      QuerySetCell(q, "col3", "Column 3 value " & i, i);
    }
    FLASH.pagesize = 1;
    return q;
  </cfscript>
  </cffunction>
</cfcomponent>
```

The value assigned to the pagesize variable in the FLASH scope will determine the number of records initially returned to the Flash movie. ColdFusion will then return that number of records, starting with the first record. Assigning a value to FLASH.pagesize is valid only if the returned value is a Query object. Otherwise, the value is ignored. If no value is set for FLASH.pagesize (default), then all the records are returned at once.

Although the initial number of records returned from a ColdFusion page or function is set in the ColdFusion code, it is typically a good idea for this value to be passed as a parameter to ColdFusion from the Flash movie in the first place. This approach is not necessarily more correct, but it does allow the page size (see the next section for more information about the page delivery mode) to be set in one location, rather than two. Following are some snippets of code that show how this is accomplished.

First, in the ActionScript:

```
// assuming a service object named srv, a response object named
// res, and a remote procedure named getPageableRS()
// passes a value of 10 to the remote procedure
srv.getPageableRS(res, {pagesize: 10});
```

Then a ColdFusion page snippet:

```
<cfset FLASH.pagesize = FLASH.params[1].pagesize>
```

Or, alternatively, a CFC function snippet:

```
<cfargument name="params" type="struct">
<cfset FLASH.pagesize = params.pagesize>
```

Processing Pageable RecordSet Objects

Once you have specified in the ColdFusion page or CFC function that only a certain number of records should be returned to the Flash movie initially, you then need to know how to handle the RecordSet object that is created. Although pageable RecordSet objects behave more or less just like non-pageable RecordSet objects, note some special considerations that need to be taken into account:

✦ How and when the records will be downloaded from the server

✦ How to watch for updates to the RecordSet object

✦ How to determine which records are available

Downloading Records

Perhaps what most distinguishes pageable RecordSet objects from their nonpageable counterparts is that you must somehow signal to the ColdFusion server when additional records should be downloaded. This is a minor task: A record only needs to be requested with the getItamAt() method. When a record is requested in this way, and that record has yet to be downloaded from the server, a request is sent to the server for that record. The ColdFusion server then returns the requested record or records to the Flash movie.

By default, each record is requested and downloaded individually when requested. However, there are three possible modes for delivery of pageable records from the ColdFusion server:

✦ ondemand: This is the default mode, in which each record is downloaded individually when requested. This mode is advantageous in that it enables the fastest download time if only one record is being used at a time. However, if many records are going to be downloaded in a short time frame, this mode can place an unnecessary burden on the server.

✦ page: In this mode, records are downloaded in groups, or pages. If a record within a page that has not yet loaded is requested within ActionScript, the entire page is fetched from the server. This mode enables multiple sequential records to be grouped and downloaded at once, to obviate the need to make individual requests to the server for each record. This is advantageous if you intend to work with or display multiple records at one time.

✦ fetchall: In this mode, the records are downloaded in the background. This can be advantageous if you know you want to download the entire record set from the server but want to have an initial number of records made available while the rest are downloading.

Note   Remember that by default, if a RecordSet is not made pageable, the RecordSet object is not available until all the records have been downloaded. Therefore, although a non-pageable RecordSet object and one in which the mode is set to fetchall may seem similar, there is a difference: The initial records of the latter are available while the rest of the RecordSet is being downloaded.

The mode of a RecordSet object can be set by using the setDeliveryMode() method. The delivery mode can be modified as often as you want once the object has been returned to Flash. When a RecordSet object is first returned to Flash, the mode defaults to ondemand.

Therefore, if you want the mode to be ondemand, you need do nothing. However, if you subsequently change the mode to page or fetchall and want to change the mode *back* to ondemand, you can do so with the following line of code (where rs is the RecordSet object):

```
rs.setDeliveryMode("ondemand");
```

When the delivery mode is set to ondemand, no other parameters are required.

Setting the delivery mode to page can be as simple as the following:

```
rs.setDeliveryMode("page");
```

When no page size is specified, the default value of 25 is used. If you want to retrieve pages of sizes *other* than 25, you can do so by specifying the desired page size as the second, optional parameter. For example, in the following line of code, the page size is set to 10:

```
rs.setDeliveryMode("page", 10);
```

Another additional option is available when the delivery mode is set to page. By default, only one page of records is downloaded at a time. However, you can also specify a number of pages to *prefetch*. This means that when a page of records is fetched from the server, an additional number of pages of records can also be prefetched such that there is always a buffer of pages already downloaded or downloading. The number of prefetch pages can be specified as the third, optional parameter when the delivery mode is set to page. In the following example, the number of prefetch pages is set to 5:

```
rs.setDeliveryMode("page", 10, 5);
```

In this example, if a requested record has not yet been downloaded, then that page of 10 records is fetched along with 5 additional pages of records. If a record is then requested from the next page of records, although the record will already have been fetched, yet another page of records will be fetched from the server to maintain the 5-page buffer of prefetched records.

Finally, you can also set the delivery mode of a RecordSet object to fetchall by simply calling the setDeliveryMode() method with a single parameter of fetchall. For example:

```
rs.setDeliveryMode("fetchall");
```

As soon as this is done, the remaining records will be fetched from the server, 25 at a time. You can, however, specify a page size value in an optional, second parameter if you want to fetch the records in groups of more or less than 25. For example, you can set the page size to 10 with the following code:

```
rs.setDeliveryMode("fetchall", 10);
```

Watching for Updates

Chapter 4 describes adding watchers to RecordSet objects using the addView() method. You use watchers to determine when RecordSet objects were updated by being sorted or by having records modified using setField(), addItem(), addItemAt(), removeItemAt(), and removeAll(). Using this same technique, you can also monitor when records are being fetched and when records have been downloaded for pageable RecordSet objects.

Note As a brief reminder, the addView() method is invoked from a RecordSet object and passed an object that will serve as the watcher.

You must then define a modelChanged() method for the watcher object. This method is automatically invoked when any of the possible RecordSet object events are triggered. The method is passed a parameter that indicates which event occurred.

When checking on updates with pageable RecordSet objects, note that three events are of primary importance:

✦ fetchRows: This event occurs when records have been requested from the server.

✦ updateRows: This event occurs when any records are updated. New records being downloaded constitutes an update.

✦ allRows: This event occurs when all the records have been downloaded for a RecordSet object.

The allRows event does not provide any additional information. However, both the fetchRows and the updateRows events provide information in the form of firstRow and lastRow properties, indicating the first and last rows that are being fetched or which have been updated. Here is an example of a watcher object that uses a trace() action to display information in the output window when the RecordSet object it is watching encounters one of these three events:

```
watcher = new Object();
watcher.modelChanged = function(info){
  if(info.event == "fetchRows"){
    trace("fetching rows " + info.firstRow + " - " + info.lastRow);
  }
  else if(info.event == "updateRows"){
    trace("rows " + info.firstRow + " - " + info.lastRow + " updated";
  }
  else if(info.event == "allRows"){
    trace("the entire record set is downloaded");
  }
}
```

Checking RecordSet Status

When you are working with pageable RecordSet objects, keep in mind that records fully downloaded can be used, but those that have not yet been fully received cannot be used. Although a record is fetched (meaning the retrieval process has begun) when it is requested in ActionScript, it will not be available immediately. Therefore, you need techniques for determining whether a record is downloaded.

Several additional methods of the RecordSet object apply when working with pageable objects. These methods are used to determine how many records have been downloaded:

✦ getNumberAvailable()

✦ isFullyPopulated()

✦ isLocal()

The `getLength()` method of a `RecordSet` object always indicates the total number of records in the fully populated object, whether or not all the records have been downloaded. Therefore, if a `RecordSet` object has 1,000 records in total, even if only one has been downloaded, the `getLength()` method will always return 1,000. Therefore, the `getLength()` method is of little benefit when trying to determine how many records have been downloaded from the server. The `getNumberAvailable()` method, in contrast, always returns the number of downloaded records. Therefore, if 10 records have been downloaded, the `getNumberAvailable()` method will return 10. Once all the records have been downloaded, the values returned by both `getLength()` and `getNumberAvailable()` will be equal.

The `isFullyPopulated()` and `isLocal()` methods essentially provide the same information. In all cases, each method will return the same value as the other. Each method returns a Boolean value indicating whether the `RecordSet` object from which the method was invoked has downloaded all the records. These methods can both be of some use because they help to determine if certain operations can be performed. As long as all the records of a `RecordSet` object have yet to be downloaded, the following methods cannot be performed on that object:

- ✦ `addItem()`
- ✦ `addItemAt()`
- ✦ `replaceItemAt()`
- ✦ `setField()`
- ✦ `removeItemAt()`
- ✦ `removeAll()`
- ✦ `filter()`
- ✦ `sort()`
- ✦ `sortItemsBy()`

Viewing Results One Page at a Time

In this exercise, you will explore pageable record sets by creating a ColdFusion Flash Remoting application in which records are browsed one page at a time. The records are downloaded to the Flash movie when they are needed, and not before.

1. In your ColdFusion webroot, create a new directory named `chapter10`.

2. Open a new ColdFusion Component document in your favorite ColdFusion editor and place in it the following code. This CFC function will create a pageable record set that can be returned to a Flash movie when called.

```
<cfcomponent>
  <cffunction name="getUsers" access="remote" returntype="query">
    <!-- this function takes one parameter - the initial page size --
>
    <cfargument name="pagesize" type="numeric" required="true">
    <cfscript>
  // names is an array with 18 names in it that will be
  // used to randomly populate a Query object. feel free
```

```
    // to use as many or as few elements in the array as you
    // want and to use any names you wish.
    names = ArrayNew(1);
      names[1] = "Arun";
      names[2] = "Tania";
      names[3] = "Elsie";
      names[4] = "Teresa";
      names[5] = "Jane";
      names[6] = "Matt";
      names[7] = "Sindhu";
      names[8] = "Joey";
      names[9] = "Robert";
      names[10] = "Snow";
      names[11] = "Simon";
      names[12] = "Carolyn";
      names[13] = "Jerry";
      names[14] = "Laura";
      names[15] = "Ryan";
      names[16] = "Peter";
      names[17] = "Jen";
      names[18] = "Michael";

    // the roles array will be used to
    // randomly populate the Query object
      roles = ArrayNew(1);
      roles[1] = "Guest";
      roles[2] = "User";
      roles[3] = "Admin";

    // create a new Query object with 5 columns
      q = QueryNew("USER_ID, USERNAME, PASSWORD, NAME, ROLE");
    // add 1000 records to the Query object
      r1 = QueryAddRow(q, 1000);
    // loop through each record of the Query object
    // and populate it
      for(i = 1; i LTE 1000; i = i + 1){
      rndmName = RandRange(1, ArrayLen(names));
      rndmRole = RandRange(1,ArrayLen(roles));
        QuerySetCell(q, "USER_ID", i, i);
        QuerySetCell(q, "USERNAME", "username" & i, i);
        QuerySetCell(q, "PASSWORD", "password" & i, i);
      QuerySetCell(q, "NAME", names[rndmName], i);
      QuerySetCell(q, "ROLE", roles[rndmRole], i);
      }
    // assign to the FLASH.pagesize variable
    // the value passed to the function from Flash
      FLASH.pagesize = pagesize;
    // return the Query object
      return q;
      </cfscript>
    </cffunction>
</cfcomponent>
```

3. Save the document as User.cfc in the chapter10 directory you created.

4. Open a new Flash document and save it as getPageableUsers.fla.

5. Rename the default layer to form. Create a new layer and name it actions.

6. On the form layer, add an instance of the ScrollPane component. Name the instance sp. Don't worry about positioning it correctly; you'll do that with ActionScript.

7. Open the Buttons library (Window⇨Common Libraries⇨Buttons). From the Circle Buttons folder, drag an instance of "circle button - next" and "circle button - previous" onto the stage on the form layer. Position both buttons near the top of the stage, with the next button on the right and the previous button on the left. Name the instances nextBtn and prevBtn, respectively.

8. On the form layer, create an instance of the ComboBox component and name it pageSizeMenu. Position the instance between the next and previous buttons. Your Flash document should now look similar to what is shown in Figure 10-1.

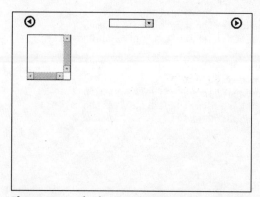

Figure 10-1: The layout of getPageableUsers.fla

9. On the actions layer, add the following code to the first frame:

```
#include "NetServices.as"

// the init() function initializes the movie
function init(){

    // set the page size to 10 to begin with
    _root.pageSize = 10;

    // usersDisplayHolder will be used to contain TextFields
    // that will hold the data from the records.
    _root.createEmptyMovieClip("usersDisplayHolder", 1);

    // these values, the column names of the RecordSet,
    // will also be used as names for the TextField objects
    // for convenience since each TextField object will
```

```
    // represent a column from the RecordSet
    var cn = new Array("USER_ID", "USERNAME", "PASSWORD", "NAME",
"ROLE");
    for(var i = 0; i < cn.length; i++){
      // create the TextField objects
      _root.usersDisplayHolder.createTextField(cn[i], i, 0, 0, 0, 0);
      _root.usersDisplayHolder[cn[i]].autoSize = true;
      _root.usersDisplayHolder[cn[i]].multiline = true;
    }

    // set the ScrollPane size and position
    _root.sp.setSize(550, 300);
    _root.sp._x = 0;
    _root.sp._y = 100;

    // set the values for the page size menu
    var pageSizes = new Array(10, 25, 50, 100);
    _root.pageSizeMenu.setDataProvider(pageSizes);
    // set the change handler for the page size menu
    _root.pageSizeMenu.setChangeHandler("onChangePageSize", _root);

    // create the watcher object for the RecordSet
    _root.usersWatcher = new Object();
    _root.usersWatcher.modelChanged = function(info){
      // when new records are downloaded update the display
      if(info.event == "updateRows"){
        _root.display();
      }
    }

    // create the response object
    _root.res = new Object();
    _root.res.onResult = function(result){
      // when the RecordSet object is returned, set
      // the delivery mode to page with a page size
      // as indicated by pageSize
      result.setDeliveryMode("page", _root.pageSize);
      // make a reference to the RecordSet object
      // on _root where it will be accessible
      _root.users = result;
      // add the watcher object
      _root.users.addView(_root.usersWatcher);
      // initialize the current record value to 0
      _root.curr = 0;
      // display the first records returned
      _root.display();
    }

    // set up the connection object
    var gwUrl = "http://localhost:8500/flashservices/gateway/";
    NetServices.setDefaultGatewayURL(gwUrl);
    _root.conn = NetServices.createGatewayConnection();
```

```
    // create the service object
    _root.srv = _root.conn.getService("chapter10.User");

    // call the getUsers() procedure and pass it
    // a page size for the initial set of records
    _root.srv.getUsers(res, _root.pageSize);

    _root.prevBtn.onRelease = function(){
      // disable the button once clicked until
      // it is enabled again after the display
      // is updated (in display() function)
      _root.prevBtn.enabled = false;
      // set the current record to one page previous
      _root.curr -= _root.pageSize;
      // if the current record is less than 0 (not a valid
      // record) then set the current record to 0
      if(_root.curr < 0){
        _root.curr = 0;
      }
      // update the display
      _root.display();
    }

    _root.nextBtn.onRelease = function(){
      // disable the button once clicked until
      // it is enabled again after the display
      // is updated (in display() function)
      _root.nextBtn.enabled = false;
      // set the current record to the next page
      _root.curr += _root.pageSize;
      // if the current record is greater than the total
      // records then set the current record to the first
      // record of the last page
      if((_root.curr + _root.pageSize) >= _root.users.getLength()){
        _root.curr = _root.users.getLength() - _root.pageSize;
      }
      // update the display
      _root.display();
    }
}


// The display() function takes care of displaying
// the current page of results
function display(){
  // check to make sure if the current number page
  // of records is greater than the number of available
  // records. if so, request the necessary records.
  // otherwise, display, display, display! :)
  if(_root.curr >= _root.users.getNumberAvailable()){
    _root.users.getItemAt(_root.curr);
  }
```

```
      else{
        var cn = _root.users.getColumnNames();
        // clear out any currently-displayed data
        for(var i = 0; i < cn.length; i++){
          _root.usersDisplayHolder[cn[i]].text = "";
        }
        // local variable that will reference
        // the records to save typing
        var r;
        // loop through the number of records to display
        for(var i = 0; i < _root.pageSize; i++){
          r = _root.users.getItemAt(_root.curr + i);
          // for each column in the record add the value
          // to the appropriate TextField (remember, TextField
          // objects have same names as columns in this example
          for(var j = 0; j < cn.length; j++){
            _root.usersDisplayHolder[cn[j]].text += r[cn[j]] + newline;
          }
        }
        // loop through the TextFields and align them
        for(var i = 0; i < cn.length; i++){
          _root.usersDisplayHolder[cn[i]]._x =
_root.usersDisplayHolder[cn[i-1]]._x + _root.usersDisplayHolder[cn[i-
1]]._width + 10;
        }
        // reset the scrollbar to the top
        _root.sp.setScrollPosition(0, 0);
        // update the scroll content of the scrollpane
        // in order to refresh the view
        _root.sp.setScrollContent(_root.usersDisplayHolder);
        // enable the buttons again
        _root.nextBtn.enabled = true;
        _root.prevBtn.enabled = true;
      }
    }

    function onChangePageSize(menu){
      // set the page size to the selected value
      _root.pageSize = menu.getValue();
      // update the page size in the delivery mode
      _root.users.setDeliveryMode("page", _root.pageSize);
      // update display
      _root.display();
    }

    // make sure to call the init() function to get
    // things started!
    init();
```

10. **Test your movie. You should be able to browse back and forth between the records. If you change the page size by selecting a different value from the menu, that change should be reflected in the display of the records.**

Summary

In this chapter, you learned how to work with pageable record sets using ColdFusion and Flash Remoting. Here are a few highlights of what you should have discovered:

✦ Using pageable record sets is a way of ensuring that only manageable amounts of data are downloaded to the Flash application at one time.

✦ By default, all the records in a `RecordSet` object are downloaded at once, but when working with large numbers of records, this can be problematic.

✦ You can create pageable record sets by setting the `FLASH.pagesize` variable in the ColdFusion application.

✦ Once a record set has been made pageable, you can manipulate the ways in which records are downloaded into Flash by using ActionScript.

✦   ✦   ✦

Creating Server-Side ActionScript

◆   ◆   ◆   ◆

In This Chapter

Discovering what
Server-Side ActionScript
(SSAS) is

Generating ASR files to
hold SSAS functionality

Using SSAS to make
HTTP requests

Using SSAS to access
databases

Looking at
undocumented,
powerful uses for SSAS

◆   ◆   ◆   ◆

Server-side ActionScript (SSAS) provides a convenient means for performing server-side actions without having to learn ColdFusion languages (CFML and CFScript) or Java. Instead, using familiar ActionScript syntax and structure, developers can perform database queries and HTTP requests. It sounds like a fantastic idea at first, but that is only the beginning of the SSAS roller coaster ride.

Despite its promise, SSAS does seem to present a couple of limitations:

+ It is available *only* for the ColdFusion MX and JRun 4 versions of Flash Remoting.

+ The functionality (that Macromedia tells you about) is limited to database queries and HTTP requests.

Furthermore, you may find that things you expect to work do not work — even though they involve valid ActionScript code.

As I indicated previously, SSAS can be a bit of a roller coaster ride initially. First it sounds like a great idea. Next, it appears to be rather limited. Then, just when you were about ready to write it off as being a waste of your time, it surprises you. In this chapter, I reveal to you not only the documented features of SSAS, but also undocumented and often powerful features of SSAS. You will also learn why certain seemingly valid code can produce unexpected errors, *and* how to avoid these pitfalls.

Introducing ActionScript on the Server

When you use ColdFusion MX or JRun 4, you can create Flash movies that invoke ActionScript functions that reside on the *server*. This section examines the following:

+ How to author ActionScript on the server

+ Determining the service and remote procedure names

Working with the Server-Side File

ActionScript on the server-side must be stored in an ActionScript Remote (ASR) file. It is simply a text file with the extension `.asr`, which contains function definitions.

When you create the functions within an ASR file, keep in mind that not all of the ActionScript classes are available in SSAS. The following classes *are* accessible:

✦ `Array`

✦ `Boolean`

✦ `Date`

✦ `Function`

✦ `Number`

✦ `Object`

✦ `String`

Note
You can create custom classes in an ASR file, but objects of these types will not be properly returned to Flash. Therefore, if you are working with custom classes in an ASR file, understand that they will be useful only on the server side.

Choosing the Correct Service and Procedure Names

As with any kind of Flash Remoting application development, knowing the correct service and procedure names for the remote procedure is vital. When working with SSAS, the service name is determined by the logical path to the ASR file, including the filename. This means that the ASR file must be placed in a directory that is accessible from a URL. In ColdFusion, this means that the ASR file must exist within the ColdFusion webroot or a subdirectory of the webroot. In JRun, it means that the ASR file must exist within a physical directory (or subdirectory) that maps to a context (a logical path) for a server in the JRun configuration.

The correct service name is the entire logical path to the ASR file and the filename (minus the `.asr` extension), with dots (periods) instead of slashes. Table 11-1 shows some examples of URLs to ASR files and the corresponding ActionScript code to access the service.

Table 11-1: Example SSAS Services

URL	ActionScript Service Object Code
`http://localhost:8500/` `chapter11/asrs/example.asr`	`srv = conn.getService("chapter11.` `asrs.example");`
`http://localhost:8200/chapter11/` `asrs/examples/ssas.asr`	`srv = conn.getService("chapter11.asrs.` `examples.ssas");`
`http://localhost:8200/` `example.asr`	`srv = conn.getService("example");`

The remote procedure name is simply the name of the function contained in the ASR that you wish to call. If you have a function named `myASRFunction()`, call it from the Flash movie in the following manner:

```
// where srv is the service object and res is the response object
srv.myASRFunction(res);
```

Making Your First ASR

In this exercise, you will practice creating an ASR file and calling its functions from a Flash Remoting movie. Its purpose is only to help you understand the basic process, as the function that will be called will not do anything that could not be done within the Flash movie itself. Once you understand how this works, you will learn how to make database queries and HTTP requests.

1. Open a new file in your favorite ActionScript editor. If you use Dreamweaver MX, select the ActionScript Remote option from the Other category (see Figure 11-1).

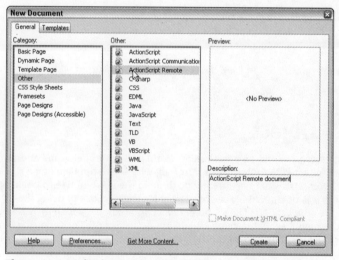

Figure 11-1: Selecting a new ActionScript Remote document in Dreamweaver

2. Save this document as `myFirstASR.asr`.

   • If you are using ColdFusion MX, save the document to a new subdirectory named `asrs` within the Wiley directory in the ColdFusion webroot.

   • If you are using JRun 4, save the document to the JRun samples server `default-ear` directory in a new subdirectory named `asrs`.

3. Create the following function definition in the document and save it:

```
function myASRFunction(val){
  return ("you entered: " + val);
}
```

4. Open a new Flash movie and enter the following code on the first frame of the default layer:

```
#include "NetServices.as"

// if you are using CF keep this URL.
// if you are using JRun, substitute 8200 for the port number
gwURL = "http://localhost:8500/flashservices/gateway/";
NetServices.setDefaultGatewayURL(gwURL);
conn = NetServices.createGatewayConnection();

srv = conn.getService("Wiley.asrs.myFirstASR");

res = new Object();
res.onResult = function(result){
  trace(result);
}
res.onStatus = function(status){
  trace(status.description);
}

srv.myASRFunction(res, "this works!");
```

5. Test your movie. You should see the following in your Output window:

```
you entered: this works!
```

Using the CF Object

Server-side ActionScript would be pointless at best if it did not offer some additional functionality over client-side ActionScript. After all, why waste time making a request to the server only to accomplish what can already be done in the Flash movie to begin with? In fact, however, SSAS (as it is documented) is exclusively for the purpose of using the CF object — an object available only in SSAS. The CF object has two methods, which provide functionality beyond what is normally available using client-side ActionScript. The following two sections examine the CF object and its two methods: http() and query().

> **Note** If you are familiar with CFML, then the http() and query() methods of the SSAS CF object will be somewhat familiar to you. These methods directly correspond to the <cfhttp> and <cfquery> tags, respectively.

Making HTTP Requests

There are several good reasons to use Flash Remoting in order to make HTTP requests:

✦ Flash sandbox security prevents you from requesting documents outside the same subdomain without using Flash Remoting.

✦ Using the SSAS http() method, you can send parameters that mimic query string variables, form-submitted variables, CGI environment variables, and cookies. Furthermore, you can mix and match — sending some of each if required. Client-side ActionScript (meaning ActionScript within the Flash movie itself) allows for query string and form-submitted variables only, and all variables must be of the same type.

✦ Client-side ActionScript does not provide a means for loading non-XML and non–name-value pair data.

The SSAS `http()` method of the `CF` object does not have any of the restrictions of the client-side counterparts. Following are just a few examples of what you can do with the `http()` method:

✦ Retrieve HTML from a local or remote server to display part or all of it within the Flash movie.

✦ Retrieve XML or name-value pair data from a document not in the same subdomain.

✦ Call a CGI script, a ColdFusion page, or another server-side application, and pass it parameters in different scopes (e.g., CGI environment variables, cookies, etc.).

Now that you have an idea of what the `http()` method does, let's look at how to use it.

The `http()` method accepts the following parameters:

✦ `url`: This string value can be the entire URL to the requested resource (e.g., `http://www.remoteserver.com/path/resource.ext`), or it can be just the protocol and server address/domain name (e.g., `http://www.remoteserver.com/`). In the latter case, you may also need to specify values for the path and file parameters (see their descriptions following this list).

✦ `method`: This should be a string value of either `post` or `get`, and it indicates the HTTP method (`GET` or `POST`)to be used for sending any parameters.

✦ `path`: If the `url` parameter did not include the logical path and filename of the resource, then you should indicate the logical path to the resource (not including the filename) as a string value in this parameter (e.g., `/path/`).

✦ `file`: If the `url` parameter did not include the logical path and filename of the resource, then you should indicate the filename as a string value in this parameter (e.g., `resource.ext`).

✦ `username`: If a username is required for the resource, then it should be passed as a parameter.

✦ `password`: If a password is required for the resource, then it should be passed as a parameter.

✦ `resolveurl`: If the data that is being retrieved includes internal, relative links (e.g., `<a href="docs/myDoc.html">`), then setting `resolveurl` to `yes` will resolve these links to absolute references based on the value of the `url` and `path` parameters in the returned value (e.g., `<a href="http://www.remoteserver.com/path/docs/myDoc.html">`). If set to `no`, or if no value is supplied, then the URLs for links are not resolved.

✦ `params`: The `params` parameter contains the values that are sent (if any) to the resource, and it should be in the form of an indexed array of objects with the following properties:

• `name`: The name that will be given to the variable being sent

• `value`: The value that will be given to the variable being sent

• `type`: The `type` property specifies the scope for the variable being sent. The possible values for type are `URL`, `FormField`, `Cookie`, and `CGI`.

The `http()` method expects parameters in one of two formats:

✦ **positional:** This means that you can pass the parameters to the method in an ordered fashion. When you do so, four options are available, depending on how many parameters you wish to pass:

- `CF.http(url);`

- `CF.http(method, url);`

- `CF.http(method, url, username, password);`

- `CF.http(method, url, params, username, password);`

You can see that when you pass positional parameters to the method, there is no option for the `path`, `file`, or `resolveurl` parameters. In order to use these parameters, you must choose the named parameter format as outlined next.

✦ **named:** When you used the named parameter format with the `http()` method, you pass to the method a single object parameter. The object should contain properties which are named to correspond to the parameters that the method accepts. For example:

```
// the value that will be passed to http()
params = new Object();
// the value for the params parameter
httpParams = new Array();
httpParams.push({name:"param1", value:"val1", type:"FormField"});
params.url = "http://www.remoteserver.com/";
params.path = "/path/";
params.file = "resource.ext";
params.method = "post";
params.username = "igoodie";
params.password = "12345";
params.resolveurl = "yes";
params.params = httpParams;
returnedContent = CF.http(params);
```

Tip   You can also pass an object literal to the `http()` method. One way is not better than the other. I simply used the Object constructor and added properties through assignment in the example because I find it easier to see than using object literal notation.

The `http()` method returns an associative array with the following seven properties:

✦ `Header`: The raw response header

✦ `Charset`: The character set used in the returned value (e.g., UTF-8)

✦ `Mimetype`: The mime type of the returned value (e.g., text/html, text/xml, image/gif, etc.)

✦ `Statuscode`: The status code (e.g., 200 OK, 500 Internal Server Error, etc.)

✦ `Responseheader`: The response header, with each key as an element of an associative array. Keys might include Date, Server, Set-Cookie, etc.

✦ `Text`: A Boolean value indicating whether or not the returned value contains text

✦ `FileContent`: The contents of the file returned

However, for reasons described later in the chapter, associative arrays in SSAS cannot be treated like associative arrays in client-side ActionScript. In order to access the elements of the associative array in SSAS, use the `get()` method. For example:

```
returnedContent = CF.http(params);
fc = returnedContent.get("FileContent");
```

On the other hand, if you simply return the entire associative array to the Flash movie, you will be able to treat it like a regular ActionScript associative array.

Querying Data Sources with ActionScript

ActionScript developers frequently want to know how they can query a database using ActionScript. There is no way to do so directly using *client-side* ActionScript. However, with the SSAS `query()` method of the `CF` object, it is possible.

Cross-Reference In order to use the `query()` method, you must assign a DSN to the data source. To do this in ColdFusion MX, see Chapter 6; to do this in JRun 4, see Chapter 12.

The `http()` method accepts the following parameters:

✦ `datasource`: The DSN of the data source as it is registered in ColdFusion MX or JRun 4

✦ `sql`: The SQL statement to execute against the data source

✦ `username`: The username for the database, if any

✦ `password`: The password matching the username given, if any

✦ `maxrows`: A number indicating the maximum number of records to return

✦ `timeout`: A number indicating the number of milliseconds to wait before timing out if no response is given

Like `http()`, the `query()` method accepts parameters in either positional or named formats. If you pass the parameters in positional format, you have four options depending on the number of parameters passed:

✦ `CF.query(datasource, sql);`

✦ `CF.query(datasource, sql, maxrows);`

✦ `CF.query(datasource, sql, username, password);`

✦ `CF.query(datasource, sql, username, password, maxrows);`

If you pass the parameters in named format, then pass them as properties of a single object. For example:

```
params = new Object();
params.datasource = "myDataSource";
params.sql = "SELECT * FROM myTable";
params.username = "igoodie";
params.password = "12345";
params.maxrows = 10;
params.timeout = 10000;
rs = CF.query(params);
```

The `query()` method returns a value that is converted into a `RecordSet` object when it is returned to Flash.

Looking More Closely at SSAS

After working with SSAS for a short time, you will likely discover that in many ways it behaves rather unlike ActionScript after all. To see how this is so, try the following three experiments. For each of the experiments, use the same ASR file—the file named ssasTests.asr saved in the asrs directory that you created in the section "Making Your First ASR."

Each experiment demonstrates a different peculiarity. The explanations for why the experiments do not work as expected appear in the section that follows all the experiments.

Experiment 1: Calling a Simple SSAS Function

In this simple exercise, you create an SSAS function that accepts an object as a parameter and returns a property of the object. It sounds simple enough. Let's see what happens.

1. Define the following function in the ssasTests.asr file and save the document:

```
function getProperty(obj){
  return obj.prop;
}
```

2. Open a new Flash document and place the following code on the first frame of the default layer. This code simply invokes the getProperty() function from the ASR file.

```
#include "NetServices.as"

gwUrl = "http://localhost:8500/flashservices/gateway/";
NetServices.setDefaultGatewayURL(gwUrl);
conn = NetServices.createGatewayConnection();

srv = conn.getService("Wiley.asrs.ssasTests");

res = new Object();
res.onResult = function(result){
  trace(result);
}
res.onStatus = function(status){
  trace(status.description);
}

param = new Object();
param.prop = "does this work?";

srv.getProperty(res, param);
```

3. Test the movie. You should get the following in the Output window:

```
undefined
```

This result is certainly curious; you expect it to return the value does this work?.

4. Modify the SSAS function as shown here and save the document:

```
function getProperty(obj){
  return obj.get("prop");
}
```

5. Test the Flash movie again. Now you should get the expected value.

Experiment 2: Querying a Database with SSAS

In this exercise, you create an SSAS function that performs a simple database query and attempts to return a single value from the returned record set.

This exercise assumes you created the WileyFlashRemoting DSN for the database created in Chapter 4.

1. Define the following function in the `ssasTests.asr` file and save the document:

```
function processQuery(){
  params = new Object();
  params.datasource = "WileyFlashRemoting";
  params.sql = "SELECT * FROM books";
  result = CF.query(params);
  return result.getItemAt(0).TITLE;
}
```

2. Open a new Flash movie and add the following code to the first frame of the default layer:

```
#include "NetServices.as"

gwUrl = "http://localhost:8500/flashservices/gateway/";
NetServices.setDefaultGatewayURL(gwUrl);
conn = NetServices.createGatewayConnection();

srv = conn.getService("Wiley.asrs.ssasTests");

res = new Object();
res.onResult = function(result){
  trace(result);
}
res.onStatus = function(status){
  trace(status.description);
}

srv.processQuery(res);
```

3. Test the movie. In the Output window, you should see the following:

```
Service threw an exception during method invocation: undefined is not
a function.
```

The ActionScript and SQL seem valid, but you still get this unusual error.

4. Modify the SSAS function as follows, save the ASR file, and test the movie again:

```
function processQuery(){
  var params = new Object();
  params.datasource = "WileyFlashRemoting";
  params.sql = "SELECT * FROM books";
  var result = CF.query(params);
  result.first();
  return result.getString("TITLE");
}
```

5. This time the Output window should show the following:

```
Complete Flash Remoting
```

Experiment 3: Performing Array Operations

In this exercise, you create an SSAS function that takes an array as a parameter and returns the array's length to the Flash movie.

1. Define the following function in the ssasTests.asr file and save the document:

```
function getLength(ar){
  return ar.length;
}
```

2. Open a new Flash movie and add the following code to the first frame of the default layer:

```
#include "NetServices.as"

gwUrl = "http://localhost:8500/flashservices/gateway/";
NetServices.setDefaultGatewayURL(gwUrl);
conn = NetServices.createGatewayConnection();

srv = conn.getService("Wiley.asrs.ssasTests");

res = new Object();
res.onResult = function(result){
  trace(result);
}
res.onStatus = function(status){
  trace(status.description);
}

ar = new Array(1,2,3);
srv.getLength(res, ar);
```

3. Test the movie. In the Output window, you should see the following:

```
undefined
```

Again, the ActionScript and SQL seem valid, but you still get this unusual error.

4. Modify the SSAS function as follows, save the ASR file, and test the movie again:

```
function getLength(ar){
  return ar.size();
}
```

5. This time the Output window should show the following:

```
3
```

Understanding the Foundations of SSAS

If you have Java programming experience, you may recognize what is happening with SSAS. Although SSAS *looks* like ActionScript and even acts like ActionScript in some ways, truth be told, it is really Java!

Caution

This is not documented — and, consequently, not supported — by Macromedia. Therefore, in future releases of Flash Remoting, server-side ActionScript might not continue to support Java functionality. It is recommended, therefore, that you not develop any critical applications that depend upon this kind of functionality. However, with that said, it seems highly unlikely that the Java functionality will actually disappear. The risk is yours to take, but it is likely not a very large risk.

The implications of this Java functionality are relatively far-reaching — about as far-reaching as Java itself. In other words, if Java can do it, you can probably do it within SSAS functions. The benefits are clear: You don't have to compile your code, and you have the added flexibility and convenience of ActionScript.

Understanding Converted Data Types

Before delving further into what extended, undocumented functionality is available in SSAS, let's first take a closer look at the data types you're most likely to use when working with the documented functionality.

Primitive data types (string, number, Boolean) can be processed in SSAS just like primitive data types in client-side ActionScript. Additionally, you can create new objects using constructors within SSAS functions (using the accessible classes listed at the beginning of this chapter) and still work with them using familiar ActionScript properties and methods. However, when you *pass objects as parameters* to a SSAS function, they are converted to Java data types. Table 11-2 summarizes these conversions.

Table 11-2: ActionScript-to-SSAS Java Data Type Conversions

ActionScript Data Type	SSAS Java Data Type
Array	java.util.ArrayList
Date	java.util.Date
Object	flashgateway.io.ASObject (Implements java.util.Map)

These conversions are the reason why experiments 1 and 3 did not initially work as you might have expected. In experiment 1, you passed an `Object` object as a parameter to an SSAS function. Because the object is converted to an `ASObject` object in SSAS, you have to use the `get()` method of that class in order to access its properties. In experiment 3, you passed the SSAS function an `Array` object, but because it is converted into an `ArrayList` object, you must use the `size()` method to retrieve the number of elements.

Tip

You can learn more about the methods of most of the Java classes mentioned in this chapter on Sun's Web site at the following URLs:

`http://java.sun.com/j2se/1.3/docs/api/` (standard edition classes and interfaces, includes `ArrayList`, `Date`, and `Map`)

`http://java.sun.com/j2ee/sdk_1.3/techdocs/api/` (enterprise edition classes and interfaces; includes `RowSet`)

Processing Record Sets in SSAS

In experiment 3, you tried to access a value from a `RecordSet` object returned from a `query()` method call. However, when you tried to do this using `RecordSet` methods, it didn't work. That's because in SSAS, returned record sets are actually of type `coldfusion.sql.Queryable`, a class that implements `javax.sql.RowSet`. Knowing this, however, it is possible to look up the methods of the `RowSet` class (such as `first()` and `getString()`) and use them within the SSAS function.

Discovering the ActionScript-to-SSAS Java Conversions

You may be wondering how I was able to convert data types from ActionScript to SSAS. It is a relatively simple process, so I will explain it briefly here.

The first thing to do is create the SSAS functions used in this discovery process. I created five of them in my approach. I begin with one function, to which I can pass an object either from Flash or from another SSAS function, and have it return that object's class information. That function, in turn, calls two others—one to return all of the interfaces the class implements and another to return the hierarchy of superclasses. I also create two more functions specifically for discovering information about the types of values returned by `http()` and `query()`. Each of these functions calls the respective method (`http()` or `query()`) and passes the returned object to the class discovery function (the first function mentioned).

Each of these functions relies on some methods of the Java `Object` and `Class` classes. All Java classes inherit from the `Object` class. In addition, the `Object` class has a method, `getClass()`, which returns a `Class` object that describes the class to which the object belongs. Here are the function definitions:

```
function getClassInfo(obj){
   var cls = obj.getClass();
   if (cls == undefined)
     return "Not an SSAS object";
```

```
    else{
      var txt = "Class Name: " + cls.getName();
      txt += getInterfaces(cls, "");
      txt += getHierarchy(cls, 0);
      return txt;
    }
}

function getInterfaces(cls, indent){
  var txt = "";
  var ntrfc = cls.getInterfaces();
  for(i in ntrfc){
    txt += "\n" + indent + " -- Implements: " + ntrfc[i];
  }
  return txt;
}

function getHierarchy(sbcls, counter){
  var indent = "";
  for(var i = 0; i < counter; i++){
    indent += "  ";
  }
  var cls = sbcls.getSuperclass();
  if (cls == undefined)
    return "";
  else{
    var txt = "\n" + indent + " ** Extends: " + cls.getName();
    txt += getInterfaces(cls, indent + "  ");
    if(counter < 4)
      txt += getHierarchy(cls, ++counter);
    return txt;
  }
}

function getHttpInfo(){
  var result = CF.http("http://www.person13.com");
  return getClassInfo(result);
}

function getQueryInfo(){
  var params = new Object();
  params.datasource = "WileyFlashRemoting";
  params.sql = "SELECT * FROM books";
  var result = CF.query(params);
  return getClassInfo(result);
}
```

Continued

Continued

In the Flash document, I then set up the connection object and service object for the ASR, and then call the SSAS functions as follows:

```
res = new Object();
res.onResult = function(result){
  trace(result);
}

srv.getClassInfo(res, new Array());
srv.getClassInfo(res, new Date());
srv.getClassInfo(res, new Object());
srv.getClassInfo(res, new Function());
srv.getQueryInfo(res);
srv.getHttpInfo(res);
```

When I run the movie, I get the following in the Output window:

```
Class Name: java.util.ArrayList
 -- Implements: interface java.util.List
 -- Implements: interface java.lang.Cloneable
 -- Implements: interface java.io.Serializable
 ** Extends: java.util.AbstractList
   -- Implements: interface java.util.List
   ** Extends: java.util.AbstractCollection
     -- Implements: interface java.util.Collection
     ** Extends: java.lang.Object
Class Name: java.util.Date
 -- Implements: interface java.io.Serializable
 -- Implements: interface java.lang.Cloneable
 -- Implements: interface java.lang.Comparable
 ** Extends: java.lang.Object
Class Name: flashgateway.io.ASObject
 ** Extends: flashgateway.util.CaseInsensitiveMap
   ** Extends: java.util.HashMap
     -- Implements: interface java.util.Map
     -- Implements: interface java.lang.Cloneable
     -- Implements: interface java.io.Serializable
     ** Extends: java.util.AbstractMap
       -- Implements: interface java.util.Map
       ** Extends: java.lang.Object
Class Name: flashgateway.io.ASObject
 ** Extends: flashgateway.util.CaseInsensitiveMap
   ** Extends: java.util.HashMap
     -- Implements: interface java.util.Map
     -- Implements: interface java.lang.Cloneable
     -- Implements: interface java.io.Serializable
     ** Extends: java.util.AbstractMap
       -- Implements: interface java.util.Map
       ** Extends: java.lang.Object
Class Name: coldfusion.sql.QueryTable
 -- Implements: interface javax.sql.RowSet
```

```
    -- Implements: interface coldfusion.wddx.RecordSet
  ** Extends: coldfusion.sql.Table
    ** Extends: coldfusion.sql.imq.imqTable
      -- Implements: interface java.io.Serializable
    ** Extends: java.lang.Object
Class Name: coldfusion.runtime.StructBean
  ** Extends: coldfusion.runtime.Scope
    -- Implements: interface coldfusion.runtime.CloneableMap
  ** Extends: java.util.AbstractMap
    -- Implements: interface java.util.Map
    ** Extends: java.lang.Object
```

Working Directly with Java Classes

Perhaps the most exciting feature of SSAS is that it exposes many classes of the Java API—particularly in the java packages (java.io, java.lang, etc.).

Note

Not all of the Java API is accessible from SSAS. I have tested many of the classes from the java.io, java.lang, java.sql, and java.util packages successfully. However, as I have not tested every class in every package, I cannot guarantee that all the classes are accessible from SSAS.

When you wish to create an object of a particular Java class using SSAS, always use the fully qualified class name. For example, in order to create a Random object in SSAS, you could use the following code:

```
var rndm = new java.util.Random();
```

If you want to retrieve the current server time (as opposed to the client time), you could use the following line of code:

```
java.lang.System.gc();
```

More Advanced SSAS Query and HTTP Requests

Now that you've gotten your feet wet with the basic theory behind "advanced" SSAS, I want to provide you with some potentially useful SSAS functions you can use for your own database queries, as well as HTTP requests.

Let's first examine a more advanced function for performing HTTP requests using the POST method. When you use the POST method, it is expected that you pass at least one parameter to the URL being called. The parameters should be, as you learned, in the form of an array of objects with name, value, and type properties. It makes the most sense in many cases to construct such an array using client-side ActionScript and pass it to the SSAS function. However, using ActionScript-only syntax and constructs, you cannot process this parameter on the server because the object is converted into an ASObject type. However, using Java constructs, it is possible to do this, as shown in the following function:

Continued

Continued

```
function post(url, httpParamsFlash){
  // the params object to be passed to http()
  var params = new Object();
  params.method = "post";
  // the URL passed to the function
  params.url = url;
  // this array will hold the http parameters
  // in the form of objects
  var httpParams = new Array();
  httpParamsAr = httpParamsFlash.toArray();
  var n, t, v, param;
  // loop through the http parameters passed from
  // Flash and populate the new array with them
  for(var i = 0; i < httpParamsAr.length; i++){
    param = httpParamsAr[i].values().toArray();
    n = param[0];
    t = param[1];
    v = param[2];
    httpParams.push({name:n, type:t, value:v});
  }
  params.params = httpParams;
  var result = CF.http(params);
  return result;
}
```

Next, let's look at more advanced functions to perform database queries. As with the previous example function, it is likely much easier to write a function for database queries that takes an object parameter with named properties corresponding to the properties of the object to be passed to the query() method (datasource, sql, etc.). This is easier because in SSAS, a function call will fail if it is not provided the correct number of parameters, and so the alternative is to write several overloaded functions accepting varying numbers of positional parameters. With this in mind, following are two custom functions that accept a single named parameter object and perform the query() method. The doSelect() method returns the record set, while the doNonSelect() function does not.

```
function doSelect(info){
  var dsn = info.get("dsn");
  var sql = info.get("sql");
  var username = info.get("username");
  var password = info.get("password");
  var maxrows = info.get("maxrows");
  var timeout = info.get("timeout");
  var params = new Object();
  params.datasource = dsn;
  params.sql = sql;
  if(username != undefined)
    params.username = username;
  if(password != undefined)
    params.password = password;
  if(maxrows != undefined)
    params.maxrows = maxrows;
```

```
      if(timeout != undefined)
        params.timeout = timeout;
      result = CF.query(params);
      return result;
    }

    function doNonSelect(info){
      var dsn = info.get("dsn");
      var sql = info.get("sql");
      var username = info.get("username");
      var password = info.get("password");
      var timeout = info.get("timeout");
      var params = new Object();
      params.datasource = dsn;
      params.sql = sql;
      if(username != undefined)
        params.username = username;
      if(password != undefined)
        params.password = password;
      if(timeout != undefined)
        params.timeout = timeout;
      result = CF.query(params);
      return result;
    }
```

Getting Servlet Information

SSAS itself is built on a class that implements `java.servlet.Servlet`. This means that servlet information is also available from SSAS. Two objects enable you to work with this information: `request` and `response`. The `request` object implements the `ServletRequest` interface and the `response` object implements the `ServletResponse` interface.

Following is an example of a function that uses the `request` object to return to the Flash movie the client's IP address:

```
    function getClientIP(){
      return request.getRemoteAddr();
    }
```

Using Typed ActionScript Objects

Because your SSAS functions can create `ASObject` objects and return them to Flash, it is possible to create typed objects using the `setType()` method within SSAS. When you do this, the returned object will be of the specified type in the client-side ActionScript, as shown in the following example.

First, let's look at the SSAS:

```
    function makeBunny(obj){
      obj.put("animalType", "bunny rabbit");
      obj.setType("Animal");
      return obj;
    }
```

Note You must use the put() method (inherited from the HashMap class) to set properties on an ASObject in SSAS. View the HashMap API at http://java.sun.com/j2se/1.4.1/docs/api/java/util/HashMap.html.

Next, here is the client-side ActionScript:

```
function Animal(){}
Animal.prototype.animalType = null;
Animal.prototype.speak = function(){
   trace("Hi! I am a " + this.animalType + ".");
}

Object.registerClass("Animal", Animal);

ares = new Object();
ares.onResult = function(result){
   trace(result.speak());
}
ares.onStatus = function(status){
   trace(status.description);
}

// where srv is a service object
srv.makeBunny(ares, new Animal());
```

When this is run, the Output window displays the following:

```
Hi! I am a bunny rabbit.
```

Note that the speak() method can be called for result within the onResult() callback method only, because the returned object is already of type Animal.

Cross-Reference For more information on the ASObject class and typed objects with ColdFusion, see Chapter 8.

Applying Advanced SSAS

In this exercise, you use SSAS to create a simple HTML editor/viewer. The application is very basic, but it illustrates some of SSAS's power.

1. Open a new ASR document for editing and save it to the ColdFusion webroot/Wiley/chapter11/asrs directory as files.asr.

2. Add the following functions to the file and save it:

```
// get the directory listing
function getDirectory(path){
   // get the directory
   var dir = new java.io.File(path);
   // get files from the directory
   var files = dir.listFiles();
   var filesHT = new java.util.Hashtable();
   // loop through all the files and add them to a
   // hashtable (associative array) with the path for
   // the key and the filename alone for the value
```

```
    for(var i = 0; i < files.length; i++){
      filesHT.put(files[i].getAbsolutePath(), files[i].getName());
    }
    // return the hashtable - will be made into
    // an associative array in Flash
    return filesHT;
}

// create a new file
function newFile(fileName, path){
  // make the file object
  var file = new java.io.File(path + fileName);
  // create the file if it doesn't exist
  file.createNewFile();
  var obj = new Object();
  obj.path = file.getAbsolutePath();
  obj.dir = getDirectory(path);
  return obj;
}

// get the contents of a file
function getFile(filePath){
  var file = new java.io.File(filePath);
  // the BufferedReader holds the contents of the file
  var rdr = new java.io.BufferedReader(new java.io.FileReader(file));
  var line = "";
  var txt = "";
  // read a line at a time
  while ((line = rdr.readLine()) != null){
    txt += line + "\n";
  }
  rdr.close();
  // return the contents as a string
  return txt;
}

// save a file
function saveFile(filePath, content){
  var file = new java.io.File(filePath);
  // the BufferedWriter allows to write to a file
  var wrtr = new java.io.BufferedWriter(new
java.io.FileWriter(file));
  wrtr.write(content);
  wrtr.close();
  return "saved";
}
```

3. Create a new directory named **SSASHtml** in your ColdFusion webroot\Wiley\chapter11 directory.

4. Open a new Flash movie and save it as `ssasHtml.fla` in the directory you created in step 3.

5. Rename the default layer to `actions`.

6. Create a new layer and name it `form`.

7. On the `form` layer, add a `ScrollPane` component instance and name it `sp`. It doesn't matter where you position it because you will use ActionScript to do that, but you might want to place it near the upper, left-hand corner just to get a sense of the layout.

8. On the `form` layer, near the bottom of the stage underneath `sp`, create a new, single-line input text field. Turn on the border for the `TextField`, and make it about the same width as the default width for the `ScrollPane`. Name this `TextField newFileName`.

9. Beneath the `newFileName TextField`, also on the `form` layer, add a `PushButton` instance and name it `newFileBtn`.

10. To the right of `sp`, add a new, multiline input `TextField`. Turn on the border for the `TextField` and make it about 300 pixels by 300 pixels (see Figure 11-2). Name the `TextField fileContents`.

11. Create a new `ScrollBar` instance by dragging it onto `fileContents`. This should automatically snap the `ScrollBar` to the `TextField`. Name the new `ScrollBar sb`.

12. Beneath `fileContents`, add two `PushButton` instances. Name them `saveBtn` and `toggleViewBtn`.

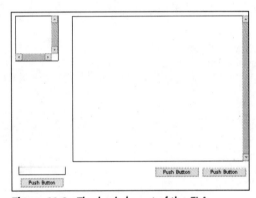

Figure 11-2: The basic layout of the FLA

13. On the first frame of the `actions` layer, add the following code:

```
#include "NetServices.as"

// this function fills the scrollpane with
// buttons that represent an index of the
// current files
function fillIndex(files){
   // creates the scroll content MC, or recreates it,
   // wiping out the old contents
   _root.createEmptyMovieClip("sc", 0);
   var count = 0;
   var mc;
   // loop through the associative array containing
   // the complete path as the key, and the file name
   // as the value
   for(var path in files){
     // create the buttons from the pushbutton symbol in the
```

```
     // library. position them, label them.
     mc = _root.sc.attachMovie("FPushButtonSymbol", "file" + count++,
count, {_y: count * 25});
     mc.setLabel(files[path]);
     // store the complete path to the file to be used
     // when opening the file
     mc.path = path;
     // when the button is pressed, open the file
     mc.onRelease = function(){
       _root.srv.getFile(fileRes, this.path);
       _root.currentFile = this.path;
     }
   }
   _root.sp.setScrollContent(_root.sc);
}

// take care of the scrollpane display
sp.setSize(110, 300);
sp._x = 10;
sp._y = 10;

// position the viewer/editor textfield
fileContents._x = 140;
fileContents._y = 10;

// position the scrollbar and make sure it
// targets fileContents
sb._x = fileContents._x + fileContents._width;
sb._y = 10;
sb.setScrollTarget(fileContents);

// the save button calls the saveFile() SSAS function
saveBtn.setLabel("save");
saveBtn.onRelease = function(){
  if(_root.currentFile != undefined)
    _root.srv.saveFile(saveRes, _root.currentFile,
_root.fileContents.text);
}

// the toggle view button toggles between HTML and text
toggleViewBtn.setLabel("toggle view");
toggleViewBtn.onRelease = function(){
  // if currently in text mode, save any edits to the
  // _root.contents variable, to retain those changes
  if(!_root.fileContents.html)
    _root.contents = _root.fileContents.text;
  // toggle the html mode of fileContents
  _root.fileContents.html = !_root.fileContents.html;
  isHtml = _root.fileContents.html;
  // disallow saving when in HTML mode
  _root.saveBtn.enabled = !isHtml;
  // if switched to HTML then set the htmlText and
  // make it not selectable. if switched to text mode
  // then do the opposite.
```

```
    if(isHtml){
      _root.fileContents.text = "";
      _root.fileContents.htmlText = _root.contents;
      _root.fileContents.selectable = false;
    }
    else{
      _root.fileContents.htmlText = "";
      _root.fileContents.text = _root.contents;
      _root.fileContents.selectable = true;
    }
}


// the new file button calls the newFile() SSAS function
newFileBtn.setLabel("new file");
newFileBtn.onRelease = function(){
  var name = _root.newFileName.text;
  if(name != ""){
    _root.srv.newFile(newRes, name, _root.path);
    _root.newFileName.text = "";
  }
}


// set up all the response objects

dirRes = new Object();
dirRes.onResult = function(result){
  _root.fillIndex(result);
}
dirRes.onStatus = function(status){
  trace(status.description);
}

fileRes = new Object();
fileRes.onResult = function(result){
  _root.fileContents.html = false;
  _root.contents = result;
  _root.fileContents.text = result;
}
fileRes.onStatus = function(status){
  trace(status.description);
}

saveRes = new Object();
saveRes.onResult = function(result){}
saveRes.onStatus = function(status){
  trace(status.description);
}

newRes = new Object();
newRes.onResult = function(result){
  dirRes.onResult(result.dir);
  _root.currentFile = result.path;
}
```

```
newRes.onStatus = function(status){
  trace(status.description);
}

function init(){
  var gwUrl = "http://localhost:8500/flashservices/gateway/";
  NetServices.setDefaultGatewayURL(gwUrl);
  var conn = NetServices.createGatewayConnection();

  _root.srv = conn.getService("Wiley.chapter11.asrs.files");
  // the path should point to the correct directory on your
  // computer. Make sure that you use double backslashes.
  _root.path =
"C:\\CFusionMX\\wwwroot\\Wiley\\chapter11\\SSASHtml\\";
  _root.srv.getDirectory(_root.dirRes, _root.path);
}

init();
```

14. Save and test the movie. At first, you probably will not have any files in the directory to edit, so you will need to create a new file. Enter a filename in the `newFileName` field and click the new file button. The file will be created, added to the index, and automatically opened for editing. Add text to the `fileContents` field and save the file. Add more files. Save, edit, and toggle between HTML and text views. Have fun.

Summary

In this chapter, you learned about server-side ActionScript, or SSAS. You learned not only about the documented methods, but also about the structure of SSAS and how to leverage it for additional and more powerful uses. Some of the key points discussed included the following:

✦ SSAS is stored in ASR files (`.asr`) in a Web-accessible directory on the server.

✦ SSAS recognizes only a subset of client-side ActionScript classes but also introduces the `CF` object with the `query()` and `http()` methods.

✦ The `query()` method enables database access using ActionScript syntax.

✦ The `http()` method enables HTTP requests to be made using ActionScript syntax.

✦ When working with SSAS, you may notice that it does not operate exactly like client-side ActionScript. A little investigation reveals that this is because SSAS is actually a wrapper for Java. As such, you can take advantage of Java functionality from within SSAS.

✦   ✦   ✦

Flash Remoting with J2EE Application Servers

Understanding Flash Remoting with J2EE

The Java 2 Platform, Enterprise Edition (J2EE), is the basis for many important technologies, including servlets, JavaServer Pages, and Enterprise JavaBeans. Flash Remoting for J2EE (including JRun) simplifies and enables the integration of your Java applications with Flash user interfaces. In this chapter you can explore the steps necessary for getting started with Flash Remoting for J2EE.

Getting Started with a J2EE Server

Flash Remoting for use with Java comes in two flavors — JRun 4 and non–JRun 4. Flash Remoting for JRun 4 comes automatically bundled with JRun 4, so no separate download or purchase is necessary. However, because Macromedia has endeavored to make Flash Remoting an open technology, there is a separate installation available that works with other J2EE application servers. Therefore, if you already use your preferred J2EE application server, Flash Remoting is also available for you.

 **Note**   Macromedia describes Flash Remoting as an open technology. This does not mean it is open source, but rather that Flash Remoting is available for many platforms (and not tied to one specific server).

Installing JRun

JRun is Macromedia's enterprise-level Java application server. If you wish to learn more about the product and/or download a 30-day trial, you can view the Macromedia JRun Web page at http://www.macromedia.com/software/jrun/.

Note   JRun has been bundled with Flash Remoting since version 4.

Installing JRun entails running a wizard that prompts you for any necessary information. JRun is supported for Windows and several Unix/Linux flavors. You may also be able to install JRun on Mac OS X, though it is not officially supported.

Choosing and Installing Another J2EE Server

If you already work with a non-JRun J2EE server, then you do not need to change it. If you do not already work with a J2EE application server, but you are interested in using something other than JRun, then you pretty much have your pick of available servers. Table 12-1 shows a partial list of some of the more popular J2EE application servers available.

Table 12-1: Non-JRun J2EE Application Servers

Product	URL	What It Does
Apache Jakarta Tomcat[a]	http://jakarta.apache.org/	Servlets and JSP
Caucho Resin[b]	http://caucho.com/resin/	Servlets and JSP, EJB (Enterprise edition only)
New Atlanta ServletExec	http://www.newatlanta.com/products/servletexec/	Servlets and JSP
Jetty[a]	http://jetty.mortbay.org/jetty/	Servlets and JSP
JBoss[a]	http://www.jboss.org/	EJB container works with Tomcat or Jetty
BEA WebLogic	http://bea.com/products/weblogic/server/	Servlets and JSP, EJB
IBM WebSphere	http://www.ibm.com/software/info1/websphere/	Servlets and JSP, EJB
Oracle 9i Application Server	http://www.oracle.com/ip/deploy/ias/	Servlets and JSP, EJB
Sybase EAServer	http://www.sybase.com/products/applicationservers/easerver	Servlets/JSP, EJB
HP AS	http://www.hpmiddleware.com/hp-as/	Servlets/JSP, EJB
Borland App Server	http://www.borland.com/bes/appserver/	Servlets/JSP, EJB
Orion	http://www.orionserver.com/	Servlets/JSP, EJB

[a]Denotes open source. Open source products are free to download and use. Generally, open source products are every bit as good as, if not better than, competing commercial products. Open source products do not always have all the graphical interfaces of commercial products and may require more editing of configuration files.

[b]Resin is not an open source product, but it is a reasonably priced, high-quality, high-performance product that is worthy of the many acknowledgments it has received.

When you work with a non-JRun server, aside from installing the application server itself, you also need to install Flash Remoting MX for Java. In order to learn more about this product, you can view the Web page at http://www.macromedia.com/software/flashremoting/.

A free trial version of Flash Remoting MX is available from the Web site as well.

Once you have acquired Flash Remoting MX for Java, run the installation. This creates a Flash Remoting MX directory (on Windows, this is created within the Program Files\Macromedia directory). The only file you need from within the installed directory is flashgateway.jar. You learn how to use this JAR file in the section "Working with Non-JRun J2EE Servers." For now, just locate the file. You can find it in the sample/WEB-INF/lib/ directory or by extracting it from the flashgateway-samples.ear file (and in turn, the archived flashgateway.war file) or the flashgateway-samples.war files.

Creating a Web Application

In order to utilize Flash Remoting, you first need to set up a Web application within your J2EE application server. Of course, you are welcome to do this any way you desire. However, to most easily follow the exercises provided throughout the book, I suggest you follow along with these instructions for creating a Web application for use with the upcoming exercises.

1. If you do not already have a directory on your hard drive named Wiley, create this directory now (i.e., C:\Wiley\).

2. Within the Wiley directory, create a Java directory.

3. Create a new directory named FR-app within the Java directory.

4. Create an app directory within the FR-app directory.

5. Create a WEB-INF directory within the app directory. At this point you should have created a directory structure as follows: Wiley\Java\FR-app\app\WEB-INF. The parent directory names are arbitrary, but the WEB-INF directory is a special name that J2EE application servers use for their Web applications.

6. Within the WEB-INF directory, create a classes directory and a lib directory. As with the name WEB-INF, the names classes and lib are special names that J2EE application servers specifically look for.

7. Within the WEB-INF directory, create a web.xml document, and place within it the following code:

```
<?xml version="1.0" encoding="UTF-8"?>
<!DOCTYPE web-app PUBLIC "-//Sun Microsystems, Inc.//DTD Web
Application 2.2//EN" "http://java.sun.com/j2ee/dtds/web-app_2_2.dtd">
<web-app>
  <display-name>My First Application</display-name>
</web-app>
```

8. If you are using JRun 4, then add a new server by following these steps (otherwise, skip to step 9):

   a. Open the JRun Management Console (JMC) and log in.

   b. Click on Create New Server (see Figure 12-1).

Figure 12-1: Clicking Create New Server

    c. A new window will appear with a form in it (see Figure 12-2). Enter Wiley for the name and C:\Wiley\Java (or the correct path to the Wiley/Java directory on your computer) for the server directory, and click Create Server.

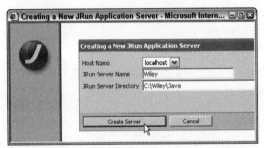

Figure 12-2: Adding new server information in JRun

    d. The next screen displays some automatically generated port numbers. Note the Web port value that is generated, as this is the port you will use to connect to the server. If you have not installed any other JRun servers, then the value will likely be 8101. Click Finish.

Note You can input a port number other than the generated value if you wish. Alternative values are not suggested here because they could potentially conflict with other programs running on your computer. The auto-generated value should be a value not currently in use on the machine, and therefore should be safe.

    e. On the left portion of the JMC, you will now see a Wiley server link. When you expand that menu, you should find a nested link to a Wiley application. Click on that link (see Figure 12-3).

    f. When you scroll down a bit on the right portion of the JMC, you should see, under the heading Web Applications, a link named My First Application. Click on this link, as shown in Figure 12-4. The name My First Application was read by the JMC from the web.xml file created in step 7.

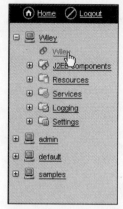

Figure 12-3: Selecting the Wiley application from the JMC

> **g.** Within the configuration for My First Application, you will find a form field named Context Path (see Figure 12-5). In this field, type **/Wiley**. This ensures that a URL such as `http://localhost:8101/Wiley` will now correspond to the Web application you have defined.
>
> **h.** Click the Apply button (not shown in the figure) at the bottom of the form.

9. If you are using a non-JRun server, configure it so that the Wiley\Java\FR-app\app directory you created maps to the context /Wiley. Following are two examples for Tomcat and Resin. If you use another server, check the Web site for this book (`www.wiley.com/compbooks/lott`) for more information.

> **a.** If you use Tomcat, configure the server.xml document found under the Tomcat installation's conf directory. Add a `<context>` element as shown in Listing 12-1 (bolded text is the content to be added):

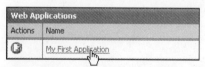

Figure 12-4: Selecting the My First Application link

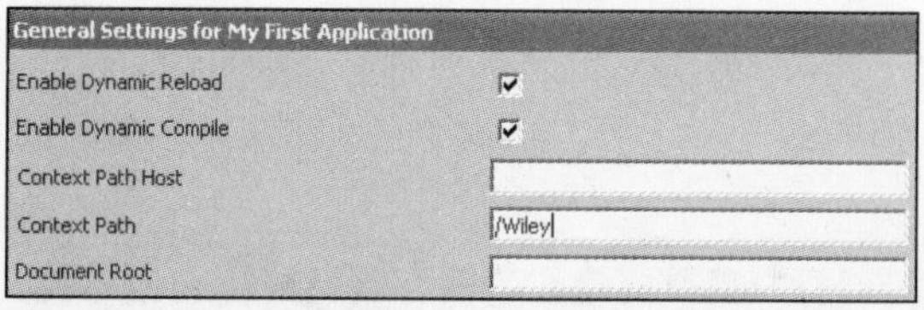

General Settings for My First Application	
Enable Dynamic Reload	☑
Enable Dynamic Compile	☑
Context Path Host	
Context Path	/Wiley
Document Root	

Figure 12-5: Entering the /Wiley context

Listing 12-1: Changes Made to Tomcat's server.xml Document

```
...
<Server port="8005" shutdown="SHUTDOWN" debug="0">
  ...
  <Service name="Tomcat-Standalone">
    ...
    <Engine name="Standalone" defaultHost="localhost"
     debug="0">
      ...
      <Host name="localhost" debug="0" appBase="webapps"
       unpackWARs="true" autoDeploy="true">
        ...
        <Context path="/Wiley"
         docBase="C:\Wiley\Java\FR-app\app\"
         debug="0"
         reloadable="true"
         crossContext="true" />
        ...
      </Host>
      ...
    </Engine>
    ...
  </Service>
  ...
</Server>
```

   b. If you are using Resin, edit the resin.conf document found in the Resin installation's conf directory. Add a <web-app> element as shown here (text that appears in bold is the content to be added):

```
...
<caucho.com>
...
<http-server>
  ...
  <host id=''>
    ...
    <web-app id='/Wiley'
     app-dir='D:\Wiley\Java\FR-app\app' />
    ...
  </host>
  ...
</http-server>
</caucho.com>
```

Installing Flash Remoting for an Application

When you have installed an application server and have successfully set up a Web application, the next step is to install the Flash Remoting gateway for each application.

Configuring JRun 4

If you use JRun 4, then your JRun servers automatically are configured to include the Flash Remoting gateway. However, I strongly encourage you to follow the instructions set forth in this section to modify the way in which JRun uses Flash Remoting. The reason is that JRun uses an EAR file by default, which can cause problems when you wish to do some things, such as use ASObject objects in your Java code. Therefore, I recommend you do the following instead:

1. Delete the deployed Flash Remoting EAR within the JRun server that is to be used. In this case, delete it from the Wiley server. You can do this from the JMC. Select the Wiley server from the menu to the left. Then, under Enterprise Applications, click the delete button, as shown in Figure 12-6.

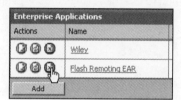

Figure 12-6: Deleting the Flash Remoting EAR

2. Open the lib directory within the JRun installation on your computer (on Windows, this is C:\JRun4\lib\ by default), and unzip the flashgateway.ear file. You can use any zip utility for this, such as WinZip.

3. Extract gateway-webapp.war from the EAR.

4. Unzip gateway-webapp.war.

5. Extract flashgateway.jar, and save it to the Web application's WEB-INF/lib directory. (You may also want to copy it to a location for easy access if you are going to use it with future Web applications.)

6. Open the Web application's web.xml file (in the WEB-INF directory), and add the following code (in bold), which maps the gateway (which is a servlet) to the context /gateway:

```
<?xml version="1.0" encoding="UTF-8"?>
<!DOCTYPE web-app PUBLIC "-//Sun Microsystems, Inc.//DTD Web
Application 2.2//EN" "http://java.sun.com/j2ee/dtds/web-app_2_2.dtd">
<web-app>
  <display-name>My First Application</display-name>
  <servlet>
    <servlet-name>FlashGatewayServlet</servlet-name>
    <servlet-class>
      flashgateway.controller.GatewayServlet
    </servlet-class>
    <init-param>
      <param-name>LOG_LEVEL</param-name>
      <param-value>Error</param-value>
    </init-param>
    <init-param>
      <param-name>DISABLE_JAVA_ADAPTERS</param-name>
      <param-value>false</param-value>
```

```
        </init-param>
        <load-on-startup>1</load-on-startup>
    </servlet>
    <servlet-mapping>
        <servlet-name>FlashGatewayServlet</servlet-name>
        <url-pattern>/gateway</url-pattern>
    </servlet-mapping>
</web-app>
```

Cross-Reference   For more information regarding web.xml and <servlet> and <servlet-mapping> elements, see Chapter 13.

Once you have configured a JRun 4 Web application to use the Flash Remoting gateway, you may need to restart the server.

Working with Non-JRun J2EE Servers

If you are working with non-JRun application servers, follow these instructions for installing the Flash Remoting gateway for a Web application.

1. Copy the flashgateway.jar file to the Web application's WEB-INF/lib directory.

2. Follow step 6 from the instructions for configuring JRun 4 in the previous section.

Depending on the application server being used, you may need to restart the server in order for the changes to be picked up.

Using Databases with J2EE

Working with databases is an important part of many applications. Some application servers provide proprietary means of working with databases. For example, JRun provides the ability to create datasources within the JMC. However, because none of these features are standardized across all application servers, this section examines how to use the JDBC API within your Java code to use databases. JDBC is a means of accessing databases when you use Java. When you work with JDBC, you need to follow these steps:

1. Load the driver.

2. Open a connection.

3. Create a statement.

4. Execute the statement.

5. Close the connection.

Note   JDBC is shorthand for Java Database Connectivity.

Loading the Driver

A driver provides a way for software to communicate with a device (such as when you install a new peripheral device on your computer) or, in this case, to a DBMS. It operates as a bridge between your application and the database. The driver that you use should be specific to the database that you use. If you are using MySQL as your database, then you can use the MySQL Connect/J driver discussed in Chapter 4. If you are using another database, then you will need to consult its documentation to determine the correct driver to use. Regardless, the driver that is used must be included in the application's classpath. This usually means placing a JAR file in the WEB-INF/lib directory, or placing the class files in the WEB-INF/classes directory unless the application server has been otherwise configured to globally include the driver across all applications.

In order to load the driver into the application, you want to create a new instance of the class. This can be accomplished with the static method forName(), of the Class class to create a Class object of the driver class, and the newInstance() method to then create the new instance. The forName() method takes a String parameter specifying the fully qualified class for the driver. For example, here is the proper way to load the driver for MySQL in your Java application:

```
Class.forName("com.mysql.jdbc.Driver").newInstance();
```

If you are using a different database, and thus a different driver, then the code remains the same, but the String value passed to forName() should indicate the correct class.

Opening a Connection

The next step in working with databases using JDBC is opening a connection. To create a java.sql.Connection object you should use the java.sql.DriverManager class's static method getConnection(). The getConnection() method takes as a parameter a String value, which specifies the connection string used to connect to your database, and returns a Connection object.

```
java.sql.Connection conn =
java.sql.DriverManager.getConnection(connectionString);
```

Consult the documentation for the driver you use in order to determine the correct connection string. If you use MySQL Connect/J, then your connection string will look something like the following:

```
String connectionString =
"jdbc:mysql://localhost:3306/WileyFlashRemoting";
```

Creating a Statement

After you have created a Connection object, you must create a java.sql.Statement object from which to execute the SQL commands. Creating a Statement object from a Connection object is simply a matter of invoking the Connection object's createStatement() method. The method takes no parameters and returns a Statement object:

```
java.sql.Statement statement = conn.createStatement();
```

Executing a Statement

From a Statement object, you can execute SQL commands on the database using a variety of methods. The two methods that will handle most situations are the executeUpdate() and executeQuery() methods.

The `executeUpdate()` method is useful for any statement that does not require a returned value containing records. For example, `UPDATE` and `DELETE` statements are well suited for use with the `executeUpdate()` method. To use the method, pass it a `String` value containing the SQL statement you wish to execute. For example:

```
statement.executeUpdate("DELETE FROM USERS");
```

The `executeQuery()` method is useful for `SELECT` statements. The `executeQuery()` method takes a String parameter containing the desired SQL statement, and it returns a `java.sql .ResultSet` object containing any records found matching the `SELECT` statement:

```
java.sql.ResultSet rs = statement.executeQuery("SELECT * FROM USERS");
```

Closing the Connection

The last step in working with a database using JDBC is to make sure that you always close the connection. Although Java does provide garbage collection, there is no way of ensuring when unused, opened database connections will be closed by that process. It is much better to call the `close()` method of the `Connection` object when you are done with it:

```
conn.close();
```

Additional information on pooling connections can be found on this book's companion Web site (`www.wiley.com/compbooks/lott`).

Summary

In this chapter, you learned about using Flash Remoting for J2EE application servers. Some of the important points to remember include the following:

✦ Flash Remoting is available for almost any J2EE application server. It comes included with JRun 4, and is available as a separate purchase when used with other application servers.

✦ Flash Remoting for Java consists of a JAR file that should be added to each Web application in which it is used.

✦ JDBC is the way in which most Java applications communicate with databases. You can use the JDBC API following the steps outlined in this chapter.

✦   ✦   ✦

Accessing Servlets and JSPs

In the early days of Web development, programmers relied heavily on CGI (Common Gateway Interface) scripts and programs developed in Perl and C++ to provide server-side functionality in Web pages. However, CGI was never particularly well suited for the kinds of applications that soon became popular. As a result, many competing technologies have arisen, such as ASP (Active Server Pages), ColdFusion, and PHP. Servlets and Java Server Pages (JSP) are the technologies for the Java platform that also belong to the same category as the preceding list. Servlets and JSPs offer many advantages, including the following:

✦ **Enhanced Power:** Servlets and JSPs are Java classes that can leverage the power of the Java API. Additionally, the servlet API offers convenient access to HTTP headers, form data, cookies, etc., making servlet and JSP programming convenient when compared with CGI programming.

✦ **Portability:** Because servlets and JSPs must adhere to a specification, a servlet or JSP developed for one server (such as Tomcat) should port quite effortlessly to any other server implementing the specification (such as JRun or Resin).

✦ **Efficient Performance:** As you will see shortly, once a servlet or JSP is first run, it remains running, and each request runs as a thread instead of a separate process. This makes servlet and JSP performance very efficient.

Using servlets and JSPs with your Flash Remoting applications offers important advantages, including the following:

✦ If you already have an application built using servlets and/or JSPs, you can quite simply leverage the functionality of this application from a Flash movie by adding just a little bit of code to the servlet and JSP sources. In this way, with minimal effort you can have both a Flash and an HTML user interface for your application.

✦ Servlets and JSPs provide convenient access to HTTP header information and other Web-specific data. For example, you can use a servlet to readily retrieve cookie data or server information, and return that to a Flash movie.

Developing Servlets

This section describes how to develop basic servlets so that you are familiar with the concepts used throughout this chapter. Developing servlets involves four basic topics:

✦ Authoring the source code

✦ Compiling the class file

✦ Deploying the servlet

✦ Invoking the servlet

Note   This section of the chapter describes basic servlet creation as it applies to servlets that are invoked from a Web browser (as opposed to being invoked from a Flash movie).

Creating the Servlet Code

A Java servlet can be defined quite simply as a Java class that extends `javax.servlet. HttpServlet` directly or indirectly. When a servlet is requested (from a Web browser or from a Flash Remoting application, for example), a new thread is opened and the servlet's `service()` method is called. The `service()` method is inherited from `HttpServlet`, and it automatically determines the type of request (such as GET or POST), and then calls the appropriate method to handle the type of request. For example, if the request type is GET, then the `doGet()` method is called. If the request type is POST, then the `doPost()` method is called.

Note   Some developers directly override the `service()` method, but in this book I override `doGet()` and/or `doPost()` instead. Additionally, you can use other methods for other types of requests. However, GET and POST are the only two we will look at in this book (because other request types are used infrequently).

The `doGet()` and `doPost()` methods each take two parameters: a `javax.servlet.http. HttpServletRequest` object and a `javax.servlet.http.HttpServletResponse` object. These objects are passed in automatically when the method is called, and they provide the means by which your servlet can interact with its requesting client. In addition, these methods each must throw both a `ServletException` and an `IOException`.

When servlets are used to write HTML output to the Web browser, they need to use a `java.io.PrintWriter` object, which can be obtained from the `HttpServletResponse` object by invoking its `getWriter()` method. Note that you should specify the content type that is returned by calling the `HttpServletResponse` object's `setContentType()` method.

Tip   When you write a servlet for use solely with Flash Remoting, and it will not interact with the Web browser whatsoever, there is no need to specify the content type or to use a `PrintWriter` object to write the output. This discussion covers typical servlets that interact with the Web browser. Later, you will learn how to easily transform these servlets so that they can interact with Flash Remoting movies as well.

Listing 13-1 shows a basic servlet that overrides both the `doGet()` and `doPost()` methods. The example shown here is a typical way to ensure that both GET and POST requests are handled in the same way.

Listing 13-1: **A basic servlet**

```
// package the class
package wiley.chapter13;

// import the packages that are used to avoid having
// to type out the fully-qualified names
import java.io.*;
import javax.servlet.*;
import javax.servlet.http.*;

// the class must extend HttpServlet
public class MyServlet extends HttpServlet{

  // doPost() calls doGet(). This way all GET and POST requests are
  // handled the same way.
  public void doPost(HttpServletRequest request, HttpServletResponse
response) throws ServletException, IOException{
    doGet(request, response);
  }

  public void doGet(HttpServletRequest request, HttpServletResponse
response) throws ServletException, IOException{
    // set the content type to text/html in most cases (though it
    // doesn't have to be, certainly)
    response.setContentType("text/html");
    // get the PrintWriter from the response object
    PrintWriter out = response.getWriter();
    out.println("<html><head><title>My Servlet</title></head>");
    out.println("<body>my servlet</body>");
    out.println("</html>");
  }

}
```

The servlet life cycle has three main parts:

✦ Initialization

✦ Invocation

✦ Termination

Every time the servlet is requested, a new thread is run and the `service()` method is called. However, the very first time that a servlet is requested, it is loaded into the JVM and the `init()` method is called. On the other end, when a servlet is unloaded, the `destroy()` method is called.

The `init()` method has two possible variations. The first one takes no parameters. When your servlet overrides this first variation of the method, it looks something like the following:

```
public void init() throws ServletException{
  // initialization code
}
```

Use the second variation when you want to initialize the servlet with parameters read from the server. This second variation is then passed a `javax.servlet.ServletConfig` parameter. When you override the method using this second variation, you must ensure that you call the `init()` method of the superclass, passing it the `ServletConfig` object. Overriding this variation looks something like the following:

```
public void init(ServletConfig config) throws ServletException{
    super.init(config);
    // initialization code
}
```

As you will learn in the section "Configuring the Application," initialization parameters can be set in the special `web.xml` file of a Web application. These values can then be read in a servlet's `init()` method using the `ServletConfig` object's `getInitParameter()` method. The method takes a string value that indicates the name of the variable to read, as shown here:

```
String myInitParamVal = config.getInitParameter("myInitParam");
```

Note　Using the `destroy()` method is a good way to take care of any tasks that should be performed when the servlet is unloaded, such as closing database connections. However, none of the examples in this chapter utilize the `destroy()` method.

Compiling the Servlet

Once you have created a servlet's source code, you next need to compile the class. Compiling the source code requires that you include the servlet classes in the CLASSPATH. The servlet classes can typically be found in a JAR file in your application server's `lib` directory. Table 13-1 shows some common servers and the name and path to the JAR file containing the needed servlet classes.

Tip　If you use Resin (and possibly some other servers), then you do not need to compile the servlet classes. Resin automatically compiles servlet source code when the servlet is requested, and it will automatically detect when changes have been made to the source code, and recompile the class.

Table 13-1: Application Servers and the Servlet JAR Files

Application Server	Path and Name of JAR File
JRun 4	*JRun Installation*/lib/jrun.jar
WebSphere 4.0.*x*	*WebSphere Installation*/AppServer/lib/j2ee.jar
JBoss 3.0.*x* /Tomcat 4.0.*x*	*JBoss Installation*/catalina/common/lib/servlet.jar
Tomcat 4.1.*x* (standalone)	*Tomcat Installation*/common/lib/servlet.jar
Resin 2.1.*x* (Enterprise Edition)	*Resin Installation*/lib/jsdk23.jar

Tip If you are using an application server other than those shown in Table 13-1, look for a JAR file that contains the `HttpServlet` class. You can view the contents of JAR files using a utility such as WinZip. For Unix you can use the `jar` command with the `-t` flag.

When you have located the JAR file containing the servlet classes, you have a few options:

✦ Include the JAR file in your computer's `CLASSPATH`.

✦ Use the `-classpath` attribute to specify the JAR file when compiling the source code.

Setting CLASSPATH and compiling

If you choose to include the JAR file in your computer's `CLASSPATH`, you can do this either from the command line or by setting it up to be processed automatically by the operating system.

If you use a Windows operating system, you can include the JAR file in the `CLASSPATH` from the command line (on the Windows taskbar, select Start⇨Run..., type **cmd,** and click OK) with the following command:

```
set CLASSPATH = %CLASSPATH%;Drive:\path\jarFileName.jar
```

For example, if you want to include jrun.jar (with a standard JRun 4 installation) in your `CLASSPATH`, you can use the following:

```
set CLASSPATH = %CLASSPATH%;C:\JRun4\lib\jrun.jar
```

When you do this, however, the `CLASSPATH` that you set only has the scope of the session from which it is set. You can test this. Open a command-line window and set the `CLASSPATH` as shown in the preceding line of code. Then execute the following:

```
echo %CLASSPATH%
```

This will display your `CLASSPATH` value. If you had any value already set for `CLASSPATH`, it will appear with `;C:\JRun4\lib\jrun.jar` appended. This is exactly what you would expect. However, if you now open up a second command-line window and execute the `echo %CLASS-PATH%` statement, you will see that the JAR file is *not* included in the `CLASSPATH` for that session.

In order to set the `CLASSPATH` value globally for a Windows NT/2000/XP computer, you can edit the system environment variables. You can accomplish this by following these steps:

1. Open the System control panel. You can access this control panel either from the Control Panel menu/window or by right-clicking My Computer (on the Desktop) and selecting Properties (see Figure 13-1).

2. Once you have the System control panel open, select the Advanced tab.

3. From the Advanced tab section of the panel, select Environment Variables (see Figure 13-2).

4. In the lower portion of the Environment Variables dialogue box is a section labeled System variables (see Figure 13-3). If the CLASSPATH variable already exists in the list, select it and click Edit. Otherwise, click New.

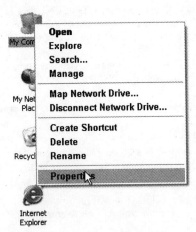

Figure 13-1: Opening the System control panel from My Computer

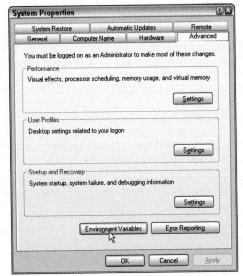

Figure 13-2: Selecting Environment Variables

Figure 13-3: The System variables list

5. In the New/Edit System Variable dialog box (see Figure 13-4), add the path and the name of the JAR file to the Variable value field. If the CLASSPATH variable already has an existing value, append the path and name of the JAR file to the end of the existing value, separating the existing and new parts with a semicolon (;). If you are creating a new variable, set the Variable field to CLASSPATH.

6. Click OK in the New/Edit System Variable dialog box, the Environment Variables dialog box, and the System Properties control panel.

Once you have set the CLASSPATH in this way, it will automatically be set for all sessions.

If you use a Unix-based operating system (including Mac OS X) and you are using csh or tcsh, you can set the CLASSPATH from the command line with the following syntax:

```
setenv $CLASSPATH:path/jarFileName.jar
```

If you want to make this setting a global, automatic setting, simply add the setenv statement to the .cshrc or .tcshrc script your shell uses on startup. You then need to execute the following command for the setting to take effect immediately:

```
source ./.cshrc
```

or

```
source ./.tcshrc
```

If you use another shell (e.g., bash), use the following command from the command line to add a JAR to your CLASSPATH:

```
set CLASSPATH=$CLASSPATH:path/jarFileName.jar
```

Edit System Variable

Variable name: CLASSPATH

Variable value: C:\JRun4\lib\jrun.jar

OK   Cancel

Figure 13-4: The Edit System Variable dialog box

And, if you want to make this setting a global, automatic setting, add the set statement to the shell script (e.g., .bashrc). It is a good idea to also add an export command to make sure the settings are picked up.

```
set CLASSPATH=$CLASSPATH:path/jarFileName.jar
export CLASSPATH
```

And if you want the settings to take place immediately after editing the shell script, run a source command from the command prompt such as

```
source ./.bashrc
```

Once you have set the CLASSPATH using either technique, you can compile your servlet source code into a class by invoking the javac utility program from the command line. To do this, simply change to the directory containing the source code, and run the javac utility, specifying the source you wish to compile, as shown in the following example:

```
javac MyServlet.java
```

When this is done, it creates a class file in the directory with the same name as the source code (for example, MyServlet.class).

Tip   If you have already been working with Java, you presumably have the Java bin directory in your system's PATH. If not, refer to Chapter 12 for a discussion of how to set this up.

Setting the Classpath during compilation

The javac utility also enables you to specify locations of classes need for the compilation of a particular file. To do this, simply add the -classpath attribute to the javac invocation and specify a list of the locations. For example, to compile MyServlet.java using jrun.jar, the javac invocation might look something like the following:

```
javac -classpath C:\JRun4\lib\jrun.jar MyServlet.java
```

Tip   If you want to add multiple paths using the -classpath attribute, simply separate them with commas.

Deploying Servlets

In order for a servlet to be accessible to a client, it must be successfully deployed. This generally involves making sure that the file is in the proper directory and that the Web application is configured so that it will associate a URL with the servlet class.

Copying the servlet classes

As you learned in Chapter 12, Web applications must have a WEB-INF directory, which in turn has both a classes and lib directory. These directories are used to store the classes used by the application—including servlets. The classes directory is used for un-JAR'ed class files, whereas the lib directory is used for storing JARs of class files.

Note   If your class is in a package and you are storing the servlet in the classes directory, you must ensure that the class file is saved within the appropriately named subdirectories corresponding to the package name. Figure 13-5 shows the basic directory structure in which MyServlet (refer to Listing 13-1) might be saved.

Figure 13-5: The MyServlet storage location

Configuring the Application

Once you have copied the class files into the appropriate location within the Web application directory structure, you next need to configure the application so that the servlet class is associated with a particular URL. The standard way of doing this is by way of a special file called web.xml.

The web.xml file should be created in the WEB-INF directory of the Web application. This file is discussed briefly in Chapter 12, so refer to that chapter for more information on the basic structure of the file. Each time you add a new servlet, you want to modify the web.xml file by adding a `<servlet>` element and a `<servlet-mapping>` element.

The `<servlet>` element is a container element that should include at least two child elements: `<servlet-name>` and `<servlet-class>`. The `<servlet-name>` element should have a value designating a unique name (within the application) for the servlet. This name should follow basic naming rules (no spaces; use numbers, letters, and underscores, etc.), but it can be any name that you choose. The `<servlet-class>` element, on the other hand, should contain a very specific value—the fully qualified class name for the servlet. If the servlet is not in a package, the value is simply the class name. If the servlet is in a package, the value should include the package name as well as the class name.

The `<servlet>` element can also contain `<init-param>` elements. These elements enable you to specify variables that can be accessed by a servlet when it is initialized. This is a convenient way to set values that might frequently change or that might vary between development and production environments so that classes don't have to be altered and recompiled when the values change. These values can be accessed using the ServletConfig object's getInitParameter() method, as described in the section "Creating a Servlet." The `<init-param>` element is a container element that should contain at least two child elements: `<param-name>` and `<param-value>`. The `<param-name>` element should have a value that indicates the name of the variable. This is the name that is specified in the getInitParameter() method call within the servlet. The `<param-value>` element should contain the value of the variable. This is the value returned by getInitParameter().

The `<servlet-mapping>` element is used to map a servlet (which must have a corresponding `<servlet>` definition) to a particular URL pattern. The `<servlet-mapping>` element is a container element that should contain at least two child elements: `<servlet-name>` and `<url-pattern>`. The `<servlet-name>` value should correspond to the name given to a servlet within its `<servlet>` definition. The `<url-pattern>` element should have the value of the URL pattern from which the servlet will be invoked. For example, if you want the servlet to be invoked from the URL http://localhost:8880/Wiley/MyServlet, then you would specify a `<url-pattern>` value of /MyServlet.

Note The URL example given above (`http://localhost:8880/Wiley/MyServlet`) assumes that the Web application being discussed is already configured (using `application.xml`) to the context `/Wiley`. (It also uses the port 8880, the default Resin port.) If you have not already configured it thus, see Chapter 12.

Listing 13-2 shows a web.xml file that configures a servlet with a class name of `wiley.chapter13.MyServlet` so that it is accessible from the URL pattern `/MyServlet`.

Listing 13-2: A Basic Servlet Configuration in web.xml

```
<?xml version="1.0" encoding="UTF-8"?>
<!DOCTYPE web-app PUBLIC "-//Sun Microsystems, Inc.//DTD Web
Application 2.2//EN" "http://java.sun.com/j2ee/dtds/web-app_2_2.dtd">
<web-app>
  <display-name>My First Application</display-name>
  <!-- this file should also include the Flash Gateway servlet
configuration as shown in chapter 12 -->
  <servlet>
    <servlet-name>MyServlet</servlet-name>
    <servlet-class>wiley.chapter13.MyServlet</servlet-class>
  </servlet>
  <servlet-mapping>
    <servlet-name>MyServlet</servlet-name>
    <url-pattern>/MyServlet</url-pattern>
  </servlet-mapping>
</web-app>
```

Invoking the Servlet

Once you have correctly configured the servlet, the only thing left to do is invoke it. Later in the chapter (in the section titled "Using Flash Remoting with Servlets and JSPs"), you will examine how to do this using Flash Remoting. For starters, however, let's invoke it from a Web browser—the "standard" way in which servlets are accessed (up to now, at least). In Listing 13-2, the servlet was mapped to the URL pattern /MyServlet. Assuming that this is done within the Web application created in Chapter 12, which is accessible from the /Wiley context, the servlet can be invoked by simply viewing http://localhost:8880/Wiley/MyServlet (or by using the appropriate port number for your application server). You should see something similar to what is shown in Figure 13-6.

Figure 13-6: Viewing MyServlet

Creating a Reporting Servlet

As you should now have the basic tools for creating and working with servlets, you can apply what you have learned by creating a slightly more complex servlet than MyServlet (refer to Listing 13-1). In this exercise, you will create ReportServlet, a servlet that reports the following:

✦ The time at which the servlet was initialized

✦ The time at which the servlet was requested

✦ The number of times the servlet has been accessed since it started running

✦ A message obtained from the web.xml file

✦ Any parameters passed to the servlet

The following steps outline the procedure for creating and using ReportServlet.

1. In the Wiley Web application's `WEB-INF/classes` directory, create a `wiley` directory, and within the `wiley` directory create a `chapter13` directory (if these directories do not already exist). These subdirectories are needed because the `servlet` that you will create will be in the `wiley.chapter13` package.

2. Open a new Java document in your favorite editor (Dreamweaver, JBuilder, Wordpad, vi, etc.), and save it as ReportServlet.java to the `chapter13` directory created in step 1.

3. In the new document, add the code from Listing 13-3 and then save it again.

Listing 13-3: ReportServlet.java Servlet Source Code

```java
package wiley.chapter13;

import java.lang.*;
import java.io.*;
import javax.servlet.*;
import javax.servlet.http.*;
import java.util.*;

public class ReportServlet extends HttpServlet{

  private Date _startTime;
  private long _count;
  private String _message;

  public void init(ServletConfig config) throws ServletException{
    super.init(config);
    // set the start time to the time when the init()
    // method is called
    _startTime = new java.util.Date();
    // initialize the count to 0
    _count = 0;
    // get the message from the web.xml file
```

Continued

Listing 13-3: *(continued)*

```
      _message = config.getInitParameter("message");
  }

  public void doPost(HttpServletRequest request, HttpServletResponse
response) throws ServletException, IOException{
    doGet(request, response);
  }

  public void doGet(HttpServletRequest request, HttpServletResponse
response) throws ServletException, IOException{
    // increment the counter for the number of times accessed
    _count++;
    // get the time that the request is made
    Date now = new java.util.Date();
    response.setContentType("text/html");
    PrintWriter out = response.getWriter();

    // output the HTML
    out.println("<html><head><title>Show Init Time</title></head>");
    out.println("<body>");
    out.println("Servlet first started: " + _startTime + "<br>");
    out.println("Current time: " + now + "<br>");
    out.println("Since started the servlet has been accessed " +
              _count + " times<br>");
    out.println("The message is: " + _message + "<br>");

    // getParameterNames() returns all the names of the parameters
    // passed to the servlet - see the servlet API for more info
    Enumeration paramNames = request.getParameterNames();
    String name;
    String[] values;
    StringBuffer valuesSb;
    while (paramNames.hasMoreElements()){
      valuesSb = new StringBuffer();
      name = (String) paramNames.nextElement();
      out.println(name + ": ");
      values = request.getParameterValues(name);
      for(int i = 0; i < values.length; i++){
        valuesSb.append(values[i]);
        if(i == values.length)
          valuesSb.append(", ");
      }
      out.println(valuesSb.toString() + "<br>");
    }
    out.println("</body></html>");
  }

}
```

4. Compile the class if necessary (Resin does not require this step). From a command line, change to the `chapter13` directory and invoke the javac utility as follows:

```
javac ReportServlet.java
```

Note

This step assumes that you have set the `CLASSPATH` to include the servlet classes. Otherwise, you will need to use the `-classpath` attribute to specify the location of the JAR file containing these classes.

5. Edit the web.xml file found in the Wiley Web application's WEB-INF directory. Listing 13-4 shows the web.xml file contents.

Listing 13-4: **web.xml for the Wiley Application**

```
<?xml version="1.0" encoding="UTF-8"?>
  <!DOCTYPE web-app PUBLIC "-//Sun Microsystems, Inc.//DTD Web
Application 2.2//EN" "http://java.sun.com/j2ee/dtds/web-app_2_2.dtd">
  <web-app>
    <display-name>My First Application</display-name>


    <servlet>
      <servlet-name>FlashGatewayServlet</servlet-name>
      <servlet-class>flashgateway.controller.GatewayServlet</servlet-
class>
      <init-param>
        <param-name>LOG_LEVEL</param-name>
        <param-value>Error</param-value>
      </init-param>
      <init-param>
        <param-name>DISABLE_JAVA_ADAPTERS</param-name>
        <param-value>false</param-value>
      </init-param>
      <load-on-startup>1</load-on-startup>
    </servlet>


    <servlet>
      <servlet-name>ReportServlet</servlet-name>
      <servlet-class>wiley.chapter13.ReportServlet</servlet-class>
      <init-param>
        <param-name>message</param-name>
        <param-value>Welcome to my Servlet</param-value>
      </init-param>
    </servlet>

    <!-- uncomment this section if you are NOT using JRun
    <servlet-mapping>
      <servlet-name>FlashGatewayServlet</servlet-name>
```

Continued

Listing 13-4: *(continued)*

```
    <url-pattern>/gateway</url-pattern>
  </servlet-mapping>
  -->

  <servlet-mapping>
    <servlet-name>ReportServlet</servlet-name>
    <url-pattern>/Report</url-pattern>
  </servlet-mapping>

</web-app>
```

6. If your application server requires that you restart it in order for it to pick up the new configuration, restart the server.

7. From a Web browser, view http://localhost:8880/Wiley/Report (use the correct port number — 8880 is the default number for Resin). Reload/refresh the page and you will see that the start time remains the same, while the request time changes and the count increases. It should look similar to what is shown in Figure 13-7.

Figure 13-7: The ReportServlet viewed in the browser

8. Add a query string to the end of the URL, such as ?param1=myVal1&param2=myVal2, and it should look something like what is shown in Figure 13-8.

Figure 13-8: The ReportServlet with parameters

Note The getParameterNames() method does not retrieve the parameter names in alphabetical order. This is why param2 is listed before param1 in Figure 13-8.

Introducing JavaServer Pages

Servlets are powerful tools for developing Web applications, but when it comes to generating HTML output, they can be a bit cumbersome. This is one of the primary reasons why developers may choose to use JavaServer Pages, or JSPs. A JSP enables the developer to combine the power of Java within a simple markup framework. In fact, JSPs look a lot like HTML pages, but with some additional elements thrown in that allow for server-side processing. This chapter does not go into detail about authoring JSPs. If you want more information about using JSPs, I recommend *JSP: JavaServer Pages* by Barry Burd (Wiley, 2001). All you really need to know for the purposes of this book is that Java code can be placed within code blocks demarcated by <% and %>, and that JSPs automatically provide for you HttpServletRequest and HttpServletResponse objects named request and response. Additionally, the response object's PrintWriter is made available automatically with the name out. For example, Listing 13-5 shows an example of a JSP that uses Java code to output the current time.

Listing 13-5: A Simple JSP (myFirstJsp.jsp)

```
<html>
  <head>
    <title>My First JSP</title>
  </head>
  <body>
    the time is: <%out.println(new java.util.Date());%>
  </body>
</html>
```

Tip You can also use a shortcut notation, rather than use the out.println() syntax. Using <%= and %> to demarcate the output block accomplishes this. For example, <%out.println(new java.util.Date());%> in Listing 13-5 could be replaced by <%=new java.util.Date()%>. Note that no semicolon is used in this shortcut technique.

JSPs should be saved in the Web application *outside* of the WEB-INF directory. For example, myFirstJsp.jsp (refer to Listing 13-5) could be saved in the application root (in the app directory if you followed the instructions in Chapter 12). In this case, the JSP is accessed in the browser at http://localhost:8880/Wiley/myFirstJsp.jsp. If you save the JSP in a subdirectory of the application root, such as a directory named myJsps, then the URL includes that directory name, as in http://localhost:8880/Wiley/myJsps/myFirstJsp.jsp.

Note JSPs actually get translated into servlets by the application server. It is even possible to view the translated servlet source code, though the location of this varies from server to server. Consult your server documentation to locate the directory in which the files are stored.

JSPs do not need to be mapped to a URL pattern as shown. However, you *can* do this if you want; doing so offers additional benefits and flexibility. For instance, the JSP can then be accessed from multiple URLs. The way in which this is accomplished is almost identical to how a servlet is mapped to a URL pattern. In the web.xml file, you need to add an additional <servlet> element for the JSP. Whereas the <servlet> element still contains the <servlet-name> child, it contains a <jsp-file> child element in place of <servlet-class>. For example:

```
<servlet>
  <servlet-name>MyJSP</servlet-name>
  <jsp-file>myFirstJsp.jsp</jsp-file>
</servlet>
```

You then need to add a `<servlet-mapping>` element for the JSP, just as if it were for a regular servlet. For example:

```
<servlet-mapping>
  <servlet-name>MyJSP</servlet-name>
  <url-pattern>/MyJSP</url-pattern>
</servlet-mapping>
```

Viewing Header Data with a JSP

In this exercise, you create a JSP that outputs the header information to the browser, displaying it in a table. You then map the JSP to a URL pattern.

1. Open a new JSP document using your favorite editor (Dreamweaver, Wordpad, vi, etc.), and save it to the Wiley Web application root as showHeaders.jsp.

2. In the new document, add the code shown in Listing 13-6 and save it.

Listing 13-6: **showHeaders.jsp**

```
<html>
<head>
<title>View All Headers</title>
</head>
<body>
Here is all the header information accessible to this JSP:<br>
<table border="1">
  <tr>
    <td><b>Header</b></td>
    <td><b>Value</b></td>
  </tr>
  <%
java.util.Enumeration headers = request.getHeaderNames();
String header, headerValue;
while(headers.hasMoreElements()){
  header = (String) headers.nextElement();
  headerValue = request.getHeader(header);
%>
  <tr>
    <td><%=header%></td>
```

```
      <td><%=headerValue%></td>
    </tr>
    <%
}
%>
</table>
</body>
</html>
```

Tip   For more information on getHeaderNames() and getHeader(), view the servlet API.

3. Open the web.xml file and add the following <servlet> and <servlet-mapping> elements:

```
<servlet>
  <servlet-name>ShowHeaders</servlet-name>
  <jsp-file>showHeaders.jsp</jsp-file>
</servlet>
<servlet-mapping>
  <servlet-name>ShowHeaders</servlet-name>
  <url-pattern>/ShowHeaders</url-pattern>
</servlet-mapping>
```

4. If necessary, restart your application server.

5. In a Web browser, view http://localhost:8880/Wiley/ShowHeaders. (As usual, modify the port number as necessary.) Figure 13-9 shows what this might look like.

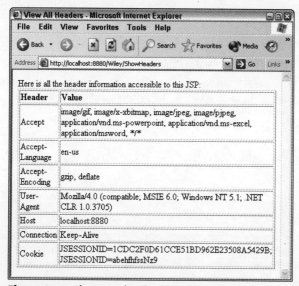

Figure 13-9: showHeaders.jsp viewed in the browser

Using Flash Remoting with Servlets and JSPs

You have now had a glimpse of how servlets and JSPs can be used to generate HTML output. However, our primary purpose in this book is to use servlets and JSPs with Flash movies. Once you have properly set up your Web application to include the Flash gateway JAR, as you did in Chapter 12, accessing servlets and JSPs is quite simple.

Choosing the Service

When you want to use a servlet or a JSP from a Flash movie, the service name should be the context for the Web application. For example, the Wiley Web application created in Chapter 12 has a context of /Wiley; therefore, the service name is Wiley. Table 13-2 shows various contexts and the corresponding service object creation codes.

Note

Remember that contexts are defined within a configuration file for the application server (such as resin.conf for Resin, or server.xml for Tomcat) or by using the administration tool for the application server, such as JRun 4. Refer to Chapter 12 for more information about how to define a context for the Web application.

Table 13-2: Contexts and Corresponding Service Names

Context (defined in application server config)	Service Object Code (ActionScript)
/MyApp	srv = conn.getService("MyApp");
/MyApp/Test	srv = conn.getService("MyApp.Test");
/Test/TestApp/Mine	srv = conn.getService("Test.TestApp.Mine");

Selecting the Procedure Name

The name given to the JSP or servlet within the <servlet> element of the web.xml document is the name by which Flash Remoting is able to call the Java class. For example, if the web.xml file contains a <servlet> element such as

```
<servlet>
  <servlet-name>MyServlet</servlet-name>
  <servlet-class>wiley.chapter13.MyServlet</servlet-class>
</servlet>
```

then the ActionScript code used to call the servlet would look something like the following:

```
srv.MyServlet(res);
```

Flash Remoting disregards any servlet mappings. In other words, if MyServlet is mapped to a URL pattern such as /MyServletMapping, it is not accessible to Flash Remoting by that name. It is accessible *only* by way of the name assigned by the <servlet-name> child of the <servlet> element.

Passing Parameters to a Servlet or JSP

When you pass parameters to a servlet or JSP page from a Flash movie, you should pass an ActionScript object with named properties in the remote procedure call. For example:

```
srv.MyServlet(res, {param1: "val1",  param2: "val2"});
```

You can then access these parameters within the servlet or JSP by way of a request object attribute named FLASH.PARAMS. You can access this attribute using the request object's getAtrribute() method. The method takes a parameter as a String, specifying the name of the attribute to retrieve (FLASH.PARAMS), and returns an Object. Here is the Java code for doing this:

```
Object flashParamsO = request.getAttribute("FLASH.PARAMS");
```

To do anything with the value returned by getAttibute(), you need to properly cast it to List. However, because your servlets and JSPs will likely be used from Web browsers, you want to make this conditional. (Otherwise, an error will occur.) Therefore, you can simply place all the processing of the Flash parameters in an if statement such as the following:

```
if(flashParamsO instanceof List){
   List flashParams = (List) flashParamsO;
   // rest of processing;
}
```

The List itself contains only one element when parameters are passed from Flash. This one element is a flashgateway.io.ASObject. You can get the ASObject by calling the get() method of the List with a parameter of 0. For example:

```
ASObject fp = flashParams.get(0);
```

The ASObject class extends the java.util.HashMap class, which means you can use the methods of the HashMap class to gain access to the parameters (and their values) stored in the ASObject as keys and values. In many cases, you will likely know the names of the parameters being passed to the servlet/JSP. In these cases, you can extract the values using the get() method of the ASObject and pass it the name of the parameter as the key value. The get() method returns the value for the given key, always as an Object. This means that you always need to cast the value to the appropriate type. Listing 13-7 shows an example of an ActionScript snippet that would call a servlet and pass it parameters of different types. Listing 13-8 then shows a Java snippet from the servlet that would receive these parameters and extract their values.

Listing 13-7: **Passing Parameters to a Servlet**

```
params = new Object();
params.myArray = new Array("a", "b", "c");
params.myString = "my string value";
params.myDate = new Date();
// service object named srv, servlet named MyParamsServlet
// response object named res
srv.MyParamsServlet(res, params);
```

Listing 13-8: **Processing Parameters in a Servlet**

```
Object flashParams0 = request.getAttribute("FLASH.PARAMS");
if (flashParams0 instanceof List){
  List flashParams = (List) flashParams0;
  ASObject fp = (ASObject)flashParams.get(0);
  ArrayList al = fp.get("myArray");
  String s = fp.get("myString");
  java.util.Date = fp.get("myDate");
}
```

You may sometimes want to iterate through parameters (passed to the servlet/JSP) whose names you do not know. You can do this using code similar to what is shown in Listing 13-9.

Listing 13-9: **Processing Unknown Parameters**

```
Object flashParams0 = request.getAttribute("FLASH.PARAMS");
if (flashParams0 instanceof List){
  List flashParams = (List) flashParams0;
  ASObject fp = (ASObject)flashParams.get(0);
  Set keys = fp.keySet();
  Iterator iter = keys.iterator();
  String s;
  Object o;
  while(iter.hasNext()){
    s = (String) iter.next();   // name of parameter
    o = fp.get(s);              // value of parameter
    // process parameter here
  }
}
```

Returning a Value to Flash

Servlets and JSPs can return a value to the calling Flash movie as well by way of the request object. Whereas retrieving parameters set from the Flash movie uses the getAttribute() method of the request object, returning a value uses the setAttribute() method of the request object. The attribute that should be set is named FLASH.RESULT. The setAttribute() method takes two parameters. The first is the String value of the name of the attribute to be set (FLASH.RESULT), and the second is the value to be assigned to the attribute. For example:

```
java.util.Date d = new java.util.Date();
request.setAttribute("FLASH.RESULT", d);
```

The method will accept any object as the second parameter, but it must be an object and not a primitive data type. For example, if you want to return an integer value to Flash, you must set the attribute to be an Integer object, and not simply an int. This is easy to do because most wrapper classes such as Integer, Float, Long, etc., have constructors that accept primitive data types as parameters. For example, you could return an integer value to Flash as shown here:

```
int myInt = 6;
request.setAttribute("FLASH.RESULT", new Integer(myInt));
```

Of course, you want to attempt to return only data types that are translatable into ActionScript. For example, although the following code snippet is perfectly allowable in Java, and will not cause any errors, it will not return any meaningful value to Flash because the gateway cannot translate a `java.io.File` object into ActionScript:

```
// this does not cause errors, but it does not return a
// meaningful ActionScript value either
java.io.File f = new java.io.File("C:\");
request.setAttribute("FLASH.RESULT", f);
```

Cross-Reference See Tables 12-2 and 12-3 for translatable data types between Java and ActionScript.

Reporting to Flash

In the section "Creating a Reporting Servlet," you made a servlet that output to the Web browser the following information:

✦ The time at which the servlet was initialized

✦ The time at which the servlet was invoked

✦ The number of times the servlet has been requested since initialization

✦ A message retrieved from the web.xml file

✦ A list of parameters and values passed to the servlet

In this exercise, you utilize the same servlet from Flash and display the results in a `TextField` object.

1. Open the ReportServlet.java file created in the section "Creating a Reporting Servlet." Edit this file so that it can also process requests from Flash movies. Listing 13-10 shows this code, with the changes from Listing 13-3 indicated in bold.

Listing 13-10: ReportServlet.java for Handling Flash Requests

```
package wiley.chapter13;

import java.lang.*;
import java.io.*;
import javax.servlet.*;
import javax.servlet.http.*;
import java.util.*;
import flashgateway.io.*;

public class ReportServlet extends HttpServlet{
```

Continued

Listing 13-10: *(continued)*

```java
private Date _startTime;
private long _count;
private String _message;

public void init(ServletConfig config) throws ServletException{
  super.init(config);
  _startTime = new java.util.Date();
  _count = 0;
  _message = config.getInitParameter("message");
}


public void doPost(HttpServletRequest request, HttpServletResponse
response) throws ServletException, IOException{
  doGet(request, response);
}

public void doGet(HttpServletRequest request, HttpServletResponse
response) throws ServletException, IOException{
  _count++;
  Date now = new java.util.Date();
  response.setContentType("text/html");
  PrintWriter out = response.getWriter();
  out.println("<html><head><title>Show Init Time</title></head>");
  out.println("<body>");
  out.println("Servlet first started: " + _startTime + "<br>");
  out.println("Current time: " + now + "<br>");
  out.println("Since started the servlet has been accessed " + _count
+ " times<br>");
  out.println("The message is: " + _message + "<br>");
  Enumeration paramNames = request.getParameterNames();
  String name;
  String[] values;
  StringBuffer valuesSb;
  while (paramNames.hasMoreElements()){
    valuesSb = new StringBuffer();
    name = (String) paramNames.nextElement();
    out.println(name + ": ");
    values = request.getParameterValues(name);
    for(int i = 0; i < values.length; i++){
      valuesSb.append(values[i]);
      if(i == values.length)
        valuesSb.append(", ");
    }
    out.println(valuesSb.toString() + "<br>");
  }
  out.println("</body></html>");
  Object flashParamsO = request.getAttribute("FLASH.PARAMS");
  Hashtable returnParams = new Hashtable();
  if (flashParamsO instanceof List){
    List flashParams = (List) flashParamsO;
```

```
ASObject aso = (ASObject)flashParams.get(0);
Set keys = aso.keySet();
Iterator iter = keys.iterator();
String s;
while(iter.hasNext()){
  s = (String) iter.next();
  if(s != null && aso != null)
    returnParams.put(s, aso.get(s));
}
}
Hashtable returnVal = new Hashtable();
returnVal.put("startTime", _startTime);
returnVal.put("currentTime", now);
returnVal.put("count", new Long(_count));
returnVal.put("message", _message);
returnVal.put("params", returnParams);
request.setAttribute("FLASH.RESULT", returnVal);
}
}
```

Note   Listing 13-10 has the servlet iterate through the parameters passed from Flash, place the parameters into a `Hashtable`, and return that value to Flash. This is not actually necessary in this particular instance because the `ASObject` itself could simply be passed back to Flash. However, this example shows you how you could iterate through all the parameters if you wanted to do any further processing.

2. Save the document, compile it (if necessary), and if it is not already in the deployment directory, copy it there. In order to compile, you need to ensure that the flashgateway.jar file and the servlet API classes are in your CLASSPATH.

3. If necessary, restart the application server.

4. Open a new Flash document and save it as reportCaller.fla.

5. Rename the default layer to form, and create a new layer named actions.

6. On the form layer, add a multilane, dynamic `TextField` object with border turned on. Name the instance `output`, and position it so that it fills the upper half of the stage, as shown in Figure 13-10. This will be where the results from the servlet are displayed.

7. On the form layer, in the lower, left portion of the stage, create two columns of three rows of single-line, input `TextField` objects with borders turned on. See Figure 13-10 for the positioning of these objects. Name the instances in the left column `paramName1`, `paramName2`, and `paramName3`, respectively, from top to bottom. In the right column, name the instances `paramVal1`, `paramVal2`, and `paramVal3`. You may also want to create static text fields above the columns as labels, as shown in Figure 13-10. These text fields enable the user to specify up to three parameters to be passed to the servlet.

8. To the right of the parameter text fields, create a `PushButton` component instance named `callServletBtn`. Figure 13-10 indicates where to position the button.

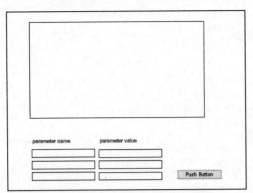

Figure 13-10: The layout of reportCaller.fla

9. On the actions layer, add the following code to the first frame:

```
#include "NetServices.as"

function init(){
  // use the proper gateway URL. The URL shown here
  // uses the default Resin port and uses the Wiley
  // context and servlet named gateway as was created
  // in chapter 12
  var gwUrl = "http://localhost:8880/Wiley/gateway";
  NetServices.setDefaultGatewayURL(gwUrl);
  var conn = NetServices.createGatewayConnection();
  _root.srv = conn.getService("Wiley");
}

res = new Object();
res.onResult = function(result){
  // result is an object with properties named
  // startTime, currentTime, count, message, and
  // params. Display these values in the output
  // text field
  _root.output.text = "Servlet First Started: " +
                      result.startTime + newline;
  _root.output.text += "Current Time: " +
                      result.currentTime + newline;
  _root.output.text += "Since started this servlet " +
                      "has been accessed " +
                      result.count + " times\n";
  _root.output.text += "The message is: " + result.message +
                      newline;
  for(var param in result.params){
    _root.output.text += param + ": " + result.params[param] +
                         newline;
  }
}
```

```
res.onStatus = function(status){
  trace(status.details);
}

callServletBtn.setLabel("call servlet");
callServletBtn.onRelease = function(){
  // if there are any parameters defined, add them
  // to an object and pass it to the servlet
  var params = new Object();
  if (_root.paramName1.text != ""){
    params[_root.paramName1.text] = _root.paramVal1.text;
  }
  if (_root.paramName2.text != ""){
    params[_root.paramName2.text] = _root.paramVal2.text;
  }
  if (_root.paramName3.text != ""){
    params[_root.paramName3.text] = _root.paramVal3.text;
  }
  // the name of the servlet defined in web.xml is ReportServlet
  _root.srv.ReportServlet(_root.res, params);
}

init();
```

10. Test the movie. If you simply click the call servlet button, it should result in something similar to what is shown in Figure 13-11. Figure 13-12 shows the results after adding parameters and clicking the button.

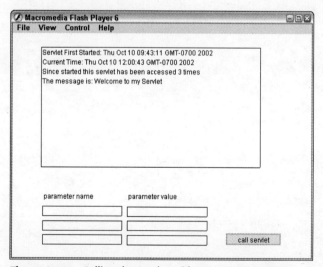

Figure 13-11: Calling the servlet without any parameters

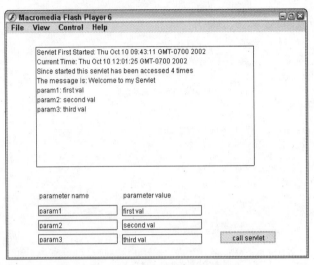

Figure 13-12: Calling the servlet with parameters

Displaying Headers in Flash

In this exercise, you call showHeaders.jsp (which you created in the section "Viewing Header Data with JSP") from a Flash movie and display the results in a text field.

1. Open showHeaders.jsp and modify the code as shown in Listing 13-11. The changes are shown in bold.

Listing 13-11: showHeaders.jsp as Modified for Use with Flash

```
<html>
<head>
<title>View All Headers</title>
</head>
<body>
Here is all the header information accessible to this JSP:<br>
<table border="1">
  <tr>
    <td><b>Header</b></td>
    <td><b>Value</b></td>
  </tr>
  <%
java.util.Enumeration headers = request.getHeaderNames();
String header, headerValue;
java.util.Hashtable returnVal = new java.util.Hashtable();
while(headers.hasMoreElements()){
  header = (String) headers.nextElement();
```

```
  headerValue = request.getHeader(header);
  returnVal.put(header, headerValue);
%>
  <tr>
    <td><%=header%></td>
    <td><%=headerValue%></td>
  </tr>
  <%
}
request.setAttribute("FLASH.RESULT", returnVal);
%>
</table>
</body>
</html>
```

2. Save the modified JSP document.

3. Open a new Flash document and save it as showHeaders.fla.

4. Rename the default layer to form and create a new layer named actions.

5. On the form layer, add a multilane, dynamic `TextField` object with border on. Name the instance `output`. Position the text field as shown in Figure 13-13.

6. Below the text field, add a `PushButton` component instance named `callJSPBtn`.

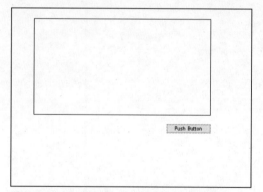

Figure 13-13: The layout of showHeaders.fla

7. On the actions layer, add the following code to the first frame:

```
#include "NetServices.as"

function init(){
  var gwUrl = "http://localhost:8880/Wiley/gateway";
  NetServices.setDefaultGatewayURL(gwUrl);
  var conn = NetServices.createGatewayConnection();
  _root.srv = conn.getService("Wiley");
}

res = new Object();
```

```
res.onResult = function(result){
  // result is an object with properties for each
  // header returned
  for(var header in result){
    _root.output.text += header + ": " + result[header] + newline;
  }
}
res.onStatus = function(status){
  trace(status.details);
}

callJSPBtn.setLabel("call JSP");
callJSPBtn.onRelease = function(){
  // the JSP servlet name is ShowHeaders (defined in web.xml)
  _root.srv.ShowHeaders(_root.res);
}

init();
```

8. Test the movie. Click the call JSP button and you should see something like what is shown in Figure 13-14.

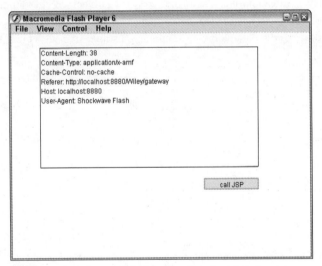

Figure 13-14: The result of a call to the showHeaders.jsp from Flash

Summary

In this chapter, you learned about using Java servlets and JSPs with Flash movies. You gained basic servlet and JSP knowledge as well as the specifics necessary to call servlets and JSPs from Flash. Some of the important highlights are as follows:

...moting with J2EE Application Servers

...d within the `wiley.chapter14` package, its service name would be `wiley.`
...yJavaClass.

...procedure name when using Java classes with Flash Remoting is simply the public
...e. For instance, if you created a service object for `MyJavaClass` named `srv`, and
...ss contains a public method named `myMethod()` (which requires no parameters),
...ash Remoting ActionScript code to call `myMethod()` would simply be as follows:

```
re res is a response object
yMethod(res);
```

...any other services that can be used with Flash Remoting (such as ColdFusion
...ents, for example), when you call a method from a Java class from a Flash movie, you
...ss it the expected number of parameters of the correct types and in the correct order.
...ans that if `myMethod()` is expecting no parameters, but you pass it one parameter:

```
.myMethod(res, "myParamVal");
```

...mote procedure invocation will fail. Moreover, parameters are accepted only when they
...assed as positional. Named parameters (e.g., {param1: "someVal", param2:
...therVal"}) will not work with Java methods.

erstanding Java Class
JavaBean Differences

...st about any Java class can be used with Flash Remoting. However, no state is necessarily
...aintained. To understand the implications of this, consider the simple Java class shown in
...Listing 14-1.

List 14-1: A Simple Java Class

```
package wiley.chapter14;

public class SimpleJavaClass{

  private String _simpleMember = null;

  public SimpleJavaClass(){}

  public void setSimpleMember(String val){
    _simpleMember = val;
  }

  public String getSimpleMember(){
    return _simpleMember;
  }

}
```

Listing 14-2 shows how this class might be used from a Flash movie.

- Servlets are Java classes that extend `HttpServlet`. They provide a powerful API for Web application development, including easy access to request and response objects.
- JSPs offer the same kind of power as servlets, with the additional benefit of being able to add presentation markup in the same file.
- Servlets and JSPs can be configured using the Web application's web.xml document. In this document, using `<servlet>` elements, you can specify a servlet name for the servlet class or JSP file. This is very important when using Flash Remoting, as the servlet name is how the Flash gateway recognizes the servlet or JSP to use.
- Parameters are passed to servlets and JSPs from Flash movies using the request object's `FLASH.PARAMS` attribute. You can access the attribute using the `getAttribute()` method.
- Values can be returned to Flash movies from servlets and JSPs using the request object's `FLASH.RESULT` attribute. You can set the attribute using the `setAttribute()` method.

♦   ♦   ♦

Interacting Java Classes JavaBeans

J ava code is always executed from a Java class,
been compiled into an intermediary language
readable language and machine-level code) that is
Java Virtual Machine (JVM). These classes general
accessible functions called *methods*. Therefore, Flas
enables you to call the public methods of any Java c
JavaBeans) that is accessible to the Web application
Flash gateway.

Accessing Java Methods from Fla

Utilizing Java class methods using Flash Remoting is relativ
straightforward. It does not require any special programming
niques to be applied to the Java classes. The Java classes nee
be altered in any way from how they would be developed if be
accessed from any other client. Therefore, when working with J
classes and Flash Remoting, you need to keep only three import
pieces of information in mind once the Java class has been succe
fully developed:

✦ Where to save the class files

✦ Determining the service name

✦ Selecting the proper procedure name

As stated already, for Java classes to be accessible to the Flash
Remoting gateway, they must be saved in a location that is accessible
to the Web application from which the gateway is running. Typically,
this means that the Java class file is saved to the application's `classes`
directory (within subdirectories corresponding to the package name if
necessary), or the class is made part of a JAR file and saved to the `lib`
directory. Unlike with servlets and JSPs, no special configuration
involving XML documents or the like is required.

The service name that the Flash Remoting gateway will use to access
the Java class is simply the fully qualified Java class name. That means
that if the Java class is named `MyJavaClass`, and it does not use any
packages, the service name you would use in your ActionScript code
would simply by `MyJavaClass`. On the other hand, if the same class

Listing 14-2: A Flash Movie Using SimpleJavaClass

```
#include "NetServices.as"

gwUrl = "http://localhost:8880/Wiley/gateway/";
NetServices.setDefaultGatewayURL(gwUrl);
conn = NetServices.createGatewayConnection();
srv = conn.getService("wiley.chapter14.SimpleJavaClass");

sRes = new Object();
sRes.onResult = function(result){
  _root.srv.getSimpleMember();
}

gRes = new Object();
gRes.onResult = function(result){
  trace(result);
}

srv.setSimpleMember("testVal");
```

If you were to test this, you would discover that the call to getSimpleMember() returns null even though setSimpleMember() was called and passed a value of testVal. This is because with a regular Java class, a new instance is created for each method call.

In order to create state you must use a JavaBean class. A JavaBean is a regular Java class that implements java.io.Serializable. When a JavaBean is used with Flash Remoting, the instance is stored in memory and a session is created so that the same JavaBean object can be called upon repeatedly. Listing 14-3 shows SimpleJavaClass made into a JavaBean simply by implementing Serializable. The modifications to the code are shown in bold.

List 14-3: A Simple JavaBean Class

```
package wiley.chapter14;

import java.io.Serializable;

public class SimpleJavaClass implements Serializable{

  private String _simpleMember = null;

  public SimpleJavaClass(){}

  public void setSimpleMember(String val){
    _simpleMember = val;
  }

  public String getSimpleMember(){
    return _simpleMember;
  }

}
```

In you were to compile `SimpleJavaClass` with the modifications shown in Listing 14-3 and then test the movie with the code from Listing 14-2 again, you would see that the returned value this time is `testVal`.

In some applications, regular Java classes are more appropriate, and in others JavaBeans are more appropriate. If you require state to be maintained, then use JavaBeans.

Reflecting On a JAR File

In this exercise, you use a regular Java class to look at the contents of a JAR file. First the application retrieves the contents of the JAR file using members of the `java.util.jar` package. Then, one of the items contained within the JAR file can be selected, and using members of the `java.lang.reflect` package, the methods within the class are displayed.

1. Create a new subdirectory named `wiley/chapter14` within the Wiley Web application's `classes` directory.

2. Open a new Java document using your favorite editor (Dreamweaver, JBuilder, vi, etc.), and save the file to the directory created in step 1 as ReadJar.java.

3. Add the code shown in Listing 14-4 to ReadJar.java and save it.

Listing 14-4: ReadJar.java

```
package wiley.chapter14;

import java.io.*;
import java.util.*;
import java.util.jar.*;
import java.lang.reflect.*;

public class ReadJar{

  // the constructor not strictly necessary for use with Flash
  // Remoting, since all methods are called as abstract
  public ReadJar(){}

  // pass the method a path to a JAR file, it returns an ArrayList
  // of the file's contents
  public ArrayList getJarContents(String path) throws Exception{
    // see API for more information on uses of each type of object
    File f = new File(path);
    JarFile jf = new JarFile(f);
    ArrayList al = new ArrayList();
    Enumeration en = jf.entries();
    JarEntry je;
    while(en.hasMoreElements()){
      je = (JarEntry) en.nextElement();
      if(!je.isDirectory())
        al.add(je.getName());
    }
    return al;
  }
```

```
// pass the method a fully-qualified class name accessible
// to the Web application and it will return an ArrayList of
// the class's methods
public ArrayList getJarFile(String fileName) throws Exception{
  Class c = Class.forName(fileName);
  Method[] methods = c.getMethods();
  ArrayList al = new ArrayList();
  for (int i = 0; i < methods.length; i++){
    al.add(methods[i].toString());
  }
  return al;
}

}
```

4. Compile the source into ReadJar.class.

5. Open a new Flash document and save it as readJar.fla.

6. Rename the default layer to form, and create a new layer named actions.

7. On the form layer, add a `ListBox` component instance in the upper, left-hand corner of the stage (see Figure 14-1). Name the instance `jarContents`.

8. Below the `ListBox` instance, create a multiline `TextField` object with border on. Name this instance `output`. Figure 14-1 shows the correct layout.

9. Drag a `ScrollBar` component instance onto the `output` object so that it snaps to it, as shown in Figure 14-1.

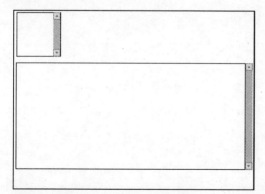

Figure 14-1: The layout of readJar.fla

10. On the first frame of the actions layer, add the following code:

```
#include "NetServices.as"

function init(){
  // resize the list box so that its contents can be read
  _root.jarContents.setSize(524, 100);
```

```
    // set the change handler for jarContents
    _root.jarContents.setChangeHandler("selectClass", _root);
    // The gateway URL in this example is set to the default port
    // for Resin (8880). You should make sure to use the correct
    // port number for your computer's configuration.
    var gwUrl = "http://localhost:8880/Wiley/gateway";
    NetServices.setDefaultGatewayURL(gwUrl);
    var conn = NetServices.createGatewayConnection();
    _root.srv = conn.getService("wiley.chapter14.ReadJar");
    // set jarFile to the path to a JAR file on your computer
    // this example shows a likely path to the flashgateway.jar
    // which may be of interest
    var jarFile = "C:\\Wiley\\Java\\FR-app\\app\\WEB-
INF\\lib\\flashgateway.jar";
    _root.srv.getJarContents(_root.jarContentRes, jarFile);
}

// a base class for response objects
function ResBase(){}
ResBase.prototype.onStatus = function(status){
  trace(status.description);
}

jarContentRes = new ResBase();
jarContentRes.onResult = function(result){
  var item;
  var dp = new Array();
  // loop through all the contents
  for(var i = 0; i < result.length; i++){
    // replace slashes with dots in the value
    item = _root.replaceSlash(result[i]);
    // make sure the value is not null, and then
    // add it to the array
    if(item != null)
      dp.push(item);
  }
  // set the newly-created array as the data
  // provider for jarContents
  _root.jarContents.setDataProvider(dp);
}

reflectRes = new ResBase();
reflectRes.onResult = function(result){
  // clear the output
  _root.output.text = "";
  // loop through results, write each line
  // to output
  for(var i = 0; i < result.length; i++){
    _root.output.text += result[i] + newline;
  }
}

// the change handler function for jarContents
function selectClass(cmpnt){
```

```
      // get the selected class name, retrieve the class
      // method definitions
      var class = cmpnt.getValue();
      _root.srv.getJarFile(_root.reflectRes, class);
    }

    function replaceSlash(val){
      var i;
      var start = 0;
      // loop through the value and replace all slashes with
      // dots
      while((i = val.indexOf("/", start)) != -1){
        val = val.substr(0, i) + "." + val.substr(i+1);
        start = i + 1;
      }
      // check to make sure the value represents a class
      // otherwise set the return value to null
      var dotClass = val.lastIndexOf(".class");
      if(dotClass == -1)
        return null;
      // chop off .class from the name
      val = val.substring(0, dotClass);
      return val;
    }

    init();
```

11. Test the movie. When the movie starts, it should retrieve the contents of the JAR file and display them in the list box. When you select one of the values from the list box, you should see the class's functions displayed in the text field below. See Figure 14-2 for an idea of what this should look like.

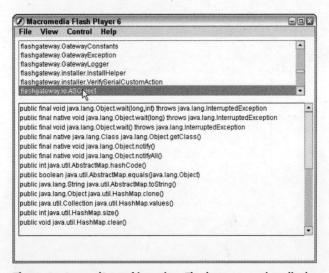

Figure 14-2: readJar.swf in action. The bottom portion displays the methods of the selected class.

Managing Users with JavaBeans

In this exercise, you use a JavaBean to create a user management system with a Flash user interface. The application enables you to add, edit, and delete users from a database table. By using a JavaBean instead of a regular Java class, you can maintain a connection to the database in between each method invocation.

1. If you did not already create the users table in the WileyFlashRemoting database in Chapter 6, do so now. You can add the table and two records using the SQL code shown in Listing 14-5. You can execute this SQL code from the DBMS command line, from a database utility, or by writing it to a file and executing the file as a script, as explained in Chapter 6 (for MySQL).

Listing 14-5: **Creating the users Table**

```
CREATE TABLE users (
  USER_ID int(10) unsigned NOT NULL  auto_increment,
  USERNAME char(50)    ,
  PASSWORD char(50)    ,
  ROLES char(50)    ,
  PRIMARY KEY (USER_ID)
)
INSERT INTO users VALUES(1,"johndoe","johnpasses","user");
INSERT INTO users VALUES(2,"ceo","ceopasses","user,admin");
```

2. Open a new Java document in your favorite editor and save it to the classes/wiley/chapter14 directory created in step 1 of the previous exercise in this chapter (see the section "Reflecting On a JAR File"). Save the file as UserBean.java.

3. Add the code from Listing 14-6 to the file and save it.

Listing 14-6: **UserBean.java**

```
package wiley.chapter14;

import java.io.*;
import java.sql.*;

public class UserBean implements Serializable{

  private Connection _connection = null;
  private Statement  statement = null;

  // a constructor with no parameters is required for a JavaBean
  public UserBean(){}
```

```
// this overloaded setConnection() requires only the
// host and database name, assuming port 3306 and no
// username and password
public void setConnection(String host, String db)
throws Exception{
  setConnection(host, "3306", db, "", "");
}


// in the example this setConnection() is called indirectly
// by way of the overloaded setConnection()
public void setConnection(String host,
                          String port,
                          String db,
                          String username,
                          String password) throws Exception{
  Class.forName("com.mysql.jdbc.Driver").newInstance();
  // create the connection string
  StringBuffer sb = new StringBuffer();
  sb.append("jdbc:mysql://");
  sb.append(host);
  sb.append(":");
  sb.append(port);
  sb.append("/");
  sb.append(db);
  sb.append("?");
  sb.append("user=");
  sb.append(username);
  sb.append("%password=");
  sb.append(password);
  // create the connection and the statement
  _connection = DriverManager.getConnection(sb.toString());
  _statement = _connection.createStatement();
}


// insert a new user based on username, password, and role(s)
public void insertUser(String username,
                       String password,
                       String role) throws Exception{
  String insertStr = "INSERT INTO USERS(USERNAME, " +
                     "PASSWORD, ROLES) VALUES('" +
                     username + "','" +
                     password + "','" +
                     role + "')";
  _statement.executeUpdate(insertStr);
}


// update an existing user given by id
public void updateUser(int id,
                       String username,
```

Continued

Listing 14-6: *(continued)*

```
                              String password,
                              String role) throws Exception{
    String updateStr = "UPDATE USERS SET USERNAME = '" +
                         username + "'," +
                         "PASSWORD = '" + password + "'," +
                         "ROLES = '" + role + "' " +
                         "WHERE USER_ID = " + id;
    _statement.executeUpdate(updateStr);
  }


  // delete a user given by id
  public void deleteUser(int id) throws Exception{
    String deleteStr = "DELETE FROM USERS WHERE USER_ID = " + id;
    _statement.executeUpdate(deleteStr);
  }


  // get all the users
  public ResultSet getUsers() throws Exception{
    String query = "SELECT * FROM USERS";
    return _statement.executeQuery(query);
  }


}
```

4. Compile the file into UserBean.class.

5. Open a new Flash document and save it as userManager.fla.

6. Rename the default layer to form, and create a new layer named actions.

7. On the form layer, add a ListBox component instance on the upper, left portion of the stage, as shown in Figure 14-3. Name the instance users.

8. Below the list box, add two PushButton component instances, as shown in Figure 14-3. Name one instance editBtn and name the other instance deleteBtn.

9. To the right of the list box, add a single-line, input TextField object with border on. Name the instance username. Figure 14-3 shows the correct layout.

10. Below username, create two more input TextField objects with border on. Make both of these password fields instead of single-line. Name these instances password and passwordConfirm. Again, Figure 14-3 shows the correct layout.

11. Add static text labels next to the three input TextField objects as shown in Figure 14-3.

12. Below the text fields, add a CheckBox component instance. Name the instance admin.

13. Below the CheckBox instance, add two PushButton component instances. Name these instances addBtn and submitChangeBtn.

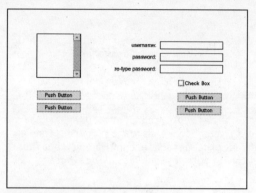

Figure 14-3: The basic form layout of
userManager.fla

14. Now, from Flash UI Components Set 2 (a download from the Macromedia Flash
    Exchange at `http://www.macromedia.com/exchange`), add a `MessageBox` component
    instance to the center of the stage as shown in Figure 14-4. Name the instance
    `messageBox`.

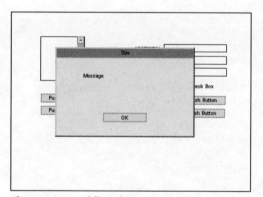

Figure 14-4: Adding the `MessageBox` component

15. On the first frame of the actions layer, add the following code:

```
// this exercise uses not only NetServices.as, but also
// DataGlue.as, so make sure to include both
#include "NetServices.as"
#include "DataGlue.as"

function init(){
  // set the check box label
  _root.admin.setLabel("Administrator");

  // initialize the movie with the message box off
```

```
    _root.messageBox._visible = false;
    // set the message and title for the message box
    _root.messageBox.setMessage("the passwords do not match");
    _root.messageBox.setTitle("mismatched passwords");

    var gwUrl = "http://localhost:8880/Wiley/gateway";
    NetServices.setDefaultGatewayURL(gwUrl);
    var conn = NetServices.createGatewayConnection();
    _root.srv = conn.getService("wiley.chapter14.UserBean");
    // call setConnection() and open a database connection
    // to the WileyFlashRemoting database running on localhost
    _root.srv.setConnection(_root.setConnRes, "localhost",
"WileyFlashRemoting");
}

// the base class for the response objects
function ResBase(){}
ResBase.prototype.onStatus = function(status){
    trace(status.details);
}

setConnRes = new ResBase();
setConnRes.onResult = function(result){
    // once the database connection has been made
    // get the list of users
    _root.srv.getUsers(_root.getUsersRes);
}

// a function used by DataGlue to format
// the users listed in the users list box
function userFormatter(record){
    // set the label to the username
    // set the data to the entire record
    o = new Object();
    o.label = record.username;
    o.data = record;
    return o;
}

getUsersRes = new ResBase();
getUsersRes.onResult = function(result){
    // when the users RecordSet is returned, display
    // formatted results in the users list box
    DataGlue.bindFormatFunction(_root.users, result,
_root.userFormatter);
}

// response object for adding, editing, or deleting
// a user
modUserRes = new ResBase();
```

```
modUserRes.onResult = function(result){
  // get new user list
  _root.srv.getUsers(_root.getUsersRes);
}


editBtn.setLabel("edit user");
editBtn.onRelease = function(){
  // get the selected user and display the
  // user info in the form to the right
  var r = _root.users.getValue();
  _root.username.text = r.username;
  _root.password.text = r.password;
  _root.passwordConfirm.text = r.password;
  // if the user is in the admin role, check
  // the box, otherwise, make sure it is unchecked
  if(r.roles.indexOf("admin") != -1)
    _root.admin.setValue(true);
  else
    _root.admin.setValue(false);
  _root.userId = r.user_id;
}


deleteBtn.setLabel("delete user");
deleteBtn.onRelease = function(){
  // get the id and call the deleteUser() method
  var id = _root.users.getValue().user_id;
  _root.srv.deleteUser(_root.modUserRes, id);
}


addBtn.setLabel("add user");
addBtn.onRelease = function(){
  _root.addEditUser("add");
}


submitChangeBtn.setLabel("submit changes");
submitChangeBtn.onRelease = function(){
  _root.addEditUser("edit");
}


function addEditUser(action){
  var un = _root.username.text;
  var pw = _root.password.text;
  var pwc = _root.passwordConfirm.text;
  var roles = "user";
  if(_root.admin.getValue())
    roles += ",admin";
  // if the passwords don't match, display the message box
  // otherwise add/update the user
  if (pw != pwc)
    _root.messageBox._visible = true;
```

```
      else{
        if(action == "add")
          _root.srv.insertUser(_root.modUserRes, un, pw, roles);
        if(action == "edit")
          _root.srv.updateUser(_root.modUserRes, _root.userId, un, pw,
roles);
        // clear the form
        _root.username.text = "";
        _root.password.text = "";
        _root.passwordConfirm.text = "";
        _root.admin.setValue(false);
      }
    }

    init();
```

16. Test the movie. You should see a list of current users in the list box when you start the movie. The initial list will likely include johndoe and ceo. Try selecting one of the users, clicking the edit user button (scc Figure 14-5), modifying the user information, and clicking the submit changes button (see Figure 14-6). Also try entering information into the form and clicking the add user button (see Figure 14-7). Lastly, select a user from the list box and click the delete user button (see Figure 14-8).

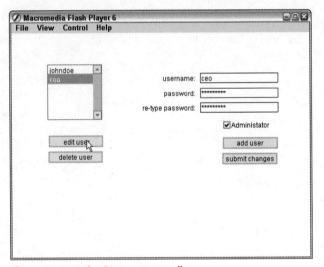

Figure 14-5: Selecting a user to edit

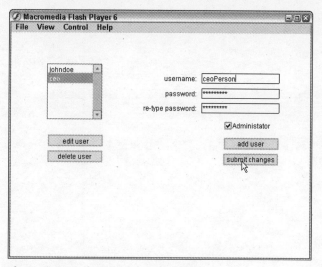

Figure 14-6: Submitting changes made to a user

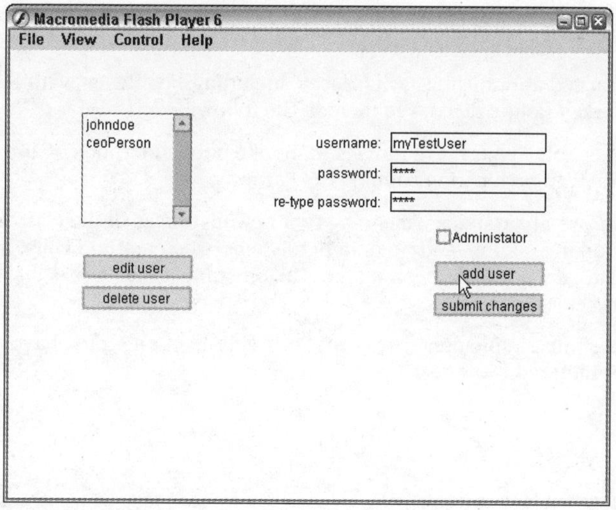

Figure 14-7: Adding a new user

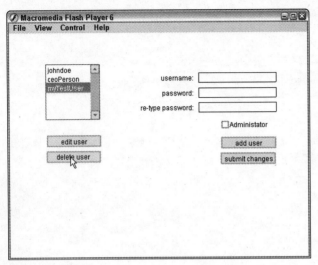

Figure 14-8: Deleting a user

Summary

In this chapter, you learned about using Java classes, including JavaBeans, with Flash Remoting. Some of the key points discussed include the following:

✦ Flash Remoting enables your Flash movies to invoke public methods of any Java class accessible to the Web application running the gateway.

✦ Regular Java classes are stateless, meaning that new instances of the class are created with each method invocation, and no data persists between method calls. JavaBeans, on the other hand, are stateful, meaning that the one object instance is maintained between method calls.

✦ JavaBean classes must implement `java.io.Serializable` and must have a constructor with no parameters.

✦   ✦   ✦

Calling Enterprise JavaBeans from Flash

✦ ✦ ✦ ✦

In This Chapter

Understanding which
Enterprise JavaBeans
can be used with Flash
Remoting

Finding the correct
service name to a
corresponding
Enterprise JavaBean

Working with various
Enterprise JavaBeans
using Flash Remoting
ActionScript

✦ ✦ ✦ ✦

Enterprise JavaBeans, or EJB, is a specification that defines application components. Despite the name, Enterprise JavaBeans are *not* JavaBeans, and other than being Java-based, they have very little else in common with JavaBeans. A description of EJB in detail is well beyond the scope of this book. If you are interested in learning more about Enterprise JavaBeans, I recommend Ed Roman, Scott Ambler, and Tyler Jewell's *Mastering Enterprise JavaBeans, Second Edition* (Wiley, 2001), which covers EJB 2.0 quite well.

When you use EJB, you need to have an EJB container. An EJB container is essentially an application server that enables you to deploy your Enterprise JavaBeans. Several EJB-compliant application servers are available, and any should work with Flash Remoting. You can find a list in Table 12-1.

Understanding EJB with Flash Remoting

You can find three kinds of EJBs in the EJB 2.0 specification:

✦ **Session Beans:** These EJBs contain functionality that is utilized within a user's session, as the name implies. They can be either stateless of stateful. A stateless Session Bean does not maintain a conversational state between calls, whereas a stateful Bean does.

✦ **Entity Beans:** These EJBs map to a particular entity (usually a database table) and model that data as Java objects. Entity Beans can be of two types: BMP (Bean Managed Persistence) or CMP (Container Managed Persistence). BMP Entity Beans are written such that the implementation of the retrieval and storage to the database is written in the Bean classes. CMP, conversely, relies on the EJB container (the application server) to implement this retrieval and storage. CMP in EJB 2.0 is a vast improvement over the 1.1 specification, and well worth looking into if you are not yet familiar with it. Unless you specifically need to write your own custom implementations, CMP is generally a better choice than BMP.

✦ **Message-Driven Beans:** These EJBs contain functionality similar to that of stateless Session Beans. However, Message-Driven Beans are invoked by sending *messages* to them. In terms of their use, a message can be sent to invoke a Message-Driven Bean, and the rest of the program can continue to run without having to wait for the EJB to complete its task. The Message-Driven Bean's functionality runs in the background.

With the use of Flash Remoting, your Flash movies can directly use stateless and stateful Session Beans as well as both BMP and CMP Entity Beans. Because Message-Driven Beans are used by way of a JMS client, your Flash movies *cannot* directly utilize them. Currently, the only way your Flash movies can use Message-Driven Beans is to write a JMS client class, and to call the methods of that class from Flash.

Using EJBs with Flash Remoting

Flash Remoting enables you to utilize deployed EJBs directly from Flash movies. Doing so is not a particularly complicated task. Regardless of whether you are using Session Beans, Entity Beans, or Message-Driven Beans, you map the ActionScript service object to the EJB in the same way. Then, depending on which type of Bean you are using, you must keep in mind specific things, as outlined in the following sections.

Obtaining the Service Reference

When you want to use an EJB directly from a Flash movie, you must first make a service object that maps to the EJB. To do this, you call the getService() method of the NetConnection instance, just as you do to obtain a service object when using Flash Remoting for any other type of server-side technology (servlet, JavaBean, etc.). The service name that you pass to getService() should be the JNDI (Java Naming and Directory Interface) name of the EJB as it is known to the EJB container. The JNDI name is the name given to the Bean in the ejb-jar.xml file within the <ejb-name> tag. For example:

```
<ejb-jar>
   <enterprise-beans>
      <session>
         <ejb-name>MyEJB</ejb-name>
         ...
      </session>
   </enterprise-beans>
</ejb-jar>
```

In this abbreviated snippet from an ejb-jar.xml file, the EJB is given the JNDI name MyEJB. Therefore, when you want to create an ActionScript service object to this EJB, you should use the following call to getService() in your Flash document:

```
srv = conn.getService("MyEJB");
```

Working with Session Beans

Session Beans are composed of at least a Bean class, a Home interface, and a Remote interface. When you create a service object in ActionScript that maps to a Session Bean, the service object is a reference to the Home interface. Therefore, if you want to invoke any of the Bean's methods, you should first obtain a reference to the Bean by calling the create() method from the Home interface.

Listing 15-1 shows a Home interface definition for an example Session Bean with a JNDI name of MySessionEJB, and Listing 15-2 shows the Bean class for the same EJB.

Listing 15-1: **MySessionEJBHome.java**

```
package wiley.chapter15;

import javax.ejb.*;
import java.rmi.Remote;
import java.rmi.RemoteException;
import java.util.*;

public interface MySessionEJBHome extends EJBHome {

  public MySessionBean create() throws CreateException,
RemoteException;

}
```

Listing 15-2: **MySessionEJBBean.java**

```
package wiley.chapter15;

import javax.ejb.*;
import java.io.Serializable;
import java.util.*;
import java.rmi.*;

public class MySessionEJBBean implements SessionBean {

  private transient SessionContext ctx;
  private transient Properties props;

  public String test(String val){
    return "val: " + val;
  }

  public void ejbActivate() {}
  public void ejbRemove() {}
  public void ejbPassivate() {}
  public void setSessionContext(SessionContext ctx) {
    this.ctx = ctx;
  }
  public void ejbCreate () {}

}
```

When the ActionScript service object is created using the JNDI name, the service object is a reference to the Home interface:

```
srv = conn.getService("MySessionEJB");
```

In order to call the `test()` method from the Bean class, you must first call the `create()` method to obtain a reference to MySessionEJBBean. Therefore, when working with Session Beans with Flash Remoting, you should always first call the `create()` method, and then wait until a successful response has been returned to Flash before calling any of the Bean methods. For example:

```
// assuming conn is a connection object to the EJB container
// get service object that maps to the Home interface
srv = conn.getService("MySessionEJB");

createRes = new Object();
createRes.onResult = function(result){
  // call the test() method of the Bean class only
  // after a successful response from the create()
  // method - which then converts the service
  // object to a reference to the Bean class
  _root.srv.test(_root.testRes,"my value");
}

testRes = new Object();
testRes.onResult = function(result){
  // outputs val: my value
  trace(result);
}

// call the create() method first, before trying to invoke
// any of the Bean methods
srv.create(createRes);
```

For an example of how to use Flash Remoting with Entity Beans, see supplemental information on the companion Web site, `www.wiley.com/compbooks/lott`.

Sending E-Mail from Flash via EJB

In this exercise, you create a stateless Session Bean that sends e-mail via the JavaMail API. The EJB code and deployment descriptor should be compatible with any EJB container. The following steps deploy the Bean in JRun 4. If you use a different EJB container, the Bean should still deploy without problems, but you will have to consult your container's documentation for instructions about how to deploy an EJB.

1. On your hard drive, you should already have a Wiley\Java directory created (i.e., C:\Wiley\Java). If not, please create this directory now.

2. Within the Wiley\Java directory, create a subdirectory named SendMailEJB.

3. Within the SendMailEJB directory, create a Wiley directory.

4. Within the Wiley directory, create a chapter15 directory.

Both the Wiley and chapter15 directories are created for the purposes of a Java package structure. The names correspond to the package name that will be used for the EJB. The SendMailEJB directory name is arbitrary. Its placement within the Wiley\Java directory is intentional for use with JRun 4 because JRun 4 will automatically pick up and deploy the EJB if it is placed in a directory within the Web application root.

5. Within the chapter15 folder created in step 4, open a text document and save it as SendMailBean.java.

6. Within SendMailBean.java, add the following code and save it:

```java
package wiley.chapter15;

import java.util.Properties;
import javax.mail.*;
import javax.mail.internet.*;
import javax.ejb.*;
import java.io.Serializable;
import java.util.*;
import java.rmi.*;

public class SendMailBean implements SessionBean {

    private transient SessionContext ctx;
    private transient Properties props;

    public void send(String to, String from, String subject, String
body, String smtp) throws Exception {

        // get system properties
        Properties props = System.getProperties();

        // set the mail server to the value passed to the method
        props.put("mail.smtp.host", smtp);

        // get the mail session
        Session session = Session.getDefaultInstance(props, null);

        // create a message within the mail session
        MimeMessage message = new MimeMessage(session);

        // Set the from address
        message.setFrom(new InternetAddress(from));

        // set the to address to the value passed to the method
        message.addRecipient(Message.RecipientType.TO, new
InternetAddress(to));

        // set the subject to the value passed to the method
        message.setSubject(subject);

        // set the body of the email to the value passed to the method
        message.setText(body);

        // send message
        Transport.send(message);
    }

    // standard, required EJB methods
```

```
        public void ejbActivate() {}
        public void ejbRemove() {}
        public void ejbPassivate() {}
        public void setSessionContext(SessionContext ctx) {
          this.ctx = ctx;
        }
        public void ejbCreate () {}

    }
```

7. Within the chapter15 folder created in step 4, open a text document and save it as SendMail.java.

8. Within SendMail.java, add the following code and save it:

```
package wiley.chapter15;

import java.rmi.RemoteException;
import java.rmi.Remote;
import javax.ejb.*;


public interface SendMail extends EJBObject, Remote {

  public void send(String to, String from, String subject, String
body, String smtp) throws RemoteException;
  }
```

9. Within the chapter15 folder created in step 4, open a text document and save it as SendMailHome.java.

10. Within SendMailHome.java, add the following code and save it:

```
package wiley.chapter15;

import javax.ejb.*;
import java.rmi.Remote;
import java.rmi.RemoteException;
import java.util.*;

public interface SendMailHome extends EJBHome {

  public SendMail create() throws CreateException, RemoteException;

}
```

11. Compile the three files created in the previous steps to SendMailBean.class, SendMail.class, and SendMailHome.class.

Note   In order to successfully compile the classes, you have to ensure that the necessary JAR files are in your CLASSPATH. These JAR files can generally be found in the lib directory of the EJB container. For example, with JRun 4, ensure that the jrun.jar file (found in the JRun 4 lib directory) is included in the CLASSPATH during compilation.

12. Within the SendMailEJB directory created in step 2, create a subdirectory named META-INF. This is the directory in which the deployment descriptors are saved.

13. Within the META-INF directory, create a new text document named ejb-jar.xml.

14. Add the following code to the ejb-jar.xml document and then save it. This simple deployment descriptor defines a stateless Session Bean with the Home and Remote interfaces and the Bean class that you created in the previous steps. It also gives the EJB a JNDI name of SendMailEJB.

```xml
<?xml version="1.0" encoding="iso-8859-1"?>

<!DOCTYPE ejb-jar PUBLIC
    '-//Sun Microsystems, Inc.//DTD Enterprise JavaBeans 1.1//EN'
    'http://java.sun.com/j2ee/dtds/ejb-jar_1_1.dtd'>

<ejb-jar>
    <enterprise-beans>
        <session>
            <ejb-name>SendMailEJB</ejb-name>
            <home>wiley.chapter15.SendMailHome</home>
            <remote>wiley.chapter15.SendMail</remote>
            <ejb-class>wiley.chapter15.SendMailBean</ejb-class>
            <session-type>Stateless</session-type>
        </session>
    </enterprise-beans>
</ejb-jar>
```

15. At this point, if you are using JRun 4, you should restart the Wiley server. When the server restarts, it should automatically detect the new EJB. Click on the Wiley server in the JMC and you should see the EJB listed under The Enterprise JavaBeans section, as shown in Figure 15-1. If you use another EJB container, you may need to JAR the files and/or use a deployment utility. Consult your EJB container's documentation for information on the specifics.

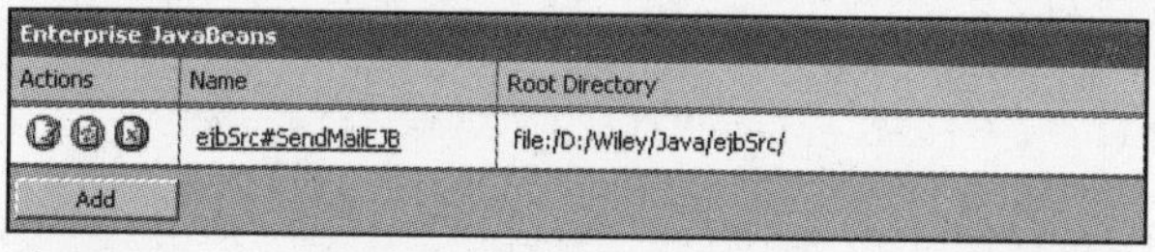

Enterprise JavaBeans		
Actions	Name	Root Directory
🔵 🔵 🔵	ejbSrc#SendMailEJB	file:/D:/Wiley/Java/ejbSrc/
Add		

Figure 15-1: The SendMailEJB listed within the Wiley server's Enterprise JavaBeans using the JMC

16. Open a new Flash document and save it as emailEJB.fla.

17. Rename the default layer to form. Add two more layers named message box and actions.

18. On the form layer, add three single-line input `TextField` objects (with border turned on) near the top of the stage, as shown in Figure 15-2. Name these instances (from top to bottom) `to`, `from`, `subject`.

19. Below the single-line `TextField` objects, add a multiline input `TextField` object with border turned on. Name this instance `message`.

20. Below message, add a `PushButton` component instance named `sendBtn`.

21. Add static text labels as shown in Figure 15-2.

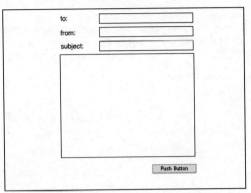

Figure 15-2: The layout of the form layer on emailEJB.fla

22. On the message box layer, add a `MessageBox` component instance (from the Flash UI Components Set 2 component set, available free from the Macromedia Exchange at `www.macromedia.com/exchange/flash`) in the center of the stage. Name this instance `mb`.

23. On the first frame of the actions layer, add the following code:

```
#include "NetServices.as"

function init(){
  // use your EJB container's gateway URL
  var gwURL = "http://localhost:8101/Wiley/gateway";
  NetServices.setDefaultGatewayURL(gwURL);
  var conn = NetServices.createGatewayConnection();

  // get a reference to the SendMailEJB Home interface by its JNDI
  // name
  _root.srv = conn.getService("SendMailEJB");

  // call the create() method to get a reference to the Bean
  _root.srv.create(_root.createRes);

  // set the title and message of the message box
  // before the create() method has returned a reference to the
  // Bean tell the user that it is loading
  _root.mb.setTitle("Mail Sender Message");
  _root.mb.setMessage("Please wait while loading ... ");
}
```

```
createRes = new Object();
createRes.onResult = function(result){
  // now that the create() method has succeeded turn off the
  // message box
  _root.mb._visible = false;
}
createRes.onStatus = function(status){
  trace(status.description);
}

sendRes = new Object();
sendRes.onResult = function(result){
  // once the send() method has successfully sent
  // the email, open the message box to tell the user
  // that the message has been sent...also clear
  // the contents of the form
  _root.mb.setMessage("Mail sent");
  _root.mb._visible = true;
  _root.to.text = "";
  _root.from.text = "";
  _root.subject.text = "";
  _root.message.text = "";
}
sendRes.onStatus = function(status){
  trace(status.description);
}

sendBtn.setLabel("send");
sendBtn.onRelease = function(){
  var to = _root.to.text;
  var from = _root.from.text;
  var subject = _root.subject.text;
  var message = _root.message.text;
  // make sure to enter your smtp server value for the
  // server variable
  var server = "your.server.here";
  // call the send() method of the EJB with the data from the
  // form
  _root.srv.send(_root.sendRes, to, from, subject, message, server);
}

// call init() to start the movie
init();
```

24. Test the movie. You should be able to send an e-mail message from Flash by way of the EJB.

Summary

In this chapter, you learned about using Enterprise JavaBeans with Flash Remoting. Some of the important highlights to remember include the following:

✦ The EJB 2.0 specification defines three kinds of EJBs: Session, Entity, and Message-Driven. Flash Remoting allows you to work directly with Session and Entity Beans, but not Message-Driven Beans.

✦ The EJB's JNDI name is the name used to create the ActionScript service object.

✦ When you create a service object for a Session Bean, it is initially a reference to the Home interface. However, once you call the `create()` method and a result is returned, the service object is a reference to the Bean.

✦   ✦   ✦

Working with JRun-Only Features

◆ ◆ ◆ ◆

In This Chapter

Learning about Flash
Remoting features
available only in JRun 4

Understanding JMX and
MBeans, as well as how
to make JRun JMX
services available to
Flash Remoting

Calling MBean methods
from Flash Remoting
movies

Integrating EJB security
using setCredentials()

◆ ◆ ◆ ◆

While the functionality available for J2EE Flash Remoting is basically the same for all J2EE application servers, a few additional features are available only in the JRun version. These features
include the following:

- ◆ Server-Side ActionScript
- ◆ Access to JMX MBeans
- ◆ Integration with EJB security

Server-Side ActionScript (SSAS) is also available in the ColdFusion
version of Flash Remoting. For more information about SSAS, refer to
Chapter 11.

Working with JMX

JMX, or Java Management Extensions, is an API for managing
resources such as an application or even a physical device attached
to a computer. Although a detailed examination isn't possible here,
JMX is a large and interesting subject, and if you want to learn more,
I recommend Mike Jasnowski's *JMX Programming* (Wiley, 2002).

Flash Remoting for JRun 4 enables you to create Flash movies that
interact with JRun JMX MBeans. An MBean is a Java class that represents a managed resource. JRun 4 uses MBeans to manage resources
such as JRun servers, Web applications, and resources such as datasources, to name a few. Using JMX enables JRun resources to be easily managed from multiple locations such as the JRun launcher and
the JMC (JRun Management Console).

Obviously, you don't want to expose all JMX functionality to just anyone, so JRun includes a security configuration for each JMX service
in the jrun.policy file (located in the JRun 4 installation's lib directory). If you open that file, you will find the following line:

```
permission jrun.security.JMXPermission
"accessMBean.DefaultDomain:service=DeployerService";
```

This line of code specifies that clients on the default domain can
access the DeployerService MBean that is part of the JRun library
of JMX MBeans. This line is included in the default JRun configuration
so that the DeployerService MBean's functionality is exposed to
Flash Remoting for the JMX example that is part of the samples
server. If you want to expose other MBeans, you can add more lines

that expose the `Interceptor` MBean and the `JMSCoreService` MBean, as shown in the following code:

```
permission jrun.security.JMXPermission
"accessMBean.DefaultDomain:service=Interceptor";
permission jrun.security.JMXPermission
"accessMBean.DefaultDomain:service=JMSCoreService";
```

You can also use the asterisk as a wildcard. For example, you can make all services available with the following line in the jrun.policy file:

```
permission jrun.security.JMXPermission
"accessMBean.DefaultDomain:service=*";
```

JRun 4 includes an entire library of JMX MBeans in its API. You can view the JRun API at `http://livedocs.macromedia.com/jrun4docs/javadocs/index.html`.

When you want to access an exposed JMX service from a Flash movie, you can do so by specifying in the jrun.policy file the service object name that corresponds to the value, as shown here:

```
srv = conn.getService("DefaultDomain:service=DeployerService");
srv = conn.getService("DefaultDomain:service=Interceptor");
srv = conn.getService("DefaultDomain:service=JMSCoreService");
```

Administering JRun from Flash

In the following exercise, you create a Flash movie that uses an existing JRun MBean (`JrunAdminService`) to manage the JRun servers in a manner similar to how it is done from the JRun launcher.

1. Open the jrun.policy file, add the following line, and save it:

```
permission jrun.security.JMXPermission
"accessMBean.DefaultDomain:service=JRunAdminService";
```

2. Open a new Flash document and save it as jmxAdmin.fla.

3. Add the `PushButton` symbol to the library. The easy way to do this is to drag an instance of the component onto the stage and then delete it from the stage. This way, there is no instance on the stage, but it has been created in the library. It will not be accessible for use with the `attachMovie()` method.

4. On the first frame of the default layer, add the following code:

```
#include "NetServices.as"

function init(){
  var gwURL = "http://localhost:8101/Wiley/gateway";
  NetServices.setDefaultGatewayURL(gwURL);
  var conn = NetServices.createGatewayConnection();

  // open a service object to the JRunAdminService
  _root.srv =
conn.getService("DefaultDomain:service=JRunAdminService");

  // create an array that will store the server names
  // retrieved from JRun
```

```
  _root.servers = new Array();

  // call the listServers() method from the MBean (see JRun API
  // for more details on the methods of the MBean)
  _root.srv.listServers(getServersRes);

  // set an interval in which the refresh() function is
  // called every 5 seconds or so
  _root.interval = setInterval(_root.refresh, 5000)
}

// when called, this method stops the server to which the
// PushButton that called it corresponds by invoking the
// MBean stopServer method with the value of the PushButton's
// sn (as in server name) custom property. This property (and
// the PushButton) is defined in the getServersRes.onResult()
// method
function stopServer(cmpnt){
  _root.srv.stopServer(_root.stopStartRes, cmpnt.sn);
}

// similar to the stopServer() function, only starts the server
function startServer(cmpnt){
  _root.srv.startServer(_root.stopStartRes, cmpnt.sn);
}

// loops through the server names in the servers array and
// call the MBean serverStatus() method for each. It creates
// a unique response object for each call using the custom
// StatusRes class that is defined below. The reason is that
// it can then be passed the name of the server through the
// constructor so that when the result is returned the response
// object can update the appropriate server's status in the
// display
function refresh(){
  for(var i = 0; i < _root.servers.length; i++){
    _root.srv.serverStatus(new _root.statusRes(_root.servers[i]),
String(_root.servers[i]));
  }
}


getServersRes = new Object();
getServersRes.onResult = function(result){
  var mc;
  // the result is an array of server names, so loop through
  // the array and create the buttons and text fields for display
  // of the servers, their status, and the ability to start and
  // stop them
  for(var i = 0; i < result.length; i++){

    // create a stop button for each server
    mc = _root.attachMovie("FPushButtonSymbol", "stop" + i, i);
    mc.setLabel("stop");
```

```
        // set the stop button's click handler to the stopServer()
        // function
        mc.setClickHandler("stopServer", _root);
        // set the sn property (as in server name) for the stop button
        mc.sn = result[i];
        // position the button below the previously created ones
        mc._y = i * 30;

        // create the start button for each server
        mc = _root.attachMovie("FPushButtonSymbol", "start" + i,
 i+result.length);
        mc.setLabel("start");
        // set the start button's click handler to the startServer()
        // function
        mc.setClickHandler("startServer", _root);
        // set the sn property for the start button
        mc.sn = result[i];
        // position the button below the previously create ones
        // and at x = 100 (to the right of the stop button)
        mc._y = i * 30;
        mc._x = 100;

        // create a text field to display the server name next to the
        // start and stop buttons
        _root.createTextField("serverName" + i, i+(result.length*2), 200,
 i * 30, 0, 0);
        _root["serverName" + i].autoSize = true;
        _root["serverName" + i].text = result[i];

        // create a text field to display the server status next to
        // each server name
        _root.createTextField("serverStatus" + result[i],
 i+(result.length*3), 250, i * 30, 0, 0);
        _root["serverStatus" + result[i]].autoSize = true;

        // add each server name to the servers array
        _root.servers.push(result[i]);
      }

      // call the refresh() function to display the status of each
      // server
      _root.refresh();
  }

  stopStartRes = new Object();
  stopStartRes.onResult = function(result){}

  // StatusRes is a class definition for the response objects
  // used by the serverStatus() service function calls
  // the constructor takes the server name so that it can be used
  // when a result is returned to onResult()
  function StatusRes(server){
    this.server = server;
  }
```

```
StatusRes.prototype.onResult = function(result){
  // set the server status text field for the appropriate
  // server to display the result of the service function
  // call
  _root["serverStatus" + this.server].text = result;
  delete this;
}

// call init() to start the movie
init();
```

5. Test your movie.

For information on working with EJB security, see the companion Web site, www.wiley.com/compbooks/lott.

Summary

In this chapter, you learned about the JRun-only features available in Flash Remoting. Important points to remember include the following:

✦ JRun 4 Flash Remoting enables three features that are not available to Flash Remoting for use with other J2EE application servers. These features include Server-Side ActionScript, JMX MBean method access, and integrated EJB security.

✦ JMX is an API for managing resources such as an application server. JMX is composed of MBeans. The JRun 4 API includes many MBeans that you can use from Flash movies.

✦ When you have made an MBean service accessible by editing the jrun.policy file, you can make calls to that MBean's methods from Flash Remoting movies.

✦   ✦   ✦

Using ASTranslator

In This Chapter

Introducing the
ASTranslator API and
understanding what it
does

Translating objects from
ActionScript to Java

Translating objects from
Java to ActionScript

When you begin working with Flash Remoting for Java in the context of actual application development, you begin to encounter what some might consider a few minor obstacles to ease of development (as well as inconsistencies with Java in general). Namely, the three issues to note are as follows:

- When passing typed objects to Java classes from Flash Remoting movies, the objects are deserialized as instances of flashgateway.io.ASObject. This does not explicitly prevent you from working with the data in a meaningful way, but it is rather inconvenient in many instances.

- When returning custom Java object types to Flash Remoting movies, the object is translated by the Flash Remoting gateway to be an ActionScript Object object, not a typed object.

Note   The only types of custom Java object types that can meaningfully be returned to Flash movies are those that implement Serializable, Dictionary, or Throwable.

- When returning a Java object that implements Serializable (a JavaBean), *all* the members — both public *and* private — of that object are returned to Flash. This is inconsistent with how Java works, and for a Java developer it is not a desirable functionality.

Here is an example of how the first issue can have an effect. If you pass an ActionScript object of type Foo (where Foo is a class defined in the Flash movie) to a Java class, then you likely want the object to be of type Foo (an instance of a custom Java class named Foo) once it is deserialized in Java. However, the object is always deserialized as ASObject instead because Flash Remoting doesn't know anything about your custom Java classes such as Foo. You can create custom code to translate the ASObject into a Foo object, but it is rather inconvenient, and it takes up development time for a rather mundane task.

Here is an example of how the second and third issues can have an effect. Consider that you have a Java class, FooBean, as shown in Listing 17-1.

Listing 17-1: **FooBean Java class**

```
public class FooBean implements Serializable {

  private String _fooPrivateOne;
  private String _fooPrivateTwo;

  public FooBean(){}

  public void setOne(String one){
    _fooPrivateOne = one;
  }

  public String getOne(){
    return _fooPrivateOne;
  }

  public void setTwo(String two){
    _fooPrivateTwo = two;
  }

  public String getTwo(){
    return _fooPrivateTwo;
  }

}
```

In your Flash movie, you have a `FooBean` ActionScript class defined and registered as shown in Listing 17-2.

Listing 17-2: **FooBean ActionScript Class**

```
function FooBean(){}
Object.registerClass("FooBean", FooBean);
```

If you returned an object of type `FooBean` from a Java class to Flash, the result would be an object of type `Object`, and *not* of type `FooBean`. This is because the Flash Remoting gateway doesn't know anything about FooBean Java objects.

Furthermore, the returned Object object would have four properties: `_fooPrivateOne`, `_fooPrivateTwo`, `one`, and `two`. The properties `one` and `two` are defined by the `get` and `set` methods of the FooBean Java class. Because the methods are publicly accessible, it is desirable that the properties `one` and `two` be included in the returned ActionScript object. However, `_fooPrivateOne` and `_fooPrivateTwo` are private members that have no business being exposed outside of the Java class. Functionally, this does not explicitly create a problem. However, it is inconsistent with how Java works, and it needlessly clutters the returned ActionScript object with unnecessary properties.

So, you ask yourself, is there any solution to this madness? And the answer is yes, there is.

Introducing ASTranslator

The folks at Carbon Five (www.carbon5.com) are serious about their J2EE, and as a result they have developed an open source Java utility API called ASTranslator specifically to resolve the previously mentioned issues with the way in which Flash Remoting handles data passed between Java classes and Flash.

Getting Started with ASTranslator

In order to obtain a copy of ASTranslator, download the JAR file from http://sourceforge .net/projects/carbonfive/ to the folder on your computer where you typically keep such files. For convenience, you may want to add the JAR to your CLASSPATH. Otherwise, you will need to specify the JAR with the -classpath flag when you run javac to compile classes that use ASTranslator.

Tip   You may also want to extract the contents of the JAR file to a location on your hard drive as it contains useful documentation.

Working with ASTranslator

When you use ASTranslator, you need to use only one class directly — com.carbonfive. flash.ASTranslator. The ASTranslator class has three methods:

✦ fromActionScript(ASObject aso): Translates an object passed to the Java class from Flash into a Java object of a custom type.

✦ fromActionScript(ASObject aso, Class class): Translates an object passed to the Java class from Flash into a Java object of type class.

✦ toActionScript(Object obj): Translates an object from a custom Java type to an ASObject to be returned to a Flash movie.

Converting from ActionScript

When you pass a typed object from a Flash movie to a Java class, it is always of type ASObject. When you pass the ASObject to the fromActionScript() method, it returns an object that you can cast to the appropriate type. For example, consider a scenario in which you have a FooBean ActionScript object (see Listing 17-2) that you pass to a Java method as follows:

```
fb = new FooBean();
// assign values to properties one and two - these properties
// match up with the get/set methods of the FooBean Java class
fb.one = "won";
fb.two = "too";
// where srv is the service object and res is the response object
srv.someJavaMethod(res, fb);
```

The Java method, someJavaMethod(), might be defined as follows *without* using ASTranslator:

```
public String someJavaMethod(ASObject aso){
  return aso.get("one");
}
```

This would return the value won—the value assigned to the one key of the ASObject passed to someJavaMethod(). (Remember, ASObject is just a fancy HashMap, so you can use the methods of HashMap, such as get().) However, it is not the most intuitive or useful way to work with the data. Instead, by using ASTranslator, you can define someJavaMethod() in a more useful way as follows.

```
//assume this class imports com.carbonfive.flash.ASTranslator
public String someJavaMethod(ASObject aso){
  ASTranslator ast = new ASTranslator();
  FooBean fb = (FooBean) ast.fromActionScript(aso);
  return fb.getOne();
}
```

This method still returns the same value—won—but in a vastly more intuitive and useful fashion—by way of the getOne() method of a correctly cast FooBean object.

The usefulness of ASTranslator's fromActionScript() method does not stop there either. It will also correctly cast any custom types that are set as members of the object passed through fromActionScript(). For example, Listing 17-3 shows a FooChildBean class, and Listing 17-4 shows FooBean rewritten such that it has get and set methods for a property of type FooChildBean.

Listing 17-3: **FooChildBean Java Class**

```
public class FooChildBean implements Serializable {

  private String _fooChildPrivateA;

  public FooChildBean(){}

  public void setA(String a){
    _fooChildPrivateA = a;
  }

  public String getA(){
    return _fooChildPrivateA;
  }

}
```

Listing 17-4: **FooBean Java Class**

```
public class FooBean implements Serializable {

  private String _fooPrivateOne;
  private String _fooPrivateTwo;
  private FooChildBean _fcbPrivate;

  public FooBean(){}
```

```
    public void setOne(String one){
      _fooPrivateOne = one;
    }

    public String getOne(){
      return _fooPrivateOne;
    }

    public void setTwo(String two){
      _fooPrivateTwo = two;
    }

    public String getTwo(){
      return _fooPrivateTwo;
    }

    public void setFcb(FooChildBean fcb){
      _fbcPrivate = fcb;
    }

    public FooChildBean getFcb(){
      return _fcbPrivate;
    }

}
```

Then, an ActionScript class must also be defined and registered for FooChildBean, as shown in Listing 17-5.

Listing 17-5: **FooChildBean ActionScript Class**

```
function FooChildBean(){}
Object.registerClass("FooChildBean", FooChildBean);
```

Now, if the FooBean object passed from ActionScript to Java has an fcb property defined of type FooChildBean, that too will be properly cast when the ASObject is run through fromActionScript(). For instance, the following ActionScript creates the FooBean object with a FooChildBean property and then passes it to a service function:

```
fb = new FooBean();
fb.one = "won";
fb.two = "too";
fb.fcb = new FooChildBean();
// assign an a property to fcb, corresponding to the getA() and
// setA() methods in the FooChildBean class
fb.fcb.a = "eh";
srv.someJavaMethod(res, fb);
```

Now consider the following definition for `someJavaMethod()`:

```
//assume this class imports com.carbonfive.flash.ASTranslator
public String someJavaMethod(ASObject aso){
  ASTranslator ast = new ASTranslator();
  FooBean fb = (FooBean) ast.fromActionScript(aso);
  return fb.getFcb().getA();
}
```

This method will return the value `eh` because that is the value that was assigned to the `a` property of the incoming `FooBean` object's `fcb` property.

Converting to ActionScript

When you wish to return a typed object to a Flash movie, all you need to do is run that object through the `toActionScript()` method of an ASTranslator object. The `toActionScript()` method takes any JavaBean-style object and returns an ASObject with the type set. When this object is returned to Flash, it will automatically be converted to an object of the appropriate type so long as an ActionScript class has been registered to the same name as the Java class.

For example, consider the `FooBean` ActionScript and Java classes defined in Listings 17-1 and 17-2, and an ActionScript service function call to a Java method defined as follows:

```
public ASObject getFooBean(){
  FooBean fb = new FooBean();
  fb.setOne("won");
  fb.setTwo("two");
  ASTranslator ast = new ASTranslator();
  return (ASObject) ast.toActionScript(fb);
}
```

If the response object in ActionScript had an `onResult()` method defined as follows:

```
res.onResult = function(result){
  trace(result instanceof FooBean);
}
```

then the output would be `true`.

Making ASTranslator Work

In general, the following guidelines for using ASTranslator will ensure that things work:

✦ Define and register an ActionScript class. This class should be registered to the *fully qualified* class name of the corresponding Java class. For example, if the `FooBean` Java class is in the `wiley.chapter17` package, then your ActionScript `registerClass()` statement should look something like:

```
Object.registerClass("wiley.chapter17.FooBean", FooBean);
```

✦ Define the ActionScript class so that it has a constructor that does not require any parameters. If your ActionScript class's constructor takes parameters and sets properties for the object, then when Flash Remoting returns the value from Java, all the properties set in the ActionScript constructor will be undefined.

✦ In order for the Java classes to correctly be converted by `ASTranslator`, they must be in the JavaBean style. That means that they must do the following:

    • Implement `Serializable`

- Use get/set methods for publicly accessible members/properties
- Have a constructor that requires no parameters

Testing ASTranslator

This section walks you through an exercise in which you can test ASTranslator for yourself. While this example illustrates the use of ASTranslator, it does not really provide any useful functionality as an application. It is solely for the purpose of helping you to understand how ASTranslator works.

1. Create a new directory named chapter17 within your Wiley Web application's WEB-INF/classes/wiley directory.

2. Open a new text document and save it as YellowPagesEntry.java to the directory created in step 1.

3. Add the code from Listing 17-6 to YellowPagesEntry.java and save the document.

Listing 17-6: **YellowPagesEntry.java**

```java
package wiley.chapter17;

public class YellowPagesEntry implements java.io.Serializable{

  private String _name;
  private int _zip;

  public YellowPagesEntry(){}

  public boolean nameContains(String matchStr){
    return (this._name.indexOf(matchStr) != -1);
  }

  public String getName(){
    System.out.println(this._name);
    return this._name;
  }

  public void setName(String name){
    this._name = name;
  }

  public int getZip(){
    return this._zip;
  }

  public void setZip(int zip){
    this._zip = zip;
  }

}
```

4. Open a new text document and save it as YellowPages.java to the directory created in step 1.

5. Add the code from Listing 17-7 to YellowPages.java and save the document.

Listing 17-7: **YellowPages.java**

```
package wiley.chapter17;

import java.util.ArrayList;

public class YellowPages implements java.io.Serializable{

  private ArrayList _entries = new ArrayList();

  public YellowPages(){}

  public void addEntry(YellowPagesEntry ype){
    this._entries.add(ype);
  }

  public ArrayList getEntries(){
    return this._entries;
  }

  public void setEntries(ArrayList entries){
    this._entries = entries;
  }

  public YellowPages findEntriesByName(String name){
    YellowPages matches = new YellowPages();
    for(int i = 0; i < this._entries.size(); i++){
      YellowPagesEntry ype = (YellowPagesEntry) this._entries.get(i);
      if(ype.nameContains(name)){
        matches.addEntry(ype);
      }
    }
    return matches;
  }

}
```

6. Open a new text document and save it as YellowPagesProcessor.java to the directory created in step 1.

7. Add the code from Listing 17-8 to YellowPagesProcessor.java and save the document.

Listing 17-8: **YellowPagesProcessor.java**

```
package wiley.chapter17;

import flashgateway.io.ASObject;
import com.carbonfive.flash.*;
import java.util.*;

public class YellowPagesProcessor {

  public YellowPagesProcessor(){}

  public ASObject find(ASObject aso, String name){
    ASTranslator ast = new ASTranslator();
    YellowPages yp = (YellowPages) ast.fromActionScript(aso);
    YellowPages result = yp.findEntriesByName(name);
    return (ASObject) ast.toActionScript(result);
  }

}
```

8. Compile the three Java files as YellowPagesEntity.class, YellowPages.class, and YellowPagesProcessor.class. Remember that in order to compile YellowPagesProcessor, javac will need to know about `ASObject` and `ASTranslator`, so make sure that the appropriate JAR files are included in your `CLASSPATH` one way or another. Additionally, in order for YellowPages.java and YellowPagesProcessor.java to compile, you need to make sure the WEB-INF\classes directory is included in the `CLASSPATH`.

9. Open a new Flash document and save it as yellowPages.fla.

10. On the first frame of the default layer, add the following code:

```
#include "NetServices.as"

function init(){
  // use your server's gateway URL
  var gwUrl = "http://localhost:8880/Wiley/gateway"
  NetServices.setDefaultGatewayURL(gwUrl);
  var conn = NetServices.createGatewayConnection();
  // create a service object that maps to YellowPagesProcessor
  _root.srv =
conn.getService("wiley.chapter17.YellowPagesProcessor");
}

function doYellowPages(){

  // create 6 YellowPagesEntry objects (see YellowPagesEntry class
  // definition following this function definition)
  ype1 = new YellowPagesEntry();
  ype1.set("AAA Ear Waxers", 90010);
  ype2 = new YellowPagesEntry();
```

```
      ype2.set("Acme Smarm School", 91602);
      ype3 = new YellowPagesEntry();
      ype3.set("Really Good Staffing", 62234);
      ype4 = new YellowPagesEntry();
      ype4.set("AAA Barn Feng Shui", 63367);
      ype5 = new YellowPagesEntry();
      ype5.set("AAA Clothes Smellers", 91356);
      ype6 = new YellowPagesEntry();
      ype6.set("Better Bowling Shoes", 90210);

      // create a YellowPages object and set its entries property
      // to an array of the 6 YellowPagesEntry objects from above
      yp = new YellowPages();
      yp.entries = new Array(ype1, ype2, ype3, ype4, ype5, ype6);

      // call the find() method of the service object and pass it
      // the YellowPages object and the search string AAA
      _root.srv.find( root.res, yp, "AAA");
  }

// define the YellowPagesEntry class
function YellowPagesEntry(){}
YellowPagesEntry.prototype.name;
YellowPagesEntry.prototype.zip;
YellowPagesEntry.prototype.set = function(name, zip){
  this.name = name;
  this.zip = zip;
}
// register YellowPagesEntry to the fully-qualified name of the
// corresponding Java class
Object.registerClass("wiley.chapter17.YellowPagesEntry",
YellowPagesEntry);

// define the YellowPages class
function YellowPages(){}
YellowPages.prototype.entries;
YellowPages.prototype.listEntries = function(){
  for(var i = 0; i < this.entries.length; i++){
    trace(this.entries[i].name);
  }
}
// register YellowPages to the fully-qualified name of the
// corresponding Java class
Object.registerClass("wiley.chapter17.YellowPages", YellowPages);

res = new Object();
res.onResult = function(result){
  // the result object automatically gets converted to
  // a YellowPages object, so you can call the listEntries()
  // method of the YellowPages ActionScript class of objects
```

```
    result.listEntries();
}

init();
doYellowPages();
```

11. Test your movie. When the server responds, it should display the following in the Output window:

```
AAA Ear Waxers
AAA Barn Feng Shui
AAA Clothes Smellers
```

This is the result because these are the two entries that match the search string provided. If you change the search string, different results will be returned.

Notice that the returned object is a `YellowPages` object, and that the `entries` array's elements are all `YellowPageEntry` objects.

Summary

In this chapter, you learned about `ASTranslator`, a useful utility API for working with Flash Remoting `ASObjects` between Java and Flash. Following are some of the important things to remember from the chapter:

✦ ActionScript typed objects sent to Java are always cast as `ASObject`. This is not the most useful form for you to be able to work with the data. `ASTranslator`'s `fromActionScript()` method helps out by converting the `ASObject` to the appropriate Java type.

✦ Custom Java object types returned to Flash movies are not properly cast even if there is a registered ActionScript class. The `ASTranslator toActionScript()` method will convert Java objects to `ASObject` types so that the Flash Remoting gateway can properly cast them in ActionScript.

✦ Returning an object by way of `ASTranslator` also ensures that only the publicly accessible properties of the Java object are returned to ActionScript, instead of exposing the private members as is normally done by the Flash Remoting gateway.

✦   ✦   ✦

Flash Remoting with .NET

Understanding Flash Remoting with .NET

✦ ✦ ✦ ✦

In This Chapter

Learning what you can expect from Flash Remoting for .NET

Setting up .NET and Flash Remoting

Creating an ASP.NET application

Accessing databases using .NET

✦ ✦ ✦ ✦

Recent years have seen a paradigm shift in the ways in which the Internet, software, and even hardware are developed and operated. Traditionally, these three entities were viewed more or less separately. However, with increasing bandwidth and numerous new protocols and formats for efficiently sharing data, the old paradigm of separation is moving toward one of integration. For example, Web-enabled cell phones already enable users to download ringtones; cars are equipped with GPS units; and some computer devices can automatically check for software updates. Therefore, it is certainly not a far stretch to envision a not-so-distant future in which common household appliances such as refrigerators will be online and able to call a repair service if problems are detected; televisions will be monitored remotely; and home heating and air conditioning systems can be controlled from work or even greater distances.

Microsoft has claimed this vision of the near future as its own creation and touts .NET as the platform that will enable it. Whether Microsoft is truly responsible for this vision is a point of contention I will leave to you. Certainly, however, as you have seen in previous chapters, .NET is not the only implementation of this vision. Web services and distributed applications are the hallmarks of .NET, but are also available as key parts of other platforms as well. That does not, however, detract from the fact that .NET *is* a major force in enabling new kinds of development and pushing forward with these ideas and technologies.

The promotion of .NET has been rather vague in its descriptions of what exactly .NET is. .NET cannot really be classified as an application server. It is more than that in some ways and less than that in others. Microsoft describes .NET as a *framework*, and so that is the word that I will use as well. From a practical standpoint, however, the .NET framework includes compilers and classes that enable you to develop .NET applications as well as a runtime environment (called the Common Language Runtime) in which the applications can be used.

Note   .NET does not include a Web server but is tethered to Internet Information Server (IIS) — Microsoft's Web server, which is included as part of the Windows operating system.

Following is a sampling of some of .NET's benefits and the things you can do using .NET:

✦ **ASP.NET:** Create Web applications using the .NET evolution of Active Server Pages. Many developers view ASP.NET as a vast improvement (both in performance as well as in development) over ASP.

✦ **ADO.NET:** Utilize database information using the Microsoft data access model.

✦ **Web Services:** Share and utilize functionality between applications.

✦ **Directory Services:** Connect to active directories such as LDAP.

✦ **Windows Forms:** Create Windows applications.

Because of the Common Language Runtime (CLR), .NET enables developers to choose between several different programming languages. If you are already familiar with Visual Basic, then you can continue to use VB for developing .NET applications. C# is a new language introduced by .NET that should appear quite familiar to those with Java experience.

 The .NET examples and exercises in this book are written using C#. You can find the VB equivalents to many of the listings on the companion Web site, www.wiley.com/compbooks/lott.

Using Flash Remoting with .NET, you can harness the power of .NET applications by way of a Flash user interface. You can use ADO.NET to enable Flash movies to interact with databases. You can utilize existing ASP.NET application logic. You can even piggyback on the .NET framework to consume Web services without any server-side scripting.

Getting Started with .NET

If you are going to use .NET with Flash Remoting, you need to do a few things in order to get started. Namely, you will want to install the .NET framework and the Flash Remoting services for .NET.

Installing .NET

The installation of .NET is a two-part process:

1. Install Internet Information Services (IIS).

2. Install the .NET Framework Standard Development Kit (SDK).

Setting Up IIS

Internet Information Services is a Web server included as a Windows component for Windows NT Server (requires the Windows NT 4.0 Option Pack), Windows 2000 Server, Windows XP Professional, and Windows .NET Server. In order to set up IIS on a computer with one of these operating systems, follow these steps:

1. Open the Control Panel. Figure 18-1 shows how to access the Control Panel from the Start menu.

Figure 18-1: Choosing the Control Panel from the Start menu

2. In the Control Panel, choose the Add or Remove Programs panel.

3. When the Add or Remove Programs panel is opened, select the Add/Remove Windows Components button from the left, as shown in Figure 18-2.

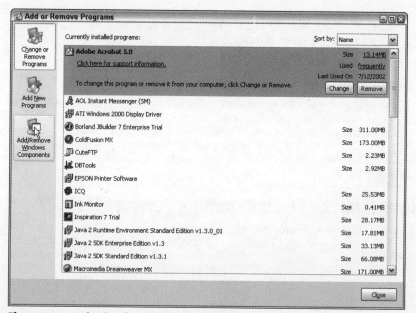

Figure 18-2: Selecting the Add/Remove Windows Components button

4. In the Windows Component Wizard, make sure that Internet Information Services is checked, as shown in Figure 18-3, and click Next.

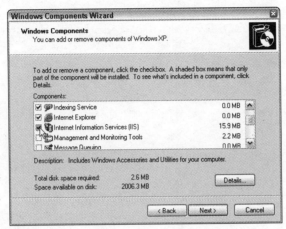

Figure 18-3: Adding Internet Information Services

5. After the installation of IIS is successfully completed, follow the prompts and close any windows and panels that you no longer need.

Note

IIS installs its directory structure, by default, in C:\Inetpub on your computer. If you used a different directory, keep that in mind and adjust accordingly when references are made throughout the upcoming chapters to the IIS installation directory.

IIS allows you to configure multiple Web sites. One default Web site is installed automatically. The default Web site's root directory is created in the wwwroot subdirectory of the IIS installation. Throughout the upcoming chapters, I assume that you are using this Web site with its default settings. Otherwise, adjust accordingly.

Setting Up the .NET Framework SDK

After you have successfully installed IIS, the next step is to install the .NET Framework SDK. If you don't have the SDK installation already on CD or on your hard drive, then you will want to download it from the Microsoft site. The SDK is a free download that you can find at http://msdn.microsoft.com/netframework/. Once you have the installation, simply run it. You will be walked through a wizard interface that will prompt you for any information required.

Installing the Flash Remoting Services for .NET

Installing Flash Remoting for .NET is a painless and simple process. If you don't already have the Flash Remoting for .NET installation, you will want to download it from the Macromedia Web site (www.macromedia.com). The developer edition is a free download. Once you have the installation file, it is simply a matter of running the executable and following the wizard prompts.

Setting Up the Application Framework

If you are going to use Flash Remoting to make calls to ASPX pages or ASP.NET DLLs, you need to first ensure that you have properly set up and configured the ASP.NET application to which the pages belong. This section describes how to successfully set up your application so that you will be able to use Flash Remoting with it.

Creating a New Application

In order for Flash Remoting to work with ASP.NET pages and DLLs, the Flash movie must be able to locate the gateway. For .NET, the gateway is made possible by way of an assembly (flashgateway.dll) located in the application's local assembly cache. This is explained in more detail in the next section. For starters, what this means is that your ASPX pages and DLLs must exist within an application. In order to create an application, you should open the Internet Information Services administrative tool (management console). You can generally access this tool from your Start menu (Start➪(All) Programs➪Administrative Tools➪Internet Information Services).

Once you have the IIS administrative tool opened, you should see an icon in the left pane labeled with your computer's name and (local computer). Next to the icon should be a plus sign, which enables you to expand the menu. In the expanded menu is another menu called Web Sites. Within Web Sites is Default Web Site. The default Web site's home directory is, by default, C:\Inetput\wwwroot. You can confirm this for yourself if you right-click on Default Web Site and choose Properties. In the new window that appears (Default Web Site Properties), select the Home Directory tab (see Figure 18-4). You can see that the local path that is used is C:\Inetput\wwwroot. When you are done, simply click Cancel.

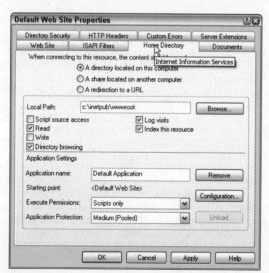

Figure 18-4: The home directory for the default Web site

If you expand the Default Web Site menu (see Figure 18-5), you will see a series of icons representing the contents of the default Web site. Some are actual subdirectories of the local path, while others are virtual directories (more on that below).

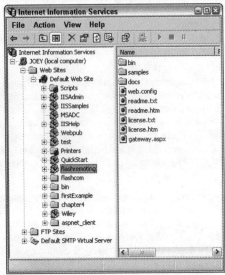

Figure 18-5: Viewing the contents of the default Web site

When you installed Flash Remoting for .NET, a directory was automatically created within your default Web site's home directory. The directory was named flashremoting. You will notice that flashremoting shows up in the IIS administration tool, but, as with some other menu items, its icon is a package icon (a box with a ball in it), instead of the folder icon used for other menu items. This icon indicates that the folder is an application starting point (the root of an application). You can change any of the directories into applications by modifying the properties for that directory. Select the flashremoting menu item, right-click on it, and select Properties. In the dialog box that appears, you will note a section labeled Application Settings in the lower portion (see Figure 18-3). Clicking the Remove button will remove the application setting from the directory. Clicking Create will create the application setting. Click Cancel when you are finished.

You may also notice that some of the menu items under Default Web Site are not physical subdirectories under the default Web site's home directory. For example, there is no directory named IISAdmin within C:\Inetpub\wwwroot. These directories are *virtual directories*. With IIS, you can enable any directory accessible from your computer to be accessible from a logical path under a Web site. To do this, use the following steps to create a virtual directory and application that you will use for exercises throughout the rest of this chapter.

1. If you haven't already done so, create a new directory named Wiley on your computer in C:\.

2. Within the Wiley directory, create a subdirectory named NET.

3. In the IIS administration tool, right-click on Default Web Site and choose New⇨ Virtual Directory. Alternatively, you can click on Default Web Site and then choose Actions⇨New⇨Virtual Directory.

4. The Virtual Directory Creation Wizard will open. Click Next.

5. In the Alias text field, enter `Wiley` and click Next.

6. In the Directory text field, enter C:\Wiley\NET (or the path to the directory you created in step 1) and click Next.

7. Leave Read and Run scripts checked and click Next.

8. Click Finish.

You should now see the Wiley virtual directory listed under Default Web Site in the IIS administration tool. You will notice that the icon indicates that the newly created virtual directory has already had the application setting applied to it.

Configuring the Application

Once you have created an application in the IIS administration tool, the next step is to configure it for use with Flash Remoting. There are two steps in this process:

✦ Setting up the local assembly cache

✦ Defining the web.config file

Creating the local assembly cache

Assembly caches are simply directories containing .NET assemblies (.dll files) that are accessible to .NET applications. ASP.NET applications can draw upon the global assembly cache as well as a local assembly cache. The global assembly cache is part of the .NET framework installation (installed under the Windows installation directory) and is accessible to *all* .NET applications. You don't have to do anything in order to make the assemblies in the global cache accessible to ASP.NET applications. Local assembly caches are those that are accessible only to an individual application.

In ASP.NET applications, the local assembly cache is composed of any assemblies placed into a directory named bin within the application's root. Therefore, if you want to create a local assembly cache for an application, the first step is to create a directory named bin in the application's root directory. The next step is to simply copy the desired assemblies into that directory.

Flash Remoting for .NET is made possible by an assembly named flashgateway.dll. You can find a copy of this file in the bin directory of the flashremoting application's root (usually C:\Inetpub\wwwroot\flashremoting\), which is created as part of the Flash Remoting for .NET installation. Any time you want to create a new ASP.NET application that uses Flash Remoting, you must include the flashgateway.dll file in that application's local assembly cache.

To set up the Wiley application's local assembly cache for use with Flash Remoting, do the following:

1. Create a new directory named bin inside the Wiley application's root (home directory). If you created this application's root according to the instructions in the previous section of this chapter, then the directory is C:\Wiley\NET.

2. Copy the flashgateway.dll file into the Wiley application's bin directory. You should be able to find the DLL in the flashremoting application's local assembly cache.

Creating the configuration file

ASP.NET applications can be configured, in part, using a special file named web.config. The web.config file is an XML file stored in the application's root directory. A large assortment of settings can be configured in this file, some of which we will look at a little later in this chapter. One setting, however, must be configured specifically in relation to Flash Remoting.

When Flash Remoting calls are made to ASPX pages, .NET must somehow know that requests to these pages should be pre-processed by the Flash Remoting service. In order to accomplish this, an HTTP Module is used. HTTP Modules can be added using the <add> subtag of the <httpModules> tag. <httpModules>, in turn, must appear within a <system.web> element. Moreover, web.config files must always have a <configuration> tag as the root element. Listing 18-1 shows a basic web.config file for an application using Flash Remoting.

Listing 18-1: **Sample web.config File**

```
<?xml version="1.0" encoding="utf-8" ?>
<configuration>
  <system.web>
    <httpModules>
      <add name="GatewayController"
type="FlashGateway.Controller.GatewayController,flashgateway" />
    </httpModules>
  </system.web>
</configuration>
```

The <add> tag has two attributes. The name attribute is simply a name given to the module so that it can be referenced later. The type attribute specifies the fully qualified class name and the assembly name, separated by a comma. In this case, the fully qualified class name for the Flash Remoting gateway is FlashGateway.Controller.GatewayController, and the assembly name is flashgateway (as in flashgateway.dll).

Therefore, in order to set up your Wiley application for use with Flash Remoting, do the following:

1. Open a new document in an editor such as Dreamweaver or Notepad.

2. Type the XML from Listing 18-1 into the new document.

3. Save the document in the Wiley application's root directory as web.config.

Accessing Databases with .NET

Microsoft's mechanism for database access is called ActiveX Data Objects for .NET (ADO.NET). ADO.NET is a collection of classes and interfaces that enable all standard database operations from within .NET applications. You can find all of these classes and interfaces within the System.Data namespace.

When you are working with databases using .NET in conjunction with Flash Remoting, there are basically four parts to consider:

✦ **The database:** The database can be of any type as long as a driver exists and is installed.

✦ **The managed provider:** This is the part that is responsible for handling the connection between the .NET application and the database, and for issuing commands via that connection.

✦ **The DataSet object:** This .NET object remains independent of the database connection that is made (and hence the managed provider used). The DataSet object is composed of DataTable objects. The DataTable object is analogous to the ActionScript RecordSet object.

✦ **The Flash client:** The DataSet object returned to the Flash client will be automatically marshaled into an array of RecordSet objects. If a DataTable object is returned to the Flash client, it will be marshaled into a single RecordSet object.

Selecting the Database

If you are working with a Microsoft database such as SQL Server, then you do not need to worry about making sure that you have the needed drivers in order to access it using ADO.NET. On the other hand, if you are using a non-Microsoft database such as MySQL, then you may need to ensure you have the proper drivers installed. As you will learn in the next section, some additional, database-specific managed providers may become available. If you use these managed providers, they should provide the needed drivers. Otherwise, you will need to make sure that you have installed the OLE DB driver for the specific DBMS you are using. For example, Chapter 4 provides instructions for downloading and installing the OLE DB driver for MySQL.

Using a Managed Provider

ADO.NET handles all the database connections and access through what are known as *managed providers*. Managed providers are simply namespaces with classes that implement common interfaces for connecting to databases and executing commands against those databases. Currently, the .NET SDK includes two managed providers: one for SQL Server and one for OLE DB–compliant data sources. Additionally, Microsoft has released an ODBC managed provider available as an add-on component for .NET.

Using any managed provider should be essentially the same as using any other managed provider. The only differences are the names of the specific classes used. For example, all managed providers should implement the System.Data.IDbConnection interface. In the SQL Server managed provider, the name of the class that implements this interface is named SqlConnection, whereas the OLE DB managed provider class that implements the interface is named OleDbConnection. The next few sections describe how to use the SQL Server and OLE DB managed providers. Once you know how to use one managed provider, that knowledge should easily transfer to using any managed provider.

 Note While it is a relatively simple task to switch databases and managed providers, be aware that some SQL commands are database-specific. This means that when you switch databases you may have to rewrite some of your SQL statements.

Before looking at the specific examples using managed providers, let's look first at the basic logic that is used. Many different variations are possible, but here I will outline three basic steps to creating a connection and executing a command using a managed provider.

1. **Create the connection:** This step involves creating the connection object for the database you wish to use. The connection object is an instance of a class that implements the System.Data.IDbConnection interface.

2. **Create the command:** In this step you create the command object that will be executed against the database (e.g., the SELECT statement, the UPDATE statement, etc.). The command object is an instance of a class that implements the System.Data.IDbCommand interface.

3. **Create the adapter:** The data adapter is used to actually execute the commands against the database, and later to fill the DataSet object. The data adapter object is an instance of a class that implements the System.Data.IDbDataAdapter interface.

The SQL Server managed provider

The SQL Server managed provider classes are all found in the System.Data.SQLClient namespace. Therefore, when you are using a SQL Server database, you will likely want to include this namespace and the System.Data namespace with the following code:

```
using System.Data;
using System.Data.SQLClient;
```

The name of the connection class in the SQL Server managed provider is SqlConnection. The constructor for this class takes a connection string passed to it as a parameter. There are many variations on the connection string, but in its simplest format, it has four parts:

✦ **Data Source:** The server name or IP address where SQL Server is running

✦ **Initial Catalog:** The name of the SQL Server database to use

✦ **User ID:** The username

✦ **Password:** The password

Here is an example of a connection object being created for a SQL Server database named myDb running on localhost with a username and password combination of igoodie and 12345:

```
String connStr = "Data Source=locahost;Initial Catalog=myDb;User
ID=igoodie;pwd=12345;";
SqlConnection conn = new SqlConnection(connStr);
```

The name of the command class in the SQL Server managed provider is SqlCommand. The constructor for this class accepts two parameters. The first parameter is a string representing the SQL command. The second parameter is the connection object. Here is an example of a SqlCommand object being created to represent a SELECT statement to be executed against the database represented by the connection object conn:

```
String sqlStr = "SELECT * FROM users";
SqlCommand cmd = new SqlCommand(sqlStr, conn);
```

The name of the adapter class for the SQL Server managed provider is SqlDataAdapter. You can create the object by calling the constructor without any parameters:

```
SqlDataAdapter adp = new SqlDataAdapter();
```

SqlDataAdapter objects have four properties that are of type SqlCommand. These properties—SelectCommand, InsertCommand, UpdateCommand, and DeleteCommand—can be assigned the value of the command objects you created. It is expected that the SQL statement provided by the command object should match the property to which it is assigned. For instance, the command object assigned to the SelectCommand property should have a

SELECT statement as its SQL command. In the following example, a `SqlDataAdapter` object named `adp` has a `SqlCommand` object named `cmd` assigned to the `SelectCommand` property:

```
adp.SelectCommand = cmd;
```

The OLE DB managed provider

The OLE DB managed provider classes are found in the `System.Data.OleDbClient` namespace. Therefore, when you are going to use this managed provider, it is a good idea to include its namespace as well as the `System.Data` namespace with the following code:

```
using System.Data;
using System.Data.OleDbClient;
```

The OLE DB connection object class is named `OleDbConnection`. You can create an object of this type using the constructor and passing it a connection string parameter. The connection string for OLE DB connection objects can have many parts, but in a simple format will likely consist of the following:

✦ **Provider:** The name of the OLE DB provider for the DBMS you are using

✦ **Data Source:** The name of the database

✦ **User ID:** The username for the database

✦ **Password:** The password for the database

Here is an example of a connection object being created for a MySQL database named myDb with a username and password combination of igoodie and 12345. The provider is MySQLProvider. This is the provider downloaded and installed in Chapter 4.

```
string connStr = "Provider=MySQLProvider;Data Source=myDb;User
ID=igoodie;Password=12345;";
OleDbConnection conn = new OleDbConnection(connStr);
```

The name of the command class in the OLE DB managed provider is `OleDbCommand`. Creating an instance of this class works just as it did with the `SqlCommand` class. Here is an example of a `OleDbCommand` object being created to represent a SELECT statement to be executed against the database represented by the connection object `conn`:

```
String sqlStr = "SELECT * FROM users";
OleDbCommand cmd = new OleDbCommand(sqlStr, conn);
```

The name of the adapter class for the OLE DB managed provider is `OleDbDataAdapter`. The `OleDbDataAdapter` class works like the `SqlDataAdapter` class:

```
OleDbDataAdapter adp = new OleDbDataAdapter();
```

Like `SqlDataAdapter` objects, `OleDbDataAdapter` objects have four properties — `SelectCommand`, `InsertCommand`, `UpdateCommand`, and `DeleteCommand` — that are used for executing statements against the database. These properties are all of type `OleDbCommand`. Here is an example in which an `OleDbDataAdapter` object named `adp` has a `OleDbCommand` object named `cmd` assigned to the `SelectCommand` property:

```
adp.SelectCommand = cmd;
```

Adding More Providers

Available from Microsoft is an add-on component for .NET that enables you to make connections to databases by way of ODBC. This add-on is available for download at `http://msdn.microsoft.com/downloads/default.asp?url=/downloads/sample.asp?url=/msdn-files/027/001/668/msdncompositedoc.xml`.

The file that you download is named `odbc_net.msi`. In order to install the file, you must have the .NET SDK already installed. If so, you merely run the file by double-clicking on it and follow the prompts of the wizard. The installation automatically includes the DLL in the general assembly cache, so you do not need to include the file in your project's source.

Additionally, for a native provider for MySQL, you can check out the dbProvider product from eInfoDesigns or MySqlDirect .NET from Core Lab. You can read more information about these products at `http://www.einfodesigns.com/dbProvider_info.aspx` and `http://crlab.com/mysqlnet/`, respectively.

Using a DataSet

DataSet objects (`System.Data.DataSet`) function more or less to contain data in table form. DataSet objects are actually containers for DataTable objects. Each DataTable can contain the data from a table in the database. You can create a new DataSet object with the following basic constructor:

```
DataSet ds = new DataSet();
```

Once you have a DataSet object, you can populate it by calling the `Fill()` method of the adapter object. The `Fill()` method is the same no matter which managed provider you are using. You can pass the method two parameters—the DataSet object to be filled, and a string value indicating the name that should be given to the table filled. Because the DataSet object is a container for DataTable objects, you must name the DataTable object that is being filled. Here is an example in which the adapter object named adp executes a SELECT statement from a command object named cmd, and then fills a table named Results in a DataSet object named ds:

```
adp.SelectCommand = cmd;
adp.Fill(ds, "Results");
```

When working with Flash Remoting, you can return either a DataSet object or a DataTable object. The DataSet object is converted into an associative array of RecordSet objects in ActionScript. DataTable objects, on the other hand, are converted into single RecordSet objects. If you want to return just a single DataTable, you can extract the DataTable from the Tables property of the DataSet object—which is a collection of DataTable objects within the DataSet. You can access the DataTables by order (integer indexes) or by name. For example, if the Results table is the only DataTable in the ds object, then you could access it either by its index:

```
DataTable dt = ds.Tables[0];
```

or by its name:

```
DataTable dt = ds.Tables["Results"];
```

Note   `DataSet` (and `DataTable`) objects are known as *disconnected*. This means that no connection is maintained between the object and the database, nor does the `DataSet` know anything about the database or the SQL commands that were used to fill it. `DataSet` objects serve simply as containers for record set data.

Converting Data Types

As with Flash Remoting for every other platform, the services for .NET automatically convert data types between the .NET application and the Flash application. Table 18-1 shows how ActionScript data types are converted to C# data types or VB data types, and Table 18-2 shows how C# data types or VB data types are converted to ActionScript data types.

Table 18-1: ActionScript to .NET Conversions

ActionScript Data Type	C# Data Type	VB Data Type
`null`	`Null`	?
`undefined`	`Undefined`	?
`Boolean`	`System.Boolean`	`Boolean`
`Number`	**Appropriate numeric type**	**appropriate numeric type**
`String`	`System.String`	`String`
`Date`	`System.DateTime`	`Date`
`Array`	`System.Collections.ArrayList`	`System.Collections.ArrayList`
`Object` (associative array)	`System.Collections.Hashtable`	`System.Collections.Hashtable`
`XML`	`System.Xml.XmlDocument`	`System.Xml.XmlDocument`
`Typed Object`	`FlashGateway.IO.ASObject`	`FlashGateway.IO.ASObject`

Table 18-2: .NET to ActionScript Conversions

C# Data Type	VB Data Type	ActionScript Data Type
`Null`	?	`Boolean`
`Bool` `System.Boolean`	`Boolean`	`Boolean`
`any numeric type`	`any numeric type`	`Number`

Continued

Table 18-2: *(continued)*

C# Data Type	VB Data Type	ActionScript Data Type
System.Char System.String	Char String	String
System.DateTime	Date	Date
any object that implements System.Collections .ICollection any array	System.Collections .ICollection object[]	Array
System.Collections .Hashtable System.Collections .IDictionary	System.Collections .Hashtable System.Collections .IDictionary	Object (associative array)
System.Xml .XmlDocument	System.Xml .XmlDocument	XML
FlashGateway .IO.ASObject	FlashGateway .IO.ASObject	typed object
System.Data .DataTable	System.Data .DataTable	RecordSet
System.Data .DataSet	System.Data .DataSet	associative array of RecordSet objects

Summary

You should now have a general understanding of what .NET is and how it can be used in relationship to Flash Remoting. Highlights of this chapter include the following points:

✦ The .NET framework is Microsoft's answer to distributed application development for the present and near future. With the use of Flash Remoting, Flash movies can make use of .NET features such as database functionality.

✦ In order to get started, you must install IIS, the .NET SDK, and Flash Remoting for .NET.

✦ In order to use ASP.NET with Flash Remoting, your ASPX pages and ASP.NET DLLs must exist within an ASP.NET application defined in IIS.

✦ Database access in .NET is made possible by way of ADO.NET. You have seen how to use managed providers to access databases. You have also learned how to fill DataSet objects and return the results to ActionScript RecordSet objects.

✦   ✦   ✦

Listing 19-3: **Adding In-Line Script**

```
<%@ Page language="C#" %>
<html>
  <body>
    <form runat="server">
      <asp:label text="This is an ASPX page" id="myLabel"
runat="server" />
    <br>
    <asp:button text="Change!" id="myButton" runat="server"
onClick="myButtonClick" />
    </form>
  </body>
</html>
<script language="C#" runat="server">
  void myButtonClick(object sender, System.EventArgs ea){
    myLabel.Text = "Wow! I changed!";
  }
</script>
```

 Note   Functions that are assigned to event handlers such as `onClick` must accept two parameters—an `object` and a `System.EventArgs` parameter.

The `myButtonClick()` function is assigned to the `myButton` `Click` event by setting the `onClick` attribute. Note also that the `label` control's `Text` property can be modified from within the in-line script.

Working with Code-Behind

In keeping with object-oriented development, you can use what is known as *code-behind*. Code-behind enables you to create a class file from which the ASPX page inherits. This way, you can keep the majority of the script out of the ASPX page. Additionally, multiple ASPX pages can inherit from a single code-behind class. This is a powerful way of sharing common functionality. When using code-behind you have at least two files — the ASPX document and a compiled class library (.dll).

First, let's look at the code-behind class. Here are a few guidelines for creating a code-behind class:

✦ It should be compiled and placed into the application's local assembly cache (bin directory).

✦ It should be inherit from the `Page` class (`System.Web.UI.Page`).

✦ Server control objects must be defined within the class.

Listing 19-4 shows an example of a code-behind class that contains the `myButtonClick()` function.

Interacting with ASP.NET Pages

✦   ✦   ✦   ✦

In This Chapter

Working with basic concepts used in creating ASPX pages

Making calls to ASPX pages from Flash movies

Including the necessary object in your ASPX pages to make them Flash Remoting-ready

Passing values to and from ASPX pages

✦   ✦   ✦   ✦

ASP.NET is designed for building applications for deployment on the Web. ASP.NET (.aspx) pages are one part of these Web applications, and are typically intended for the presentation of the application within a Web browser. As such, ASPX pages typically contain layout information and additional content for display in the Web browser. They are not intended to be called as procedures, because doing so is rather less efficient than calling an assembly method. That said, however, it makes sense to be able to call ASPX pages as remote procedures via Flash Remoting, in order to leverage preexisting logic and programming within a Flash user interface. For instance, you or your company may already have an existing application that uses ASPX pages as the user interface. If so, with just a little modification you could call those pages as remote procedures from a Flash movie. By doing so, you effectively have both an ASP.NET and a Flash user interface that utilizes the same underlying application structure.

The Anatomy of ASP.NET

An ASP.NET application can contain many parts, but for our purposes in this chapter, we'll look at the following:

✦ Basic structure and directives

✦ Server controls

✦ Render blocks

✦ In-line script

✦ Code-behind

Examining ASPX Page Structure

In its simplest form, an ASPX page is simply composed of HTML. All HTML elements are valid elements of ASPX pages. Therefore, for example, the code shown in Listing 19-1 would be perfectly valid ASPX code.

Listing 19-1: **A Simple ASPX Page**

```
<html>
  <body>
    This is an ASPX page
  </body>
</html>
```

In addition to basic HTML elements are many other ASPX-specific elements. Among those that pertain to the entire page are elements called *directives*. ASPX pages actually get compiled into classes, and directives are a way of taking care of classlike settings within the ASPX tag-based structure. For instance, using the Page directive, you can specify inheritance (as you will see in the code-behind section of this chapter). All directives are indicated by an opening <%@ and a closing %>. Here is an example of a basic Page directive that specifies the language (C#) for the page:

```
<%@ Page language="C#" %>
```

Directives can be placed anywhere within the ASPX document, but are conventionally placed at the top.

Adding Server Controls

Server controls are ASP.NET elements that provide an easy way to programmatically affect what is displayed in the page (as well as the behavior of the page). For example, using the button control, you can create a button on a page to which you can assign actions (such as submitting a form). You could also create text that can be programmatically altered (color, content, alignment, etc.) using the label control. A large assortment of server controls is available, but all of them should adhere to the following rules:

✦ The control code must appear inside a <form> tag, with the runat attribute set to server.

✦ The control tag must be properly terminated. Either the opening tag must be matched correctly to a closing tag, or the tag must be terminated by an ending forward slash.

✦ The control element itself should have its runat attribute set to server (this is in addition to the runat attribute's being set in the <form> tag).

✦ The control element should also have a value assigned to the id attribute if it is to be controlled programmatically.

When displayed in the browser, Listing 19-2 creates effectively the same result as the code from Listing 19-1, but does it using a label control. However, as you will see in just a moment, the label control allows for greater programmatic control.

Listing 19-2: **Adding a label Control**

```
<%@ Page language="C#" %>
<html>
  <body>
    <form runat="server">
      <asp:label text="This is an ASPX page" id="myLabel"
runat="server" />
    </form>
  </body>
</html>
```

Understanding Render Blocks

In ASP (before .NET), the only way to add programming logic and dynamic output to a page was by way of render blocks. In ASPX pages, you have other options, but render blocks can still be useful. Render blocks are demarcated by <% and %>. In between these opening and closing marks, you can place programming code (using the language specified in the Page directive). Here is an example of code in a render block that calculates the current date and time:

```
<%
System.DateTime dt = DateTime.Now;
%>
```

You can also use a variation on the render block to output a value within the ASPX page. Placing the value to be output between <%= and %> will accomplish this. For example:

```
<%@ Page language="C#" %>
<html>
  <body>
    <%
    System.DateTime dt = DateTime.Now;
    %>
    Right now it is: <%=dt%>
  </body>
</html>
```

Using In-Line Script

In-line script allows C#, Visual Basic, or any of the other ASP.NET-supported languages to be inserted into an ASPX page. In-line script should be positioned between the opening and closing <script> tags. The <script> tag should have two attributes. The language attribute should be set to indicate the programming language that will be used, and the runat attribute should be set to server.

Within the in-line script, you can add functions that can be assigned to server control events. For example, the button control can cause a Click event to occur. You can define a function and then assign that function to be called when the Click event occurs. Listing 19-3 shows how this can be done, adding to the code from Listing 19-2 (changes in bold).

Listing 19-4: **A Simple Code-Behind Class**

```
namespace Wiley.Chapter19 {

  public class FirstCodeBehind : System.Web.UI.Page {

    protected System.Web.UI.WebControls.Label myLabel;

    protected void myButtonClick(object sender, System.EventArgs ea){
    myLabel.Text = "Wow! I changed!";
    }


    }

}
```

The ASPX page that uses the code-behind class must inherit it. You can do this simply by specifying the fully qualified class name in the inherits attribute of the Page directive. Listing 19-5 shows an ASPX page that inherits the code-behind class shown in Listing 19-4.

Listing 19-5: **An ASPX Page Inheriting a Code-Behind Class**

```
<%@ Page language="C#" inherits="Wiley.Chapter19.FirstCodeBehind" %>
<html>
  <body>
    <form runat="server">
      <asp:label text="This is an ASPX page" id="myLabel"
runat="server" />
      <br>
      <asp:button text="Change!" id="myButton" runat="server"
onClick="myButtonClick" />
    </form>
  </body>
</html>
```

By default, certain events are handled automatically by the ASPX page. For example, the Load event is automatically handled, and any additional handlers that are assigned within control tags (such as with onClick attributes) are configured. However, when you are using code-behind classes, it is a good idea to explicitly do all of this. The reason for this is two-fold. First of all, explicitly wiring up methods to handle events allows you more control over the way the page is processed than allowing the events to be automatically handled. Second, many ASPX editors (such as VS.NET) automatically write the code this way, and so it is good to familiar-ize yourself with the process so that you can understand code generated by those editors.

In order to accomplish this, the first thing you should do is turn off the autowiring in the ASPX page. Autowiring simply means that certain events (`Init`, `Load`, `DataBinding`, `PreRender`, `Dispose`, and `Error`) are automatically handled by default. However, you want the capability to write your own code to handle these events. To turn off autowiring, simply set the `autoEventWireup` attribute to false in the `Page` directive. For example:

```
<%@ Page language="C#" inherits="Wiley.Chapter19.FirstCodeBehind"
autoEventWireup="false" %>
```

When you turn off autowiring, you need to modify the code-behind class. Here is a brief overview of the changes:

✦ Add a constructor. Within the constructor, assign a method to handle the `Page.Init` event.

✦ Within the method that handles the `Init` event, assign methods to any additional events that should be handled. This should include handling the `Page.Load` event.

✦ Within the method that handles the `Load` event, take care of any page view needs, such as setting label control values.

Listing 19-6 shows a reworking of the ASPX page from Listing 19-5. In this example, the autowiring is set to false, the text attribute is removed from the label control tag, and the event handler assignment is removed from the button control tag.

Listing 19-6: **A Non-Autowired ASPX Page**

```
<%@ Page language="C#" inherits="Wiley.Chapter19.FirstCodeBehind"
autoEventWireup="false" %>
<html>
  <body>
    <form runat="server">
      <asp:label id="myLabel" runat="server" />
    <br>
    <asp:button text="Change!" id="myButton" runat="server"
onClick="myButtonClick" />
    </form>
  </body>
</html>
```

Listing 19-7 shows the code-behind class that accompanies the ASPX page from Listing 19-6.

Listing 19-7: **A Complete Code-Behind Class**

```
namespace Wiley.Chapter19 {

  using System;
  using System.Web.UI.WebControls;
```

```
public class FirstCodeBehind : System.Web.UI.Page {

  protected Label myLabel;
  protected Button myButton;

  public FirstCodeBehind(){
    Page.Init += new System.EventHandler(initPage);
  }

  protected void initPage(object sender, EventArgs ea){
    Page.Load += new System.EventHandler(loadPage);
    myButton.Click += new System.EventHandler(myButtonClick);
  }

  protected void loadPage(object sender, EventArgs ea){
    myLabel.Text = "This is an ASPX page";
  }

  protected void myButtonClick(object sender, EventArgs ea){
    myLabel.Text = "Wow! I changed!";
  }

}

}
```

Creating Simple ASP.NET Applications

As stated previously, the real advantage of using Flash Remoting with ASP.NET pages is the capability to leverage existing ASPX page functionality from your Flash movies. In order to see how this works, I am first going to walk you through creating some small ASP.NET-only applications. Later in this chapter, you will revisit these examples by calling them from Flash movies.

Counting Users

In this exercise, you create an ASPX page that displays how many users are currently using the application—whether the sessions are opened on the same machine or halfway across the world. In order to do this, you will need to use the Global.asax file.

The Global.asax file is a special file that, when placed in the application's root directory, is automatically run by .NET. Into this file you can place some special methods that are automatically wired up to application and session events. In this exercise, you use the `Application_Start` method, the `Session_Start` method, and the `Session_End` method. The names of these methods describe the events to which they are wired.

The basic idea is that when the application is first started (meaning when the very first request is made), you set an application-wide variable to 0 to initialize the number of users to 0. Each time a session is started, the application-wide variable indicating the number of users will be incremented. This is also when you set the timeout for each session to 1 minute. This means that after one minute of inactivity, the session will end. When the sessions end, one user is automatically subtracted from the application-wide variable.

Note Because sessions encompass all open browser windows of the same browser program, you need at least two browser programs to test this exercise (or two different computers). I provide instructions in this exercise for how to do this with two different browser programs on the same computer. It is tested using Internet Explorer 6 and Netscape 4.7. You could also use Opera or any other program or versions.

The following steps outline the creation of a user-counter application as described in the preceding paragraphs:

1. Open a new document in your favorite ASPX editor (Dreamweaver MX, WordPad, etc.), and save it as Global.asax in the Wiley application root directory.

2. Add the following code to the Global.asax file:

```
<%@ Import namespace="System.IO" %>
<script language="C#" runat="server">

    // called when the application first starts
    void Application_Start(object sender, EventArgs ea){
      // initialize this application-wide variable to 0;
      Application["users"] = 0;
    }

    // called for each new user session
    void Session_Start(object sender, EventArgs ea){
      // increment the user variable
      Application["users"] = (int) Application["users"] + 1;
      // set the session to timeout after a minute
      Session.Timeout = 1;
    }

    // called after session times out
    void Session_End(object sender, EventArgs ea){
      // decrement the user variable
      Application["users"] = (int) Application["users"] - 1;
    }

</script>
```

Note `Application` and `Session` are predefined variables available from any ASPX page and from the Global.asax file for any ASP.NET application. Values added to the collection do not preserve their type, so when retrieving the value, you have to cast it correctly (as in (int) `Application["users"]`).

3. Save the Global.asax file.

4. Open a new ASPX document and save it as currentUsers.aspx in the Wiley application root directory.

5. In this document, add the following code:

```
<%@ Page Language="C#" %>
<html>
<head>
<title>Users</title>
</head>
<body>
<%
// get number of users
int usersNum = (int) Application["users"];
string verb = "are";
string plural = "s";
// choose correct subject/verb agreement
if(usersNum == 1){
    verb = "is";
    plural = "";
}

%>
There <%=verb%> currently <%= usersNum%> user<%=plural%> online.
</body>
</html>
```

6. Save the document.

7. In your first browser program (I am using IE), open
http://localhost/Wiley/currentUsers.aspx. It should say the following:

```
There is currently 1 user online
```

Figure 19-1 shows what this looks like.

Figure 19-1: Browser 1, one session open

8. In your second browser program (I am using Netscape), open the same URL. It should read as follows:

```
There are currently 2 users online
```

Figure 19-2 shows what this looks like.

Figure 19-2: Browser 2, two
sessions open

9. Return to the first browser and refresh the view. This browser should also now indicate
   two online users (see Figure 19-3).

Figure 19-3: Browser 1, two
sessions open

10. If you want, you can wait for a minute or two and then refresh one or the other browser
    windows. Only one session should then be open (because the sessions timeout after a
    minute according to the settings in Global.asax).

Making a Guestbook

In this exercise, you use a code-behind class and some simple server controls in an ASAX
page to create a guestbook application. This application performs three main functions:

- ✦ Enables the user to add a new guestbook entry
- ✦ Lists an index of current entries
- ✦ Enables the user to view an entry by selecting it from the index

This application is more advanced than the previous one. In presenting it, I am assuming that
you are familiar enough with C# to understand it. However, the following two concepts may
be new to you even if you are familiar with C#:

✦ Using the <appSettings> section of the web.config file for the application, it is possible to create some variables that are accessible throughout the application. This is similar to creating an element within the `Application` collection. The value is then accessible from any ASPX page in the application by way of the `System.Configuration.ConfigurationSettings.AppSettings` collection.

✦ In this exercise, you read and write from files. This is accomplished with the `StreamReader` and `StreamWriter` objects (both classes are part of the `System.IO` namespace).

  • The `StreamReader` constructor is overloaded to accept a `FileStream` parameter (which is obtained in this case by way of the `File.OpenRead()` method). You can then read the file all at once with the `StreamReader` object's `ReadToEnd()` method. Once you are done with the `StreamReader` object, call the `Close()` method.

  • The `StreamWriter` constructor is overloaded to accept a string specifying the file to which to write. You can then call the `Write()` and `WriteLine()` methods of the object to write to the file. When you are done, you should call the `Close()` method.

The following steps walk you through the process of creating a guestbook application:

1. Create a new directory in the Wiley application root named guestBookEntries.

2. Open a new document in your favorite ASPX/Text/XML editor and save it to the Wiley application root directory as web.config.

3. Add the following code to the document. This will add to the `AppSettings` collection a key named `path`, which will hold the value of the path to the guestBookEntries directory.

```
<?xml version="1.0" encoding="utf-8" ?>
<configuration>

  <appSettings>
    <add key="path" value="C:\\Wiley\\guestBookEntries\\" />
  </appSettings>


</configuration>
```

Note   Make sure that the value for the path correctly indicates the path to guestBookEntries for *your* application if it differs from what is shown here. The backslashes are doubled because the single backslash is interpreted as part of an escape sequence.

4. Save web.config.

5. Open a new document and save it to the Wiley application root as guestBook.aspx.

6. Add the following code to the document and then save it. This ASPX page uses a code-behind class named `GuestBook`, which you will define next. All this page does is create the controls and lay out the page.

```
<%@ Page Language="C#" inherits="Wiley.Chapter19.GuestBook"
autoEventWireup="false" %>
<html>
<head>
<title>Guestbook</title>
```

```
  </head>
  <body>
    <form runat="server">
      <asp:label id="entry" runat="server" />
    <hr>
    <b>Make a guestbook entry</b><br>
    Name:<br>
    <asp:textbox id="name" runat="server" />
    <br>
      Message:<br>
    <asp:textbox textmode="multiline" rows="5" columns="50"
id="message" runat="server" />
    <br>
    <asp:button Text="Add Entry" ID="addButton" runat="server" />
    <hr>
    <b>Select an entry to view</b><br>
    <asp:label id="entries" runat="server" />
    </form>
  </body>
</html>
```

7. Open a new document in your favorite C#/text editor and save it as GuestBook.cs to the Wiley application's `bin` directory.

8. In the new document, add the following code:

```csharp
namespace Wiley.Chapter19 {

  using System;
  using System.IO;
  using System.Web.UI.WebControls;
  using System.Text;

  // the code-behind class must inherit from Page
  public class GuestBook : System.Web.UI.Page {

    // create the members of the class
    protected TextBox message;
  protected TextBox name;
  protected Button addButton;
    protected Label entries;
  protected Label entry;
  protected string path;

    // the constructor simply wires the Init event to
    // the initPage() method
    public GuestBook(){
    Page.Init += new EventHandler(initPage);
    }

    // the initPage() method wires the Load event and
    // assigns the path value obtained from the web.config file
    protected void initPage(object sender, EventArgs ea){
      Page.Load += new EventHandler(loadPage);
```

5. In this document, add the following code:

```
<%@ Page Language="C#" %>
<html>
<head>
<title>Users</title>
</head>
<body>
<%
// get number of users
int usersNum = (int) Application["users"];
string verb = "are";
string plural = "s";
// choose correct subject/verb agreement
if(usersNum == 1){
  verb = "is";
  plural = "";
}

%>
There <%=verb%> currently <%= usersNum%> user<%=plural%> online.
</body>
</html>
```

6. Save the document.

7. In your first browser program (I am using IE), open
http://localhost/Wiley/currentUsers.aspx. It should say the following:

```
There is currently 1 user online
```

Figure 19-1 shows what this looks like.

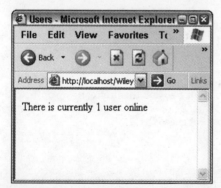

Figure 19-1: Browser 1, one session open

8. In your second browser program (I am using Netscape), open the same URL. It should
read as follows:

```
There are currently 2 users online
```

Figure 19-2 shows what this looks like.

Figure 19-2: Browser 2, two sessions open

9. Return to the first browser and refresh the view. This browser should also now indicate two online users (see Figure 19-3).

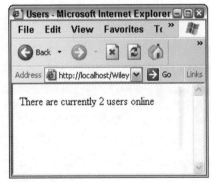

Figure 19-3: Browser 1, two sessions open

10. If you want, you can wait for a minute or two and then refresh one or the other browser windows. Only one session should then be open (because the sessions timeout after a minute according to the settings in Global.asax).

Making a Guestbook

In this exercise, you use a code-behind class and some simple server controls in an ASAX page to create a guestbook application. This application performs three main functions:

✦ Enables the user to add a new guestbook entry

✦ Lists an index of current entries

✦ Enables the user to view an entry by selecting it from the index

This application is more advanced than the previous one. In presenting it, I am assuming that you are familiar enough with C# to understand it. However, the following two concepts may be new to you even if you are familiar with C#:

```csharp
        path = (string)
System.Configuration.ConfigurationSettings.AppSettings["path"];
    }

    // when the page is loaded assign the event handler method
    // to the button click and call the showEntries() method
    // which will display the index of entries
    protected void loadPage(object sender, EventArgs ea){
    addButton.Click += new EventHandler(addEntry);
    showEntries();
    }

    // shows the index of entries
    protected void showEntries(){
    // clear out any existing LinkButtons
    entries.Controls.Clear();
    LinkButton lb;
    // ar is a string array of the entries
    // gathered from the index file
    // each entry is in the format:
    // filename,entryUserName
    string[] ar = getEntries();
    string es;
    string[] s;
    if(ar != null){
      // loop through all the entries
        for(int i = 0; i < ar.Length; i++){
      es = (string) ar[i];
      // split the string into the filename and
      // the entry user name
        s = es.Split(new Char[] {','});
      // create a new LinkButton
      lb = new LinkButton();
      // the LinkButton text should contain the entry
      // user name
        lb.Text = s[1] + "<br>\n";
      // the ID of the LinkButton should be the filename
      lb.ID = s[0];
      // assign a event handler to the Click event
        lb.Click += new EventHandler(viewEntry);
      // add the LinkButton to the entries control
        entries.Controls.Add(lb);
    }
    }
    }

    // get the entries from the index file
    protected string[] getEntries(){
      string file = path + "entriesIndex.txt";
      string[] entriesAr = null;
      if(File.Exists(file)){
        // open the file
      StreamReader sr = new StreamReader(File.OpenRead(file));
```

```
        StringBuilder sb;
        // read the contents of the file into a StringBuilder
          sb = new StringBuilder(sr.ReadToEnd());
        sr.Close();
        // split the contents into an array
        entriesAr = sb.ToString().Trim().Split(new Char[] {'\r'});
        for(int i = 0; i < entriesAr.Length; i++){
          // remove any beginning/ending whitespace
          entriesAr[i].Trim();
        }
          }
        return entriesAr;
  }

  // add a new entry from the submitted form
  protected void addEntry(object sender, EventArgs ea){
    // call the writeFile() method with the values
    // from the form
    writeFile(name.Text, message.Text);
    // update the view of the entries index
    showEntries();
    // clear the form
    name.Text = "";
    message.Text = "";
  }

  // view a single entry
  protected void viewEntry(object sender, EventArgs ea){
    // determine which LinkButton was clicked
    LinkButton slb = (LinkButton) sender;
    // get the entry from the specified filename (same
    // as the LinkButton ID in this application
    string s = getEntry(slb.ID);
    // display the entry
    entry.Text = "<b>Selected entry</b><br>\r" + s;
  }

  // get the entry from the file
  private string getEntry(string fileName){
    // retrieve the contents of the specified file
    StreamReader sr = new StreamReader(File.OpenRead(path + fileName
+ ".txt"));
    StringBuilder sb = new StringBuilder(sr.ReadToEnd());
    // return the file contents formatted as HTML
    return sb.Replace("\r", "<br>").ToString();
  }

  // write the new entry to a file
    private void writeFile(string nm, string mssg){
      // get the date and time now
    DateTime dt = DateTime.Now;
```

```
      // the file name will be in based on the
      // date and time, ensuring that it is unique
        string fileName = dt.ToString("ddMMyy_hhmmss");
      // open the new file
      StreamWriter sw = new StreamWriter(path + fileName + ".txt");
      sw.WriteLine(nm);
      sw.WriteLine(dt.ToString());
      sw.Write(mssg);
      sw.Close();
      // open the index file and append the new entry information
      StreamWriter index = new StreamWriter(path + "entriesIndex.txt",
true);
      index.Write(fileName + "," + nm + "\r");
      index.Close();
      }

  }

}
```

9. Save the document.

10. Compile the class into an assembly named GuestBook.dll. One way to do this is from the command line. You can open a command prompt (Start menu⇨Run), change to the proper directory (cd \Wiley\NET\bin), and then type csc /t:library GuestBook.cs and press Enter.

11. Copy GuestBook.dll to the Wiley application's bin directory.

12. In your Web browser, view http://localhost/Wiley/guestBook.aspx (see Figure 19-4). You should be able to add a new entry and then view any added entries by clicking the link from the index (see Figure 19-5).

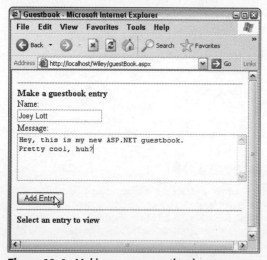

Figure 19-4: Making a new guestbook entry

Figure 19-5: Viewing added entries

Calling ASP.NET Pages

You now know how to properly configure your ASP.NET application for use with Flash Remoting, and it is hoped that you have completed two simple ASPX exercises. Now you only need to learn how to work with an ASP.NET application from Flash by calling it as a remote procedure. In this section, you will examine the following:

✦ Connecting to the gateway

✦ Determining the correct service and procedure name within ActionScript when attempting to call an ASPX page as a remote procedure

✦ Accepting parameters in an ASPX page from Flash

✦ Returning a value to Flash

✦ Using special ASP.NET syntax for returning `DataSet` and `DataTable` objects

Using the Correct Gateway URL

The first thing you need to know in order to successfully use Flash Remoting with ASP.NET is the proper gateway URL to use in creating your ActionScript connection object. The ASP.NET gateway can be determined by Flash Remoting if it is provided with any ASPX page in the application's root directory (so long as the application includes flashservices.dll in the local assembly cache.) Although you can use any ASPX page in the root directory, I like to create a blank file named flashgateway.aspx just for this purpose.

For example, if I have created an application with a logical path of /Wiley (as in http://local-host/Wiley) that maps to the directory C:\Wiley\NET, then I would create a new ASPX document in C:\Wiley\NET named flashgateway.aspx. This file does not need to contain anything special. It must merely reside in the application's root directory. That is the only condition placed upon it. If I then want to call any ASPX pages from the Wiley application, I can use the following as my gateway URL for creating my connection object:

```
http://localhost/Wiley/flashgateway.aspx
```

Choosing the Service and Procedure Name

The next step in properly calling an ASPX page via Flash Remoting is determining which service name and procedure name to use. This is relatively simple:

✦ The service name is determined by the logical path to the ASPX file. In the service name, however, all separating forward slashes should be dots. Table 19-1 shows a few examples of URLs to ASPX pages and the corresponding service object code for those pages in ActionScript.

✦ The procedure name is determined by the name of the ASPX file itself. Table 19-2 shows a few examples of ASPX pages and the corresponding procedure calls in ActionScript.

Table 19-1: Example ASPX Page Services

URL	ActionScript Service Object Code
http://localhost/Chapter19/ examples/example1.aspx	srv = conn.getService("Chapter19.examples");
http://localhost/Chapter19/ examples/moreExamples/page.aspx	srv = conn.getService("Chapter19. examples.moreExamples");
http://localhost/coolStuff.aspx	srv = conn.getService("");

Table 19-2: Examples of ASPX Pages as AS Procedures

ColdFusion Page Name	ActionScript Procedure Call
example1.aspx	srv.example1(res);
page.aspx	srv.page(res);
coolStuff.aspx	srv.coolStuff(res);

Let's walk through a simple example. If I have created an ASPX page named myPage.aspx in the Wiley application's root directory, here is how I might call it from a Flash movie:

```
#include "NetServices.as"
// I use an ASPX page in the application's root as the
// gateway URL
```

```
gwUrl = "http://localhost/Wiley/flashgateway.aspx";
NetServices.setDefaultGatewayURL(gwUrl);
conn = NetServices.createGatewayConnection();

// create the service object
srv = conn.getService("Wiley");

// create the response object
res = new Object();
res.onResult = function(result){}

// call the ASPX page with no parameters
srv.myPage(res);
```

Setting Up the ASPX Page

Communication between ASPX pages and Flash movies takes place using a FlashGateway .Flash object. The FlashGateway.Flash class is part of the flashgateway.dll assembly. Therefore, in order to accept parameters or return values, an ASPX page must have a Flash object created within it. There are two ways to do this:

✦ Use the Register directive in the page

✦ Call the Flash constructor within a render block, an in-line script block, or a code-behind class.

Using the Register directive

Let's first look at using the Register directive to create a Flash object in your ASPX pages. The syntax of a Register directive is similar to that of any other directive (such as a Page directive). It begins with <%@ and ends with %>. With the Register directive, we want to associate a particular namespace from a particular assembly with a tag prefix in the ASPX page. In the case of Flash Remoting, we want to associate the FlashGateway namespace from the flashgateway.dll assembly with a tag prefix. The tag prefix is arbitrary. Macromedia uses the tag prefix Macromedia, so that is what is used here. The following Register directive creates the desired association:

```
<%@ Register TagPrefix="Macromedia" Namespace="FlashGateway"
Assembly="flashgateway" %>
```

The TagPrefix attribute value is arbitrary; however, the Namespace and Assembly attributes should always have these same values (FlashGateway and flashgateway, respectively).

Once you have the tag prefix associated with the namespace, you can create an object (a Flash control) with a <Macromedia:Flash> tag (or <MyTagPrefix:Flash> if you chose a different tag prefix). You want to assign a value to an ID and a runat attribute. The ID is arbitrary. It is the name given to the object should you need to reference it in your code. The runat attribute should always be set to server. Here is an example of a Flash control tag that creates a new control (object) named flash:

```
<Macromedia:Flash ID="flash" runat="server" />
```

You will learn how to use this control when we get to passing parameters and returning values.

Calling the Flash constructor

If you are using code-behind or simply want to create the Flash object in a render block or in-line script block, you can also simply call the constructor, as shown in the following example:

```
FlashGateway.Flash flash = new FlashGateway.Flash();
```

That is all you need to do in order to create the Flash object.

Passing Parameters

Passing parameters to an ASPX page from a Flash movie is nothing unusual or new. You simply pass the parameters to the page in the ActionScript remote procedure call. Handling those parameters in the ASPX page requires a little bit of explanation, however.

If you are passing parameters to an ASPX page, you have no choice but to process them from within a render block, an in-line script block, or a code-behind class. The parameters are passed to the ASPX page by way of the Flash object's Params property. The Params property is an object that implements IList (like an ArrayList), but that automatically preserves the object types. Therefore, you can access the elements of the Params list as you would an array; you don't have to worry about properly casting the elements you retrieve, and the list can contain mixed types (string, int, DateTime, XML, etc.). The elements of the Params list appear in the order in which they are passed from the ActionScript procedure call.

In order to see how this works, let's look at an example. The following snippet of ActionScript code calls an ASPX page named myPage.aspx and passes it three parameters — a string, an Array object, and a Date object:

```
// assumes res is the response object and
// srv is the service object
srv.myPage(res, "a string", new Array(1,2,3), new Date());
```

In the ASPX page or its code-behind class, you could then access these parameters as follows:

```
// assuming you have a Flash object named flash
string s = flash.Params[0];
System.Collections.ArrayList al = flash.Params[1];
System.DateTime dt = flash.Params[2];
```

Because you will likely always want your ASPX pages to work both when called from Flash or when viewed in a Web browser, keep in mind that the Flash object's Params property may not always contain any elements. In fact, it will contain elements only when it is passed parameters from your Flash movie. When viewed directly from the Web browser (with no Flash movie involved), however, your ASPX page will not have been passed any parameters from a Flash movie. If you attempt to access an element of the Params list, you will cause an error. Therefore, it is a good idea to always enclose any code that processes Params elements within an if statement that checks to see if any elements exist. You can do this simply by using a conditional statement that confirms that the Params object's Count property indicates the proper number of elements. In the following example, the elements of the Params list are processed only if the Count property is greater than 0:

```
if(flash.Params.Count > 0){
   string s = flash.Params[0];
   System.Collections.ArrayList al = flash.Params[1];
   System.DateTime dt = flash.Params[2];
}
```

Returning a Value

If you want to return a value to the Flash movie from an ASPX page, you have a few options:

✦ You can return a string value placed between opening and closing Flash control tags.

✦ You can assign the value to the Flash object's Result property.

Tip

If you are returning record sets to Flash, you have another option available to you, which is covered in the next section.

Using control tags

It is possible to return a string value to a Flash movie using no script (render block, in-line, or code-behind). You can simply enclose any text you want returned between opening and closing Flash control tags, as shown in the following example:

```
<Macromedia:Flash ID="flash" runat="server">
This text will get returned to Flash
</Macromedia:Flash>
```

Using the Result property

The more robust way to return data to a Flash movie from an ASPX page is by assigning the value to the Flash object's Result property. Clearly, in order to accomplish this, you must use scripting of some kind, whether that is in a render block, in in-line script, or in a code-behind class. Here is an example in which the server time is returned to a Flash movie by way of the Result property:

```
flash.Result = DateTime.Now;
```

You can return only one value per request, so assigning multiple values to the Result property will not return multiple values. Only the value held by the Result property when the page has completed executing is returned to the Flash movie. For instance, in the following example, only the string some value is returned to the Flash movie:

```
flash.Result = DateTime.Now;
flash.Result = 5;
flash.Result = "some value";
```

Of course, this in no way restricts you from returning multiple values wrapped in an object such as an ArrayList. In the following example, a single value is returned, but with three elements:

```
System.Collections.ArrayList al = new System.Collections.ArrayList();
al.Add(DateTime.Now);
al.Add(5);
al.Add("some value");
flash.Result = al;
```

Adding a Flash User Interface to ASP.NET

Earlier in this chapter, you completed two exercises in which you created ASPX pages. Now let's revisit them and modify them slightly so that they function as they did previously *and* include Flash user interfaces added via Flash Remoting.

For an exercise on counting users in Flash, see the companion Web site, www.wiley.com/compbooks/lott.

Making a Flash Guestbook

In this exercise, you modify the GuestBook.cs code-behind class to process Flash calls (while still functioning properly when called from a Web browser). By then creating a Flash user interface, you will have both a Flash and an HTML version of the guestbook.

1. Open the GuestBook.cs file in your favorite C# editor.

2. Modify the loadPage() method as shown here so that it can determine the proper course of action depending on whether Flash is calling the page or not:

```
protected void loadPage(object sender, EventArgs ea){
  FlashGateway.Flash flash = new FlashGateway.Flash();
  if(flash.Params.Count > 0){
    string action = (string) flash.Params[0];
    if(action == "writeEntry"){
      string nameFlash = (string) flash.Params[1];
      string messageFlash = (string) flash.Params[2];
      writeFile(nameFlash, messageFlash);
    }
    if(action == "listEntries" || action == "writeEntry"){
      flash.Result = getEntries();
    }
    if(action == "getEntry"){
      string fileNameFlash = (string) flash.Params[1];
      flash.Result = getEntry(fileNameFlash);
    }
  }
  else{
    addButton.Click += new EventHandler(addEntry);
    showEntries();
  }
}
```

3. Save the file. Then compile it. You need to be sure to provide the compiler with information as to where it can find flashgateway.dll. Use the following command to compile the code:

```
csc /t:library /r:flashgateway.dll GuestBook.cs
```

You will find guestBook_starter.fla on this book's companion Web site, www.wiley.com/compbooks/lott.

4. Download the file guestBook_starter.fla from the Web site and open the file in Flash.

5. On frame 1 of the actions layer, add the following code:

```
#include "NetServices.as"

gwUrl = "http://localhost/Wiley/flashgateway.aspx";
NetServices.setDefaultGatewayURL(gwUrl);
conn = NetServices.createGatewayConnection();
```

```
srv = conn.getService("Wiley");

// set up the response objects for the three kinds
// of requests (adding a new entry, listing
// entries index, and viewing an entry)
resAdd = new Object();
resAdd.onResult = function(result){
  var spc = _root.spContent;
  // the result should be send to the
  // resList.onResult() method which displays
  // the index of entries
  _root.resList.onResult(result);
  // reset the forms and index up to the top of
  // the screen
  spc.addForm._y = 0;
  spc.entries._y = spc.addForm._y + spc.addForm._height + 10;
}
resAdd.onStatus = function(status){
  trace(status.description);
}

resEntry = new Object();
resEntry.onResult = function(result){
  var spc = _root.spContent;
  // display the selected entry
  _root.spContent.entry.htmlText = "<b>Selected entry</b><br>";
  _root.spContent.entry.htmlText += result;
  // move the form and index down to
  // accommodate the selected entry output
  spc.addForm._y = spc.entry._height + 10;
  spc.entries._y = spc.addForm._y + spc.addForm._height + 10;
  // add the text format to the entry
  spc.entry.setTextFormat(_root.tf);
  // scroll back to the top
  _root.sp.setScrollPosition(0);
  // update the view in the scroll pane
  _root.sp.setScrollContent(_root.spContent);
}
resEntry.onStatus = function(status){
  trace(status.description);
}


resList = new Object();
resList.onResult = function(result){
  var spc = _root.spContent;
  var mc;
  // loop through all the indexes
  for(var i = 0; i < result.length; i++){
    // split the element into the filename and the
    // user name
    s = result[i].split(".");
    // create the new button and position it
    // FPushButtonSymbol is the linkage name
```

```
        // for the PushButton symbol already in the
        // library
        mc = spc.entries.attachMovie("FPushButtonSymbol",
                                     "entry" + i,
                                     i,
                                     {_y: (i * 25) + 30});
        // add the label to the button
        mc.setLabel(s[1]);
        // add the file property to the button
        mc.file = s[0];
        // when the button is released, call the ASPX page
        // with the getEntry parameter and the filename
        mc.onRelease = function(){
          _root.srv.guestBookFlash(_root.resEntry,
                                   "getEntry",
                                   this.file);
        }
      }
    }
    // update scroll view
    _root.sp.setScrollContent(spc);
  }
  resList.onStatus = function(status){
    trace(status.description);
  }

  // get the initial list of entries
  srv.guestBookFlash(resList, "listEntries");

  // position the scrollpane and set the size
  sp._x = 0;
  sp._y = 0;
  sp.setSize(550, 400);
  // set the scroll content
  sp.setScrollContent(spContent);
  // entry is a TextField used to hold the selected
  // entry
  spContent.createTextField("entry", 0, 0, 0, 0, 0);
  spContent.entry.autoSize = true;
  spContent.entry.html = true;

  // set up the textformat object
  tf = new TextFormat();
  tf.font = "_sans";

  // this if for the button in the add form
  spContent.addForm.addButton.onRelease = function(){
    // if the name TextField is filled out
    if(this._parent.nameField.text != ""){
    // call the ASPX page to write the new entry
    // passing the name and message entered by the user
    _root.srv.guestBookFlash(_root.resAdd,
                             "writeEntry",
                             this._parent.nameField.text,
                             this._parent.messageField.text);
```

```
        // clear the form
        this._parent.nameField.text = "";
        this._parent.messageField.text = "";
    }
}
```

6. Test the movie. Try adding new entries (see Figure 19-6) and viewing previously entered entries (see Figure 19-7).

Note   You may find that you have problems viewing the PushButton instances in the ScrollPane. This is a known bug in earlier revisions of the Flash 6 player. If you update your player, this will be resolved. See the companion Web site for a link for updating your player.

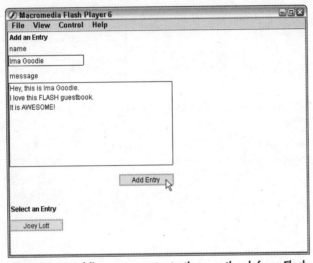

Figure 19-6: Adding a new entry to the guestbook from Flash

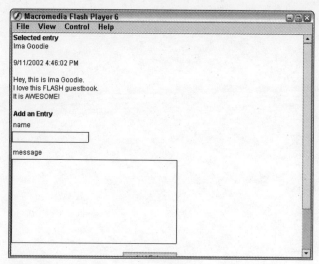

Figure 19-7: Viewing an entry in Flash

Summary

In this chapter, you explored concepts relating to ASP.NET and Flash Remoting. Here are a few of the key points from the chapter:

✦ Existing ASPX pages can be modified in such a way that they can be both viewed in the Web browser *and* utilized by Flash Remoting applications.

✦ ASP.NET pages utilize elements such as Web controls, script blocks, and code-behind classes.

✦ ASPX pages can be called from Flash Remoting movies using the following: an ASPX page in the application root as the gateway, the logical path as the service name, and the page filename as the remote procedure name.

✦ ASPX pages called from Flash Remoting movies must include a `FlashGateway.Flash` object in order to receive and return parameters.

✦   ✦   ✦

Using .NET Library Assemblies

Assemblies are the main building blocks of all .NET applications, and so it is important that Flash Remoting enable Flash movies to interact with assemblies. You can use Flash Remoting to make a call to any public method of any class contained in a DLL that resides in the ASP.NET application's local assembly cache. No special techniques need to be used to call methods within an assembly. Values are passed to and from methods in standard ways. You do not have to use Flash.Params and Flash.Result, as you would with ASPX pages. Therefore, this chapter does not cover most of the techniques used to create DLLs that can be used by Flash Remoting. If you want a good book about .NET programming in C#, I recommend *C# Bible* by Jeff Ferguson et al. (Wiley, 2002).

Calling Assembly Methods

As with any Flash Remoting remote procedure call, you need to determine two important pieces of information when calling .NET assembly methods — the service name and the remote procedure name. The service name is the fully qualified class name of the class within the assembly. The remote procedure name is, quite simply, the name of the method defined in the assembly. Listing 20-1 shows the source code for a simple assembly.

Listing 20-1: **The Source of a Simple Assembly**

```
namespace Wiley.Chapter20 {
  public class Simple {
    public string getValue(){
      return "simple value";
    }
  }
}
```

If you wanted to invoke the getValue() method in the assembly for which the source code is shown in Listing 20-1, you would use the following ActionScript snippet to create the service object and invoke the method:

```
// conn and res are assumed to be defined as the connection
// object and response object
srv = conn.getService("Wiley.Chapter20.Simple");
srv.getValue(res);
```

Creating an MP3 player

As it is easy to use a .NET assembly with Flash Remoting, let's simply dive in with an exercise. In this section, you create a Flash MP3 player that uses a .NET assembly to determine the available files and retrieve the metadata (which includes the track title and artist name, for example) for each of them.

Note   The 40 revision of the Flash 6 player added the id3 property to Sound objects. This property enables direct access to the same metadata that this exercise exposes through the use of a DLL. However, there is no way to directly access the MP3 metadata from Flash using earlier revisions of the Flash 6 player, and so this exercise enables you to still make this information available to older revisions.

1. Create a new directory named music in the Wiley Web application directory (C:\Wiley\NET\).

2. Open the web.config file created in Chapter 19 (step 3 of the section "Making a Guestbook"), and add the line of code shown in bold here (the ellipses indicate where the full contents are not displayed):

```
<?xml version="1.0" encoding="utf-8" ?>
<configuration>

  <appSettings>
    <add key="path" value="D:\\Wiley\\NET\\guestBookEntries\\" />
    <add key="musicDir" value="D:\\Wiley\\NET\\music\\" />
  </appSettings>


...


</configuration>
```

This will set a value for the directory that the application will search for MP3 files.

3. Open a new .NET assembly source document and save it to the Wiley Web Application local assembly cache directory (bin) as MusicGetter.cs.

4. In the document, add the following code and save it:

```
namespace Wiley.Chapter20 {

  using System.IO;
  using System.Collections;
  using System.Text;

  public class MusicGetter {

    // this method returns a listing of the MP3 files and
    // their metadata as a Hashtable (which become an
    // Object in ActionScript
```

```
public Hashtable getAvailableSongs(){
  Hashtable ht = new Hashtable();
  // getDir() is a private method that returns the
  // music directory set in the web.config file
  string dir = getDir();
  // get all the files in the directory
  string[] files = Directory.GetFiles(dir);
  // loop through and add all MP3 files to the
  // Hashtable with the filename as the key and
  // the value as the metadata retrieved by way
  // of the getSongInfo() private method
  for(int i = 0; i < files.Length; i++){
    if(files[i].IndexOf(".mp3") != -1){
      ht.Add(files[i], getSongInfo(files[i]));
    }
  }
  return ht;
}

// get a Hashtable of the file's metadata
private Hashtable getSongInfo(string file){
  Hashtable ht = new Hashtable();
  ht.Add("file", file);
  // MP3 files have an embedded ID3 tag that you
  // can read using the following code
  FileStream fs = new FileStream(file, FileMode.Open);
  byte[] buff = new byte[128];
  fs.Seek(-128, SeekOrigin.End);
  fs.Read(buff, 0, 128);
  fs.Close();
  Encoding  instEncoding = new ASCIIEncoding();
  string tag = instEncoding.GetString(buff);

  // tag is the resulting string value of the ID3 tag
  // that has been read from the MP3 file. If the tag
  // contains values, populate the Hashtable with
  // those values
  if (tag.Substring(0,3) == "TAG") {
    ht.Add("title", tag.Substring(  3, 30).Trim());
    ht.Add("artist", tag.Substring( 33, 30).Trim());
    ht.Add("album", tag.Substring( 63, 30).Trim());
    ht.Add("year", tag.Substring( 93, 4).Trim());
  }
  else {
    ht.Add("title", "");
    ht.Add("artist", "");
    ht.Add("album", "");
    ht.Add("year", "");
  }
  return ht;
}

// read the directory from the web.config file
private string getDir(){
```

```
        return (string)
System.Configuration.ConfigurationSettings.AppSettings["musicDir"];
    }

  }

}
```

5. Compile the source into a DLL named MusicGetter.dll. You can do this from the command line by changing to the Wiley Web application bin directory and typing csc /t:library MusicGetter.cs.

6. Open a new Flash document and save it as mp3Player.fla.

7. Modify the document settings (Modify⇨Document) so that the stage measures 300 pixels by 150 pixels.

8. Rename the default layer to playerControls, and create a new layer named actions.

9. On the playerControls layer, add a ComboBox component instance in the upper-left portion of the stage. Name the instance songList. (See Figure 20-1 for layout.)

10. To the right of the songList instance, add a PushButton component instance (see Figure 20-1) and name it loadBtn.

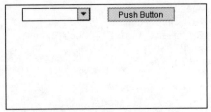

Figure 20-1: Layout of mp3Player.fla through step 10

11. Add a song play progress bar.

   a. Below the songList and loadBtn instances, draw a line about 200 pixels wide. The exact length is not important.

   b. Select the line and convert it to a MovieClip symbol (F8) named bar.

   c. Select the instance of the bar symbol and convert it to a MovieClip symbol as well. Name the symbol progressBar. You should now have a symbol named progressBar that contains an instance of the bar symbol.

   d. Name the progressBar symbol instance (the instance on the Main Timeline) progressBar.

   e. Edit in place the progressBar instance.

   f. Name the bar symbol instance bar.

   g. Rename the default layer within the symbol to bar, and create a new layer named progress. Lock the bar layer.

h. On the progress layer, draw a rectangle over the `bar` instance as shown in Figure 20-2. This rectangle does not need to be a specific width, as that will be controlled with ActionScript. However, you may want to draw something that roughly matches what is shown in Figure 20-2.

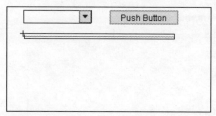

Figure 20-2: Layout of mp3Player.fla through step 11h

i. Select the rectangle drawn in the previous step and convert it to a MovieClip symbol. Name the symbol progress, and be sure to set the registration point to the left side, as shown in Figure 20-3. This is important so that when the progress indicator moves, its left side remains fixed.

Figure 20-3: Converting the rectangle to a symbol and setting the registration to the left side

j. Name the instance of the progress symbol `progress`.

12. Return to the Main Timeline.

13. On the playerControls layer, add a dynamic `TextField` object below the `progressBar` instance. The size is not important because this will be controlled by ActionScript.

14. On the actions layer, add the following code to the first frame:

```
#include "NetServices.as"

function init(){
   // create the holder MovieClip for the Sound object
   _root.createEmptyMovieClip("songHolder", 1);
   // create the Sound object, and target it to songHolder
   _root.mySong = new Sound(songHolder);

   // configure the TextField object to be multiline with
   // word wrap off and auto-size on
   _root.title.multiline = true;
   _root.title.wordWrap = false;
   _root.title.autoSize = true;
```

```
  // initialize the progress bar so that it is aligned
  // and not visible to start
  _root.progressBar.progress._x = _root.progressBar.bar._x;
  _root.progressBar.progress._visible = false;

  var gwUrl = "http://localhost/Wiley/flashgateway.aspx";
  NetServices.setDefaultGatewayURL(gwUrl);
  var conn = NetServices.createGatewayConnection();
  _root.srv = conn.getService("Wiley.Chapter20.MusicGetter");
  _root.srv.getAvailableSongs(res);
}

res = new Object();
res.onResult = function(result){
  var title;
  var songs = new Array();
  // the result is an object with keys and values
  // for each available song. Loop through all the
  // songs
  for(var i in result){
    // if the song has a title, use that. Otherwise, if no
    // title exists, use the file name
    if(result[i].title != ""){
      title = result[i].title;
    }
    else{
      title = i;
    }
    // add the song to an array of objects with label of
    // the song's title, and data of the metadata for the
    // mp3
    songs.push({label: title, data: result[i]});
  }
  // set the songList data provider to the songs array
  _root.songList.setDataProvider(songs);
}
res.onStatus = function(status){
  trace(status.description);
}

loadBtn.setLabel("play song");
loadBtn.onRelease = function(){
  // when a user clicks to load a song, make the progress
  // bar visible
  _root.progressBar.progress._visible = true;
  // get the selected song, and load it into mySong
  var song = _root.songList.getSelectedItem();
  _root.mySong.loadSound(song.data.file, true);

  // continuously update the progress bar based on
  // the loaded song's position and duration properties
```

```
_root.songHolder.onEnterFrame = function(){
    var p = _root.mySong.position;
    var d = _root.mySong.duration;
    var pr = _root.progressBar.progress;
    var pbw = _root.progressBar.bar._width;
    pr._width = (p/d) * pbw;
}
// set the TextField to output information about the
// current mp3. the year and album information are also
// returned if available, and you could display those
// as well if you want
_root.title.text = "Now Playing: " + newline;
_root.title.text += "Title: " + song.label + newline;
_root.title.text += "Artist: " + song.data.artist;
}

// don't forget to call init()!
init();
```

15. Copy the desired MP3 files to the music directory within the Wiley Web application. (If you don't have any MP3 files, you can find some for download at MP3.com.)

16. Test the movie. The names of available MP3 tracks will automatically load in the menu. Select one and click the button. The track information will display, the song will begin playing, and the progress bar will move. See Figure 20-4 for an example of the MP3 player in action.

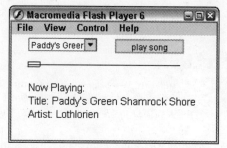

Figure 20-4: The MP3 player in action

Working with Typed Objects

Using the .NET `FlashGateway.IO.ASObject` class, it is possible to send typed objects between Flash movies and .NET applications and back again. There are two different processes—one for sending typed objects to a .NET application and one for returning typed objects to a Flash movie. However, in both cases, you must be sure to create the class for the typed object and register that class in ActionScript.

Defining and Registering the ActionScript Class

Whether you are defining and registering an ActionScript class for use with .NET, another technology (such as Java), or strictly within Flash, the process is the same.

✦ Define the class, complete with constructor, properties, and methods.

✦ Assign the properties that should be registered to the class `prototype`.

✦ Call `Object.registerClass()`.

Listing 20-2 shows a simple example of a class that is defined and registered in ActionScript.

Listing 20-2: Defining and Registering a Simple ActionScript Class

```
// the constructor
function CatalogueItem(name){
  this.name = name;
}
// define a property, name
CatalogueItem.prototype.name = null;
// define a method, describe()
CatalogueItem.prototype.describe = function(){
  trace(this.name);
}
// register the class to the name CatalogueItem
Object.registerClass("CatalogueItem", CatalogueItem);
```

Sending a Typed Object to .NET

When you want to send a typed object to .NET, there are two stages — the sending of the object and the .NET receipt of the object. The sending part is very straightforward. You simply create the object and pass it to the remote procedure as you would any other kind of object or primitive data type.

When you wish to receive a typed object within a .NET application, you must create a .NET class that mirrors the ActionScript class. The .NET mirror class needs to have the same name. The properties that you want to use must also be defined with the same names. For example, you could define a .NET mirror class to the CatalogueItem ActionScript class from Listing 20-2 as shown in Listing 20-3.

Listing 20-3: CatalogueItem .NET Class

```
public class CatalogueItem {

  public string name;
  public CatalogueItem(){}

}
```

You can then define a method in a .NET application to expect a parameter of that type. Listing 20-4 shows an example of this. This listing shows the entire assembly definition, including the mirror class (`CatalogueItem`).

Listing 20-4: **Receiving a Typed Object**

```
namespace Wiley.Chapter20 {

  public class CatalogueItem {

    public string name;
    public CatalogueItem(){}

  }

  public class Catalogue {

    public string parseItem(CatalogueItem it){
      return it.name;
    }

  }

}
```

If you then call the `parseItem()` method from Listing 20-4 from a Flash movie, with the `CatalogueItem` class registered as shown in Listing 20-2, everything will work smoothly. For example:

```
// where srv is the service object
res = new Object();
res.onResult = function(result){
  trace(result);
}
srv.parseItem(res, new CatalogueItem("my catalogue item"));
// results in my catalogue item being displayed in the
// output window
```

Returning a Typed Object to Flash

.NET applications can also return typed objects to Flash movies. When you wish to do this, however, you must directly use a `FlashGateway.IO.ASObject` object. Since the `ASObject` class implements the `ICollection` interface, it provides all the properties and methods available to all classes that implement `ICollection`, such as the `Add()` method. Using the `Add()` method, you can add properties to the object. Additionally, the `ASObject` class has an `ASType` property that enables you to assign a type to the object. The type should be a string that corresponds to the ActionScript class as it is registered in the Flash movie. Listing 20-5 shows a .NET method that will return a `CatalogueItem` object to Flash with a `name` property set to `my .NET catalogue item`.

Listing 20-5: **Returning a Typed Object**

```
public FlashGateway.IO.ASObject getItem(){
  FlashGateway.IO.ASObject o = new FlashGateway.IO.ASObject();
  o.Add("name", "my .NET catalogue item");
  o.ASType = "CatalogueItem";
  return o;
}
```

Listing 20-6 shows what you should expect when you call such a method from a Flash movie.

Listing 20-6: **Getting a Typed Object from .NET**

```
// srv is the service object, CatalogueItem is registered
res = new Object();
res.onResult = function(result){
  // call the describe() method defined for CatalogueItem
  // objects
  result.describe();
}
srv.getItem(res);
// will display my .NET catalogue item in the Output window
```

Summary

In this chapter, you learned how to use .NET DLLs with Flash Remoting. To recap, here are some of the important points discussed throughout the chapter:

✦ Flash Remoting enables you to call the public methods of any .NET assembly within the local assembly cache of a .NET Web application. In ActionScript, you reference the fully qualified class name as the service.

✦ In most cases, no special Flash Remoting–specific code is required in your .NET assemblies.

✦ You can pass typed objects to .NET assembly methods from Flash. In order to do so, the ActionScript class must be registered and there must be a mirror class in .NET.

✦ You can return typed objects to Flash movies from .NET by using an ASObject object and setting its ASType property to match the name of the registered ActionScript class.

✦   ✦   ✦

Consuming .NET Web Services

Microsoft .NET is a platform designed specifically with Web services in mind. As you will learn in this chapter, it provides many tools and utilities that make creating and consuming Web services accessible to the developer.

In Chapter 9, you learned about how to consume Web services from Flash movies when using Flash Remoting for .NET. This chapter serves as a companion to Chapter 9, extending concepts introduced in that chapter. In this chapter, you learn about the following topics:

- ✦ Developing .NET Web services for use with Flash Remoting
- ✦ Using .NET to proxy Web services that cannot be directly consumed by Flash movies

Creating .NET Web Services

Custom .NET Web services can be a powerful resource for many applications, including Flash Remoting movies. Not only will a well-developed Web service be accessible to your Flash Remoting movies, it can be made accessible as a service for others as well.

.NET Web services are created using ASMX documents. ASMX documents enable you, the developer, to create a .NET class (or classes) as you are already accustomed to doing. The .NET framework then automatically generates the actual, more complicated, Web service assembly source and compiles it when it is first requested.

An ASMX document is a plaintext document in which you define the methods of the Web service. The ASMX document is saved in the same locations where you save ASPX documents. Keep in mind the following rules when developing an ASMX document:

- ✦ The document should begin with a `WebService` directive.
- ✦ The document should include the `System.Web.Services` namespace.
- ✦ The Web service methods should be encapsulated within a public class.
- ✦ Each Web service method should be flagged with the following attribute: `[WebMethod]` (in C#) or `<WebMethod()>` (in Visual Basic).

Optionally, you can also specify the target namespace that will be used by the Web service. By default, the value http://tempuri.org/ is used. In order to specify the target namespace, add an attribute prior to the class declaration, as shown here for C#:

```
[WebService(Namespace="http://wiley.com/completeflashremoting/")]
```

or as follows in VB:

```
<WebService(Namespace="http://wiley.com/completeflashremoting/")>
```

Listing 21-1 shows a simple ASMX document that defines a SimpleService Web service.

Listing 21-1: A SimpleService.asmx file

```
<%@ WebService language="C#" class="SimpleService" %>

using System.Web.Services;

[WebService(Namespace="http://wiley.com/completeflashremoting/")]
public class SimpleService {

  [WebMethod]
  public string showValue(string input){
    return "Your value is " + input;
  }


}
```

Testing a Web Service

The .NET framework provides a simple way to test your Web services. By entering the URL to the ASMX document in a Web browser, you can view a special .NET Web service interface (see Figure 21-1).

Figure 21-1: The .NET Web service method list

This interface first displays a list of the available Web service methods. Clicking on one of the methods in the list provides you with an interface via which you can test the method (see Figure 21-2).

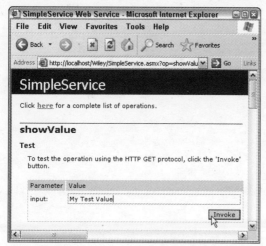

Figure 21-2: The .NET Web service method test interface

When you click the invoke button, a new Web browser window is spawned, containing the outgoing SOAP message generated by the method (see Figure 21-3).

Figure 21-3: The outgoing SOAP message created by the .NET Web service method test

Generating WSDL

Another nice feature of working with .NET Web services is that they automatically generate their own WSDL documents. If you append ?wsdl to the ASMX URL, the WSDL document is output (see Figure 21-4).

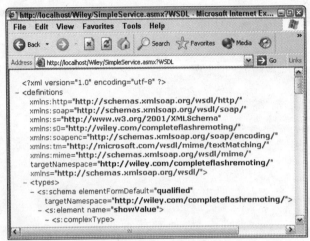

Figure 21-4: A WSDL document automatically generated from the ASMX file

Making a Horoscope Web Service

In this exercise, you use .NET to create a Web service that returns a horoscope read from an XML file. The Flash interface consists of a drop-down menu that is populated by an array returned by the Web service containing the available signs of the Zodiac. The user can select one and request the horoscope for the sign from the Web service. The application then displays that value.

1. Create a new directory within the Wiley Web application root named horoscopes.

2. Create a new XML document and save it as horoscopes.xml in the new horoscopes directory.

3. In the XML document, add the code in Listing 21-2 and save it.

Listing 21-2: **horoscopes.xml**

```
<?xml version="1.0" encoding="iso-8859-1"?>
<horoscope>
  <sign name="Aries" value="You are going to have a wonderful day." />
  <sign name="Taurus" value="Unexpected good comes your way." />
  <sign name="Gemini" value="Things are definitely in your favor." />
  <sign name="Cancer" value="Follow your highest dreams for they are
coming true." />
  <sign name="Leo" value="Today is a day to live and love." />
  <sign name="Virgo" value="Everyone supports you in your truest
desires." />
  <sign name="Libra" value="Everything just gets better and better." />
  <sign name="Scorpio" value="Expect good things now." />
```

```
    <sign name="Sagittarius" value="Love and other good surprises are
yours." />
    <sign name="Capricorn" value="Set your sights high and watch them
manifest." />
    <sign name="Aquarius" value="You and everyone you know is prospered
beyond even your greatest hopes." />
    <sign name="Pisces" value="Life is working for you in every possible
good way." />
</horoscope>
```

4. Add a new key named horoscopesDir to the web.config file, to contain the value of the directory that contains the horoscopes.xml file, and save the document. The following code shows in bold the code to add to the web.config file.

```
<?xml version="1.0" encoding="utf-8" ?>
<configuration>

  <appSettings>
  ...
  <add key="horoscopesDir"
       value="D:\\Wiley\\NET\\horoscopes\\" />
  </appSettings>
  ...
</configuration>
```

5. Open a new ASMX document and save it to the Wiley Web application root as Horoscope.asmx.

6. In the document, add the code in Listing 21-3 and then save it.

Listing 21-3: **Horoscope.asmx**

```
<%@ WebService Language="C#" class="Horoscope" %>

using System.Web.Services;
using System.Xml;
using System.Collections;
using System.Text;

[WebService(Namespace="http://wiley.com/completeflashremoting/")]
public class Horoscope {

  // get an array of signs for which horoscopes are
  // available
  [WebMethod]
  public ArrayList getSigns(){
    ArrayList al = new ArrayList();
    // get the directory for the XML document
```

Continued

Listing 21-3: *(continued)*

```
    string dir = (string)
System.Configuration.ConfigurationSettings.AppSettings["horoscopesDir"]
;
    // create a reader for the document
    XmlTextReader reader = new XmlTextReader(dir + "horoscopes.xml");
    reader.WhitespaceHandling = WhitespaceHandling.None;
    StringBuilder sb;
    // loop through all the elements of the XML document
    while(reader.Read()){
      // if the element is a sign element, add the name
      // attribute value to the ArrayList
      if(reader.Name == "sign"){
        al.Add(reader.GetAttribute("name"));
      }
    }
    reader.Close();
    return al;
  }

  // get an array of all the horoscopes
  [WebMethod]
  public ArrayList getHoroscopes(){
    ArrayList al = new ArrayList();
    string dir = (string)
System.Configuration.ConfigurationSettings.AppSettings["horoscopesDir"]
;
    XmlTextReader reader = new XmlTextReader(dir + "horoscopes.xml");
    reader.WhitespaceHandling = WhitespaceHandling.None;
    StringBuilder sb;
    while(reader.Read()){
      if(reader.Name == "sign"){
        sb = new StringBuilder();
        sb.Append(reader.GetAttribute("name"));
        sb.Append(": ");
        sb.Append(reader.GetAttribute("value"));
        al.Add(sb.ToString());
      }
    }
    reader.Close();
    return al;
  }

  // get a string value of one of the horoscopes
  [WebMethod]
  public string getHoroscope(string sign){
    string val = "";
```

```
    string dir = (string)
System.Configuration.ConfigurationSettings.AppSettings["horoscopesDir"]
;
    XmlTextReader reader = new XmlTextReader(dir + "horoscopes.xml");
    reader.WhitespaceHandling = WhitespaceHandling.None;
    StringBuilder sb;
    while(reader.Read()){
      if(reader.Name == "sign" && reader.GetAttribute("name").Trim() ==
sign){
        sb = new StringBuilder();
        sb.Append(reader.GetAttribute("name"));
        sb.Append(": ");
        sb.Append(reader.GetAttribute("value"));
        val = sb.ToString();
        break;
      }
    }
    reader.Close();
    return val;
  }

}
```

7. Open a new Flash document and save it as horoscopes.fla.

8. Rename the default layer to form, and create a new layer named actions.

9. On the form layer, add a `ComboBox` component in the upper, left-hand portion of the stage (see Figure 21-5). Name the instance `signsMenu`.

10. To the right of the `ComboBox`, add a `PushButton` component instance (see Figure 21-5), and name it `selectBtn`.

11. Below the `ComboBox`, add a dynamic `TextField` instance (see Figure 21-5). Name the instance `horoscope`.

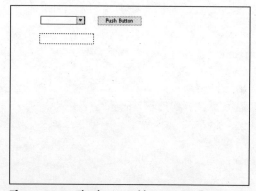

Figure 21-5: The layout of horoscope.fla

12. On the actions layer, add the following code:

```
#include "NetServices.as"

function init(){

  _root.horoscope.multiline = true;
  _root.horoscope.autoSize = true;

  gwUrl = "http://localhost/Wiley/flashgateway.aspx";
  NetServices.setDefaultGatewayURL(gwUrl);
  var conn = NetServices.createGatewayConnection();
  // the wsdl URL is to the auto-generated document from
  // the ASMX
  var wsdl = "http://localhost/Wiley/Horoscope.asmx?wsdl";
  srv = conn.getService(wsdl);

  // initialize the movie by calling the getSigns() method
  // to return the available signs
  srv.getSigns(signsRes);
}

// when the array of signs is returned, use it to populate
// the signsMenu
signsRes = new Object();
signsRes.onResult = function(result){
  // add the additional option for all signs at once
  result.push("all signs");
  _root.signsMenu.setDataProvider(result);
}
signsRes.onStatus = function(status){
  trace(status.description);
}

// when a single horoscope is returned, display the
// value in the TextField
oneRes = new Object();
oneRes.onResult = function(result){
  _root.horoscope.text = result;
}
oneRes.onStatus = function(status){
  trace(status.description);
}

// when all the horoscopes are returned in an array,
// loop through them and display them on lines in
// the TextField
allRes = new Object();
allRes.onResult = function(result){
```

```
      for(var i = 0; i < result.length; i++){
        _root.horoscope.text += result[i] + newline;
      }
  }
  allRes.onStatus = function(status){
    trace(status.description);
  }

  selectBtn.setLabel("get horoscope");
  selectBtn.onRelease = function(){
    // get the selected sign
    var sign = _root.signsMenu.getValue();
    // if all signs is selected, call getHoroscopes(), else
    // call getHoroscope() with the selected sign
    if(sign == "all signs")
      _root.srv.getHoroscopes(_root.allRes);
    else
      _root.srv.getHoroscope(_root.oneRes, sign);
  }

  init();
```

13. Test the movie. It might take a moment on the initial test for the menu to populate because the Web service needs to compile and perform its own initialization tasks. Once the menu is populated, select a sign and click the button. Figure 21-6 shows an example of how your movie should look.

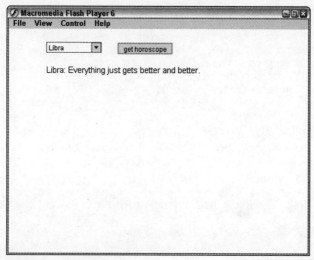

Figure 21-6: Testing the movie

Working with Typed Objects

In addition to working with standard types of objects and values with a .NET Web service method, you may want to also work with parameters of custom types. This may involve passing parameters to a Web service method from a Flash movie or returning a typed object to a Flash movie.

Passing Typed Parameters

Passing a typed object to a .NET Web service involves three main steps:

✦ Creating and registering the ActionScript class that defines the type of object you wish to send to the Web service

✦ Defining the .NET mirror class with the same name as the registered ActionScript class

✦ Creating the Web service method to expect a parameter of the .NET mirror class type

Listing 21-4 shows an example of defining and registering an ActionScript class.

Listing 21-4: An ActionScript Class Definition and Registration

```
function MyType(val){
  this.myTypeProperty = val;
}
// you must define all properties for the prototype
MyType.prototype.myTypeProperty;

// register the class. The first parameter determines the
// name of the object type that will be sent to the Web
// service, and the second parameter is a reference to the
// ActionScript class
Object.registerClass("MyType", MyType);
```

Listing 21-5 shows an example of an ASMX document that contains both the Web service class and the mirror class for the ActionScript class, MyType. Alternatively, you could create the mirror class in a separate document and compile it separately.

Listing 21-5: A .NET ASMX with a Corresponding Class Definition

```
<%@ WebService language="C#" class="MyWebService" %>

using System.Web.Services;

public class MyType {

  private myTypeProperty;

  public MyType(){}
```

```
    public string getDescription(){
      return "the object says: " + this.myTypeProperty;
    }

  }

  public class MyWebService {

    [WebMethod]
    public string getTypeDescription(MyType obj){
      return obj.getDescription();
    }


  }
```

Based on Listings 21-2 and 21-3, the ActionScript code in Listing 21-6 shows how it might all be put into action.

Listing 21-6: Passing a Typed Object to a Web Service

```
// document in which MyType is defined and registered
// srv is the service object to the Web service and res
// is the response object

mt = new MyType("this is my custom type");
srv.getTypeDescription(res);
// returns - the object says: this is my custom type
```

Returning Typed Objects

Currently, there is no known way for a .NET Web service to return a typed object to Flash. This is because .NET Web services do not allow ASObject data types to be passed in and out.

Consuming Web Services with .NET

Some Web services do not return usable values to Flash when consumed directly. In these cases, it can be helpful to use .NET to consume the Web service and then return the results in a usable form to the Flash movie.

You can create a .NET class to consume a Web service relatively easily because .NET provides a utility, wsdl.exe, that automatically generates the necessary proxy class for you based on the WSDL document (or XSD schema or DISCO document) for the service. The wsdl.exe utility can be invoked from the command line. A handful of options are available for it. Some of them are relevant to our discussion here, while others are not. If you want a list of the options, simply type the following:

```
wsdl /?
```

The two options applicable to our discussion are /language and /namespace. By default, the language used is C#, so it is not necessary to specify the language option if you wish to use C#. However, you can specify C# explicitly with /language:CS. If you wish to use Visual Basic, you can use the /language:VB option.

The default namespace used by classes output by wsdl.exe is the global namespace. If you wish to specify another namespace, you can use the /namespace option. You can set the namespace to Wiley.Chapter21, for instance, with the /namespace:Wiley.Chapter21 option.

Invoke the wsdl.exe utility with the name, wsdl, followed by the options (if any), and then the URL to the WSDL document (or other allowable document). For example:

```
wsdl /language:CS /namespace:Wiley.Chapter21
http://localhost/Wiley/SimpleService.asmx?wsdl
```

This in turn generates an assembly source document based on the name of the Web service — for example, SimpleService.cs. You need to compile this generated proxy assembly source.

Once you have a compiled proxy assembly, you can create a .NET resource that uses it. The resource that uses the proxy assembly can be of most any type — ASPX, ASMX, DLL, etc. — but in most cases, when you are working with Flash Remoting, it is easiest to create a DLL for this purpose.

Searching Amazon with .NET

The best way to understand how to consume a Web service from .NET is to dive right into an example. In this exercise, you use .NET to consume the Amazon Web service and return the results to a Flash movie. At the time of this writing, the Amazon Web service is an example of a service that does not return usable results to Flash when consumed directly.

Note   You need to register with Amazon.com's associates program (free). To do so, go to http://associates.amazon.com. Once you have signed up and are logged on, go to their Web services page (http://associates.amazon.com/exec/panama/associates/ntg/browse/-/1067662/103-5686734-5679061) and get a developer's token (free), which you will need to complete this exercise.

1. From the command line, change directories to the Wiley Web application bin directory and then type the following:

```
wsdl /language:CS /namespace:Wiley.Chapter21
http://soap.amazon.com/schemas2/AmazonWebServices.wsdl
```

If you are using Visual Basic, simply change the language option from CS to VB.

2. Compile the resulting document (AmazonSearchService.cs or AmazonSearchService.vb).

3. Open the AmazonSearchService source code.

4. Open a new C# (or Visual Basic) document and save it to the Wiley Web application bin directory as AmazonSearch.cs (or AmazonSearch.vb).

5. Analyzing the AmazonSearchService source code, you will see that you need the following classes in order to perform a keyword search operation with the Amazon Web service: AmazonSearchService, ProductInfo (for the returned value), and KeywordRequest (for the parameters sent to the service).

6. Add the following code to AmazonSearch.cs:

```
namespace Wiley.Chapter21{

  // import FlashGateway.IO because you will use ASObject
  using FlashGateway.IO;

  public class AmazonSearch{

    // doKeyWordSearch gets called from the Flash movie
    // with an object containing the parameters to send
    // to the service. The method returns a ProductInfo
    // object
    public ProductInfo doKeywordSearch(ASObject paramC){

      // extract all the values passed from Flash
      string keyword = (string) paramC["keyword"];
      string page = (string) paramC["page"];
      string mode = (string) paramC["mode"];
      string tag = (string) paramC["tag"];
      string type = (string) paramC["type"];
      string devtag = (string) paramC["devtag"];


      // create the AmazonSearchService object
      AmazonSearchService aws = new AmazonSearchService();

      // create the KeywordRequest object that is used
      // to send the parameters to the
      // KeywordSearchRequest() method
      KeywordRequest kwr = new KeywordRequest();
      kwr.keyword = keyword;
      kwr.page = page;
      kwr.mode = mode;
      kwr.tag = tag;
      kwr.type = type;
      kwr.devtag = devtag;


      // call the service method through the proxy
      ProductInfo pi = aws.KeywordSearchRequest(kwr);
      // return the result to Flash
      return pi;
    }

  }
}
```

7. Save and compile the AmazonSearch assembly to AmazonSearch.dll. You need to make sure to include a reference to both flashgateway.dll and to AmazonSearchService.dll when you run the compiler. For example:

```
csc /t:library /r:flashgateway.dll,AmazonSearchService.dll
AmazonSearch.cs
```

8. To create the Flash document, refer to the exercise in Chapter 9 under the section "Searching Amazon via Proxy" and follow steps 3 through 18. The only change you need to make is to the code in step 17, as shown in bold here:.

```
#include "NetServices.as"

function init(){
  ...
  gwUrl = "http://localhost/Wiley/flashgateway.aspx";
  _root.srv = conn.getService("Wiley.chapter21.AmazonSearch");
}
...
```

Summary

.NET Web services are a powerful tool for use with your Flash Remoting movies. In this chapter, you learned how to create your own .NET Web services and how to consume Web services using .NET. Specific highlights from this chapter to take note of include the following:

✦ .NET Web services are authored in ASMX documents. These documents must include a WebService directive, import the System.Web.Services namespace, and should include the [WebMethod] (or <WebMethod()> for VB) attribute for each method that you wish to make available through the Web service.

✦ Typed objects can be passed to .NET Web services from Flash movies when the ActionScript class is registered and a mirror class has been defined in .NET.

✦ Some Web services do not return usable results to Flash when consumed directly. You can use .NET to consume the Web service and return the results to Flash in these cases.

✦   ✦   ✦

Building Remoting Applications

Developing Flash E-Commerce

Whether it is called e-commerce, m-commerce, or any of the other buzzwords applied to the buying and selling of products and services on the Internet, it represents a tremendous portion of the business found on the World Wide Web today. In this chapter, you build an application that can serve as the foundation of your online store — whether you are selling T-shirts, insurance, books on psychic powers, or custom dog collars.

Architecting the Application

There is always more than one way to create an application. Therefore, it is a good idea for you to create a map of what you are going to create and how — *before* you begin writing any code. The next several sections walk you through one approach to the development of a Flash Remoting e-commerce application. Specifically, I outline the desired functionality, the pieces of the application, and how it all fits together to form a whole. I also discuss the reasons behind some of the choices, as well as the strengths and weaknesses of those choices.

Specifying Functionality

Before you can build something, you have to know *what* you want to build and what you want it to do. Ideally, any applications you build should be highly scalable and extensible, making the adding of functionality later not only possible, but easy. However, the purpose of an application must be understood from the beginning. For example, no matter how well designed a factory for making cars is, it will not function very well for printing books.

One of the easiest ways to define the essence of an application is to simply list the functionality you want included in the application. For the example application outlined in this chapter, I include the following list of functionality. The functionality is organized into two categories: administration and storefront.

✦ Administration

- Add/modify/remove categories of the store (e.g., jewelry, toys, music)
- Add/modify/remove items of the store (assigned to categories from above)
- View orders that have been placed

✦ Storefront

- Browse items by category
- Add items to the shopping cart
- View/modify the shopping cart
- Register users
- Log in users
- Checkout/submit order
- Calculate shipping and handling costs

Note   The preceding list of functionality includes most of the basic, core functionality of an e-commerce application. One element that is not included in this list (and consequently in the application in this chapter) is the capability to process credit card transactions. This is because processing credit card transaction requires that you have the appropriate arrangements made—that is, an account with a credit card processing company. Although this functionality is not included in the application, you can easily include it if you have made the proper arrangements.

The Application Overview

I have chosen to design the application in four main parts:

✦ **Database:** The entire contents of the store (categories and items) are saved and retrieved from a database. This provides standardized, efficient, and quick access to the data. In addition to the store contents, user and order information is also stored in the database.

✦ **CFC/Java class/.NET DLL:** Depending on your chosen platform, you need only choose one of these options to build your e-commerce application. Contained within this portion is all the logic needed to perform the data access.

✦ **Administrative Flash movie:** I opted to provide access to the administrative functionality in one Flash movie. This way, I didn't need to restrict access to that functionality on the server side by creating administrative accounts (usernames and passwords). For the example application, this is fine. However, for added security, you may find that you want to add password protection to that functionality.

✦ **Storefront Flash movie:** The storefront Flash movie is the user interface to the e-commerce application whereby users can browse and shop available categories and items. All the stateful information (such as logged in user, shopping cart data, etc.) is maintained within this movie, rather than on the server.

Creating the Database

The database is the foundation of the application. It is essential that the database be well designed in order for the rest of the application to function properly. For the sake of ease, I chose to simply add tables (all of which I have named with the ECOMM prefix) to the existing WileyFlashRemoting database created in Chapter 4. Therefore, if you have not already created this database, you should follow the instructions in that chapter for setting it up.

Figure 22-1 outlines the tables and columns used by the e-commerce application. You can see the conceptual relationships between some of the columns in the tables. These relationships are *not* enforced within the database itself. However, a visual representation of the relationships can be helpful in order to understand how the tables work together.

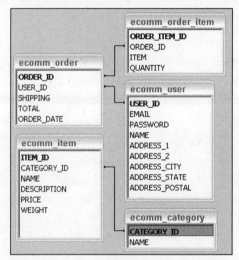

Figure 22-1: The tables of the database for the ecomm application

Table 22-1 lists the tables and their columns, along with a brief description of each column.

Table 22-1: The Tables of the Database

Table	Column	Description
ECOMM_CATEGORY	CATEGORY_ID	The primary key identifying a unique category
ECOMM_CATEGORY	NAME	The name of a product category (e.g., housewares, clothing, books)
ECOMM_ITEM	ITEM_ID	The primary key identifying a unique item
ECOMM_ITEM	CATEGORY_ID	The ID of the category to which the item belongs
ECOMM_ITEM	NAME	The name of the item

Continued

Table 22-1: *(continued)*

Table	Column	Description
ECOMM_ITEM	DESCRIPTION	A description of the item
ECOMM_ITEM	PRICE	The price per item
ECOMM_ITEM	WEIGHT	The weight (in pounds) per item (for calculating shipping costs)
ECOMM_USER	USER_ID	The primary key identifying a unique user
ECOMM_USER	EMAIL	The user's e-mail address—used as the login
ECOMM_USER	PASSWORD	The password with which the user logs in
ECOMM_USER	NAME	The user's name
ECOMM_USER	ADDRESS_1	The user's street address
ECOMM_USER	ADDRESS_2	The second line (if any) of the street address
ECOMM_USER	ADDRESS_CITY	The city for the user's address
ECOMM_USER	ADDRESS_STATE	The state for the user's address
ECOMM_USER	ADDRESS_POSTAL	The postal/zip code for the user's address
ECOMM_ORDER	ORDER_ID	The primary key identifying a unique order
ECOMM_ORDER	USER_ID	The ID of the user who placed the order
ECOMM_ORDER	SHIPPING	The shipping costs for the order
ECOMM_ORDER	TOTAL	The total costs (not including shipping) for the order
ECOMM_ORDER	ORDER_DATE	The date the order was placed
ECOMM_ORDER_ITEM	ORDER_ITEM_ID	The primary key identifying an item included in the order
ECOMM_ORDER_ITEM	ORDER_ID	The ID of an order to which an order item belongs
ECOMM_ORDER_ITEM	ITEM	The name of the item in the order
ECOMM_ORDER_ITEM	QUANTITY	The quantity of the item ordered

Once you have a basic understanding of the database tables you want to create, the next step is to actually create them. Listing 22-1 includes the SQL code for creating all of the tables necessary. You can execute each `CREATE` statement from the command line of your DBMS, or you can place the contents of the entire listing in a text file and run that file from the command line (if that functionality is available to your DBMS).

Listing 22-1: **The SQL to Generate the ecomm Tables**

```
CREATE TABLE ecomm_category (
  CATEGORY_ID int(10) unsigned NOT NULL  auto_increment,
  NAME varchar(50) NOT NULL   ,
  PRIMARY KEY (CATEGORY_ID)
);

CREATE TABLE ecomm_item (
  ITEM_ID int(10) unsigned NOT NULL  auto_increment,
  CATEGORY_ID int(10) unsigned NOT NULL  DEFAULT '0' ,
  NAME varchar(50) NOT NULL  ,
  DESCRIPTION varchar(255)   ,
  PRICE float(5,2) unsigned NOT NULL  DEFAULT '0.00' ,
  WEIGHT int(10) unsigned NOT NULL  DEFAULT '0'  ,
  PRIMARY KEY (ITEM_ID)
);

CREATE TABLE ecomm_order (
  ORDER_ID int(10) unsigned NOT NULL  auto_increment,
  USER_ID int(10) unsigned NOT NULL  DEFAULT '0' ,
  SHIPPING float(10,2) unsigned NOT NULL  DEFAULT '0.00' ,
  TOTAL float(12,2) unsigned NOT NULL  DEFAULT '0.00' ,
  ORDER_DATE datetime NOT NULL  DEFAULT '0000-00-00 00:00:00'  ,
  PRIMARY KEY (ORDER_ID)
);

CREATE TABLE ecomm_order_item (
  ORDER_ITEM_ID int(10) unsigned NOT NULL  auto_increment,
  ORDER_ID int(10) unsigned NOT NULL  DEFAULT '0' ,
  ITEM varchar(50) NOT NULL  ,
  QUANTITY int(10) unsigned NOT NULL  DEFAULT '0'  ,
  PRIMARY KEY (ORDER_ITEM_ID)
);

CREATE TABLE ecomm_user (
  USER_ID int(10) unsigned NOT NULL  auto_increment,
  EMAIL varchar(50) NOT NULL  ,
  PASSWORD varchar(50) NOT NULL  ,
  NAME varchar(50) NOT NULL  ,
  ADDRESS_1 varchar(50) NOT NULL  ,
  ADDRESS_2 varchar(50)    ,
  ADDRESS_CITY varchar(50) NOT NULL  ,
  ADDRESS_STATE varchar(50) NOT NULL  ,
  ADDRESS_POSTAL int(10) unsigned NOT NULL  DEFAULT '0'  ,
  PRIMARY KEY (USER_ID)
);
```

Developing the Server-Side Application

The server-side portion of the application is what performs the database access. Whether you are using ColdFusion, Java, or .NET, the functionality is the same. In Table 22-2, you can see a list of the methods, the parameters, and the data returned.

Note   The data types are listed as the Java types. The `String` type corresponds to `string` in both ColdFusion and .NET. The `int` and `float` types correspond to the `numeric` type in ColdFusion (and are the same in .NET and Java). The `ArrayList` type corresponds to the `Array` type in ColdFusion (and is also `ArrayList` in .NET). Finally, `ResultSet` corresponds to `Query` in ColdFusion, and `DataTable` in .NET.

Table 22-2: The Server-Side Functions

Function Name	Parameters	Return Type
addCategory	String name	Void
addItem	String name	
String description		
int categoryId		
float price		
int weight	Void	
modifyCategory	int categoryId	
String name	Void	
modifyItem	int itemId	
String name		
String description		
int categoryId		
float price		
int weight	Void	
removeCategory	int categoryId	Void
removeItem	int itemId	Void
getCategories		ResultSet
getCategoryItems		ResultSet
getItem	int itemId	ResultSet
register	String email	
String password		
String name		

Function Name	Parameters	Return Type
String address1		
String address2		
String city		
String state		
int zip	Void	
login	String email	
String password	ResultSet	
deleteUser	int userId	ResultSet
getUsers		ResultSet
placeOrder	int userId	
float shipping		
float total		
ArrayList items	Void	
getOrders		ResultSet
getOrder	int orderId	ResultSet

The server-side portion of the application is developed using your chosen platform. The following three sections provide instructions for creating this portion in ColdFusion, Java, and .NET. Locate the appropriate section and follow the instructions given.

Creating the ColdFusion Component

If you use ColdFusion, follow these steps:

1. Within the ColdFusion webroot, you should already have a directory named Wiley. If not, create this directory.

2. Within the Wiley directory, create a chapter22 directory.

3. Within the chapter22 directory, create a new CFC document named CFRMXComm.cfc.

4. Add the code from Listing 22-2 to CFRMXComm.cfc and save the document.

Listing 22-2: **CFRMXComm.cfc**

```
<cfcomponent>

  <!-- add a new category to the store -->
  <cffunction name="addCategory" access="remote"
            returntype="void">
```

Continued

Listing 22-2: *(continued)*

```
    <cfargument name="name" type="string" required="true">
    <cfquery datasource="WileyFlashRemoting">
      INSERT INTO ECOMM_CATEGORY(NAME) VALUES('#name#')
    </cfquery>
</cffunction>

<!-- add a new item to the store -->
<cffunction name="addItem" access="remote" returntype="void">
  <cfargument name="name" type="string" required="true">
  <cfargument name="description" type="string" required="true">
  <cfargument name="categoryId" type="numeric" required="true">
  <cfargument name="price" type="numeric" required="true">
  <cfargument name="weight" type="numeric" required="true">
  <cfquery datasource="WileyFlashRemoting">
    INSERT INTO ECOMM_ITEM(NAME, DESCRIPTION,
                            CATEGORY_ID, PRICE, WEIGHT)
    VALUES('#name#', '#description#', #categoryId#,
          #price#, #weight#)
  </cfquery>
</cffunction>
<!-- modify the name of an existing category -->
<cffunction name="modifyCategory" access="remote"
            returntype="void">
  <cfargument name="categoryId" type="numeric"
              required="true">
  <cfargument name="name" type="string" required="true">
  <cfquery datasource="WileyFlashRemoting">
    UPDATE ECOMM_CATEGORY SET NAME = '#name#'
    WHERE CATEGORY_ID = #categoryId#
  </cfquery>
</cffunction>

<!-- modify the values of an existing item -->
<cffunction name="modifyItem" access="remote"
            returntype="void">
  <cfargument name="itemId" type="numeric"
              required="true">
  <cfargument name="name" type="string" required="true">
  <cfargument name="description" type="string"
              required="true">
  <cfargument name="categoryId" type="numeric"
              required="true">
  <cfargument name="price" type="numeric"
              required="true">
  <cfargument name="weight" type="numeric"
              required="true">
  <cfquery datasource="WileyFlashRemoting">
    UPDATE ECOMM_ITEM
```

```
      SET NAME = '#name#',
      DESCRIPTION = '#description#',
      CATEGORY_ID = #categoryId#,
      PRICE = #price#,
      WEIGHT = #weight#
      WHERE ITEM_ID = #itemId#
  </cfquery>
</cffunction>

<!-- remove a category from the store - NOTE: this does
     not remove the items within the category -->
<cffunction name="removeCategory" access="remote"
            returntype="void">
  <cfargument name="categoryId" type="numeric"
              required="true">
  <cfquery datasource="WileyFlashRemoting">
    DELETE FROM ECOMM_CATEGORY
    WHERE CATEGORY_ID = #categoryId#
  </cfquery>
</cffunction>

<!-- remove an item -->
<cffunction name="removeItem" access="remote"
            returntype="void">
  <cfargument name="itemId" type="numeric"
              required="true">
  <cfquery datasource="WileyFlashRemoting">
    DELETE FROM ECOMM_ITEM
    WHERE ITEM_ID = #itemId#
  </cfquery>
</cffunction>

<!-- get all the categories -->
<cffunction name="getCategories" access="remote"
            returntype="query">
  <cfquery datasource="WileyFlashRemoting"
           name="categories">
    SELECT * FROM ECOMM_CATEGORY
  </cfquery>
  <cfreturn #categories#>
</cffunction>

<!-- get all the items in a category -->
<cffunction name="getCategoryItems" access="remote"
            returntype="query">
  <cfargument name="categoryId" type="numeric"
              required="true">
  <cfquery datasource="WileyFlashRemoting" name="items">
    SELECT *
    FROM ECOMM_ITEM
    WHERE CATEGORY_ID = #categoryId#
```

Continued

Listing 22-2: *(continued)*

```
      </cfquery>
      <cfreturn #items#>
   </cffunction>


   <!-- get an item -->
   <cffunction name="getItem" access="remote"
               returntype="query">
      <cfargument name="itemId" type="numeric"
                  required="true">
      <cfquery datasource="WileyFlashRemoting" name="item">
         SELECT * FROM ECOMM_ITEM
         WHERE ITEM_ID = #itemId#
      </cfquery>
      <cfreturn #item#>
   </cffunction>


   <!-- register a new user -->
   <cffunction name="register" access="remote"
               returntype="void">
      <cfargument name="email" type="string"
                  required="true">     <cfargument name="password"
type="string"
                  required="true">
      <cfargument name="name" type="string" required="true">
      <cfargument name="address1" type="string"
                  required="true">
      <cfargument name="address2" type="string"
                  required="true">
      <cfargument name="city" type="string" required="true">
      <cfargument name="state" type="string"
                  required="true">
      <cfargument name="zip" type="numeric" required="true">
      <cfquery datasource="WileyFlashRemoting">
         INSERT INTO ECOMM_USER(EMAIL, PASSWORD, NAME,
                              ADDRESS_1, ADDRESS_2,
                              ADDRESS_CITY, ADDRESS_STATE,
                              ADDRESS_POSTAL)
         VALUES('#email#', '#password#', '#name#',
               '#address1#', '#address2#', '#city#',
               '#state#', #zip#)
      </cfquery>
   </cffunction>


   <!-- login a user. if the username and password match
        then the user's record is returned -->
   <cffunction name="login" access="remote"
               returntype="query">
      <cfargument name="email" type="string"
```

```
                    required="true">
  <cfargument name="password" type="string"
              required="true">
  <cfquery datasource="WileyFlashRemoting" name="user">
    SELECT * FROM ecomm_user
    WHERE EMAIL = '#email#' AND
    PASSWORD = '#password#'
  </cfquery>
  <cfreturn #user#>
</cffunction>

<!-- place an order. pass in the userId, shipping costs,
     total costs, and an array of structs of the items
     in the order -->
<cffunction name="placeOrder" access="remote"
            returntype="void">
  <cfargument name="userId" type="numeric"
              required="true">
  <cfargument name="shipping" type="numeric"
              required="true">
  <cfargument name="total" type="numeric"
              required="true">
  <cfargument name="items" type="array" required="true">
  <cfset timestampVal = CreateODBCDateTime(Now())>

  <!-- these database actions should be performed
       together, and no other user should be able to
       access this code while another is performing
       these inserts. The reason being that
       the new order_id must be accurately
       associated. -->
  <cflock timeout="10">
    <!-- insert the order -->
    <cfquery datasource="WileyFlashRemoting">
      INSERT INTO ECOMM_ORDER(USER_ID, SHIPPING, TOTAL,
                              ORDER_DATE)
      VALUES(#userId#, #shipping#, #total#,
             #timestampVal#)
    </cfquery>

    <!-- get the new order id -->
    <cfquery datasource="WileyFlashRemoting"
             name="orderId">
      SELECT MAX(ORDER_ID) AS ID
      FROM ECOMM_ORDER
    </cfquery>

    <!-- for all the items in the order, insert them
         into the database -->
    <cfloop from="1" to="#ArrayLen(items)#" index="i">
      <cfquery datasource="WileyFlashRemoting">
```

Continued

Listing 22-2: *(continued)*

```
        INSERT INTO ECOMM_ORDER_ITEM(ORDER_ID, ITEM,
                                     QUANTITY)
        VALUES(#orderId.ID#, '#items[i].item#',
               '#items[i].quantity#')
      </cfquery>
    </cfloop>
  </cflock>
</cffunction>

<!-- get all the orders -->
<cffunction name="getOrders" access="remote"
            returntype="query">
  <cfquery datasource="WileyFlashRemoting"
           name="orders">
    SELECT * FROM ECOMM_ORDER, ECOMM_USER
    WHERE ECOMM_USER.USER_ID = ECOMM_ORDER.USER_ID
  </cfquery>
  <cfreturn orders>
</cffunction>

<!-- get the items from an order -->
<cffunction name="getOrder" access="remote"
            returntype="query">
  <cfargument name="orderId" type="numeric"
              required="true">
  <cfquery datasource="WileyFlashRemoting" name="order">
    SELECT * FROM ECOMM_ORDER_ITEM
    WHERE ECOMM_ORDER_ITEM.ORDER_ID = #orderId#
  </cfquery>
  <cfreturn order>
</cffunction>

</cfcomponent>
```

Creating the Java Class

If you are using a J2EE application server, follow these steps:

1. Within the Web application's WEB-INF/classes, you should already have a Wiley directory. If you do not, create it.

2. Create a chapter22 directory within the Wiley directory.

3. Create a new Java file named CFRMXComm.java in the chapter22 directory.

4. Add the code from Listing 22-3 to the CFRMXComm.java document and save it.

Listing 22-3: **CFRMXComm.java**

```java
package wiley.chapter22;

import java.io.*;
import java.sql.*;
import java.util.*;
import flashgateway.io.ASObject;

public class CFRMXComm {

  // create the Statement object to be used for the
  // database calls
  public Statement makeStatement() throws Exception{
    Class.forName("com.mysql.jdbc.Driver").newInstance();
    String connStr = "jdbc:mysql://localhost/WileyFlashRemoting";
    Connection connection = DriverManager.getConnection(connStr);
    Statement statement = connection.createStatement();
    return statement;
  }

  // executes a SQL statement on the database and does
  // not return a result (ie - INSERT, DELETE, UPDATE)
  public void update(String sql) throws Exception{
    Statement statement = makeStatement();
    statement.executeUpdate(sql);
  }

  // executes a SQL statement on the database and returns
  // a result (ie - SELECT)
  public ResultSet query(String sql) throws Exception{
    Statement statement = makeStatement();
    return statement.executeQuery(sql);
  }

  // add a new category to the store
  public void addCategory(String name) throws Exception{
    StringBuffer sb = new StringBuffer();
    sb.append("INSERT INTO ECOMM_CATEGORY(NAME) VALUES('");
    sb.append(name);
    sb.append("')");
    update(sb.toString());
  }

  // add a new item to the store
  public void addItem(String name, String description, int categoryId,
float price, int weight) throws Exception{
    StringBuffer sb = new StringBuffer();
    sb.append("INSERT INTO ECOMM_ITEM(NAME, DESCRIPTION, CATEGORY_ID,
PRICE, WEIGHT) VALUES('");
```

Continued

Listing 22-3: *(continued)*

```java
    sb.append(name);
    sb.append("', '");
    sb.append(description);
    sb.append("', ");
    sb.append(categoryId);
    sb.append(", ");
    sb.append(price);
    sb.append(", ");
    sb.append(weight);
    sb.append(")");
    update(sb.toString());
  }

  // modify the name of an existing category
  public void modifyCategory(int categoryId, String name) throws
Exception{
    StringBuffer sb = new StringBuffer();
    sb.append(" UPDATE ECOMM_CATEGORY SET NAME = '");
    sb.append(name);
    sb.append("' WHERE CATEGORY_ID = ");
    sb.append(categoryId);
    update(sb.toString());
  }

  // modify the values of an existing item
  public void modifyItem(int itemId, String name,
                         String description,
                         int categoryId, float price,
                         int weight) throws Exception{
    StringBuffer sb = new StringBuffer();
    sb.append("UPDATE ECOMM_ITEM SET NAME = '");
    sb.append(name);
sb.append("', DESCRIPTION = '");
    sb.append(description);
    sb.append("',  CATEGORY_ID = ");
    sb.append(categoryId);
    sb.append(", PRICE = ");
    sb.append(price);
    sb.append(", WEIGHT = ");
    sb.append(weight);
    sb.append(" WHERE ITEM_ID = ");
    sb.append(itemId);
    System.out.println(sb.toString());
    update(sb.toString());
  }

  // remove a category from the store - NOTE: this does
  // not remove the items within the category
```

```java
public void removeCategory(int categoryId) throws Exception{
  StringBuffer sb = new StringBuffer();
  sb.append("DELETE FROM ECOMM_CATEGORY WHERE CATEGORY_ID = ");
  sb.append(categoryId);
  update(sb.toString());
}

// remove an item
public void removeItem(int itemId) throws Exception{
  StringBuffer sb = new StringBuffer();
  sb.append("DELETE FROM ECOMM_ITEM WHERE ITEM_ID = ");
  sb.append(itemId);
  update(sb.toString());
}

// get all the categories
public ResultSet getCategories() throws Exception{
  StringBuffer sb = new StringBuffer();
  sb.append("SELECT * FROM ecomm_category");
  return query(sb.toString());
}

// get all the items within a category
public ResultSet getCategoryItems(int categoryId) throws Exception{
  StringBuffer sb = new StringBuffer();
  sb.append("SELECT * FROM ecomm_item WHERE CATEGORY_ID = ");
  sb.append(categoryId);
  return query(sb.toString());
}

// get an item based on the id
public ResultSet getItem(int itemId) throws Exception {
  StringBuffer sb = new StringBuffer();
  sb.append("SELECT * FROM ecomm_item WHERE ITEM_ID = ");
  sb.append(itemId);
  return query(sb.toString());
}

// register a new user
public void register(String email, String password,
                     String name, String address1,
                     String address2, String city,
                     String state,
                     int zip) throws Exception{
  StringBuffer sb = new StringBuffer();
  sb.append(" INSERT INTO ecomm_user(EMAIL, PASSWORD, NAME, ");
  sb.append("ADDRESS_1, ADDRESS_2, ADDRESS_CITY, ADDRESS_STATE, ");
  sb.append("ADDRESS_POSTAL) VALUES('");
  sb.append(email);
  sb.append("', '");
  sb.append(password);
```

Continued

Listing 22-3: *(continued)*

```java
        sb.append("', '");
        sb.append(name);
        sb.append("', '");
        sb.append(address1);
        sb.append("', '");
        sb.append(address2);
        sb.append("', '");
        sb.append(city);
        sb.append("', '");
        sb.append(state);
        sb.append("', ");
        sb.append(zip);
        sb.append(")");
        update(sb.toString());
    }

    // login a user. if the username and password match then
    // the user's record is returned
    public ResultSet login(String email, String password) throws
Exception{
        StringBuffer sb = new StringBuffer();
        sb.append("SELECT * FROM ecomm_user WHERE EMAIL = '");
        sb.append(email);
        sb.append("' AND PASSWORD = '");
        sb.append(password);
        sb.append("'");
        return query(sb.toString());
    }

    // place an order. pass in the userId, shipping costs,
    // total costs, and an array of structs of the items in
    // the order
    public void placeOrder(int userId, float shipping, float total,
ArrayList items) throws Exception{
        // synchronize to ensure the database operations in
        // the group can only be accessed by one user at
        // a time
        synchronized(this){

        StringBuffer sb = new StringBuffer();
        sb.append("INSERT INTO ecomm_order(USER_ID, SHIPPING, TOTAL,
ORDER_DATE) VALUES(");
        sb.append(userId);
        sb.append(", ");
        sb.append(shipping);
        sb.append(", ");
        sb.append(total);
        sb.append(", '");
```

```
      sb.append(new java.sql.Timestamp(System.currentTimeMillis()));
      sb.append("')");
      update(sb.toString());

      // get the new order id
      ResultSet rs = query("SELECT max(ORDER_ID) AS ID FROM
ecomm_order");
      rs.first();
      int id = rs.getInt("ID");

      // loop through all the items in the ArrayList, and
      // insert them into the database
      Object[] o = items.toArray();
      for(int i = 0; i < o.length; i++){
        sb = new StringBuffer();
        sb.append("INSERT INTO ecomm_order_item(ORDER_ID, ITEM, QUANTITY)
VALUES(");
         sb.append(id);
        sb.append(", '");
        sb.append(((ASObject) o[i]).get("item"));
        sb.append("', '");
        sb.append(((ASObject) o[i]).get("quantity"));
        sb.append("')");
        update(sb.toString());
      }

      }
   }

   // get all the orders
   public ResultSet getOrders() throws Exception{
     StringBuffer sb = new StringBuffer();
     sb.append("SELECT * FROM ecomm_order, ecomm_user ");
     sb.append("WHERE ecomm_user.USER_ID = ecomm_order.USER_ID");
     return query(sb.toString());
   }

   // get all the items from an order
   public ResultSet getOrder(int orderId) throws Exception {
     StringBuffer sb = new StringBuffer();
     sb.append("SELECT * FROM ecomm_order_item WHERE ORDER_ID = ");
     sb.append(orderId);
     return query(sb.toString());
   }

}
```

5. Compile CFRMXComm.java into CFRMXComm.class, and keep it within the same chapter 22 directory.

Tip   If you do not have the flashgateway.jar file in your CLASSPATH, be sure to include it by way of the -classpath flag of javac when compiling CFRMXComm.java because the class uses `ASObject` objects.

Creating the .NET Assembly

If you use .NET, follow these steps:

1. Within the .NET Wiley Web application's bin directory (see Chapter 18 for details on setting this up), create a new assembly source document named CFRMXComm.cs (or CFRMXComm.vb).

2. In the CFRMXComm.cs document, add the code from Listing 22-4 and save it.

Web Resource   The VB version of this code can be found on the companion Web site, www.wiley.com/ compbooks/lott.

Listing 22-4: **CFRMXComm.cs**

```
namespace wiley.chapter22 {

  using System.Data;
  using System.Data.OleDb;
  using System.Text;
  using FlashGateway.IO;
  using System.Collections;

  public class CFRMXComm {

  // creates the connection object that is used to make
  // database queries. This code uses OleDb. If you are
  // using SQL Server then adjust appropriately (see
  // chapter 18), or if you are using a database other
  // than MySQL then adjust appropriately.
  private OleDbConnection makeConnection(){
     string connStr = "Server=localhost;Provider=MySQLProv;Data
Source=WileyFlashRemoting";
     return new OleDbConnection(connStr);
  }

  // run a SQL statement on the database and return
  // a result (ie - SELECT)
  private DataTable query(string sql){
    OleDbConnection conn = makeConnection();
    OleDbCommand cmd = new OleDbCommand(sql, conn);
    OleDbDataAdapter adp = new OleDbDataAdapter();
    adp.SelectCommand = cmd;
    DataSet ds = new DataSet();
    adp.Fill(ds, "Results");
    return ds.Tables[0];
  }
```

```
// run a SQL statement on the database and do not
// return a result (ie - INSERT, UPDATE, DELETE)
private void update(string sql){
   OleDbConnection conn = makeConnection();
   OleDbCommand cmd = new OleDbCommand(sql, conn);
   OleDbDataAdapter adp = new OleDbDataAdapter();
   adp.InsertCommand = cmd;
}

// add a new category to the store
public void addCategory(string name) {
   StringBuilder sb = new StringBuilder();
   sb.Append("INSERT INTO ECOMM_CATEGORY(NAME) VALUES('");
   sb.Append(name);
   sb.Append("')");
   update(sb.ToString());
}

// add a new item to the store
public void addItem(string name, string description,
                    int categoryId, float price,
                    int weight) {
   StringBuilder sb = new StringBuilder();
   sb.Append("INSERT INTO ECOMM_ITEM(NAME, DESCRIPTION, CATEGORY_ID,
PRICE, WEIGHT) VALUES('");
   sb.Append(name);
   sb.Append("', '");
   sb.Append(description);
   sb.Append("', ");
   sb.Append(categoryId);
   sb.Append(", ");
   sb.Append(price);
   sb.Append(", ");
   sb.Append(weight);
   sb.Append(")");
   update(sb.ToString());
}

// modify an existing category
public void modifyCategory(int categoryId, string name){
   StringBuilder sb = new StringBuilder();
   sb.Append(" UPDATE ECOMM_CATEGORY SET NAME = '");
   sb.Append(name);
   sb.Append("' WHERE CATEGORY_ID = ");
   sb.Append(categoryId);
   update(sb.ToString());
}

// modify an existing item
public void modifyItem(int itemId, string name,
                       string description,
```

Continued

Listing 22-4: *(continued)*

```
                         int categoryId, float price,
                         int weight) {
  StringBuilder sb = new StringBuilder();
  sb.Append("UPDATE ECOMM_ITEM SET NAME = '");
  sb.Append(name);
  sb.Append("', DESCRIPTION = '");
  sb.Append(description);
  sb.Append("',  CATEGORY_ID = ");
  sb.Append(categoryId);
  sb.Append(", PRICE = ");
  sb.Append(price);
  sb.Append(", WEIGHT = ");
  sb.Append(weight);
  sb.Append(" WHERE ITEM_ID = ");
  sb.Append(itemId);
  update(sb.ToString());
}

// remove a category from the store - NOTE: this does
// not remove the items within the category
public void removeCategory(int categoryId) {
  StringBuilder sb = new StringBuilder();
  sb.Append("DELETE FROM ECOMM_CATEGORY WHERE CATEGORY_ID = ");
  sb.Append(categoryId);
  update(sb.ToString());
}

// remove an item
public void removeItem(int itemId) {
  StringBuilder sb = new StringBuilder();
  sb.Append("DELETE FROM ECOMM_ITEM WHERE ITEM_ID = ");
  sb.Append(itemId);
  update(sb.ToString());
}
// get all the categories
public DataTable getCategories() {
  StringBuilder sb = new StringBuilder();
  sb.Append("SELECT * FROM ecomm_category");
  return query(sb.ToString());
}

// get all the items within a category
public DataTable getCategoryItems(int categoryId) {
  StringBuilder sb = new StringBuilder();
  sb.Append("SELECT * FROM ecomm_item WHERE CATEGORY_ID = ");
  sb.Append(categoryId);
  return query(sb.ToString());
}
```

```
    // get an item based on the id
    public DataTable getItem(int itemId) {
      StringBuilder sb = new StringBuilder();
      sb.Append("SELECT * FROM ecomm_item WHERE ITEM_ID = ");
      sb.Append(itemId);
      return query(sb.ToString());
    }


    // register a new user
    public void register(string email, string password, string name,
string address1, string address2, string city,
                        string state, int zip) {
      StringBuilder sb = new StringBuilder();
      sb.Append(" INSERT INTO ecomm_user(EMAIL, PASSWORD, NAME, ");
      sb.Append("ADDRESS_1, ADDRESS_2, ADDRESS_CITY, ADDRESS_STATE, ");
      sb.Append("ADDRESS_POSTAL) VALUES('");
      sb.Append(email);
      sb.Append("', '");
      sb.Append(password);
      sb.Append("', '");
      sb.Append(name);
      sb.Append("', '");
      sb.Append(address1);
      sb.Append("', '");
      sb.Append(address2);
      sb.Append("', '");
      sb.Append(city);
      sb.Append("', '");
      sb.Append(state);
      sb.Append("', ");
      sb.Append(zip);
      sb.Append(")");
      update(sb.ToString());
    }


    // login a user. if the username and password match then
    // the user's record is returned
    public DataTable login(string email, string password) {
      StringBuilder sb = new StringBuilder();
      sb.Append("SELECT * FROM ecomm_user WHERE EMAIL = '");
      sb.Append(email);
      sb.Append("' AND PASSWORD = '");
      sb.Append(password);
      sb.Append("'");
      return query(sb.ToString());
    }


    // place an order. pass in the userId, shipping costs,
    // total costs, and an array of structs of the items in
    // the order
```

Continued

Listing 22-4: *(continued)*

```
   public void placeOrder(int userId, float shipping,
                          float total, ArrayList items){
     StringBuilder sb = new StringBuilder();
     sb.Append("INSERT INTO ecomm_order(USER_ID, SHIPPING, TOTAL,
ORDER_DATE) VALUES(");
     sb.Append(userId);
     sb.Append(", ");
     sb.Append(shipping);
     sb.Append(", ");
     sb.Append(total);
     sb.Append(", '");
     sb.Append(System.DateTime.Now);
     sb.Append("')");
     update(sb.ToString());

     // get the new order id
     DataTable dt = query("SELECT max(ORDER_ID) AS ID FROM
ecomm_order");
     DataRow dr = dt.Rows[0];
     int id = (int)dr["ID"];

     // loop through all the items in the ArrayList and add
     // them to the database
     for(int i = 0; i < items.Count; i++){
       sb = new StringBuilder();
       sb.Append("INSERT INTO ecomm_order_item(ORDER_ID, ITEM, QUANTITY)
VALUES(");
        sb.Append(id);
        sb.Append(", '");
        sb.Append(((ASObject)items[i])["item"]);
        sb.Append("', '");
        sb.Append(((ASObject)items[i])["quantity"]);
        sb.Append("')");
        update(sb.ToString());
     }
   }
// get all the orders
   public DataTable getOrders() {
     StringBuilder sb = new StringBuilder();
     sb.Append("SELECT * FROM ecomm_order, ecomm_user ");
     sb.Append("WHERE ecomm_user.USER_ID = ecomm_order.USER_ID");
     return query(sb.ToString());
   }

   // get the items in an order
   public DataTable getOrder(int orderId)  {
     StringBuilder sb = new StringBuilder();
     sb.Append("SELECT * FROM ecomm_order_item WHERE ORDER_ID = ");
```

```
        sb.Append(orderId);
        return query(sb.ToString());
    }


    }
}
```

3. Compile CFRMXComm.cs (or CFRMXComm.vb) to CFRMXComm.dll, and keep it in the same bin directory as the source.

Tip   Be sure to include the /r switch when compiling CFRMXComm.dll to point to the flashgateway.dll because the class uses ASObject objects.

Authoring the Administration Flash Movie

The next step in creating the example application is to make the administration Flash movie. The administration movie consists of four main parts that are spread over four frames on the Main Timeline. These parts are as follows:

✦ **Main menu:** The administrator can choose to add/modify/remove categories and items, as well as view orders.

✦ **Category form:** This form enables the administrator to add new categories and modify existing categories.

✦ **Item form:** This form enables the administrator to add new items and modify existing items.

✦ **View orders page:** This "page" consists of two scroll panes — one to list the orders, and another to view the details of a selected order.

To create this movie, follow these steps.

1. Open a new Flash document and save it as cfrmxCommAdmin.fla.

2. Rename the default layer form. Add three additional layers named frame actions, actions, and labels.

3. On frames one through four of the form, frame actions, and labels layers, create empty keyframes; and on the actions layer, create regular frames (non-keyframes) through frame four.

4. On the labels layer, give the frames labels (from frame one to frame four) of mainMenu, category, item, and orders.

5. On the first frame of the form layer, add seven PushButton component instances. Position the instances as shown in Figure 22-2 and name them categoryAddBtn, categoryModifyBtn, categoryRemoveBtn, itemAddBtn, itemModifyBtn, itemRemoveBtn, and ordersBtn.

6. Add three ComboBox component instances. Position these instances as shown in Figure 22-2 and name them categoryMenu, itemCategoryMenu, and itemMenu.

7. Add static text labels as shown in Figure 22-2.

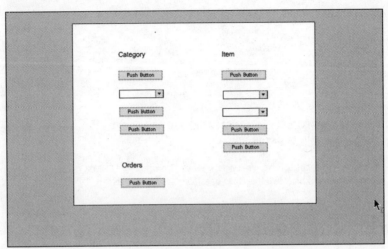

Figure 22-2: The layout of frame one of cfrmxCommAdmin.fla

8. On frame two of the form layer, add a single-line input TextField object with border turned on. Name this instance name. Position the object in the center of the stage as shown in Figure 22-3.

9. Add a PushButton component instance below the name instance. Name the button instance submitBtn.

10. Add static text labels as shown in Figure 22-3.

11. On frame three of the form layer, add four input TextField objects with border turned on. Position them as shown in Figure 22-4. The first, third, and fourth objects should be single-line, while the second is a multiline TextField. Name the instances (from top to bottom) name, description, price, and weight.

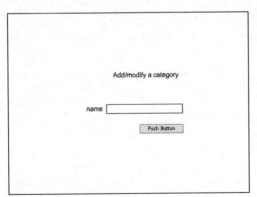

Figure 22-3: The layout of frame two of cfrmxCommAdmin.fla

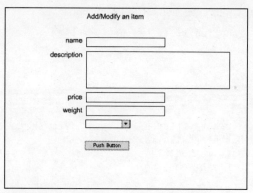

Figure 22-4: The layout of frame three of cfrmxCommAdmin.fla

12. Below the `TextField` objects add a `ComboBox` component instance. Name this instance `addItemCategoryMenu`.

13. Below the `ComboBox` instance, add a `PushButton` component instance. Name the instance `submitBtn`.

14. On the fourth frame of the form layer, add a `ListBox` component instance. Name the instance `ordersMenu`. The position does not matter because it will be repositioned by ActionScript.

15. Add a `ScrollPane` component instance. Name the instance `orderSp`. The position does not matter because, as with `ListBox`, this object will be repositioned by ActionScript.

16. Add a `PushButton` component instance in the lower, right corner of the stage as shown in Figure 22-5. Name the instance `returnBtn`.

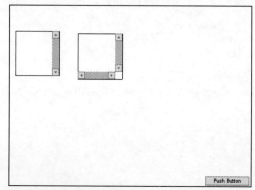

Figure 22-5: The layout of frame four of cfrmxCommAdmin.fla

17. On frame one of the frame actions layer, add the following code:

```
// only call the init function if it has not yet been
// called
if(!inited){
  inited = true;
  init();
}

// if the categories have not yet been retrieved from the
// server then do so, but otherwise, simply call the
// refreshItemCategories() method. This avoids making
// unnecessary calls to Flash Remoting
if(!categoriesInited){
  categoriesInited = true;
  srv.getCategories(getCategoriesRes);
}
else{
  refreshItemCategories();
}

// set the change handler for itemCategoryMenu to a
// function named onItemCategory(). This function (defined
// on the actions layer) changes the items menu contents
// when an item category is selected
_root.itemCategoryMenu.setChangeHandler("onItemCategory");

// stop the timeline
stop();

// when clicking the categoryAddBtn set a variable,
// action, to add and go to the category form. The
// value add let's the category "page" know that it
// is adding a new category, not modifying one
categoryAddBtn.setLabel("add new");
categoryAddBtn.onRelease = function(){
  _root.action = "add";
  _root.gotoAndStop("category");
}

// pretty much the same thing as categoryAddBtn, except
// for adding a new item
itemAddBtn.setLabel("add new");
itemAddBtn.onRelease = function(){
  _root.action = "add";
  _root.gotoAndStop("item");
}

// set action to modify (as opposed to add), get the
// selected category from the menu, and go to the
// category form
categoryModifyBtn.setLabel("modify");
```

```
categoryModifyBtn.onRelease = function(){
  _root.action = "modify";
  _root.selectedCategory = _root.categoryMenu.getSelectedItem();
  _root.gotoAndStop("category");
}


// set the action to modify (not add), and call the
// getItem() service method to get the data for the item
// that is being modified
itemModifyBtn.setLabel("modify");
itemModifyBtn.onRelease = function(){
  _root.action = "modify";
  _root.srv.getItem(_root.getItemRes,
parseInt(_root.itemMenu.getValue()));
}


// call the removeCategory() service method and pass it
// the id of the selected category
categoryRemoveBtn.setLabel("remove");
categoryRemoveBtn.onRelease = function(){
  var categoryId = parseInt(_root.categoryMenu.getValue());
  _root.srv.removeCategory(_root.removeCategoryRes, categoryId);
}


// call the removeItem() service method and pass it the
// id of the selected item.
itemRemoveBtn.setLabel("remove");
itemRemoveBtn.onRelease = function(){
  _root.itemCategoryId = _root.itemCategoryMenu.getValue();
  var itemId = _root.itemMenu.getValue();
  _root.srv.removeItem(_root.removeItemRes, itemId);
}


// call the getOrders() service method and go to the
// orders "page"
ordersBtn.setLabel("view orders");
ordersBtn.onRelease = function(){
  _root.srv.getOrders(_root.getOrdersRes);
  _root.gotoAndStop("orders");
}
```

18. On frame two of the frame actions layer, add the following code:

```
// if the action is modify then populate the form with the
// selected category data
if(action == "modify"){
  name.text = selectedCategory.label;
}


// submit the data to the server
submitBtn.setLabel("submit");
submitBtn.onRelease = function(){
  // set categoriesInited to false so that the categories
```

```
// will be retrieved from the server instead of using
// the cached version
_root.categoriesInited = false;
var n = _root.name.text;

// if the action is add then call the addCategory()
// service method. Otherwise call modifyCategory()
if(_root.action == "add"){
  _root.srv.addCategory(_root.addCategoryRes, n);
}
else{
  _root.srv.modifyCategory(_root.addCategoryRes,
parseInt(_root.selectedCategory.data), n);
  }
}
```

19. On frame three of the frame actions layer, add the following code:

```
// populate the menu with the values from the categoriesRS
// RecordSet object that is saved on _root when the
// categories are retrieved (see getCategoriesRes on
// actions layer)
DataGlue.bindFormatStrings(_root.addItemCategoryMenu,
                           categoriesRS, "#NAME#",
                           "#CATEGORY_ID#");

// if the action is modify then populate the form
if(action == "modify"){
  priceVal = parseFloat(selectedItem.PRICE);
  priceVal *= 100;
  priceVal = Math.round(priceVal)/100;
  name.text = selectedItem.NAME;
  description.text = selectedItem.DESCRIPTION;
  price.text = priceVal;
  weight.text = selectedItem.WEIGHT;

  // set the selected item from the menu
addItemCategoryMenu.setSelectedIndex(selectedItem.categoryIndex);
  }

// submit the data to the server
submitBtn.setLabel("submit");
submitBtn.onRelease = function(){
  var n = _root.name.text;
  var d = _root.description.text;
  var c = parseInt(_root.addItemCategoryMenu.getValue());
  var p = parseFloat(_root.price.text);
  var w = parseInt(_root.weight.text);

  // delete the itemsByCategory array element that
  // represents the category to which this item belongs.
  // ItemsByCategory is a cached version of the items by
  // category, and deleting the category element forces
```

```
// the application to look up the category's items when
// they are next requested. This is important since the
// value will be changed.
delete _root.itemsByCategory[c];

// if the action is add then call the addItem() service
// method. Otherwise, call the modifyItem() service
// method
if(action == "add"){
  _root.srv.addItem(_root.addItemRes, n, d, c, p, w);
}
else{
  _root.srv.modifyItem(_root.addItemRes,
parseInt(_root.selectedItem.ITEM_ID), n, d, c, p, w);
  }
}
```

20. On frame four of the frame actions layer, add the following code:

```
// set the sizes and position of the ListBox and
// ScrollPane
ordersMenu.setSize(500, 100);
ordersMenu._x = 25;
ordersMenu._y = 25;

orderSp.setSize(500, 230);
orderSp._x = 25;
orderSp._y = 130;

// when an item from ordersMenu is selected the getOrder()
// function (defined on actions) should be called
ordersMenu.setChangeHandler("getOrder");

// return to the main menu when clicked
returnBtn.setLabel("return");
returnBtn.onRelease = function(){
  _root.gotoAndStop("mainMenu");
}
```

21. On the first frame (the only keyframe) of the actions layer, add the following code:

```
#include "NetServices.as"
#include "DataGlue.as"

// the toDollar() method is added to the Number
// class, and it makes sure that the number never
// has more than 2 decimal places
Number.prototype.toDollar = function(){
  var da = Math.round(this * 100)/100;
  return da;
}

function init(){
  _root.itemsByCategory = new Object();
```

```
    // use the correct gateway URL for your application
    // server
    var gwURL = "http://localhost:8880/Wiley/gateway";
    NetServices.setDefaultGatewayURL(gwURL);
    var conn = NetServices.createGatewayConnection();

    // the service name is slightly different for each
    // platform. Shown is the service name for Java. For CF
    // use: Wiley.chapter22.CFRMXComm and for .NET use:
    // Wiley.Chapter22.CFRMXComm
    _root.srv = conn.getService("wiley.chapter22.CFRMXComm");
}

// this function is called when a new itemCategoryMenu
// value is selected and populates the itemMenu with the
// items for the selected category
function onItemCategory(menu){
  var i = parseInt(menu.getValue());

  // itemsByCategory is an array that stores the cached
  // values for items by category. This alleviates the
  // need to make calls to the database every time the
  // menu value is changed. If no element exists for the
  // category, however, then make a call to the
  // getCategoryItems() service method. Otherwise, simply
  // populate the menu with the cached values
  if(_root.itemsByCategory[i] == undefined){
    _root.srv.getCategoryItems(_root.getCategoryItemsRes, i);
  }
  else{
    DataGlue.bindFormatStrings(_root.itemMenu,
_root.itemsByCategory[i], "#NAME#", "#ITEM_ID#");
  }
}

// this function populates the categoryMenu and
// itemCategoryMenu with the values that had previously
// been retrieved from the database, rather than having
// to make a database call again
function refreshItemCategories(){
  DataGlue.bindFormatStrings(_root.categoryMenu, _root.categoriesRS,
"#NAME#", "#CATEGORY_ID#");
  DataGlue.bindFormatStrings(_root.itemCategoryMenu,
_root.categoriesRS, "#NAME#", "#CATEGORY_ID#");
  _root.onItemCategory(_root.itemCategoryMenu);
}

// this function is called when an item from the
// ordersMenu is selected. Call the getOrder() service
// method with the id of the selected order
function getOrder(menu){
```

```
  _root.selectedOrder = menu.getValue();
  var id = parseInt(menu.getValue().ORDER_ID);
  _root.srv.getOrder(_root.getOrderRes, id);
}

// after addItem() has been called, return to the
// main menu
addItemRes = new Object();
addItemRes.onResult = function(result){
  _root.gotoAndStop("mainMenu");
}

// after addCategory() has been called, return to the
// main menu
addCategoryRes = new Object();
addCategoryRes.onResult = function(result){
  _root.gotoAndStop("mainMenu");
}

getCategoriesRes = new Object();
getCategoriesRes.onResult = function(result){
  // save the categories RecordSet to a variable
  // on _root for later use
  _root.categoriesRS = result;

  // populate categoryMenu and itemCategoryMenu
  DataGlue.bindFormatStrings(_root.categoryMenu, result, "#NAME#",
"#CATEGORY_ID#");
  DataGlue.bindFormatStrings(_root.itemCategoryMenu, result,
"#NAME#", "#CATEGORY_ID#");
}

getCategoryItemsRes = new Object();
getCategoryItemsRes.onResult = function(result){
  var cid = result.getItemAt(0).CATEGORY_ID;

  // itemsByCategory is an associative array of cached
  // items by category. Add the RecordSet to the array
  // with a key of the category id
  _root.itemsByCategory[cid] = result;

  // populate itemMenu
  DataGlue.bindFormatStrings(_root.itemMenu, result, "#NAME#",
"#ITEM_ID#");
}

// getItem() is called when modifying an existing item, so
// upon retrieving the record set the selectedItem
// variable on _root to the record for the item and add to
// it the index (not the category id) of the selected
// category from the menu, then go to the item form
getItemRes = new Object();
```

```
getItemRes.onResult = function(result){
  _root.selectedItem = result.getItemAt(0);
  _root.selectedItem.categoryIndex =
_root.itemCategoryMenu.getSelectedIndex();
  _root.gotoAndStop("item");
}

// call getCategories() to update the category listing
removeCategoryRes = new Object();
removeCategoryRes.onResult = function(result){
  _root.srv.getCategories(_root.getCategoriesRes);
}

// remove the cached element from itemsByCategory for the
// category to which the removed item belonged, then
// call refreshItemCategories() to update the display
removeItemRes = new Object();
removeItemRes.onResult = function(result){
  delete _root.itemsByCategory[_root.itemCategoryId];
  _root.refreshItemCategories();
}

// format function for DataGlue
function formatOrders(order){
  o = new Object();
  o.label = order.NAME + "..." + order.ORDER_DATE;
  o.data = order;
  return o;
}

// populate ordersMenu
getOrdersRes = new Object();
getOrdersRes.onResult = function(result){
  DataGlue.bindFormatFunction(_root.ordersMenu, result,
_root.formatOrders);
}

getOrderRes = new Object();
getOrderRes.onResult = function(result){
  // create an order MovieClip, and populate it
  // dynamically with the values from the order
  // start by creating the text fields
  var order = _root.createEmptyMovieClip("order", 1);
  order.createTextField("orderDate", 1, 0, 0, 0, 0);
  order.createTextField("itemNames", 2, 0, 0, 0, 0);
  order.createTextField("itemQuantities", 3, 0, 0, 0, 0);
  order.createTextField("total", 4, 0, 0, 0, 0);
  order.createTextField("shipping", 5, 0, 0, 0, 0);
  order.createTextField("userInfo", 6, 0, 0, 0, 0);
  order.itemNames.autoSize = true;
  order.itemNames.text = "ITEM\n";
  order.itemQuantities.autoSize = true;
```

```
      order.itemQuantities.text = "QUANTITY\n";
      var item;

      // fill itemNames and itemQuantities with the values for
      // all the order items
      for(var i = 0; i < result.getLength(); i++){
        item = result.getItemAt(i);
        order.itemNames.text +=  item.ITEM + newline;
        order.itemQuantities.text += item.QUANTITY + newline;
      }
      order.orderDate.autoSize = true;
      order.orderDate.text = "DATE: " + _root.selectedOrder.ORDER_DATE;
      order.itemNames._y = order.orderDate._height + 5;
      order.itemQuantities._y = order.itemNames._y;
      order.itemQuantities._x = order.itemNames._x +
  order.itemNames._width + 5;
      order.shipping.autoSize = true;
      order.shipping.text = "shipping: " +
  parseFloat(_root.selectedOrder.SHIPPING).toDollar();
      order.shipping._y = order.itemNames._y + order.itemNames._height;
      order.total.autoSize = true;
      order.total.text = "total (not including shipping): " +
  parseFloat(_root.selectedOrder.total).toDollar();
      order.total._y = order.shipping._y + order.shipping._height + 5;
      order.userInfo.autoSize = true;
      order.userInfo.text = "SHIP TO:\n";
      order.userInfo.text += _root.selectedOrder.NAME + newline;
      order.userInfo.text += _root.selectedOrder.ADDRESS_1 + newline;
      order.userInfo.text += _root.selectedOrder.ADDRESS_2 + newline;
      order.userInfo.text += _root.selectedOrder.ADDRESS_CITY + ", ";
      order.userInfo.text += _root.selectedOrder.ADDRESS_STATE + newline;
      order.userInfo.text += _root.selectedOrder.ADDRESS_POSTAL;
      order.userInfo._y = order.total._y + order.total._height + 5;

      // set the scroll content of orderSp to the order
      // MovieClip
      _root.orderSp.setScrollContent(order);
  }
```

22. Test the movie. You should add categories and items to the database through this inter-
    face so that it will be populated when you have completed the storefront movie. Click
    the add new button for categories to add a new category to the store. You should see a
    form like the one shown in Figure 22-6. Once you have filled out the form, click the sub-
    mit button. This should return you to the main menu, where you should now see the
    new category in the category menus.

    Next, add a new item by clicking the add new button for items. You should then see a
    form like the one shown in Figure 22-7. Fill out the form and click the submit button.

    At this point, you may want to add more categories and items. You may also want to
    experiment with modifying and deleting items and categories.

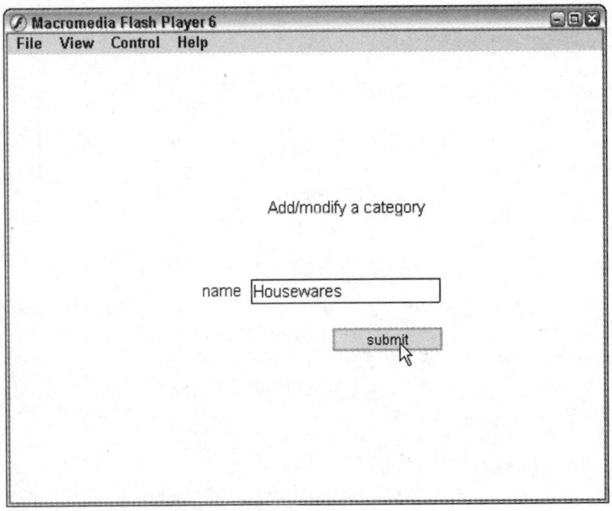

Figure 22-6: Adding a new category

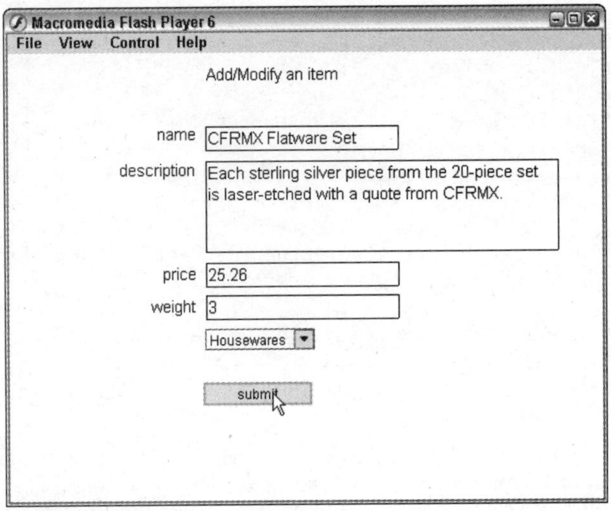

Figure 22-7: Adding a new item

Building the Storefront Flash Movie

The storefront movie is the remaining piece of the entire application. This movie uses only one frame on the Main Timeline, and loads various content into scroll panes. The storefront calculates the shipping cost as the UPS ground shipping based on a ServiceObjects (www.serviceobjects.com) Web service named DOTS for Shipping Comparison (www. serviceobjects.com/products/dots_shipping.asp). In order to use this service, you should sign up for a trial license key from their Web site. You may also want to analyze the WSDL document to understand the request and response data types for the Web service.

To create the storefront movie, complete the following steps:

Note   Unless otherwise noted, set the font size of all the TextField objects to 12.

1. Open a new Flash document and save it as storeFront.fla.

2. Rename the default layer to form, and create a new layer named actions.

3. Create a new Movie Clip symbol (Insert⇨New Symbol), and name the symbol CategoryItem. CategoryItem is going to be a component that will display the data for each item in a category.

4. Edit the CatgoryItem symbol.

5. Rename the default layer to background. Create three additional layers named text, button, and actions.

6. On the background layer, draw a light-gray rectangle (with no outline). Make the rectangle 400 pixels by 51 pixels and position it such that the upper, left corner is at 0,0.

7. Select the rectangle and convert it to a Movie Clip symbol named Background.

8. Name the instance of Background background.

9. On the text layer, add a dynamic TextField object (with border turned off) that is about 270 pixels long, and position it at about 5,5. Name this instance display.

10. Also on the text layer, to the right of display, add an input TextField object with border turned on. Name this instance quantity. Add a static text label next to the input field as shown in Figure 22-8.

11. On the button layer, add a PushButton component instance positioned in the lower, right corner of the background rectangle as shown in Figure 22-8. Name this instance addBtn.

Figure 22-8: The layout of CategoryItem

12. On the first frame of the actions layer, add the following code:

```
// the code must appear between #initclip and #endinitclip
// so that it executes before the code on the main
// timeline
#initclip

// this is a component, so it should extend MovieClip
CategoryItem.prototype = new MovieClip();

function CategoryItem(){
  this.display.wordWrap = true;
```

```
  // ensure only numeric values get input into
  // quantity
  this.quantity.restrict = "0-9";
}


// set label and click handler for addBtn
// this is in onLoad() rather than the constructor
// because onLoad() executes only once the MovieClip
// has actually loaded, whereas the constructor is called
// beforehand. If this code was placed in the constructor
// then it would not have the desired effect because
// addBtn would not yet have loaded
CategoryItem.prototype.onLoad = function(){
  this.addBtn.setLabel("add");
  this.addBtn.setClickHandler("addItem", this);
}


// add an item to the shopping cart. sCart is the
// reference to the shopping cart component set by
// the setShoppingCart() method (see following)
CategoryItem.prototype.addItem = function(){
  this.sCart.addItem(this.data, parseInt(this.quantity.text));
}


// set the data for the instance - populate the
// text fields with the values for the specific
// item
CategoryItem.prototype.setData = function(item){
  this.data = item;
  var price = Math.round(item.PRICE * 100)/100;
  this.display.text = item.NAME + newline;
  this.display.text += item.DESCRIPTION + newline;
  this.display.text += "$" + price;
  this.display._height = this.display.textHeight + 5;
  this.background._height = this.display._height + 5;
}


// set the shopping cart reference
CategoryItem.prototype.setShoppingCart = function(sc){
  this.sCart = sc;
}


// register the class
Object.registerClass("CategoryItem", CategoryItem);

#endinitclip
```

13. Select the linkage properties for CategoryItem and check the Export for ActionScript and Export on first frame options. Set the linkage identifier to CategoryItem. The linkage properties can be opened from the library. Select the symbol and choose Linkage from the library's menu.

14. From the library, select CategoryItem and duplicate the symbol. You can do this by right-clicking on the symbol and choosing from the menu that appears, or by selecting the symbol icon and then choosing duplicate from the library menu. Name the new, duplicated symbol `ShoppingCartItem`.

15. Edit `ShoppingCartItem`.

16. Keep `display` in the same position, but shorten its length to about 150 pixels.

17. Move `quantity`, the static text label, and the `PushButton` instance to the left, as shown in Figure 22-9.

18. Rename the `PushButton` instance to `removeBtn`.

19. On the text layer, add a dynamic `TextField` object with border turned off. Position the object to the right of `quantity` as shown in Figure 22-9. Name this instance `totals`.

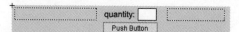

Figure 22-9: The layout of ShoppingCartItem

20. On the first frame of the actions layer, replace the code that is there with the following:

```
#initclip

ShoppingCartItem.prototype = new MovieClip();

function ShoppingCartItem(){
  this.display.multiline = true;
  this.display.wordWrap = true;
  this.quantity.restrict = "0-9";
  this.totals.multiline = true;
  this.totals.wordWrap = true;

  // color the background light blue
  var c = new Color(this.background);
  c.setRGB(0xC1D6FD);
}

ShoppingCartItem.prototype.onLoad = function(){
  this.removeBtn.setLabel("remove");
  this.removeBtn.setClickHandler("removeItem", this);

  // when the quantity is changed by the user call the
  // showTotals() method (defined later)
  this.quantity.parent = this;
  this.quantity.onChanged = function(){
    this.parent.showTotals();
  }
}

// set the instance's parent shopping cart and the id of
// the instance within the shopping cart
```

```
ShoppingCartItem.prototype.setCart = function(cart, id){
  this.cart = cart;
  this.cartId = id;
}


// remove this item from the shopping cart by calling
// the shopping cart's updateTotal() method to subtract
// the item's total as well as the removeItem() method
// Then call the MovieClip removeMovieClip() method to
// remove the component instance
ShoppingCartItem.prototype.removeItem = function(){
  this.cart.updateTotal(-this.total);
  this.cart.removeItem(this.cartId);
  this.removeMovieClip();
}


// show the cost for the item given the selected
// quantity
ShoppingCartItem.prototype.showTotals = function(){
  // set pTotal (as in previous total) to the total prior
  // to the update
  var pTotal = this.total;

  // set total to the quantity times the price per item
  this.total = parseInt(this.quantity.text) * this.price;

  // if the total is not a number then set it to 0
  if (isNaN(this.total)){
    this.total = 0;
  }

  // display the total
  this.totals.text = "total for item: $" + this.total;
  this.totals._height = this.totals.textHeight + 5;

  // call the shopping cart's updateTotal() method with
  // the new total minus the previous total
  this.cart.updateTotal(this.total - pTotal);
}


// set the data for the item
ShoppingCartItem.prototype.setData = function(item, quantity){
  this.data = item;
  this.quantity.text = quantity;
  this.price = parseFloat(item.PRICE).toDollar();
  this.showTotals();
  this.display.text = item.NAME + newline;
  this.display.text += "$" + this.price + " each";
  this.display._height = this.display.textHeight + 5;
  if (this.display._height + 5 > this.background._height){
    this.background._height = this.display._height + 5;
  }
}
```

```
// set a reference to the shopping cart to which this
// item belongs
ShoppingCartItem.prototype.setShoppingCart = function(shoppingCart){
  this.shoppingCart = shoppingCart;
}

// register the class
Object.registerClass("ShoppingCartItem", ShoppingCartItem);

#endinitclip
```

21. Select the linkage properties for ShoppingCartItem and check the Export for ActionScript and Export on first frame options. Set the linkage identifier to ShoppingCartItem.

22. Duplicate the ShoppingCartItem symbol, and name the duplicate ShoppingCartFooter.

23. Edit ShoppingCartFooter.

24. Delete totals, quantity, and the static text label.

25. Rename the PushButton instance checkoutBtn.

26. Move display and checkoutBtn so that they are positioned as shown in Figure 22-10.

Figure 22-10: The layout of ShoppingCartFooter

27. On the first frame of the actions layer, replace the existing code with the following:

```
#initclip

ShoppingCartFooter.prototype = new MovieClip();

function ShoppingCartFooter(){
  this.total = 0;
  this.display.multiline = false;
  this.display.autoSize = true;
  this.display.text = "total: no items added";
  var c = new Color(this.background);
  c.setRGB(0xC1D6FD);
}

ShoppingCartFooter.prototype.onLoad = function(){
  this.checkoutBtn.setLabel("checkout");
  this.checkoutBtn.setClickHandler("checkout", this._parent);
}

// this method displays the total for the entire shopping // cart
ShoppingCartFooter.prototype.updateTotal = function(val){
  this.total += val;
```

```
    this.display.text = "total: $" + this.total.toDollar();
}

Object.registerClass("ShoppingCartFooter", ShoppingCartFooter);

#endinitclip
```

28. Select the linkage properties for `ShoppingCartFooter` and check the Export for ActionScript and Export on first frame options. Set the linkage identifier to `ShoppingCartFooter`.

29. Create a new Movie Clip symbol named `ShoppingCart`.

30. Edit `ShoppingCart`.

31. On the first frame of the default layer, add the following code:

```
#initclip

ShoppingCart.prototype = new MovieClip();

function ShoppingCart(){
  // initialize with a count of 0 items
  this.count = 0;

  // items is an array of all the items in the cart
  this.items = new Array();

  // add a footer
  this.attachMovie("ShoppingCartFooter", "footer", 0);
  this.footer._y = 5;
}

// called when adding an item to the cart
ShoppingCart.prototype.addItem = function(addedItem, quantity){
  var c = this.count;

  // attach a new item component
  var item = this.attachMovie("ShoppingCartItem", "item" + c, c + 1);

  // set the item's cart reference to this and the id to
  // the item count
  item.setCart(this, c);

  // position the new item to below the last
  // previously added item
  item._y = this["item" + (c - 1)]._y + this["item" + (c -
1)]._height + 5;

  // increment the count
  this.count++;

  // pass the values along to the new shopping cart item
  item.setData(addedItem, quantity);
```

```
      // position the footer below the new item
      this.footer._y += item._height + 5;

      // set the scroll pane content to this to update the
      // view
      this.sp.setScrollContent(this);

      // add the item to the items array. Elements of the
      // are objects with a cartId property and an item
      // property that is a reference to the ShoppingCartItem
      // instance
      this.items.push({cartId: c, item: item});
   }

// remove an item from the cart
ShoppingCart.prototype.removeItem = function(id){
   var move = false;
   var h;
   // loop through the items in the cart
   for(var i = 0; i < this.items.length; i++){
      // if current item in loop has a cart id matching
      // the one passed to the method for removal then
      // get that instance's height, remove it from the
      // items array, and set move to true
      if(this.items[i].cartId == id){
         h = this.items[i].item._height + 5;
         this.items.splice(i, 1);
         move = true;
      }
      // if move is true then move the instance up by the
      // value of the height of the removed ShoppingCartItem
      // instance. Move is only true after the removed item
      // has been encountered in the loop, so only items
      // after that one are moved up
      if(move){
         this.items[i].item._y -= h;
      }
   }
   this.footer._y -= h;
}

ShoppingCart.prototype.updateTotal = function(val){
   this.footer.updateTotal(val);
}

// set a reference to the shopping cart's scroll pane (if
// any)
ShoppingCart.prototype.setScrollPane = function(sp){
   this.sp = sp;
}

// call the checkout function that is set by
// setCheckoutHandler()
```

```
ShoppingCart.prototype.checkout = function(){
  this.checkoutRef();
}

// set a reference to a function that is called
// when ready to checkout
ShoppingCart.prototype.setCheckoutHandler = function(functionRef){
  this.checkoutRef = functionRef;
}

Object.registerClass("ShoppingCart", ShoppingCart);

#endinitclip
```

32. Create a new Movie Clip symbol named `LoginForm`.

33. Edit `LoginForm`.

34. Add two single-line input `TextField` objects with border turned on, and position them as shown in Figure 22-11. Name these instances (from top to bottom) `email` and `password`.

35. Add two `PushButton` component instances and position them as shown in Figure 22-11. Name these instances (from top to bottom) `loginBtn` and `registerBtn`.

36. Add static text labels as shown in Figure 22-11.

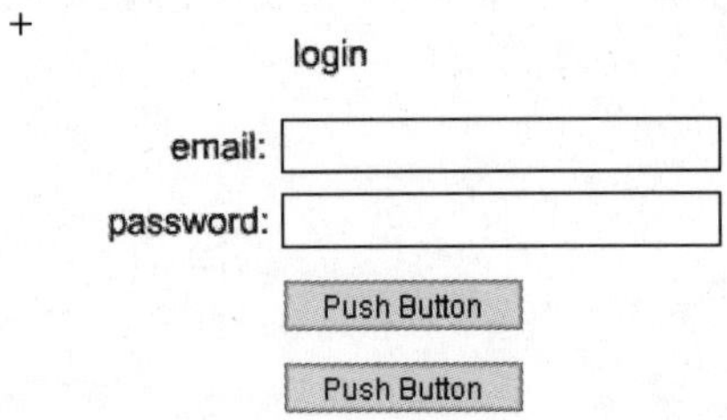

Figure 22-11: The layout of LoginForm

37. Select the linkage properties for `LoginForm` and check the Export for ActionScript and Export on first frame options. Set the linkage identifier to `LoginForm`.

38. Create a new Movie Clip symbol named `RegistrationForm`.

39. Edit `RegistrationForm`.

40. Add nine input `TextField` objects with border turned on. Position them as shown in Figure 22-12. From top to bottom name the instances `email`, `password`, `confirm`, `name`, `address1`, `address2`, `city`, `state`, `zip`.

41. Make `password` and `confirm` both password fields. Make the rest of the instances single-line fields.

42. Add a `PushButton` component instance below the `TextField` objects as shown in Figure 22-12. Name the instance `submitBtn`.

43. Add static text labels as shown in Figure 22-12.

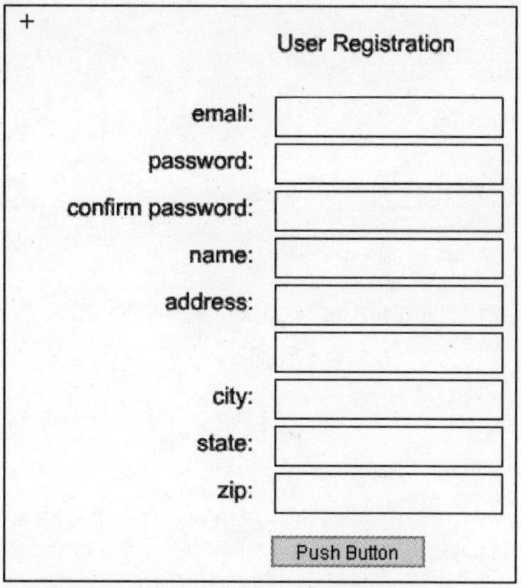

Figure 22-12: The layout of RegistrationForm

44. Select the linkage properties for RegistrationForm and check the Export for ActionScript and Export on first frame options. Set the linkage identifier to `RegistrationForm`.

45. Return to the Main Timeline.

46. On the form layer, add three `ScrollPane` component instances. The position of these instances does not matter because they will be controlled by ActionScript. Name these instances `navSp`, `mainSp`, and `scSp`. The `navSp` scroll pane will contain the navigational buttons for the categories. The `mainSp` scroll pane will be where your application displays the items, the login and registration forms, and the checkout information. The `scSp` scroll pane will contain the user's shopping cart contents.

47. On the first frame of the actions layer, add the following code:

```
#include "NetServices.as"

// same function as was defined in the admin movie
Number.prototype.toDollar = function(){
  var da = Math.round(this * 100)/100;
  return da;
}

function init(){

  // initialize the sizes and positions of the scroll
  // panes
  _root.navSp._x = 10;
  _root.navSp._y = 50;
  _root.navSp.setSize(100, 300);
```

```
        _root.mainSp._x = 115;
        _root.mainSp._y = 5;
        _root.mainSp.setSize(400, 200);

        _root.scSp._x = 115;
        _root.scSp._y = 210;
        _root.scSp.setSize(400, 185);

        // create a ShoppingCart instance, set its checkout
        // handler function and its scroll pane
        var sc = _root.attachMovie("ShoppingCart", "sCart", 1);
        _root.scSp.setScrollContent(sc);
        sc.setCheckoutHandler(_root.checkout);
        sc.setScrollPane(_root.scSp);

        // set gateway URL to the correct URL for your
        // application server
        var gwURL = "http://localhost:8880/Wiley/gateway";
        NetServices.setDefaultGatewayURL(gwURL);
        var conn = NetServices.createGatewayConnection();

        // shown is correct for Java
        // for CF: Wiley.chapter22.CFRMXComm
        // for .NET: Wiley.Chapter22.CFRMXComm
        _root.srv = conn.getService("wiley.chapter22.CFRMXComm");

        // get the categories
        _root.srv.getCategories(_root.getCategoriesRes);

        // set the Web service service
        _root.wSrv =
conn.getService("http://ws2.serviceobjects.net/pc/packcost.asmx?WSDL"
);
}

// checks to see if _root.user is a valid user
function isLoggedIn(){
    return (_root.user.USER_ID != undefined)
}

// the checkout() function is called by the shopping cart
// when the user clicks on the checkout button
function checkout(){
    // if the user is logged in proceed to checkout page
    // otherwise, go to login form
    if(_root.isLoggedIn()){
        // if you use CF or .NET then use uncommented line
        // but if you use Java then comment out the
        // uncommented line, and uncomment the commented line
        _root.makeCheckoutForm();
        //_root.makeCheckoutForm(0);
```

```
    }
    else{
      _root.makeLoginForm();
    }
}

function makeLoginForm(){
  // attach the LoginForm and set it to be the mainSp
  // scroll pane's content
  var main = _root.attachMovie("LoginForm", "main", 3);
  _root.mainSp.setScrollContent(main);

  // this is a trick to set the label once the button has
  // loaded. Otherwise, setLabel() would be called too
  // soon
  main.registerBtn.onLoad = function(){
    this.setLabel("register");
  }
  main.registerBtn.onRelease = function(){
    _root.makeRegisterForm();
  }
  main.loginBtn.onLoad = function(){
    this.setLabel("login");
  }

  // login the user with the entered email and password
  // by calling the login() service method
  main.loginBtn.onRelease = function(){
    var email = this._parent.email.text;
    var password = this._parent.password.text;
    _root.srv.login(_root.loginRes, email, password);
  }
}

function makeRegisterForm(){

  // attach the RegistrationForm and set it to be
  // the scroll content for mainSp
  var main = _root.attachMovie("RegistrationForm", "main", 3);
  _root.mainSp.setScrollContent(main);

  main.submitBtn.onLoad = function(){
    this.setLabel("submit");
  }

  // call the register() service method
  main.submitBtn.onRelease = function(){
    var email = this._parent.email.text;
    var password = this._parent.password.text;
    var name = this._parent.name.text;
    var address1 = this._parent.address1.text;
```

```
        var address2 = this._parent.address2.text;
        var city = this._parent.city.text;
        var state = this._parent.state.text;
        var zip = parseInt(this._parent.zip.text);
        _root.srv.register(_root.registerRes, email,
                            password, name,
                            address1, address2,
                            city, state, zip);
    }
}

function makeCheckoutForm(shipping){
  // if shipping is not defined then get the shipping
  // information first
  if(shipping == undefined){
    // this should only get called for CF and .NET users
    // if you are using Java then you cannot directly call
    // the Web service, and this will not work. By calling
    // makeCheckoutForm() with the parameter 0 (see
    // checkout() function) the shipping costs are set to
    // 0 and the code in this if statement is never
    // encountered

    // the items from the shopping cart
    var sci = _root.sCart.items;
    var weight = 0;

    // loop through all the items and total up the weight
    for(var i = 0; i < sci.length; i++){
      weight += parseInt(sci[i].item.data.WEIGHT) *
parseInt(sci[i].item.quantity.text);
    }

    // params is the parameter passed to the Web service.
    // the property names and data type are defined
    // by the WSDL. For simplicity set the from city,
    // state, and postal code as shown here (pretend all
    // the items get shipped from Los Angeles). Also, the
    // application is only set up in this example to take
    // US addresses, so you can hardcode the US value for
    // from and to countries. Carriers is set to 2 for
    // UPS.
    var params = new Object();
    params.Weight = weight;
    params.FromCity = "Los Angeles";
    params.FromStateProv = "CA";
    params.FromPostalCode = "90010";
    params.FromCountry = "US";
    params.ToCity = _root.user.ADDRESS_CITY;
    params.ToStateProv = _root.user.ADDRESS_STATE;
    params.ToPostalCode = String(_root.user.ADDRESS_POSTAL);
```

```
    params.ToCountry = "US";
    params.Carriers = 2;
    // your license key in place of the X's
    params.LicenseKey = "XXXX-XXXX-XXXX";
    _root.wSrv.GetShippingRates(_root.shippingRes, params);
  }
  else{
    // if the shipping is already calculated then display
    // the checkout confirmation page

    // set a shipping property of the shopping cart to the
    // shipping cost
    _root.sCart.shipping = shipping;

    // create a MovieClip and populate it with TextField
    // objects and a PushButton
    var main = _root.createEmptyMovieClip("main", 3);
    main.createTextField("itemNames", 1, 0, 0, 0, 0);
    main.createTextField("itemPrices", 2, 0, 0, 0, 0);
    main.createTextField("itemQuantities", 3, 0, 0, 0, 0);
    main.createTextField("itemTotals", 4, 0, 0, 0, 0);
    main.createTextField("shipping", 5, 0, 0, 0, 0);
    main.createTextField("userInfo", 6, 0, 0, 0, 0);
    main.attachMovie("FPushButtonSymbol", "submitBtn", 7);

    var sci = _root.sCart.items;

    // itemNames, itemPrices, itemQuantities, and
    // itemTotals are four TextField object that are
    // arranged as columns next to one another so that
    // the values inserted into each line up - name, price
    // quantity, total - for each item
    main.itemNames.autoSize = true;
    main.itemNames.text = "ITEM\n";
    main.itemPrices.autoSize = true;
    main.itemPrices.text = "PRICE\n";
    main.itemQuantities.autoSize = true;
    main.itemQuantities.text = "QUANTITY\n";
    main.itemTotals.autoSize = true;
    main.itemTotals.text = "\n";
    var total = 0;

    // loop through all the items from the shopping cart
    // and add values to the column TextField objects
    for(var i = 0; i < sci.length; i++){
      main.itemNames.text += sci[i].item.data.NAME + newline;
      main.itemPrices.text += sci[i].item.data.PRICE.toDollar() +
newline;
      main.itemQuantities.text += sci[i].item.quantity.text +
newline;
      main.itemTotals.text += sci[i].item.total + newline;
```

```
        // calculate the total for all items by adding this
        // item's cost to the running total
        total += parseFloat(sci[i].item.total);
    }

    // set the total property of the shopping cart to the
    // total calculated from the for loop
    _root.sCart.total = total;

    // position the column TextField objects
    main.itemPrices._x = main.itemNames._width + 5;
    main.itemQuantities._x = main.itemPrices._x +
main.itemPrices._width + 5;
    main.itemTotals._x = main.itemQuantities._x +
main.itemQuantities._width + 5;

    // display the shipping costs
    main.shipping.autoSize = true;
    main.shipping.text = "shipping: " + shipping;
    main.shipping._y = main.itemPrices._height;

    // display the user (ship to) information
    main.userInfo.autoSize = true;
    main.userInfo.text = "SHIP TO:\n";
    main.userInfo.text += _root.user.NAME + newline;
    main.userInfo.text += _root.user.ADDRESS_1 + newline;
    main.userInfo.text += _root.user.ADDRESS_2 + newline;
    main.userInfo.text += _root.user.ADDRESS_CITY + ", ";
    main.userInfo.text += _root.user.ADDRESS_STATE + newline;
    main.userInfo.text += _root.user.ADDRESS_POSTAL;
    main.userInfo._y = main.shipping._y + main.shipping._height + 5;

    main.submitBtn._y = main.userInfo._y + main.userInfo._height + 5;
    main.submitBtn.setLabel("submit");
    main.submitBtn.onRelease = function(){
      var uid = parseInt(_root.user.USER_ID);
      var ship = parseFloat(_root.sCart.shipping);
      var total = parseFloat(_root.sCart.total);

      // create an array of order items with item (name)
      // and quantity properties
      var items = new Array();
      var sci = _root.sCart.items;
      for(var i = 0; i < sci.length; i++){
        items[i] = new Object();
        items[i].item = sci[i].item.data.NAME;
        items[i].quantity = parseInt(sci[i].item.quantity.text);
      }
      // call the placeOrder() service method
      _root.srv.placeOrder(_root.placeOrderRes, uid, ship, total,
items);
```

```
    }
    _root.mainSp.setScrollContent(main);
  }
}


getCategoriesRes = new Object();
getCategoriesRes.onResult = function(result){
  var btn;
  // create a MovieClip and fill it with PushButton
  // instances for each category
  var nav = _root.createEmptyMovieClip("nav", 2);
  for(var i = 0; i < result.getLength(); i++){
    btn = nav.attachMovie("FPushButtonSymbol",
                    "category" + i,
                    i,
                    {_x: 0, _y: i * 25});
    btn.setLabel(result.getItemAt(i).NAME);
    btn.categoryId = result.getItemAt(i).CATEGORY_ID;
    // when the button is clicked, call the
    // getCategoryItems() service method
    btn.onRelease = function(){
      _root.srv.getCategoryItems(_root.getCategoryItemsRes,
this.categoryId);
    }
  }
  // set the MovieClip to be the scroll content of navSp
  _root.navSp.setScrollContent(nav);
}


getCategoryItemsRes = new Object();
getCategoryItemsRes.onResult = function(result){
  var item;
  // create a MovieClip and fill it with CategoryItem
  // instances for each item in the category
  _root.createEmptyMovieClip("main", 3);
  for(var i = 0; i < result.getLength(); i++){
    item = _root.main.attachMovie("CategoryItem", "item" + i, i);
    item._y = _root.main["item" + (i-1)]._y + _root.main["item" + (i-
1)]._height + 5;
    item.setData(result.getItemAt(i));
    item.setShoppingCart(_root.sCart);
  }
  // set the MovieClip to be the scroll content of mainSp
  _root.mainSp.setScrollContent(_root.main);
}


// once a user has registered, display the login form
registerRes = new Object();
registerRes.onResult = function(){
  _root.makeLoginForm();
}
```

```
// once the user has tried to login, set the returned
// record to the user object, and then call the checkout()
// function. If the login was unsuccessful then checkout()
// automatically makes the login form again
loginRes = new Object();
loginRes.onResult = function(result){
  _root.user = result.getItemAt(0);
  _root.checkout();
}

shippingRes = new Object();
shippingRes.onResult = function(result){
  var shipping;
  // loop through the results, and find the one with
  // service of 03 (ground shipping)
  for(var i in result.rate){
    if(result.rate[i].service == "03"){
      shipping = parseFloat(result.rate[i].postage);
      break;
    }
  }
  // as long as there was not an error then call
  // makeCheckoutForm() with the shipping cost value
  if(result.error == undefined){
    _root.makeCheckoutForm(shipping);
  }
}

// when an order has been placed then display a thank you
// message
placeOrderRes = new Object();
placeOrderRes.onResult = function(result){

  var main = _root.createEmptyMovieClip("main", 3);
  _root.main.createTextField("message", 1, 0, 0, 0, 0);
  main.message.text = "Thank you for your order.";
  main.message.autoSize = true;
  _root.mainSp.setScrollContent(main);
}

// call the init() method to get the movie started
init();
```

48. Test the movie. When the movie starts, you should see a list of buttons on the left side—one for each category. By clicking on the category, the items in that category will be retrieved and displayed in the main scroll pane. You can then enter a quantity and click the add button for an item, as shown in Figure 22-13.

Once items have been added to the shopping cart, they are displayed in the bottom scroll pane. You then have the option of removing those items by clicking the remove button, or modifying the quantity as shown in Figure 22-14. The total for the item and the shopping cart is automatically re-totaled.

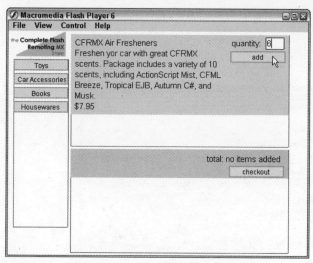

Figure 22-13: Adding an item to the shopping cart

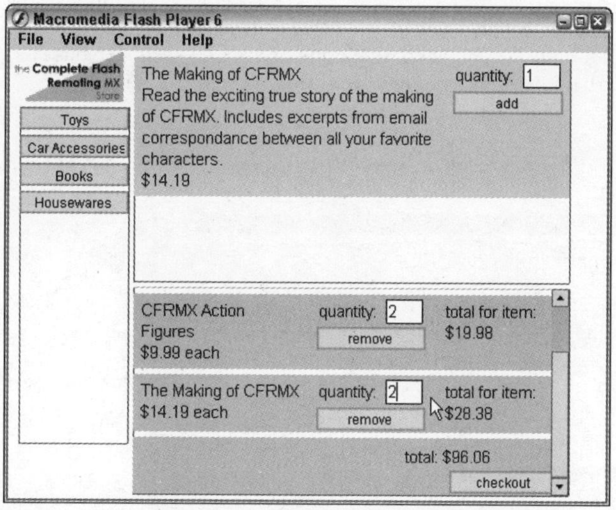

Figure 22-14: Entering a new quantity for an item in the shopping cart recalculates the totals.

Once you have completed adding items to the shopping cart, you can click the checkout button. This will automatically prompt you to log in. Because you likely have not yet created an account, you should click the register button. This takes you to the registration form. After you have filled out and submitted the form, you will be redirected back to the login form. Log in and you should see a confirmation screen like the one shown in Figure 22-15.

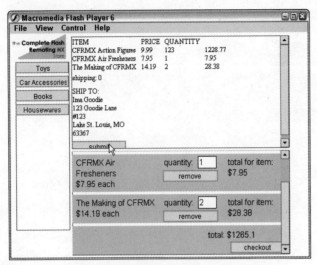

Figure 22-15: The confirmation screen

After submitting the order from the confirmation screen, you might want to open the administration movie and click the view orders button. You should see then a listing of all the orders that have been placed. Click one of the items from the list to display the order details in the bottom scroll pane, as shown in Figure 22-16.

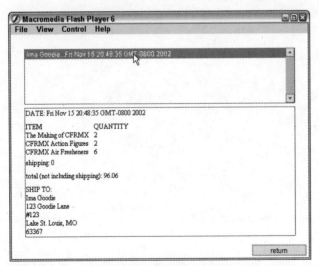

Figure 22-16: Viewing the order details in the administration movie

Summary

In this chapter you created an e-commerce application using a Flash Remoting. The application uses a database to store and retrieve information about the items in the store as well as the users and their orders. You created a Flash movie to serve as the administrative interface for the store, through which you can add, modify, and remove items as well as view orders that have been placed. You also created a Flash interface through which users can browse through the contents of the store and make purchases.

✦　　✦　　✦

Making a Messageboard

✦ ✦ ✦ ✦

In This Chapter

Understanding the overview of the messageboard application

Creating a database for the application

Developing the service functions

Authoring the Flash user interface movies and integrating them with the server-side service

✦ ✦ ✦ ✦

A popular and useful application often included in Web sites is a messageboard system. Messageboards can be found on numerous sites covering a wide variety of subjects, from support forums such as those at Macromedia to discussions about parenting and spirituality, such as those found on Oprah.com. Numerous sites, such as EZBoard.com, offer users the expertise to set up forums for whatever topics they choose to discuss. With Flash Remoting, you can now quite effectively create a messageboard system that uses a Flash user interface — setting it apart from most existing messageboard systems.

Designing the Application

There are always as many ways to create an application as there are people, and so there is no one, "right" way to approach the task. The example used throughout this chapter presents the way in which I created the application. Therefore, the first thing you should do is gain a general overview of how the messageboard is structured, as well as the desired functionality.

Specifying Functionality

A messageboard application can contain various kinds of functionality, ranging from simple to complex. Some functionality is obvious, such as the ability to create a thread and a message. An additional feature offered by some systems includes subscribing to a thread (meaning that you get an e-mail notification when a new reply is posted to the thread). The messageboard system you create in this chapter can be considered a version 1.0 application. The feature set includes a few "extras," but you may want to create additional releases of the application to which you add more features, as discussed later in the chapter. Following is a list of the basic features included in the application outlined in this chapter:

✦ Administration

- Add/modify/delete forums (A messageboard can contain many forums, which provide order and structure to the threads they contain.)

- Delete users

- Toggle administrative privileges for users

✦ Messageboard

- Register new users

- Log in existing users

- Select a forum

- Create a new thread

- Browse threads

- Reply to a thread

- Delete a message (for original author and administrators only)

Looking at the Application Overview

This application was designed with four main parts:

✦ **Database:** Some messageboard systems use databases, whereas others use text files. The advantage of using text files is that they do not require a database to be installed. However, using a database results in easier, more powerful functionality, not to mention faster access time. For this reason, and because even if you don't already have a database system you can follow the directions in Chapter 4 to set one up, I have opted to use a database rather than text files for storing the messageboard data.

✦ **CFC/Java class/.NET DLL:** Depending on your platform, you will probably want to use only one of these options. I designed the example application in this chapter so that only one CFC/class/DLL contains all the methods used by the program.

✦ **Administrative Flash movie:** This movie contains administrative functionality as outlined in the previous section.

✦ **Messageboard Flash movie:** This movie contains the messageboard functionality as outlined in the previous section.

Creating the Database

The database is the foundation of the entire application. Therefore, you should look at this portion of the development first. Although you have many different ways to approach the database schema for the messageboard application, I have chosen one that is simplistic and avoids redundancy as much as possible. Figure 23-1 illustrates the tables of the database. The bold column names are the primary keys. Although I chose not to enforce any relationships within the database itself, Figure 23-1 does illustrate the ways in which the fields of the tables relate conceptually.

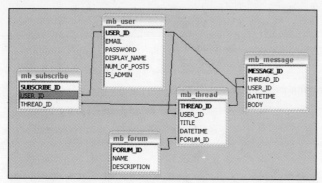

Figure 23-1: The tables of the database for the messageboard application

Table 23-1 describes each of the tables and their columns.

Table 23-1: The Tables of the Messageboard Database

Table	Column	Description
MB_USER	USER_ID	Unique numeric ID for the user
MB_USER	EMAIL	The user's e-mail address. This is used as the username for logging in.
MB_USER	PASSWORD	The user's password
MB_USER	DISPLAY_NAME	The user's name as it will appear on his or her posts
MB_USER	NUM_OF_POSTS	The number of posts the user has made
MB_USER	IS_ADMIN	1 if the user is an administrator, 0 otherwise
MB_FORUM	FORUM_ID	Unique numeric ID for the forum
MB_FORUM	NAME	The name of the forum
MB_FORUM	DESCRIPTION	A brief description of the forum
MB_THREAD	THREAD_ID	Unique numeric ID for the thread
MB_THREAD	USER_ID	The ID of the user who created the thread
MB_THREAD	TITLE	The title of the thread
MB_THREAD	DATETIME	The date and time that the thread was created
MB_THREAD	FORUM_ID	The ID of the forum in which the thread appears
MB_MESSAGE	MESSAGE_ID	Unique numeric ID for the message
MB_MESSAGE	THREAD_ID	The ID of the thread in which the message appears
MB_MESSAGE	USER_ID	The ID of the user who posted the message
MB_MESSAGE	DATETIME	The date and time the message was posted

Continued

Table 23-1: *(continued)*

Table	Column	Description
MB_MESSAGE	BODY	The contents of the message itself
MB_SUBSCRIBE	SUBSCRIBE_ID	Unique numeric ID for the subscription to a thread
MB_SUBSCRIBE	USER_ID	The ID of the user who subscribed to the thread
MB_SUBSCRIBE	THREAD_ID	The ID of the thread to which the user subscribed

In order to create the database tables, you can choose to either download a copy of the database from the Web site for this book, or you can execute the SQL statements shown in Listing 23-1. If you execute the SQL statements, you can run them one at a time from the command line of the RDBMS, or you can save them to a text file and run that file from the command line of the RDBMS. Please note that I have added these tables to the existing WileyFlashRemoting database set up in Chapter 4. If you have not yet created this database, you will need to do so prior to running this SQL code. The SQL creates only the new tables, not a new database.

Listing 23-1: **The SQL to Generate the Messageboard Tables**

```
CREATE TABLE mb_forum (
  FORUM_ID int(10) unsigned NOT NULL  auto_increment,
  NAME varchar(50) NOT NULL,
  DESCRIPTION varchar(255),
  PRIMARY KEY (FORUM_ID)
);

CREATE TABLE mb_message (
  MESSAGE_ID int(10) unsigned NOT NULL  auto_increment,
  THREAD_ID int(10) unsigned NOT NULL  DEFAULT '0',
  USER_ID int(10) unsigned NOT NULL  DEFAULT '0',
  DATETIME datetime NOT NULL  DEFAULT '0000-00-00 00:00:00',
  BODY text NOT NULL,
  PRIMARY KEY (MESSAGE_ID)
);

CREATE TABLE mb_subscribe (
  SUBSCRIBE_ID int(10) unsigned NOT NULL  auto_increment,
  USER_ID int(10) unsigned NOT NULL  DEFAULT '0',
  THREAD_ID int(10) unsigned NOT NULL  DEFAULT '0',
  PRIMARY KEY (SUBSCRIBE_ID)
);

CREATE TABLE mb_thread (
  THREAD_ID int(10) unsigned NOT NULL  auto_increment,
  USER_ID int(10) unsigned NOT NULL  DEFAULT '0',
  TITLE varchar(50) NOT NULL,
```

```
    DATETIME datetime NOT NULL  DEFAULT '0000-00-00 00:00:00',
    FORUM_ID int(10) unsigned NOT NULL  DEFAULT '0',
    PRIMARY KEY (THREAD_ID)
);

CREATE TABLE mb_user (
    USER_ID int(10) unsigned NOT NULL  auto_increment,
    EMAIL varchar(50) NOT NULL,
    PASSWORD varchar(50) NOT NULL,
    DISPLAY_NAME varchar(50) NOT NULL,
    NUM_OF_POSTS int(10) unsigned NOT NULL  DEFAULT '0',
    IS_ADMIN tinyint(1) unsigned NOT NULL  DEFAULT '0',
    PRIMARY KEY (USER_ID)
);
```

Developing the Server-Side Application

The next step in creating the messageboard is to create the server-side logic. The following three sections outline the equivalent code for ColdFusion, Java, and .NET. You need to create only one of these, so choose the section that is appropriate for you depending on your preferred platform, and follow the instructions. In each case, I have opted to create only one file (component/class/assembly) to contain all the methods utilized by the Flash movies.

Note

The code for all three platforms contains some SQL code that may be specific to MySQL. This is because some of the SQL commands are complex, including joins and other more advanced SQL constructs. If you are not using MySQL and you find that the SQL does not work for your database, please go to the Web site for this book and request and/or download the SQL that works for your particular DBMS. If you adapt the code to work for your DBMS, please feel free to submit it to the Web site for other readers.

Creating the ColdFusion Component

If you use ColdFusion, follow these steps:

1. Within the ColdFusion webroot, you should already have a directory named Wiley. If not, create this directory.

2. Within the Wiley directory, create a chapter23 directory.

3. Within the chapter23 directory, create a new CFC document named MessageBoard.cfc.

4. Add the code from Listing 23-2 to MessageBoard.cfc and save the document.

Listing 23-2: **MessageBoard.cfc**

```
<cfcomponent>
  <!-- creates a new forum given a name and description-->
  <cffunction name="createForum" access="remote" returntype="boolean">
```

Continued

Listing 23-2: *(continued)*

```
    <cfargument name="name" type="string" required="true">
    <cfargument name="description" type="string" required="true">
    <cftry>
      <cfquery datasource="WileyFlashRemoting">
      INSERT INTO MB_FORUM(NAME, DESCRIPTION)
      VALUES('#name#', '#description#')
      </cfquery>
      <cfreturn true>
      <cfcatch>
        <cfreturn false>
      </cfcatch>
    </cftry>
  </cffunction>

  <!-- delete a forum -->
  <cffunction name="deleteForum" access="remote" returntype="boolean">
    <cfargument name="forumId" type="numeric" required="true">
    <cftry>
      <!-- deletes the forum -->
      <cfquery datasource="WileyFlashRemoting">
        DELETE FROM MB_FORUM WHERE FORUM_ID = #forumId#
      </cfquery>
      <!-- get all the messages from all the threads
           within the forum -->
      <cfquery datasource="WileyFlashRemoting" name="messages">
      SELECT MB_MESSAGE.MESSAGE_ID
      FROM MB_THREAD, MB_MESSAGE
      WHERE MB_THREAD.FORUM_ID = #forumId#
      AND MB_MESSAGE.THREAD_ID = MB_THREAD.THREAD_ID
      </cfquery>
      <!-- loop through all the messages, and call the
           deleteMessage function for each of them -->
      <cfloop query="messages">
      <cfinvoke method="deleteMessage">
        <cfinvokeargument name="messageId"
value="#messages.MESSAGE_ID#">
      </cfinvoke>
      </cfloop>
      <cfreturn true>
    <cfcatch>
      <cfreturn false>
    </cfcatch>
    </cftry>
  </cffunction>

  <!-- modify the name and description of an existing
       forum -->
  <cffunction name="modifyForum" access="remote" returntype="boolean">
```

```
      <cfargument name="forumId" type="numeric" required="true">
      <cfargument name="name" type="string" required="true">
      <cfargument name="description" type="string" required="true">
      <cftry>
        <cfquery datasource="WileyFlashRemoting">
        UPDATE MB_FORUM SET NAME = '#name#', DESCRIPTION =
'#description#' WHERE
        FORUM_ID = #forumId#
        </cfquery>
        <cfreturn true>
        <cfcatch>
          <cfreturn false>
        </cfcatch>
      </cftry>
    </cffunction>


    <!-- retrieve all the forums -->
    <cffunction name="getForums" access="remote" returntype="query">
      <!-- this is a complex SQL statement that
           retrieves all the forums as well as the
           number of threads within the forum
           and the time and date of the last post
           within the forum -->
      <cfquery datasource="WileyFlashRemoting" name="forums">
      SELECT MB_FORUM.*,
      count(MB_THREAD.THREAD_ID) AS THREAD_COUNT,
      UNIX_TIMESTAMP(max(MB_THREAD.DATETIME))
      AS LAST_POST_DATE
      FROM MB_FORUM
      LEFT JOIN MB_THREAD ON
      MB_THREAD.FORUM_ID = MB_FORUM.FORUM_ID
      GROUP BY MB_FORUM.FORUM_ID
      </cfquery>
      <cfreturn #forums#>
    </cffunction>


    <!-- gets all the threads for a forum -->
    <cffunction name="getThreads" access="remote" returntype="query">
      <cfargument name="forumId" type="numeric" required="true">
      <!-- another complex SQL statement that
           gets the threads as well as the author and time
           and date of the last post to each thread -->
      <cfquery datasource="WileyFlashRemoting" name="threads">
      SELECT MB_THREAD.*,
      MB_USER.DISPLAY_NAME AS AUTHOR,
      count(MB_MESSAGE.MESSAGE_ID) AS REPLIES,
      UNIX_TIMESTAMP(max(MB_MESSAGE.DATETIME))
      AS LAST_POST_TIME
      FROM MB_THREAD, MB_USER
      LEFT JOIN MB_MESSAGE ON
      MB_MESSAGE.THREAD_ID = MB_THREAD.THREAD_ID
```

Continued

Listing 23-2: *(continued)*

```
      WHERE MB_THREAD.FORUM_ID = #forumId# AND
      MB_USER.USER_ID = MB_THREAD.USER_ID
      GROUP BY MB_THREAD.THREAD_ID
      </cfquery>
      <cfreturn #threads#>
</cffunction>

<!-- posts a new thread -->
<cffunction name="postThread" access="remote" returntype="boolean">
  <cfargument name="forumId" type="numeric" required="true">
  <cfargument name="userId" type="numeric" required="true">
  <cfargument name="title" type="string" required="true">
  <cfargument name="body" type="string" required="true">
  <cftry>
    <cfset timestampVal = CreateODBCDateTime(Now())>
    <!-- cflock ensures that only one user can run this
         code at a time to ensure no conflicts -->
    <cflock timeout="10">
      <!-- insert the thread -->
      <cfquery datasource="WileyFlashRemoting">
      INSERT INTO
      MB_THREAD(FORUM_ID, USER_ID, TITLE, DATETIME)
      VALUES(#forumId#, #userId#, '#title#', #timestampVal#)
      </cfquery>
      <!-- get the thread id -->
      <cfquery datasource="WileyFlashRemoting" name="newThread">
      SELECT max(THREAD_ID) AS NEW_ID FROM MB_THREAD
      </cfquery>
      <!-- call the postMessage function to add the
           message for the thread -->
      <cfinvoke method="postMessage">
        <cfinvokeargument name="threadId" value="#newThread.NEW_ID#">
        <cfinvokeargument name="userId" value="#userId#">
        <cfinvokeargument name="body" value="#body#">
      </cfinvoke>
    </cflock>
    <cfreturn true>
    <cfcatch>
      <cfreturn false>
    </cfcatch>
  </cftry>
</cffunction>

<!-- add a new message to a thread -->
<cffunction name="postMessage" access="remote" returntype="boolean">
  <cfargument name="threadId" type="numeric" required="true">
  <cfargument name="userId" type="numeric" required="true">
  <cfargument name="body" type="string" required="true">
```

```
    <cftry>
      <cfset timestampVal = CreateODBCDateTime(Now())>
      <!-- insert the message -->
      <cfquery datasource="WileyFlashRemoting">
      INSERT INTO
      MB_MESSAGE(THREAD_ID, USER_ID, BODY, DATETIME)
      VALUES(#threadId#, #userId#, '#body#', #timestampVal#)
      </cfquery>
      <!-- update the author's number of posts value -->
      <cfquery datasource="WileyFlashRemoting">
      UPDATE MB_USER
      SET NUM_OF_POSTS = NUM_OF_POSTS + 1
      WHERE USER_ID = #userId#
      </cfquery>
      <!-- run the subscriptions for any users subscribed
           to the thread to let them know of a new
           reply -->
      <cfinvoke method="runSubscriptions">
        <cfinvokeargument name="threadId" value="#threadId#">
      </cfinvoke>
      <cfreturn true>
      <cfcatch>
        <cfreturn false>
      </cfcatch>
    </cftry>
  </cffunction>

  <!-- get the messages for a thread -->
  <cffunction name="getMessages" access="remote" returntype="query">
    <cfargument name="threadId" type="numeric" required="true">
    <!-- get the messages for the thread, including author
         display names and their number of posts -->
    <cfquery datasource="WileyFlashRemoting" name="messages">
    SELECT MB_MESSAGE.*,
    MB_USER.DISPLAY_NAME,
    MB_USER.NUM_OF_POSTS
    FROM MB_MESSAGE, MB_USER
    WHERE MB_MESSAGE.THREAD_ID = #threadId# AND
    MB_USER.USER_ID = MB_MESSAGE.USER_ID
    </cfquery>
    <cfreturn #messages#>
  </cffunction>

  <!-- delete a message -->
  <cffunction name="deleteMessage" access="remote"
returntype="boolean">
    <cfargument name="messageId" type="numeric" required="true">
    <cftry>
      <!-- get the thread ID for this message -->
      <cfquery datasource="WileyFlashRemoting" name="tid">
      SELECT THREAD_ID
```

Continued

Listing 23-2: *(continued)*

```
          FROM MB_MESSAGE
          WHERE MESSAGE_ID = #messageId#
          </cfquery>
          <!-- check how many messages exist for the thread-->
          <cfquery datasource="WileyFlashRemoting" name="count">
          SELECT count(MESSAGE_ID) AS MCOUNT
          FROM MB_MESSAGE
          WHERE THREAD_ID = #tid.THREAD_ID[1]#
          </cfquery>
          <!--- delete the message -->
          <cfquery datasource="WileyFlashRemoting">
          DELETE FROM MB_MESSAGE
          WHERE MB_MESSAGE.MESSAGE_ID = #messageId#
          </cfquery>
          <!-- if there was only one message (the one deleted)
               in the thread, delete the thread -->
          <cfif #count.MCOUNT# LTE 1>
            <cfquery datasource="WileyFlashRemoting">
            DELETE FROM MB_THREAD
            WHERE THREAD_ID = #tid.THREAD_ID[1]#
            </cfquery>
          </cfif>
          <cfreturn true>
      <cfcatch>
        <cfreturn false>
      </cfcatch>
      </cftry>
  </cffunction>

  <!-- set a user's admin privileges -->
  <cffunction name="toggleUserPriv" access="remote" returntype="query">
    <cfargument name="userId" type="numeric" required="true">
    <cfargument name="isAdmin" type="numeric" required="true">
    <cfquery datasource="WileyFlashRemoting">
    UPDATE MB_USER
    SET IS_ADMIN = #isAdmin#
    WHERE USER_ID = #userId#
    </cfquery>
    <cfinvoke method="getUsers" returnvariable="users">
    </cfinvoke>
    <cfreturn #users#>
  </cffunction>

  <!-- delete a user -->
  <cffunction name="deleteUser" access="remote" returntype="query">
    <cfargument name="userId" type="numeric" required="true">
    <cfquery datasource="WileyFlashRemoting">
    DELETE FROM MB_USER
    WHERE USER_ID = #userId#
```

```
    </cfquery>
    <cfinvoke method="getUsers" returnvariable="users">
    </cfinvoke>
    <cfreturn #users#>
  </cffunction>


  <!-- get all the users from the database -->
  <cffunction name="getUsers" access="remote" returntype="query">
    <cfquery datasource="WileyFlashRemoting" name="users">
    SELECT * FROM MB_USER
    </cfquery>
    <cfreturn #users#>
  </cffunction>


  <!-- login a user, return their information -->
  <cffunction name="login" access="remote" returntype="query">
    <cfargument name="username" type="string" required="true">
    <cfargument name="password" type="string" required="true">
    <cfquery datasource="WileyFlashRemoting" name="user">
    SELECT * FROM MB_USER WHERE EMAIL = '#username#' AND PASSWORD =
'#password#'
    </cfquery>
    <cfreturn #user#>
  </cffunction>


  <!-- register a new user -->
  <cffunction name="registerUser" access="remote" returntype="boolean">
    <cfargument name="display" type="string" required="true">
    <cfargument name="email" type="string" required="true">
    <cfargument name="password" type="string" required="true">
    <cftry>
      <cfquery datasource="WileyFlashRemoting" name="user">
      INSERT INTO MB_USER(DISPLAY_NAME, EMAIL, PASSWORD)
      VALUES('#display#', '#email#', '#password#')
      </cfquery>
      <cfreturn true>
      <cfcatch>
        <cfreturn false>
      </cfcatch>
    </cftry>
  </cffunction>


  <!-- subscribe a user to a thread -->
  <cffunction name="subscribe" access="remote" returntype="boolean">
    <cfargument name="threadId" type="numeric" required="true">
    <cfargument name="userId" type="numeric" required="true">
    <cftry>
      <!-- check to see if the user is already
           subscribed to the thread -->
      <cfquery datasource="WileyFlashRemoting" name="subscriptions">
      SELECT * FROM MB_SUBSCRIBE
```

Continued

Listing 23-2: *(continued)*

```
            WHERE THREAD_ID = #threadId# AND
            USER_ID = #userId#
            </cfquery>
            <!-- if the user is not subscribed already
                 subscribe the user -->
            <cfif #subscriptions.RecordCount# EQ 0>
              <cfquery datasource="WileyFlashRemoting">
              INSERT INTO MB_SUBSCRIBE(THREAD_ID, USER_ID)
              VALUES(#threadId#, #userId#);
              </cfquery>
            </cfif>
            <cfreturn true>
            <cfcatch>
              <cfreturn false>
            </cfcatch>
        </cftry>
    </cffunction>

    <!-- run the subscriptions for a thread -->
    <cffunction name="runSubscriptions" access="remote"
returntype="boolean">
        <cfargument name="threadId" type="numeric" required="true">
        <cftry>
            <!-- select all the emails of subscribed users
                 and the title of the thread -->
            <cfquery datasource="WileyFlashRemoting" name="emailInfo">
              SELECT MB_USER.EMAIL, MB_THREAD.TITLE
              FROM MB_USER, MB_THREAD, MB_SUBSCRIBE
              WHERE MB_SUBSCRIBE.THREAD_ID = #threadId# AND
              MB_USER.USER_ID = MB_SUBSCRIBE.USER_ID AND
              MB_THREAD.THREAD_ID = #threadId#
            </cfquery>
            <!-- for each subscriber, send an email -->
            <cfloop query="emailInfo">
              <cfmail from="mb@myMessageBoard.com"
                      to="#emailInfo.EMAIL#"
                      server="your.smtp.server.goes.here"
                      subject="new reply to subscribed thread">
                There is a new reply posted to the thread titled
#emailInfo.TITLE#
              </cfmail>
            </cfloop>
        <cfreturn true>
        <cfcatch>
        <cfreturn false>
        </cfcatch>
        </cftry>
    </cffunction>
</cfcomponent>
```

Creating the Java Class

If you are using a J2EE application server, follow these steps:

1. Within the Web application's WEB-INF/classes, you should already have a Wiley directory. If you do not, create it now.

2. Create a chapter23 directory within the Wiley directory.

3. Create a new Java file named MessageBoard.java in the chapter23 directory.

4. Add the code from Listing 23-3 to the MessageBoard.java document, and save it.

Listing 23-3: MessageBoard.java

```java
package wiley.chapter23;

import java.io.*;
import java.sql.*;
import javax.mail.*;
import javax.mail.internet.*;
import java.util.*;

public class MessageBoard {

    // create the Statement object to be used for the database calls
    private Statement makeStatement() throws Exception{
        // this code assumes you are using the MySQL
        // WileyFlashRemoting database that was created in
        // chapter 4. Otherwise you will need to adjust it
        // appropriately.
        Class.forName("com.mysql.jdbc.Driver").newInstance();
        String connStr = "jdbc:mysql://localhost/WileyFlashRemoting";
        Connection connection = DriverManager.getConnection(connStr);
        Statement statement = connection.createStatement();
        return statement;
    }

    // executes a SQL statement on the database and does
    // not return a result (ie - INSERT, DELETE, UPDATE)
    private void update(String sql) throws Exception{
        System.out.println(sql);
        Statement statement = makeStatement();
        statement.executeUpdate(sql);
    }

    // executes a SQL statement on the database and returns
    // a result (ie - SELECT)
    private ResultSet query(String sql) throws Exception{
        Statement statement = makeStatement();
        return statement.executeQuery(sql);
    }
```

Continued

Listing 23-3: *(continued)*

```java
  // inserts a new forum into the database
  public void createForum(String name, String description) throws
Exception{
    StringBuffer sb = new StringBuffer();
    sb.append("INSERT INTO MB_FORUM(NAME, DESCRIPTION) VALUES('");
    sb.append(name);
    sb.append("', '");
    sb.append(description);
    sb.append("')");
    update(sb.toString());
  }

  // deletes a forum from the database
  public void deleteForum(int forumId) throws Exception{

    // delete the forum
    StringBuffer sb = new StringBuffer();
    sb.append("DELETE FROM MB_FORUM WHERE FORUM_ID = ");
    sb.append(forumId);
    update(sb.toString());

    // select all the messages from any threads in the
    // forum
    sb = new StringBuffer();
    sb.append("SELECT MB_MESSAGE.MESSAGE_ID FROM MB_THREAD, MB_MESSAGE
WHERE MB_THREAD.FORUM_ID = ");
    sb.append(forumId);
    sb.append(" AND MB_MESSAGE.THREAD_ID = MB_THREAD.THREAD_ID");
    ResultSet rs = query(sb.toString());

    // loop through the messages, and call deleteMessage()
    // for each
    while(rs.next()){
      deleteMessage(rs.getInt("MESSAGE_ID"));
    }
  }

  // modify the values for an existing forum
  public void modifyForum(int forumId, String name, String description)
throws Exception{
    StringBuffer sb = new StringBuffer();
    sb.append("UPDATE MB_FORUM SET NAME = '");
    sb.append(name);
    sb.append("', DESCRIPTION = '");
    sb.append(description);
    sb.append("' WHERE FORUM_ID = ");
    sb.append(forumId);
    update(sb.toString());
  }
```

```
    // get all the forums
    public ResultSet getForums() throws Exception{

        // the SQL statement here is a complex one using
        // joins to get not only the forums, but also the
        // number of threads and the date and time of the most
        // recent post for the forum
        StringBuffer sb = new StringBuffer();
        sb.append("SELECT MB_FORUM.*, ");
        sb.append("count(MB_THREAD.THREAD_ID) AS THREAD_COUNT, ");
        sb.append("UNIX_TIMESTAMP(max(MB_THREAD.DATETIME)) AS
LAST_POST_DATE ");
        sb.append("FROM MB_FORUM LEFT JOIN MB_THREAD ON ");
        sb.append("MB_THREAD.FORUM_ID = MB_FORUM.FORUM_ID ");
        sb.append("GROUP BY MB_FORUM.FORUM_ID");
        return query(sb.toString());
    }


    // get the threads for a forum
    public ResultSet getThreads(int forumId) throws Exception{

        // this is another complex SQL statement that uses a
        // join to get the threads as well as the number of
        // replies and the date and time of the most recent
        // post
        StringBuffer sb = new StringBuffer();
        sb.append("SELECT MB_THREAD.*, ");
        sb.append("MB_USER.DISPLAY_NAME AS AUTHOR, ");
        sb.append("count(MB_MESSAGE.MESSAGE_ID) AS REPLIES, ");
        sb.append("UNIX_TIMESTAMP(max(MB_MESSAGE.DATETIME)) AS
LAST_POST_TIME ");
        sb.append("FROM MB_THREAD, MB_USER ");
        sb.append("LEFT JOIN MB_MESSAGE ON ");
        sb.append("MB_MESSAGE.THREAD_ID = MB_THREAD.THREAD_ID ");
        sb.append("WHERE MB_THREAD.FORUM_ID = ");
        sb.append(forumId);
        sb.append(" AND MB_USER.USER_ID = MB_THREAD.USER_ID ");
        sb.append("GROUP BY MB_THREAD.THREAD_ID");
        return query(sb.toString());
    }

    // inserts a new thread into the database
    public void postThread(int forumId, int userId, String title, String
body) throws Exception{

        // synchronize to ensure the database operations in
        // the group can only be accessed by one user at
        // a time
        synchronized(this){

        // insert the thread
        StringBuffer sb = new StringBuffer();
```

Continued

Listing 23-3: *(continued)*

```java
    sb.append("INSERT INTO MB_THREAD(FORUM_ID, USER_ID, TITLE,
DATETIME) VALUES(");
    sb.append(forumId);
    sb.append(", ");
    sb.append(userId);
    sb.append(", '");
    sb.append(title);
    sb.append("', '");
    sb.append(new java.util.Date());
    sb.append("')");
    update(sb.toString());

    // get the ID of the new thread
    ResultSet rs = query("SELECT max(THREAD_ID) AS NEW_ID FROM
MB_THREAD");
    rs.first();

    // insert a new message for the thread
    postMessage(rs.getInt("NEW_ID"), userId, body);
    }
  }

  // inserts a new message for a thread
  public void postMessage(int threadId, int userId, String body) throws
Exception{

    // insert the new message
    StringBuffer sb = new StringBuffer();
    sb.append("INSERT INTO MB_MESSAGE(THREAD_ID, USER_ID, BODY,
DATETIME) VALUES(");
    sb.append(threadId);
    sb.append(", ");
    sb.append(userId);
    sb.append(", '");
    sb.append(body);
    sb.append("', '");
    sb.append(new java.sql.Timestamp(System.currentTimeMillis()));
    sb.append("')");
    update(sb.toString());

    // update the user's number of posts
    sb = new StringBuffer();
    sb.append("UPDATE MB_USER SET NUM_OF_POSTS = NUM_OF_POSTS + 1 ");
    sb.append("WHERE USER_ID = ");
    sb.append(userId);
    update(sb.toString());

    // run the subscriptions on the thread to notify any
    // subscribed users that a new reply has been added
```

```
      runSubscriptions(threadId);
   }


   // get all the messages for a thread
   public ResultSet getMessages(int threadId) throws Exception{
      StringBuffer sb = new StringBuffer();
      sb.append("SELECT MB_MESSAGE.*, MB_USER.DISPLAY_NAME,
MB_USER.NUM_OF_POSTS ");
      sb.append("FROM MB_MESSAGE, MB_USER ");
      sb.append("WHERE MB_MESSAGE.THREAD_ID = ");
      sb.append(threadId);
      sb.append(" AND MB_USER.USER_ID = MB_MESSAGE.USER_ID ");
      sb.append("ORDER BY MB_MESSAGE.DATETIME");
      return query(sb.toString());
   }


   // delete a message from a thread
   public void deleteMessage(int messageId) throws Exception{

      // get the thread ID for the message
      StringBuffer sb = new StringBuffer();
      sb.append("SELECT THREAD_ID FROM MB_MESSAGE WHERE MESSAGE_ID = ");
      sb.append(messageId);
      ResultSet rs = query(sb.toString());

      rs.first();

      // get the number of messages in the thread
      sb = new StringBuffer();
      sb.append("SELECT count(MESSAGE_ID) AS MCOUNT ");
      sb.append("FROM MB_MESSAGE WHERE THREAD_ID = ");
      sb.append(rs.getInt("THREAD_ID"));
      ResultSet rs2 = query(sb.toString());

      // delete the message
      sb = new StringBuffer();
      sb.append("DELETE FROM MB_MESSAGE  WHERE MB_MESSAGE.MESSAGE_ID =
");
      sb.append(messageId);
      update(sb.toString());

      rs2.first();

      // if it was the only message in the thread, delete
      // the thread
      if(rs2.getInt("MCOUNT") <= 1){
        sb = new StringBuffer();
        sb.append("DELETE FROM MB_THREAD  WHERE THREAD_ID = ");
        sb.append(rs.getInt("THREAD_ID"));
        update(sb.toString());
      }
   }
```

Continued

Listing 23-3: *(continued)*

```
// set the admin privileges for a user
 public ResultSet toggleUserPriv(int userId, int isAdmin) throws
Exception{
   StringBuffer sb = new StringBuffer();
   sb.append("UPDATE MB_USER SET IS_ADMIN = ");
   sb.append(isAdmin);
   sb.append(" WHERE USER_ID = ");
   sb.append(userId);
   update(sb.toString());

   return getUsers();
 }

 // delete a user
 public ResultSet deleteUser(int userId) throws Exception{
   StringBuffer sb = new StringBuffer();
   sb.append("DELETE FROM MB_USER WHERE USER_ID = ");
   sb.append(userId);
   update(sb.toString());

   return getUsers();
 }

 // get all the users
 public ResultSet getUsers() throws Exception{
   return query("SELECT * FROM MB_USER");
 }

 // login a user, return the user's info
 public ResultSet login(String username, String password) throws
Exception{
   StringBuffer sb = new StringBuffer();
   sb.append("SELECT * FROM MB_USER WHERE EMAIL = '");
   sb.append(username);
   sb.append("' AND PASSWORD = '");
   sb.append(password);
   sb.append("'");
   return query(sb.toString());
 }

 // register a new user
 public void registerUser(String display, String email, String
password) throws Exception{
   StringBuffer sb = new StringBuffer();
   sb.append("INSERT INTO MB_USER(DISPLAY_NAME, EMAIL, PASSWORD)
VALUES('");
   sb.append(display);
   sb.append("', '");
```

```
    sb.append(email);
    sb.append("', '");
    sb.append(password);
    sb.append("')");
    update(sb.toString());
}

// subscribe a user to a thread
public void subscribe(int threadId, int userId) throws Exception{

    // check to see if the user is already subscribed
    // to the thread
    StringBuffer sb = new StringBuffer();
    sb.append("SELECT * FROM MB_SUBSCRIBE  WHERE THREAD_ID = ");
    sb.append(threadId);
    sb.append(" AND  USER_ID = ");
    sb.append(userId);
    ResultSet rs = query(sb.toString());

    // if the user is not already subscribed, subscribe
    // them
    if(!rs.next()){
      sb = new StringBuffer();
      sb.append("INSERT INTO MB_SUBSCRIBE(THREAD_ID, USER_ID)
VALUES(");
      sb.append(threadId);
      sb.append(", ");
      sb.append(userId);
      sb.append(")");
      update(sb.toString());
    }
}

// run the subscriptions on a thread
public void runSubscriptions(int threadId) throws Exception{

    // get the email and thread title for all the
    // subscriptions for a thread
    StringBuffer sb = new StringBuffer();
    sb.append("SELECT MB_USER.EMAIL, MB_THREAD.TITLE ");
    sb.append("FROM MB_USER, MB_THREAD, MB_SUBSCRIBE ");
    sb.append("WHERE MB_SUBSCRIBE.THREAD_ID = ");
    sb.append(threadId);
    sb.append(" AND MB_USER.USER_ID = MB_SUBSCRIBE.USER_ID");
    sb.append(" AND  MB_THREAD.THREAD_ID = ");
    sb.append(threadId);
    ResultSet rs = query(sb.toString());
```

Continued

Listing 23-3: *(continued)*

```java
    // for each subscription send an email
    while(rs.next()){
      sendEMail(rs.getString("EMAIL"), rs.getString("TITLE"));
    }
  }

  // sends an email for a subscription to a user
  public void sendEMail(String to, String title) throws
MessagingException {
    Properties props = new Properties();
    props.put("mail.smtp.host", "your.smtp.host.here");
    Session session = Session.getDefaultInstance(props, null);
    Message msg = new MimeMessage(session);
    InternetAddress addressFrom = new
InternetAddress("mb@myMessageBoard.com");
    msg.setFrom(addressFrom);
    InternetAddress[] addressTo = new InternetAddress[1];
    addressTo[0] = new InternetAddress(to);
    msg.setRecipients(Message.RecipientType.TO, addressTo);
    msg.setSubject("new reply to subscibed thread");
    StringBuffer sb = new StringBuffer();
    sb.append("There is a new reply posted to the thread titled ");
    sb.append(title);
    msg.setContent(sb.toString(), "text/plain");
    Transport.send(msg);
  }

}
```

5. Compile MessageBoard.java into MessageBoard.class, and keep it within the same chapter23 directory.

Creating the .NET Assembly

If you use .NET, follow these steps:

1. Within the .NET Wiley Web application's bin directory (see Chapter 18 for details on setting this up), create a new assembly source document named MessageBoard.cs (or MessageBoard.vb).

2. In the MessageBoard.cs document, add the code from Listing 23-4 and save it.

The VB version of this code can be found on the companion Web site, www.wiley.com/compbooks/lott.

Listing 23-4: **MessageBoard.cs**

```
namespace wiley.chapter23 {

  using System.Data;
  using System.Data.OleDb;
  using System.Text;
  using System.Web.Mail;

  public class MessageBoard {

  // creates the connection object that is used to make
  // database queries. This code uses OleDb. If you are
  // using SQL Server then adjust appropriately (see
  // chapter 18), or if you are using a database other
  // than MySQL then adjust appropriately.
  private OleDbConnection makeConnection(){
    string connStr = "Server=localhost;Provider=MySQLProv;Data
Source=WileyFlashRemoting";
    return new OleDbConnection(connStr);
  }


  // run a SQL statement on the database and return
  // a result (ie - SELECT)
  private DataTable query(string sql){
    OleDbConnection conn = makeConnection();
    OleDbCommand cmd = new OleDbCommand(sql, conn);
    OleDbDataAdapter adp = new OleDbDataAdapter();
    adp.SelectCommand = cmd;
    DataSet ds = new DataSet();
    adp.Fill(ds, "Results");
    return ds.Tables[0];
  }


  // run a SQL statement on the database and do not
  // return a result (ie - INSERT, UPDATE, DELETE)
  private void update(string sql){
    OleDbConnection conn = makeConnection();
    OleDbCommand cmd = new OleDbCommand(sql, conn);
    OleDbDataAdapter adp = new OleDbDataAdapter();
    adp.InsertCommand = cmd;
  }


  // insert a new forum
  public void createForum(string name, string description){
    StringBuilder sb = new StringBuilder();
    sb.Append("INSERT INTO MB_FORUM(NAME, DESCRIPTION) VALUES('");
    sb.Append(name);
    sb.Append("', '");
    sb.Append(description);
```

Continued

Listing 23-4: *(continued)*

```
    sb.Append("')");
    update(sb.ToString());
  }

  // delete a forum
  public void deleteForum(int forumId) {

    // delete the forum
    StringBuilder sb = new StringBuilder();
    sb.Append("DELETE FROM MB_FORUM WHERE FORUM_ID = ");
    sb.Append(forumId);
    update(sb.ToString());

    // select all the messages from the threads within
    // the forum
    sb = new StringBuilder();
    sb.Append("SELECT MB_MESSAGE.MESSAGE_ID FROM MB_THREAD, MB_MESSAGE
WHERE MB_THREAD.FORUM_ID = ");
    sb.Append(forumId);
    sb.Append(" AND MB_MESSAGE.THREAD_ID = MB_THREAD.THREAD_ID");
    DataTable dt = query(sb.ToString());

    // delete each message
    foreach (DataRow dr in dt.Rows){
      deleteMessage((int) dr["MESSAGE_ID"]);
    }
  }

  // modify the values for an existing forum
  public void modifyForum(int forumId, string name, string description)
{
    StringBuilder sb = new StringBuilder();
    sb.Append("UPDATE MB_FORUM SET NAME = '");
    sb.Append(name);
    sb.Append("', DESCRIPTION = '");
    sb.Append(description);
    sb.Append("' WHERE FORUM_ID = ");
    sb.Append(forumId);
    update(sb.ToString());
  }

  // get all the forums
  public DataTable getForums() {

    // this is a complex SQL statement with a join that
    // gets all the forum data plus the number of threads
    // in the forum and the date and time of the most
    // recent thread
```

```
      StringBuilder sb = new StringBuilder();
      sb.Append("select MB_FORUM.*, ");
      sb.Append("count(MB_THREAD.THREAD_ID) AS THREAD_COUNT, ");
      sb.Append("UNIX_TIMESTAMP(max(MB_THREAD.DATETIME)) AS
LAST_POST_DATE ");
      sb.Append("from MB_FORUM LEFT JOIN MB_THREAD ON ");
      sb.Append("MB_THREAD.FORUM_ID = MB_FORUM.FORUM_ID ");
      sb.Append("GROUP BY MB_FORUM.FORUM_ID");
      return query(sb.ToString());
   }

   // get all the threads for a forum
   public DataTable getThreads(int forumId) {

      // this is another complex SQL statement that uses a
      // join to get not only the threads, but also the name
      // of the author, the number of replies, and the time
      // and date of the latest post
      StringBuilder sb = new StringBuilder();
      sb.Append("SELECT MB_THREAD.*, ");
      sb.Append("MB_USER.DISPLAY_NAME AS AUTHOR, ");
      sb.Append("count(MB_MESSAGE.MESSAGE_ID) AS REPLIES, ");
      sb.Append("UNIX_TIMESTAMP(max(MB_MESSAGE.DATETIME)) AS
LAST_POST_TIME ");
      sb.Append("FROM MB_THREAD, MB_USER ");
      sb.Append("LEFT JOIN MB_MESSAGE ON ");
      sb.Append("MB_MESSAGE.THREAD_ID = MB_THREAD.THREAD_ID ");
      sb.Append("WHERE MB_THREAD.FORUM_ID = ");
      sb.Append(forumId);
      sb.Append(" AND MB_USER.USER_ID = MB_THREAD.USER_ID ");
      sb.Append("GROUP BY MB_THREAD.THREAD_ID");
      return query(sb.ToString());
   }


   // post a new thread
   public void postThread(int forumId, int userId, string title, string
body) {

      // lock the database operations so they can only be
      // accessed by one user at a time
      lock(this) {

         // insert the new thread
         StringBuilder sb = new StringBuilder();
         sb.Append("INSERT INTO MB_THREAD(FORUM_ID, USER_ID, TITLE,
DATETIME) VALUES(");
         sb.Append(forumId);
         sb.Append(", ");
         sb.Append(userId);
         sb.Append(", '");
```

Continued

Listing 23-4: *(continued)*

```
      sb.Append(title);
      sb.Append("', '");
      sb.Append(System.DateTime.Now);
      sb.Append("')");
      update(sb.ToString());

      // get the new thread ID
      DataTable dt = query("SELECT max(THREAD_ID) AS NEW_ID FROM
MB_THREAD");
      DataRow dr = dt.Rows[0];

      // post the message to the thread
      postMessage((int)dr["NEW_ID"], userId, body);
   }
 }

  // post a new reply (message) to a thread
  public void postMessage(int threadId, int userId, string body) {

    // insert the message
    StringBuilder sb = new StringBuilder();
    sb.Append("INSERT INTO MB_MESSAGE(THREAD_ID, USER_ID, BODY,
DATETIME) VALUES(");
    sb.Append(threadId);
    sb.Append(", ");
    sb.Append(userId);
    sb.Append(", '");
    sb.Append(body);
    sb.Append("', '");
    sb.Append(System.DateTime.Now);
    sb.Append("')");
    update(sb.ToString());

    // increment the author's number of posts
    sb = new StringBuilder();
    sb.Append("UPDATE MB_USER SET NUM_OF_POSTS = NUM_OF_POSTS + 1 ");
    sb.Append("WHERE USER_ID = ");
    sb.Append(userId);
    update(sb.ToString());

    // run the subscriptions for the thread to notify
    // subscribed users that a new reply has been posted
    runSubscriptions(threadId);
  }

  // get the messages for a  thread
  public DataTable getMessages(int threadId) {
    StringBuilder sb = new StringBuilder();
```

```
      sb.Append("SELECT MB_MESSAGE.*, MB_USER.DISPLAY_NAME,
MB_USER.NUM_OF_POSTS ");
      sb.Append("FROM MB_MESSAGE, MB_USER ");
      sb.Append("WHERE MB_MESSAGE.THREAD_ID = ");
      sb.Append(threadId);
      sb.Append(" AND MB_USER.USER_ID = MB_MESSAGE.USER_ID ");
      sb.Append("ORDER BY MB_MESSAGE.DATETIME");
      return query(sb.ToString());
   }

   // delete a message
   public void deleteMessage(int messageId) {

      // get the thread ID for the message
      StringBuilder sb = new StringBuilder();
      sb.Append("SELECT THREAD_ID FROM MB_MESSAGE WHERE MESSAGE_ID = ");
      sb.Append(messageId);
      DataTable dt = query(sb.ToString());

      DataRow dr = dt.Rows[0];

      // get the number of messages for the thread
      sb = new StringBuilder();
      sb.Append("SELECT count(MESSAGE_ID) AS MCOUNT ");
      sb.Append("FROM MB_MESSAGE WHERE THREAD_ID = ");
      sb.Append(dr["THREAD_ID"]);
      DataTable dt2 = query(sb.ToString());

      // delete the message
      sb = new StringBuilder();
      sb.Append("DELETE FROM MB_MESSAGE  WHERE MB_MESSAGE.MESSAGE_ID =
");
      sb.Append(messageId);
      update(sb.ToString());

      DataRow dr2 = dt2.Rows[0];

      // if the message was the only one in the thread,
      // also delete the thread
      if((int)dr["MCOUNT"] <= 1){
        sb = new StringBuilder();
        sb.Append("DELETE FROM MB_THREAD  WHERE THREAD_ID = ");
        sb.Append(dr["THREAD_ID"]);
        update(sb.ToString());
      }
   }

   // set the admin privileges for a user
   public DataTable toggleUserPriv(int userId, int isAdmin) {
      StringBuilder sb = new StringBuilder();
      sb.Append("UPDATE MB_USER SET IS_ADMIN = ");
```

Continued

Listing 23-4: *(continued)*

```
    sb.Append(isAdmin);
    sb.Append(" WHERE USER_ID = ");
    sb.Append(userId);
    update(sb.ToString());

    return getUsers();
  }

  // delete a user
  public DataTable deleteUser(int userId) {
    StringBuilder sb = new StringBuilder();
    sb.Append("DELETE FROM MB_USER WHERE USER_ID = ");
    sb.Append(userId);
    update(sb.ToString());

    return getUsers();
  }

  // get all the users
  public DataTable getUsers() {
    return query("SELECT * FROM MB_USER");
  }

  // login a user, return the user info
  public DataTable login(string username, string password) {
    StringBuilder sb = new StringBuilder();
    sb.Append("SELECT * FROM MB_USER WHERE EMAIL = '");
    sb.Append(username);
    sb.Append("' AND PASSWORD = '");
    sb.Append(password);
    sb.Append("'");
    return query(sb.ToString());
  }

  // register a new user
  public void registerUser(string display, string email, string
password) {
    StringBuilder sb = new StringBuilder();
    sb.Append("INSERT INTO MB_USER(DISPLAY_NAME, EMAIL, PASSWORD)
VALUES('");
    sb.Append(display);
    sb.Append("', '");
    sb.Append(email);
    sb.Append("', '");
    sb.Append(password);
    sb.Append("')");
    update(sb.ToString());
  }
```

```
// subscribe to a thread
public void subscribe(int threadId, int userId) {
  StringBuilder sb = new StringBuilder();
  sb.Append("SELECT * FROM MB_SUBSCRIBE  WHERE THREAD_ID = ");
  sb.Append(threadId);
  sb.Append(" AND  USER_ID = ");
  sb.Append(userId);
  DataTable dt = query(sb.ToString());
  if(!(dt.Rows.Count > 0)){
    sb = new StringBuilder();
    sb.Append("INSERT INTO MB_SUBSCRIBE(THREAD_ID, USER_ID)
VALUES(");
    sb.Append(threadId);
    sb.Append(", ");
    sb.Append(userId);
    sb.Append(")");
    update(sb.ToString());
  }
}


// run the subscriptions for a thread
public void runSubscriptions(int threadId) {

  // get the thread title and the emails for all
  // subscribed users
  StringBuilder sb = new StringBuilder();
  sb.Append("SELECT MB_USER.EMAIL, MB_THREAD.TITLE ");
  sb.Append("FROM MB_USER, MB_THREAD, MB_SUBSCRIBE ");
  sb.Append("WHERE MB_SUBSCRIBE.THREAD_ID = ");
  sb.Append(threadId);
  sb.Append(" AND MB_USER.USER_ID = MB_SUBSCRIBE.USER_ID");
  sb.Append(" AND  MB_THREAD.THREAD_ID = ");
  sb.Append(threadId);
  DataTable dt = query(sb.ToString());

  // for all the subscribers, send the email
  foreach(DataRow dr in dt.Rows){
    sendEMail((string)dr["EMAIL"], (string)dr["TITLE"]);
  }
}

// send the email for a subscription
public void sendEMail(string to, string title) {
  StringBuilder sb = new StringBuilder();
  sb.Append("There is a new reply posted to the thread titled ");
  sb.Append(title);
  MailMessage mail = new MailMessage();
  mail.To = to;
  mail.From = "mb@myMessageBoard.com";
  mail.BodyFormat = MailFormat.Text;
```

Continued

Listing 23-4: *(continued)*

```
mail.Subject = "new reply to subscibed thread";
mail.Body = sb.ToString();
SmtpMail.SmtpServer = "mail.pacbell.net";
SmtpMail.Send(mail);


    }



    }
}
```

3. Compile MessageBoard.cs (or MessageBoard.vb) to MessageBoard.dll, and keep it in the same bin directory as the source.

Authoring the Administration Flash Movie

The next step in creating the messageboard application is to make the administration Flash movie. To do this, follow these steps:

1. Open a new Flash document and save it as messageBoardAdmin.fla.

2. Rename the default layer form. Add three additional layers named frame actions, actions, and labels.

3. Select the first frame of the labels layer, and in the Properties panel, name the frame mainMenu.

4. On the form layer, add a ComboBox component instance on the upper, left part of the stage, as shown in Figure 23-2. Name this instance forumsMenu.

5. Below the forumsMenu instance, add three PushButton component instances as shown in Figure 23-2. Name these instances modifyForumBtn, newForumBtn, and deleteForumBtn, in order from top to bottom.

6. To the right of forumsMenu, add another ComboBox component instance as shown in Figure 23-2. Name the instance usersMenu.

7. Below usersMenu, add two PushButton component instances. Name these instances toggleAdminBtn and deleteUserBtn.

8. Add new, empty keyframes to frame 2 on the labels, frame actions, and form layers. Add a new regular frame (not a keyframe) to frame 2 on the actions layer.

9. Select frame 2 on the labels layer, and in the Properties panel, give it the label forum.

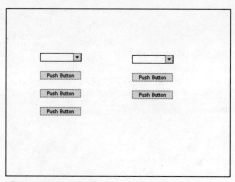

Figure 23-2: The layout of frame 1 of the administration movie

10. On frame 2 of the form layer, add a single-line, input `TextField` object with border turned on. Name the instance `name`, and position it near the center and to the right, as shown in Figure 23-3.

11. Below `name`, add a multiline, input `TextField` object with border turned on as shown in Figure 23-3. Name the instance `description`.

12. Add a `PushButton` component instance below the `TextField` objects as shown in Figure 23-3. Name the instance `submitBtn`.

13. Add static text labels as shown in Figure 23-3.

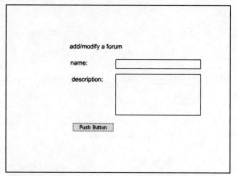

Figure 23-3: The layout of frame 2 of the administration movie

14. On frame 1 of the actions layer (there is only one keyframe on this layer), add the following code:

```
#include "NetServices.as"
#include "DataGlue.as"
```

```
function init(){
  // adjust the gateway URL appropriately
  var gwURL = "http://localhost:8101/Wiley/gateway";
  NetServices.setDefaultGatewayURL(gwURL);
  var conn = NetServices.createGatewayConnection();
   // the service name shown here is for the Java version.
   // in ColdFusion wiley should be Wiley, and in .NET
   // it should be Wiley.Chapter23.MessageBoard
   _root.srv = conn.getService("wiley.chapter23.MessageBoard");
}

// a formatter function used by DataGlue
function formatForumsMenu(forum){
  o = new Object();
  o.label = forum.NAME;
  o.data = forum;
  return o;
}

// a formatter function used by DataGlue
function formatUsersMenu(user){
  o = new Object();
  var lbl = user.EMAIL;
  if (user.IS_ADMIN){
    lbl = "*" + lbl;
  }
  o.label = lbl;
  o.data = user;
  return o;
}

// call getForums() and getUsers() to refresh the menus
function refreshView(){
  _root.srv.getForums(_root.getForumsRes);
  _root.srv.getUsers(_root.usersRes);
}

// the response object for the call to getForums()
getForumsRes = new Object();
getForumsRes.onResult = function(result){
  // display the forums in forumsMenu
  DataGlue.bindFormatFunction(_root.forumsMenu, result,
_root.formatForumsMenu);
}

// the response object for createForum()
createForumRes = new Object();
createForumRes.onResult = function(result){
  // returns the movie playhead to the mainMenu
  // labeled frame and refreshes the menu views
  _root.gotoAndStop("mainMenu");
  _root.refreshView();
}
```

```
// the response object for deleteForum()
deleteForumRes = new Object();
deleteForumRes.onResult = function(result){
  // refresh the menu views
  _root.refreshView();
}


// the response object for both toggleUserPriv() and
// deleteUser()
usersRes = new Object();
usersRes.onResult = function(result){
  // show the users in usersMenu
  DataGlue.bindFormatFunction(_root.usersMenu, result,
_root.formatUsersMenu);
}
```

15. On frame 1 of the frame actions layer, add the following code:

```
// if the movie has not yet been initialized, call init()
// and call refreshView(). Set inited to true so this
// code is only called once per session
if(!inited){
  inited = true;
  init();
  refreshView();
}


modifyForumBtn.setLabel("modify");
modifyForumBtn.onRelease = function(){
  // get the selected forum
  _root.selectedForum = _root.forumsMenu.getValue();
  // set a variable, action, to keep track of whether
  // the forum is being created or modified
  _root.action = "modify";
  // go to the forum label
  _root.gotoAndStop("forum");
}


newForumBtn.setLabel("create new");
newForumBtn.onRelease = function(){
  // set action to create to keep track of the fact that
  // the forum is being created, not modified.
  _root.action = "create";
  // go to the forum label
  _root.gotoAndStop("forum");
}


deleteForumBtn.setLabel("delete forum");
deleteForumBtn.onRelease = function(){
  // get the selected forum ID and call deleteForum()
  var id = _root.forumsMenu.getValue().FORUM_ID;
  _root.srv.deleteForum(_root.deleteForumRes, id);
}
```

```
toggleAdminBtn.setLabel("toggle admin");
toggleAdminBtn.onRelease = function(){
  // get the selected user's ID
  var id = _root.usersMenu.getValue().USER_ID;
  // set isAdmin to the opposite of the current value
  // of IS_ADMIN for the user. Because IS_ADMIN is either
  // 0 or 1, this expression will reverse that value.
  var isAdmin = Math.abs(_root.usersMenu.getValue().IS_ADMIN - 1);
  // call toggleUserPriv with the new value for IS_ADMIN
  _root.srv.toggleUserPriv(_root.usersRes, id, isAdmin);
}

deleteUserBtn.setLabel("delete");
deleteUserBtn.onRelease = function(){
  // get the selected user's ID, and call deleteUser()
  var id = _root.usersMenu.getValue().USER_ID;
  _root.srv.deleteUser(_root.usersRes, id);
}

// make sure to stop the playback of the Main Timeline
this.stop();
```

16. Add the following code to frame 2 of the frame actions layer:

```
// if the action variable is set to modify then fill the
// form with the current values of the selected forum
if(action == "modify"){
  name.text = selectedForum.NAME;
  description.text = selectedForum.DESCRIPTION;
}

submitBtn.setLabel("submit");
submitBtn.onRelease = function(){
  var n = _root.name.text;
  var d = _root.description.text;
  // if the action variable is set to create, call
  // createForum(), else call modifyForum()
  if(_root.action == "create"){
    _root.srv.createForum(_root.createForumRes, n, d);
  }
  else{
    var id = _root.selectedForum.FORUM_ID;
    _root.srv.modifyForum(_root.createForumRes, id, n, d);
  }
}
```

17. Test the movie. Click on the create new button. The forum form should appear as shown in Figure 23-4. Fill out the form and click the submit button. You may want to add multiple forums. If you decide you want to modify a forum's name or description, you can select it from the forum menu. You can also delete a forum you no longer want. The users menu will remain empty for now, but you will revisit it after creating the front end for the messageboard.

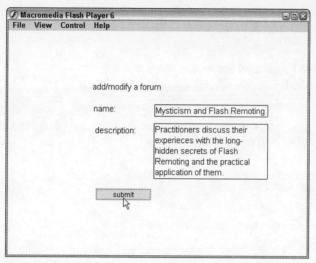

Figure 23-4: Adding a new forum with the administration movie

Building the Messageboard Flash Movie

The remaining step is to now create the messageboard's user interface Flash movie. To do this, complete the following steps:

Note   Unless otherwise noted, set the font size in all the `TextField` objects to 12.

1. Open a new Flash document and save it as messageBoard.fla.

2. Rename the default layer to form, and create a new layer named actions.

3. Create a new Movie Clip symbol (Insert⇨New Symbol), and name the symbol Forum. Forum is going to be a component that displays the forum information.

4. Edit the Forum symbol.

5. Rename the default layer to background. Create three additional layers named outline, text, and actions.

6. On the background layer, draw a light-gray rectangle that is 540 pixels wide and 72 pixels high, positioned so that its upper, left corner is at 0,0. Select the rectangle and convert it to a Movie Clip symbol named ForumBG. Name the instance of ForumBG `background`.

7. On the outline layer, draw a black, unfilled rectangle that outlines `background`. Then, draw two vertical lines as shown in Figure 23-5.

Figure 23-5: The background and outline layers of
the Forum component

8. On the text layer, add three dynamic `TextField` objects — one in each of the segments, as shown in Figure 23-6. Name the instances `nameDesc`, `threadCount`, and `lastPostDate`, from left to right.

Figure 23-6: Adding the TextField objects to the
Forum component

9. On the first frame of the actions layer, add the following code to define the component:

```
// make sure to enclose the code in #initclip
// and #endinitclip
#initclip

// make the Forum class inherit from MovieClip
Forum.prototype = new MovieClip();

// this constructor is automatically called whenever a new
// instance of the Forum component is created
function Forum(){
  // set up the TextField objects
  this.nameDesc.multiline = true;
  this.nameDesc.wordWrap = true;
  this.threadCount.autoSize = true;
  this.lastPostDate.multiline = true;
  this.lastPostDate.autoSize = true;
  // create a Color object for the background
  // so that it can change color when rolled over
  this.bgCol = new Color(this.background);
}

// a method used to format time values so that
// 1 becomes 01, 2 becomes 02, etc.
Forum.prototype.formatTime = function(val){
  if(val >= 10){
    return val;
  }
  else{
    return "0" + val;
  }
}
```

```
    // set the data for the instance
    Forum.prototype.setData = function(forum){
      this.data = forum;
      this.id = forum.FORUM_ID;
      var timeDate = new Date();
      // the LAST_POST_DATE value is in seconds...
      // convert to milliseconds and pass to setTime()
      timeDate.setTime(forum.LAST_POST_DATE * 1000);
      // display the forum data in the text fields
      this.nameDesc.text = forum.NAME + newline;
      this.nameDesc.text += forum.DESCRIPTION;
      // use a TextFormat object to make the title
      // a larger and bolder font
      var tf = new TextFormat();
      tf.size = 15;
      tf.bold = true;
      var len = forum.NAME.length;
      this.nameDesc.setTextFormat(0, len, tf);
      this.threadCount.text = "threads:\n" + forum.THREAD_COUNT;
      if (forum.LAST_POST_DATE != null){
      this.lastPostDate.text = "most recent thread: \n"
      this.lastPostDate.text += (timeDate.getMonth()+1) +
                    "/" + timeDate.getDate() + "/" +
                    timeDate.getFullYear() + newline +
                    this.formatTime(timeDate.getHours()) +
                    ":" +
                    this.formatTime(timeDate.getMinutes());
      }
    }

    // on rollover make the forum light blue
    Forum.prototype.onRollOver = function(){
      this.bgCol.setRGB(0xA9C4FA);
    }

    // on rollout, restore to light gray
    Forum.prototype.onRollOut = function(){
      this.bgCol.setRGB(0xE0DFE3);
    }

    // register the class to the name Forum
    Object.registerClass("Forum", Forum);

    #endinitclip
```

10. Open the Linkage Properties for the Forum symbol and set the symbol to Export for ActionScript and Export in first frame. Set the linkage identifier to Forum.

11. Create a new Movie Clip symbol (Insert➪New Symbol) and name it Thread. Thread is the component for threads within a forum, with similar functionality to the Forum component.

12. Edit the Thread symbol.

13. Rename the default layer to background. Create three additional layers named outline, text, and actions.

14. On the background layer, draw a light-gray rectangle measuring 540 pixels by 30 pixels, with the upper, left corner at 0,0. Select the rectangle and convert it to a Movie Clip symbol named ThreadBG. Name the instance of the symbol background.

15. On the outline layer, draw a black, unfilled rectangle with the same dimensions as background (so that it outlines the MovieClip instance). Draw three vertical lines as shown in Figure 23-7.

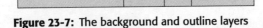

Figure 23-7: The background and outline layers of the Thread component

16. On the text layer, add four dynamic TextField objects as shown in Figure 23-8. Name these instances title, author, replies, and lastPost, from left to right.

Figure 23-8: Adding TextField objects to the Thread component

17. Add the following code to the first frame of the actions layer:

```
// much of this component definition is similar to
// the definition of Forum. If you have questions
// that comments in this code don't address,
// refer to the comments in the Forum code.
#initclip

Thread.prototype = new MovieClip();

function Thread(){
  this.bgCol = new Color(this.background);
}

Thread.prototype.formatTime = function(val){
  if(val >= 10){
    return val;
  }
  else{
    return "0" + val;
  }
}

Thread.prototype.setData = function(thread){
  this.data = thread;
  this.id = thread.THREAD_ID;
  var timeDate = new Date();
```

```
        timeDate.setTime(thread.LAST_POST_TIME * 1000);
        this.title.text = thread.TITLE;
        this.author.text = thread.AUTHOR;
        this.replies.text = thread.REPLIES;
        this.lastPost.text = (timeDate.getMonth()+1) + "/" +
                      timeDate.getDate() + "/" +
                      timeDate.getFullYear() + newline +
                      this.formatTime(timeDate.getHours()) +
                      ":" +
                      this.formatTime(timeDate.getMinutes()));
    }

Thread.prototype.onRollOver = function(){
    this.bgCol.setRGB(0xA9C4FA);
}

Thread.prototype.onRollOut = function(){
    this.bgCol.setRGB(0xE0DFE3);
}

Object.registerClass("Thread", Thread);

#endinitclip
```

18. Open the Linkage Properties for the Thread symbol and set the symbol to Export for ActionScript and Export in first frame. Set the linkage identifier to Thread.

19. Create a new Movie Clip symbol (Insert⇨New Symbol) and name it Message. Message is the component for messages (posts) within a thread.

20. Edit the Message symbol.

21. Rename the default layer to background. Create three additional layers named text, button, and actions.

22. Draw a light-gray rectangle measuring 540 pixels by 100 pixels, with the upper, left corner at 0,0. Select the rectangle and convert it to a Movie Clip symbol named MessageBG. Name the instance of the symbol background.

23. On the text layer, add two dynamic TextField objects as shown in Figure 23-9. Name these instances postInfo and message, from left to right.

24. Open the Buttons library (Window⇨Common Libraries⇨Buttons), and on the button layer, add an instance of the "Oval buttons - blue" button as shown in Figure 23-9. Name the instance deleteBtn.

25. Resize the deleteBtn instance to 33% using the transform tool, and add a static text field to label the button delete.

Figure 23-9: Adding TextField objects and button to the Message component

26. Add the following code to the first frame of the actions layer:

```
// as with the Thread component definition, much of this
// code is similar to Forum. If you have questions
// about some uncommented code refer back to the comments
// in the code for Forum
#initclip

Message.prototype = new MovieClip();

function Message(){
  this.message.wordWrap = true;
  this.message.autoSize = false;
  this.postInfo.autoSize = true;
  // make the delete button invisible to start
  this.deleteLabel._visible = false;
  this.deleteBtn._visible = false;
}

Message.prototype.setData = function(message){
  this.data = message;
  // if the message's author is the user who is
  // currently logged in or if the current user
  // has administrative privileges, turn on the
  // delete button
  if(_root.user.USER_ID == message.USER_ID ||
    _root.user.IS_ADMIN == 1){
    this.deleteBtn._visible = true;
    this.deleteLabel._visible = true;
    this.deleteBtn.onRelease = function(){
      // when the button is clicked, call the
      // deleteMessage() method of the service
      _root.srv.deleteMessage(_root.deleteMessageRes,
this._parent.data.MESSAGE_ID);
    }
  }
  this.postInfo.text = "author: ";
  this.postInfo.text += message.DISPLAY_NAME + newline;
  this.postInfo.text += "posts: ";
  this.postInfo.text += message.NUM_OF_POSTS;
  this.message.text = message.BODY;
  // set the height of the message text field to the
  // height of its text plus a buffer of 5 pixels
  this.message._height = this.message.textHeight + 5;
  // get the height of the message textfield plus the button
  var h = this.message._height + this.deleteBtn._height + 5;
  // if the post info text field has a greater height
  // use that instead
  if (this.postInfo._height > h){
    h = this.postInfo._height;
  }
```

```
    // set the background to the height of the message
    this.background._height = h;
    // draw an outline
    this.drawOutline(h);
  }

  Message.prototype.drawOutline = function(h){
    // create the holder MovieClip
    this.createEmptyMovieClip("outline", 1);
    with (this.outline){
      lineStyle(1, 0, 100);
      // draw an outline around the background
      // rectangle
      lineTo(540, 0);
      lineTo(540, h);
      lineTo(0, h);
      lineTo(0, 0);
      var w = this.message._x - 5;
      // draw a line between the post info and message
      moveTo(w, 0);
      lineTo(w, h);
    }
  }

  Object.registerClass("Message", Message);

  #endinitclip
```

27. Open the Linkage Properties for the Message symbol and set the symbol to Export for ActionScript and Export in first frame. Set the linkage identifier to Message.

28. Create a new Movie Clip symbol named TextLink. This symbol is a component that is used to create navigation elements for the messageboard. Instances will be created dynamically to enable the user to navigate up and down through selected forums, threads, and messages.

29. Edit TextLink.

30. Rename the default layer to text, and create another layer named actions.

31. On the text layer, add a dynamic TextField object named linkText with border turned off. Position the object at 0,0. The size of it does not matter, as it will be determined with ActionScript.

32. On the first frame of the Actions layer, add the following code:

```
// as with the other component definitions, much of this
// code is similar to Forum. If you have questions
// about some uncommented code refer back to the comments
// in the code for Forum
#initclip

TextLink.prototype = new MovieClip();
```

```
function TextLink(){
  this.linkText.autoSize = true;
}

// this method sets the text value and defines a callback
// function that is invoked when the component instance
// is clicked
TextLink.prototype.setLink = function(label, functionRef){
  this.linkText.text = label;
  this.onRelease = function(){
    // invoke the callback function when clicked
    functionRef.call();
    // get the depth of this instance
    var depth = this.getDepth();
    // loop through all the other MovieClip instances
    // in the parent, and if any have a greater depth,
    // delete them.
    for(var i in this._parent){
      if(this._parent[i].getDepth() > depth){
        this._parent[i].removeMovieClip();
      }
    }
    this._parent.currentDepth = depth + 1;
  }
}

TextLink.prototype.onRollOver = function(){
  this.linkText.textColor = 0x0000FF;
}

TextLink.prototype.onRollOut = function(){
  this.linkText.textColor = 0x000000;
}

Object.registerClass("TextLink", TextLink);

#endinitclip
```

33. Open the Linkage Properties for the TextLink symbol and set the symbol to Export for ActionScript and Export in first frame. Set the linkage identifier to TextLink.

34. Create a new Movie Clip symbol named ThreadMessageHolder. This symbol contains the header information for a thread.

35. Edit ThreadMessageHeader.

36. Rename the default layer to background. Create two additional layers named text and buttons.

37. On the background layer, draw a light-gray rectangle with black outline that is 540 pixels by 100 pixels. Align the upper, left corner of the rectangle to 0,0.

38. On the text layer, create a dynamic `TextField` object about 510 pixels by 60 pixels. Name the instance `headerText`, and position it as shown in Figure 23-10.

39. On the buttons layer, add two instances of the "Oval buttons - blue" symbol as shown in Figure 23-10. Name these instance `subscribeBtn` and `replyBtn`, and create static text labels next to each.

Figure 23-10: The layout of ThreadMessageHolder

40. Create a new Movie Clip symbol named LoginForm. This is the form the user will use to log in.

41. Edit LoginForm.

42. Rename the default layer to form.

43. Add an input `TextField` object to the layer with border turned on. Name the instance username. Position the instance as shown in Figure 23-11. (Pay special attention to the positioning relative to the symbol's registration point.)

44. Add a password `TextField` object just below `usename` as shown in Figure 23-11. Name the instance `password`.

45. Add a `PushButton` component instance below the `TextField` objects. Name the instance `submitBtn`.

46. Add static text labels as shown in Figure 23-11.

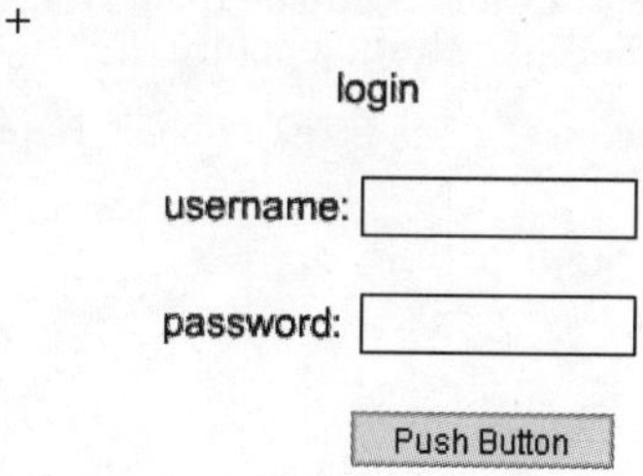

+

login

username: ☐

password: ☐

[Push Button]

Figure 23-11: The LoginForm

47. Create a new Movie Clip symbol named RegisterForm. This is the form the user will use to register a new user.

48. Edit RegisterForm.

49. Rename the default layer to form.

50. Add two input `TextField` objects to the layer, with border turned on. Name the instances `displayName` and `email`. Position the instances as shown in Figure 23-12. (Pay special attention to the positioning relative to the symbol's registration point.)

51. Add two password `TextField` objects just below `email` as shown in Figure 23-12. Name the instances `password` and `confirm`.

52. Add a `PushButton` component instance below the `TextField` objects. Name the instance `submitBtn`.

53. Add static text labels as shown in Figure 23-12.

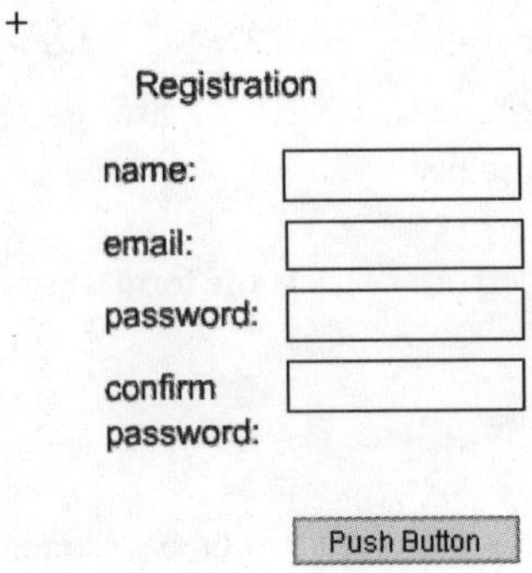

+

Registration

name:

email:

password:

confirm
password:

Push Button

Figure 23-12: The RegisterForm

54. Create a new Movie Clip symbol named RegisterForm. This is the form the user will use to post a reply to a thread.

55. Edit ReplyForm.

56. Rename the default layer to form.

57. Add a multiline input `TextField` object to the layer, with border turned on. Name the instance `message`. Position the instance as shown in Figure 23-13. (Pay special attention to the positioning relative to the symbol's registration point.)

58. Add a `PushButton` component instance below the `TextField` object. Name the instance `submitBtn`.

59. Add a static text label as shown in Figure 23-13.

+

type your message below:

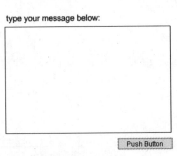

Push Button

Figure 23-13: The ReplyForm

60. Create a new Movie Clip symbol named ThreadForm. This is the form the user will use to post a new thread.

61. Edit ThreadForm.

62. Rename the default layer to form.

63. Add a single-line input TextField object to the layer, with border turned on. Name the instance title, and position it as shown in Figure 23-14. (Pay special attention to the positioning relative to the symbol's registration point.)

64. Add a multiline input TextField object with border turned on just below title. Name the instance message.

65. Add a PushButton component instance below the TextField objects. Name the instance submitBtn.

66. Add static text labels as shown in Figure 23-14.

Figure 23-14: The ThreadForm

67. Create a new Movie Clip symbol named ThreadsHeader. This symbol is used at the top of the list of threads for a selected forum. It includes the button that enables a user to post a new thread.

68. Edit ThreadsHeader.

69. Rename the default layer to background. Create two additional layers named text and button.

70. On the background layer, draw a light-purple rectangle with black outline measuring 540 pixels by 30 pixels. Position this rectangle so that the upper, left corner is at 0,0.

71. Draw three black, vertical lines across the rectangle as shown in Figure 23-15.

72. On the text layer, add static text labels as shown in Figure 23-15.

73. On the button layer, add an instance of the "Oval buttons - blue" symbol below the rectangle, as shown in Figure 23-15. Name the instance newThreadBtn.

74. Add a static text label next to the Button instance, as shown in Figure 23-15.

Figure 23-15: The layout of ThreadsHeader

75. Return to the Main Timeline.

76. On the form layer, add a `ScrollPane` component instance named `sp`. The position will be set by ActionScript. The scroll pane is the place where all the forms and components will be loaded by way of ActionScript.

77. In the upper, right corner of the stage, add two instances of "Oval buttons - blue." Name the instances `loginBtn` and `registerBtn`.

78. Add static text labels next to the buttons, as shown in Figure 23-16.

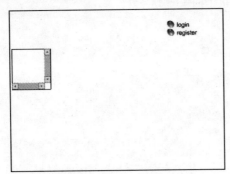

Figure 23-16: The layout on the Main Timeline for messageBoard.fla

79. On the actions layer, add the following code:

```
#include "NetServices.as"

function init(){
    // this gateway URL should be the same one you used in
    // the administration movie.
    var gwURL = "http://localhost:8880/Wiley/gateway";
    NetServices.setDefaultGatewayURL(gwURL);
    var conn = NetServices.createGatewayConnection();

    // set the size and position of the scroll pane
    _root.sp.setSize(540, 300);
    _root.sp._x = 5;
    _root.sp._y = 100;

    // create the MovieClip that will be used for loading
    // the content and that will be set as the scroll
    // content for the scroll pane
```

```
    _root.createEmptyMovieClip("mb", 1);
    // the service name should be the same as you used in
    // the administration movie.
    _root.srv = conn.getService("wiley.chapter24.MessageBoard");

    // call the makeForumsList() function to start out
    _root.makeForumsList();

    // set the handlers for the buttons
    _root.loginBtn.onRelease = _root.makeLoginForm;
    _root.registerBtn.onRelease = _root.makeRegisterForm;
}

// this function is called by others to clear out the
// contents of the mb MovieClip
function clearMB(){
  for(var mc in _root.mb){
    _root.mb[mc].removeMovieClip();
  }
}

// check if the user is logged in. when a user
// successfully logs in, the user information is stored in
// _root.user. If the _root.user.EMAIL value is defined,
// then they are logged in.
function isLoggedIn(){
  if(_root.user.EMAIL != undefined){
    return true;
  }
  else{
    return false;
  }
}

// make the original navigation holder MovieClip in the
// upper left corner (at 0,0 by default), and add to it a //
navigation element called >>home that calls the
// makeForumsList() function when clicked.
function makeNav(){
  _root.createEmptyMovieClip("nav", 2);
  _root.addNav(">>home", _root.makeForumsList, 1);
}

// add a new navigation element to the navigation holder
// MovieClip
function addNav(link, func, level){
  // create a new TextLink instance in the nav holder
  var tl = _root.nav.attachMovie("TextLink", "tl" + level, level);
  // call the setLink() method of the new TextLink
  // component instance.
  tl.setLink(link, func);
```

```
    // set the _y value so that the navigation links don't
    // overlap
    tl._y = level * tl._height;
  }


  // basically, makes the "home" page by clearing the mb
  // MovieClip, calling the makeNav() function to create a
  // fresh navigation, and call the getForums() service
  // function.
  function makeForumsList(){
    _root.clearMB();
    _root.makeNav();
    _root.srv.getForums(_root.getForumsRes);
  }


  // when a forum is selected its data is stored to
  // _root.selectedForum. This function calls the
  // getThreads() service function, passing it the ID for
  // the selected Forum
  function makeThreadsList(){
    _root.srv.getThreads(_root.getThreadsRes,
                         _root.selectedForum.FORUM_ID);
  }


  // when a thread is selected its data is stored to
  // _root.selectedThread. This function calls the
  // getMessages() service function, passing it the ID
  // for the selected thread
  function makeMessagesList(){
    _root.srv.getMessages(_root.getMessagesRes,
                          _root.selectedThread.THREAD_ID);
  }


  // load the login form into the scrollpane holder
  // MovieClip and sets the values for the submit button
  function makeLoginForm(){
    _root.clearMB();
    var form = _root.mb.attachMovie("LoginForm", "form", 1);
    // this is a little trick to ensure the setLabel() ]
    // method is called after the component has loaded.
    // Otherwise, because of load order issues, the
    // setLabel() method is called before the component has
    // loaded.
    form.submitBtn.onLoad = function(){
      this.setLabel("submit");
    }
    form.submitBtn.onRelease = function(){
      // when a user attempts to login, clear any user that
      // is currently logged in.
      _root.user = null;
```

```
      // call the login() service function with the username
      // and password that the user entered.
      var un = this._parent.username.text;
      var pw = this._parent.password.text;
      _root.srv.login(_root.loginRes, un, pw);
    }
    _root.sp.setScrollContent(_root.mb);
  }


  // loads the registration form into the scrollpane holder
  // MovieClip
  function makeRegisterForm(){
    _root.clearMB();
    var form = _root.mb.attachMovie("RegisterForm", "form", 1);
    // this is the same trick as was employed in
    // makeLoginForm()
    form.submitBtn.onLoad = function(){
      this.setLabel("submit");
    }
    form.submitBtn.onRelease = function(){
      var disp = this._parent.displayName.text;
      var email = this._parent.email.text;
      var pw = this._parent.password.text;
      var cpw = this._parent.confirm.text;
      // make sure the passwords match, then call the
      // registerUser() service function
      if(pw == cpw){
        _root.srv.registerUser(_root.registerRes, disp, email, pw);
      }
    }
    _root.sp.setScrollContent(_root.mb);
  }


  // loads the new thread form into the scroll pane holder
  // MovieClip
  function makeNewThreadForm(){
    _root.clearMB();
    // make sure the user is logged in first. If they are,
    // load the form, otherwise, call makeLoginForm()
    if(_root.isLoggedIn()){
      var form = _root.mb.attachMovie("ThreadForm", "form", 1);
      form.submitBtn.onLoad = function(){
        this.setLabel("submit");
      }
      form.submitBtn.onRelease = function(){
        var fid = _root.selectedForum.FORUM_ID;
        var uid = _root.user.USER_ID;
        var title = this._parent.title.text;
        var body = this._parent.message.text;
        _root.srv.postThread(_root.postMessageRes, fid, uid, title,
body);
```

```
      }
    }
    else{
      _root.makeLoginForm();
    }
    _root.sp.setScrollContent(_root.mb);
}

// load the reply form
function makeReplyForm(){
  _root.clearMB();
  // make sure the user is logged in before allowing a
  // reply. Otherwise, call makeLoginForm();
  if(_root.isLoggedIn()){
    var form = _root.mb.attachMovie("ReplyForm", "form", 1);
    form.submitBtn.setLabel("submit");
    form.submitBtn.onRelease = function(){
      var tid = _root.selectedThread.THREAD_ID;
      var uid = _root.user.USER_ID;
      var body = this._parent.message.text;
      _root.srv.postMessage(_root.postMessageRes, tid, uid, body);
    }
  }
  else{
    _root.makeLoginForm();
  }
  _root.sp.setScrollContent(_root.mb);
}

// after a new user registers, go to the login form
registerRes = new Object();
registerRes.onResult = function(result){
  _root.makeLoginForm();
}

// after a new message is posted, go to the threads list
// for the current forum
postMessageRes = new Object();
postMessageRes.onResult = function(result){
  _root.makeThreadsList();
}

// when the list of forums is retrieved, populate the
// scroll pane with them using the Forum component
getForumsRes = new Object();
getForumsRes.onResult = function(result){
  var forum, height;
  // loop through the returned forums
  for(var i = 0; i < result.getLength(); i++){
    // get the height of the forum component
    height = _root.mb["forum" + (i - 1)]._height - 1;
```

```
    // create a new component within mb and position it at
    // the bottom of the list
    forum = _root.mb.attachMovie("Forum", "forum" + i, i, {_y: i *
height});
    // call the setData() method of the Forum component
    // instance, and pass it the record for the current
    // forum from the list
    forum.setData(result.getItemAt(i));
    // when clicked, set the selectedForum value, add a
    // navigation element, and call makeThreadsList()
    forum.onRelease = function(){
      _root.selectedForum = this.data;
      _root.addNav(">>" + _root.selectedForum.NAME,
                   _root.makeThreadsList,
                   2);
      _root.makeThreadsList();
    }
  }
  // set the scroll content for sp so that it updates the
  // scroll view
  _root.sp.setScrollContent(_root.mb);
  // the page variable is used to keep track of which page
  // is currently being viewed
  _root.page = "forums";
}

// list the threads retrieved for a forum
getThreadsRes = new Object();
getThreadsRes.onResult = function(result){
  _root.clearMB();
  // add the ThreadsHeader instance
  header = _root.mb.attachMovie("ThreadsHeader", "header", 0);
  // set the newThreadBtn to set page to newThread, and to
  // call the makeNewThreadForm() function
  header.newThreadBtn.onRelease = function(){
    _root.page = "newThread";
    _root.makeNewThreadForm();
  }
  var y = header._height;
  // loop through all the threads returned from
  // the service function
  for(var i = 0; i < result.getLength(); i++){
    // create a new Thread component instance
    thread = _root.mb.attachMovie("Thread",
                                  "thread" + i,
                                  (i+1),
                                  {_y: y});
    // call the setData() method of the Thread
    // instance with the value of the current thread
    // record
    thread.setData(result.getItemAt(i));
```

```
      // when the thread is clicked set the selectedThread
      // value, add a navigation element, and call
      // makeMessagesList()
      thread.onRelease = function(){
        _root.selectedThread = this.data;
        _root.addNav(">>" + _root.selectedThread.TITLE,
                     _root.makeMessagesList,
                     3);
        _root.makeMessagesList();
      }
      y = thread._y + thread._height - 1;
    }
    _root.sp.setScrollContent(_root.mb);
    _root.page = "threads";
}

// list the messages for a selected thread
getMessagesRes = new Object();
getMessagesRes.onResult = function(result){
  _root.clearMB();
  var dateTime, message;
  // add the ThreadMessageHeader
  var header = _root.mb.attachMovie("ThreadMessageHeader", "header",
1);
  // set the header text to display the title and original
  // author of the thread
  header.headerText.text = _root.selectedThread.TITLE + newline;
  header.headerText.text += _root.selectedThread.AUTHOR;
  // make the reply form when the replyBtn is clicked
  header.replyBtn.onRelease = function(){
    _root.page = "reply";
    _root.makeReplyForm();
  }
  // allow the user to subscribe to the thread if
  // they are logged in. Otherwise, go to the login
  // form
  header.subscribeBtn.onRelease = function(){
    _root.page = "subscribe";
    if(_root.isLoggedIn()){
      _root.srv.subscribe(_root.subscribeRes,
_root.selectedThread.THREAD_ID, _root.user.USER_ID);
    }
    else{
      _root.makeLoginForm();
    }
  }
  // loop through all the messages returned from the
  // service function
  for(var i = 0; i < result.getLength(); i++){
    // create a Message instance
    message = _root.mb.attachMovie("Message", "message" + i, i + 2);
```

```
      // set the data of the component instance to the
      // current message record
      message.setData(result.getItemAt(i));
      // if the message is the first in the list then
      // set its position just under the header, otherwise
      // set its position to be under the previous message
      if(i == 0){
        message._y = header._height + 10;
      }
      else{
        message._y = _root.mb["message" + (i-1)]._y +
_root.mb["message" + (i-1)]._height + 10;
      }
    }
    _root.sp.setScrollContent(_root.mb);
    _root.page = "messages";
}

// process a user being logged in
loginRes = new Object();
loginRes.onResult = function(result){
    // set the _root.user variable to the returned
    // user data RecordSet object
    _root.user = result.getItemAt(0);
    // if the user is successfully logged in
    // determine what to do next based on the value
    // of the _root.page variable. This allows for a
    // user to be automatically returned to the place
    // they were last before they logged in.
    if(_root.isLoggedIn()){
      switch(_root.page){
        case "forums":
          _root.makeForumsList();
          break;
        case "threads":
          _root.makeThreadsList();
          break;
        case "subscribe":
          _root.srv.subscribe(_root.subscribeRes,
_root.selectedThread.THREAD_ID, _root.user.USER_ID);
        case "messages":
          _root.makeMessagesList();
          break;
        case "newThread":
          _root.makeNewThreadForm();
          break;
        case "reply":
          _root.makeReplyForm();
      }
    }
    else{
```

```
   }
 }

 // after a message is deleted call makeThreadsList)()
 deleteMessageRes = new Object();
 deleteMessageRes.onResult = function(result){
   _root.makeThreadsList();
 }

 // don't need to do anything after a user subscribes
 subscribeRes = new Object();
 subscribeRes.onResult = function(result){}

 // call init() to start the movie
 init();
```

80. Test your movie! When it starts, you should see a list of the forums you created in the administration movie. An example is shown in Figure 23-17.

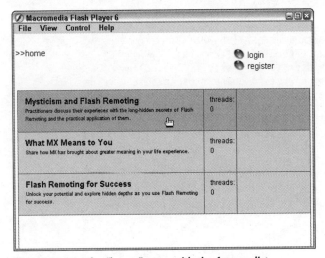

Figure 23-17: The "home" page with the forums list

When you select a forum, it will take you to the list of threads for that forum. Obviously, because you have just created this system, there will not yet be any threads. If you click on the post new thread button (see Figure 23-18), however, you can post a new thread in the forum.

The system automatically checks to make sure that you are logged in before allowing you to post a new thread. Because you have not yet logged in, you will be automatically redirected to the login form. However, you will need to register first. Click the register button at the upper, right corner of the window to be taken to the registration form (see Figure 23-19).

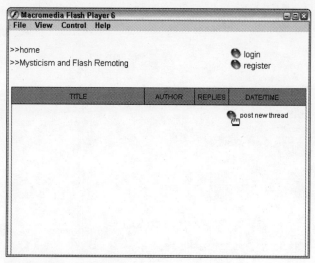

Figure 23-18: Selecting to post a new thread

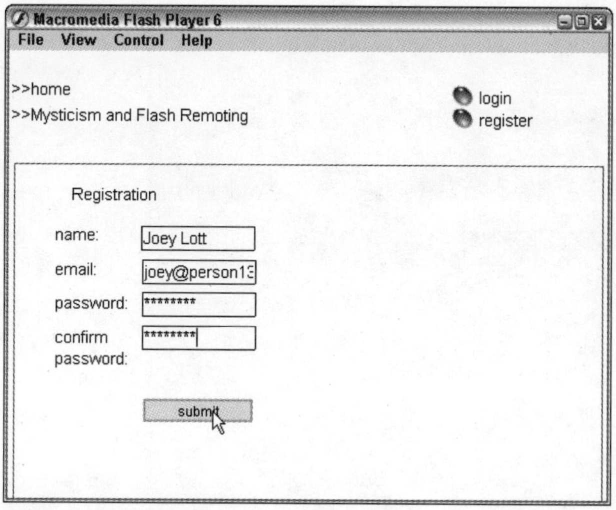

Figure 23-19: Registering as a new user

Once you register, you will be redirected to the login form. Fill out the information you entered in the registration form and click submit. You should then be redirected automatically to the new thread form page, as shown in Figure 23-20.

After you fill out the new thread form and click submit, you will be directed back to the thread list for the selected forum. In Figure 23-21, you can see how your new thread will appear in the list.

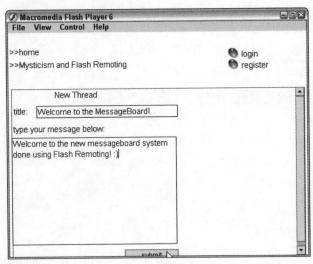

Figure 23-20: Posting a new thread

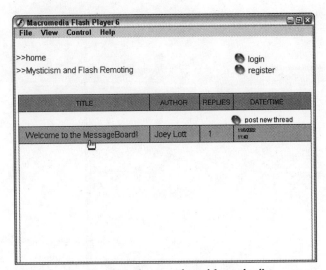

Figure 23-21: Choosing the new thread from the list

Clicking on the thread from the list takes you to the thread page with a list of the messages. Because you are the author of the message, you have the option of deleting it (see Figure 23-22). However, if you were logged in as another user, you could not delete the message (unless the user had administrative privileges).

If you click on the >>home navigation link as shown in Figure 23-22, you will be returned to the "home" page.

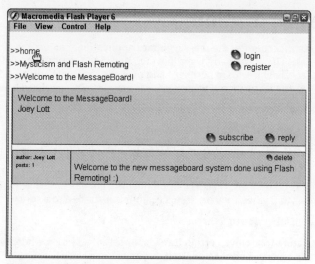

Figure 23-22: Returning to the home page

In Figure 23-23, you can see that the "home" page now reflects the changes you have made. The forum lists the number of threads and the date and time of the most recent thread.

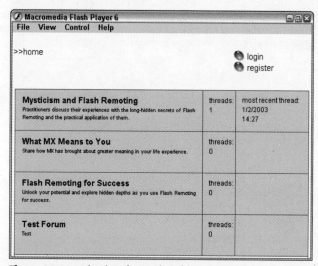

Figure 23-23: Viewing the updated home page

81. At this point, you may also want to experiment by adding more users and then setting administrative privileges for some of the users in the administration movie.

Extending the Application

As mentioned earlier in this chapter, the messageboard application you just created can be considered a 1.0 version. There are many ways in which you could improve upon this system once you have it in place. Feel free to experiment and make adjustments and modifications to suit your needs, adding any features you want.

Here is a list of just a few suggestions for consideration:

✦ Allow users to modify their registration.

✦ Allow users to have their e-mail displayed along with their posts or to keep that information private if they desire.

✦ Use a MessageBox component (Flash UI Components 2) to alert users when the login was unsuccessful, and when they have successfully subscribed to a thread.

✦ Allow a user to unsubscribe to a thread.

✦ Allow administrators to archive certain threads, or set up a system whereby threads are automatically archived after an allotted period of time.

Summary

In this chapter, you have created [0]a messageboard application [0]using Flash Remoting. You created database tables into which the messageboard posts and user information are stored and retrieved. You then created an administrative Flash movie that enables you to add, modify, and delete the available forums as well as delete users and toggle administrative authority for current users. Finally, you created a Flash user interface for the messageboard that allows users to register, log in, and post new threads and replies.

✦　　✦　　✦

Creating an E-mail Client

E-mail is a technology that continues to be of critical importance to the Internet. Users often check their e-mail using a client that runs on their computer, such as Outlook or Eudora. Although this works great for reading messages on a personal computer at home or at the office, it does not enable a user to read his or her e-mail from any other locations. The need to be able to read e-mail from any location made Web-based e-mail clients popular. With this in mind, you can now create a Flash interface for a Web-based e-mail client.

Designing the Application

The first step in any application development process is to design and architect the entire application. I usually divide this process into two categories:

+ Determining the desired functionality

+ Creating an overview (perhaps a flowchart) of how the pieces work together

Specifying Functionality

The functionality of a basic e-mail client doesn't need to be complex. For more complicated clients with larger feature sets, you might want to include the functionality listed in the section "Extending the E-mail Client." For the application that you build in this chapter, however, the following functionality is covered:

+ Connecting to the server with a username and password: In order to retrieve the e-mail for a user, you must enable the user to specify the server (in this case, it must be a POP3 server, so no Hotmail or Yahoo! accounts) and the username and password for the account.

+ Retrieving basic information about all messages in the inbox: Generally, you want an e-mail client to list all the messages in the inbox — displaying the sender's address, the subject, and the date sent.

✦ ✦ ✦ ✦

In This Chapter

Planning the creation of a Flash Remoting e-mail client

Creating the server-side portion of the application to retrieve and send e-mail messages

Authoring a Flash user interface and integrating it using Flash Remoting

✦ ✦ ✦ ✦

✦ Retrieving the entire contents of an individual message when selected: When a user selects a message from the inbox list, you want to be able to display that entire e-mail.

✦ Deleting a message from the server: You will undoubtedly want to be able to delete all those unsolicited commercial e-mails you receive, as well as any other unwanted messages.

✦ Replying to an e-mail message: This feature should enable the creation of a new e-mail message based on information (recipient and subject) to which the user is responding. The new message also includes the contents of the original e-mail message in the body of the reply.

✦ Composing a new e-mail message: This feature enables a user to create a new, blank e-mail message.

Looking at the Application Overview

This application has three parts:

✦ **The e-mail server:** This is an integral part of the application. Although it may seem obvious, it is worth pointing out just to be clear. In order for you to successfully test this application, you need an e-mail account on a POP3 server. Typically, if you have an e-mail account with an ISP, then your account is a POP3 account. You need to know three pieces of information with regard to this: the server URL or IP address, the username for the account (often, though not always, the e-mail address), and the password for the account. If you are unsure of this information and you use an e-mail client such as Outlook, check in the client program's accounts settings for the information that it is using.

✦ **The server-side application code:** Depending on whether you are using ColdFusion, .NET, or Java, you should create a ColdFusion Component, a DLL, or a Java class, respectively, that contains all the necessary methods for interacting with the e-mail server.

✦ **The Flash movie:** This is the user interface for the other two parts of the application. It is the way in which the user utilizes all the functionality you have built.

Creating the Server-Side Application Code

The following three sections cover all that you need to do in order to create the server-side portion of your e-mail client application. You need to complete only one of the three (ColdFusion, .NET, or Java) parts, so select the heading that pertains to you and follow the instructions.

Creating the ColdFusion Component

If you use ColdFusion, follow these steps:

1. Within the ColdFusion webroot, you should already have a directory named Wiley. If not, create this directory.

2. Within the Wiley directory, create a chapter24 directory.

3. Within the `chapter24` directory, create a new CFC document named FlashMail.cfc.

4. Add the code from Listing 24-1 to FlashMail.cfc and save the document.

Listing 24-1: FlashMail.cfc

```
<cfcomponent>

  <!-- retrieves all the messages in the inbox
       for an account specified by a host (server),
       username, and password -->
  <cffunction name="getMessages"
              access="remote"
              returntype="array">
    <cfargument name="username"
                type="string"
                required="true">
    <cfargument name="password"
                type="string"
                required="true">
    <cfargument name="host" type="string" required="true">
    <!-- the cfpop tag contacts the specified server,
         connects to the account given by the username and
         password, and then if the action is
         GETHEADERONLY, it retrieves the headers for all
         the messages and saves them to a query with a
         name indicated by the name attribute value -->
    <cfpop server="#host#"
        username="#username#"
        password="#password#"
        action="GETHEADERONLY"
        name="messages">
    <!-- messagesArray is the array that will be returned
         to Flash -->
    <cfset messagesArray = ArrayNew(1)>
    <!-- loop through all the messages retrieved from the
         cfpop call -->
    <cfloop query="messages">
      <cfscript>
        // create a struct and add to it the values for
        // the current message (messageNumber, from,
        // subject, date are the names of the values
        // returned according to the ColdFusion API. View
        // the CFML reference for more information on
        // cfpop). Then add the struct to the array that
        // gets returned to Flash
        mStruct = StructNew();
        mStruct.id = messages.messageNumber;
        mStruct.from = messages.from;
        mStruct.subject = messages.subject;
```

Continued

Listing 24-1: *(continued)*

```
        mStruct.sent = messages.date;
        ArrayAppend(messagesArray, mStruct);
    </Cfscript>
  </cfloop>
  <cfreturn messagesArray>
</cffunction>

<!-- get a single message based on an id and return it
     to Flash -->
<cffunction name="getMessage"
            access="remote"
            returntype="struct">
  <cfargument name="username"
              type="string"
              required="true">
  <cfargument name="password"
              type="string"
              required="true">
  <cfargument name="host" type="string" required="true">
  <cfargument name="id" type="numeric" required="true">

  <!-- connect to the server with cfpop again, but this
       time set action to GETALL and messagenumber to
       the id of a specific message. This will then
       retrieve the entire contents of that
       one message -->
  <cfpop server="#host#"
         username="#username#"
         password="#password#"
         action="GETALL"
         messagenumber="#id#"
         name="message">
  <cfscript>
    // create a struct with the from address, subject,
    // and body of the email message for returning to
    // Flash
    mStruct = StructNew();
    mStruct.from = message.from;
    mStruct.subject = message.subject;
    mStruct.body = message.body;
  </cfscript>
  <cfreturn mStruct>
</cffunction>

<!-- send an email -->
<cffunction name="sendEmail"
            access="remote"
            returntype="void">
```

```
         <cfargument name="to" type="string" required="true">
         <cfargument name="from" type="string" required="true">
         <cfargument name="subject"
                   type="string"
                   required="true">
         <cfargument name="body" type="string" required="true">
         <cfargument name="host" type="string" required="true">

         <!-- cfmail is the tag that is used to send email
             using ColdFusion. You need to specify the to,
             from, subject, and server. Then place the body of
             the email between the opening and closing cfmail
             tags -->
         <cfmail to="#to#"
               from="#from#"
               subject="#subject#"
               server="#host#">
         #body#
         </cfmail>
</cffunction>

<!-- delete a message from the server -->
<cffunction name="deleteMessage"
            access="remote"
            returntype="array">
         <cfargument name="username"
                   type="string"
                   required="true">
         <cfargument name="password"
                   type="string"
                   required="true">
         <cfargument name="host" type="string" required="true">
         <cfargument name="id" type="numeric" required="true">

         <!-- use cfpop to delete the message by specifying
             action as DELETE and messagenumber as the id of
             the message to delete -->
         <cfpop server="#host#"
               username="#username#"
               password="#password#"
               action="DELETE"
               messagenumber="#id#">

         <!-- call the getMessages function and return that
             value to Flash -->
         <cfinvoke method="getMessages"
                  returnvariable="messages">
           <cfinvokeargument name="username"
                           value="#username#">
           <cfinvokeargument name="password"
                           value="#password#">
```

Continued

Listing 24-1: *(continued)*

```
        <cfinvokeargument name="host" value="#host#">
    </cfinvoke>
    <cfreturn messages>
  </cffunction>

</cfcomponent>
```

Creating the Java Class

If you are using a J2EE application server, follow these steps:

1. If you do not already have the JavaMail API installed, download it and install it now. You can download it from Sun's Web site at http://java.sun.com/products/javamail/. You will want to extract the contents and then copy the JAR files (mail.jar, pop3.jar, and smtp.jar specifically) to a location within your CLASSPATH. I recommend that you copy these files to the jre/lib/ext directory of your JDK installation.

Note The JavaMail API documentation is available at http://java.sun.com/products/ javamail/1.3/docs/javadocs/index.html. You may want to view this for reference as to what particular classes do.

2. Within the Web application's WEB-INF/classes, you should already have a Wiley directory. If you do not, create it.

3. Create a chapter24 directory within the Wiley directory.

4. Create a new Java file named FlashMail.java in the chapter24 directory.

5. Add the code from Listing 24-2 to the FlashMail.java document and save it.

Listing 24-2: **FlashMail.java**

```
package wiley.chapter24;

import java.io.*;
import java.net.*;
import java.text.*;
import javax.mail.*;
import javax.mail.internet.*;
import java.util.*;

public class FlashMail {

  public FlashMail(){}

  // this method is used by the public method to retrieve
```

```
  // the user's inbox
  private Folder connect(String un, String pw, String host) throws
Exception{

    // the Session object provides access to the Store
    // object - which is what connects to the server
    Session session =
Session.getDefaultInstance(System.getProperties(), null);

    // get the Store object, specify a POP3 protocol
    Store store = session.getStore("pop3");

    // connect to the server with the username and
    // password provided
    store.connect(host, un, pw);

    // with a POP3 account there is only one folder - the
    // INBOX. Retrieve this Folder
    Folder inbox = store.getFolder("INBOX");

    // open the inbox for read/write access
    inbox.open(Folder.READ_WRITE);
    return inbox;
  }

  // get all the messages in the inbox
  public ArrayList getMessages(String un, String pw, String host)
throws Exception{

    // call the connect() method to get the Folder object
    Folder inbox = connect(un, pw, host);

    // get all the messages from the inbox
    Message[] messages = inbox.getMessages();
    Hashtable ht;
    ArrayList al = new ArrayList();

    // loop through all the messages
    for(int i = 0; i < messages.length; i++){

      // create a new Hashtable and add to it the keys
      // subject, from, and sent with the values from the
      // message
      ht = new Hashtable();
      ht.put("id", new Integer(messages[i].getMessageNumber()));
      ht.put("subject", messages[i].getSubject());
      ht.put("from", messages[i].getFrom()[0].toString());
      ht.put("sent", messages[i].getSentDate());
      // add to the ArrayList the message's Hashtable
      al.add(ht);
    }
```

Continued

Listing 24-2: *(continued)*

```
    // close the inbox Folder and return the ArrayList of
    // message Hashtables
    inbox.close(true);
    return al;
}

// get a single message
public Hashtable getMessage(String un, String pw, String host, int
id) throws Exception{

    // call the connect() method to get the inbox
    Folder inbox = connect(un, pw, host);

    // get the message with indicated id
    Message m = inbox.getMessage(id);
    String body;

    // if the mime type is text/plain then the body is
    // retrieved by getContent(). But if the message is
    // multipart then process it with the
    // getMultipartContent() function (defined next), and
    // otherwise, simply convert the value that
    // getContent() returns to a String
    if(m.isMimeType("text/plain")){
      body = (String)m.getContent();
    }
    else if(m.isMimeType("multipart/*")){
      body = getMultipartContent((Multipart)m.getContent());
    }
    else{
      body = m.getContent().toString();
    }

    // create a Hashtable for the message, fill it with
    // keys from, subject, and body
    Hashtable ht = new Hashtable();
    ht.put("from", m.getFrom()[0].toString());
    ht.put("subject", m.getSubject());
    ht.put("body", body);

    // close the inbox and return the message Hashtable
    inbox.close(true);
    return ht;
}

// a private method used by getMessage() to extract the
// content of a message that is multipart
private String getMultipartContent(Multipart mp) throws Exception{
```

```
      String ct;
      StringBuffer sb = new StringBuffer();

      // get the parts contained within the message
      int c = mp.getCount();
      MimeBodyPart mbp;
      sb.append("this message contains multiple parts\n");

      // loop through each part of the message
      for(int i = 0; i < c; i++){
        sb.append("------------------ part ");
        sb.append((i + 1));
        sb.append(" ------------------\n");
        mbp = (MimeBodyPart)mp.getBodyPart(i);

        // if the content type of the message part is
        // text of some kind then append that content
        // to the StringBuffer, otherwise, indicate that it
        // is of a type that cannot be viewed
        ct = mbp.getContentType();
        if(ct.startsWith("text/")){
          sb.append((String)mbp.getContent());
        }
        else{
          sb.append("This part of the message contains an attachment, and
cannot be viewed");
        }
      }
      return sb.toString();
  }

  // send an email
  public void sendEmail(String to, String from, String subject, String
body, String host) throws Exception{
      Properties props = System.getProperties();

      // set the host to use
      props.put("mail.smtp.host", host);

      Session session = Session.getDefaultInstance(props, null);

      // create the new message and fill its contents
      MimeMessage message = new MimeMessage(session);
      message.setFrom(new InternetAddress(from));
      message.addRecipient(Message.RecipientType.TO, new
InternetAddress(to));
      message.setSubject(subject);
      message.setText(body);
      // send the message
      Transport.send(message);
  }
```

Continued

Listing 24-2: *(continued)*

```
// delete a message
public ArrayList deleteMessage(String un, String pw, String host, int
id) throws Exception{

    // get the Folder object
    Folder inbox = connect(un, pw, host);

    // get the message with the specified id
    Message m = inbox.getMessage(id);

    // set the deleted flag to true
    m.setFlag(Flags.Flag.DELETED, true);

    // close the inbox to finalize the deletion
    inbox.close(true);

    // return the value from getMessages()
    return getMessages(un, pw, host);
}

}
```

---

6. Compile FlashMail.java into FlashMail.class, and keep it within the same chapter 24 directory.

Creating the .NET Assembly

If you use .NET, follow these steps:

1. Within the .NET Wiley Web application's bin directory (see Chapter 18 for details on setting this up), create a new assembly source document named FlashMail.cs (or FlashMail.vb).

2. In the FlashMail.cs document, add the code from Listing 24-3 and save it.

Web Resource

The VB version of this code can be found on the companion Web site, www.wiley.com/ compbooks/lott.

Listing 24-3: **FlashMail.cs**

```
using System;
using System.IO ;
using System.Net;
using System.Net.Sockets;
using System.Text;
```

```
using System.Collections;
using System.Web.Mail;

namespace Wiley.Chapter24 {

  public class FlashMail: System.Object{

    public FlashMail(){}

    // get all the messages from the inbox
    public ArrayList getMessages(String username, String password,
String host) {

      // TcpClient is the object by which the connection
      // to the server (via sockets) is made
      TcpClient tcpClient = new TcpClient();

      // the NetworkStream object is the way in which data
      // is sent across the socket connection
      NetworkStream netStream = null;

      // the makeConnection() method is a private method
      // that makes the socket connection and logs in the
      // user. the TcpClient and NetworkStream objects are
      // passed to it by reference, so they can be used
      // within this method after they are set in the
      // private method
      makeConnection(ref tcpClient, ref netStream, username, password,
host);

      // writeToNetStream is a private method that sends
      // commands to the server, and readFromNetStream is
      // a private method that reads the value from the
      // NetworkStream object. The STAT command returns
      // the basic status of the user's inbox - including
      // the number of messages.
      writeToNetStream(ref netStream, "STAT");
      string returnMsg = readFromNetStream(ref netStream);

      // The value returned from the STAT command can be
      // split into an array with values delimited by a
      // space, and the second element will be the number
      // of messages on the server
      string[] messagesData = returnMsg.Split(new char[] {' '});
      int count=Int32.Parse(messagesData[1]);

      ArrayList message =  new ArrayList();
      Hashtable ht;
      string s;
      ArrayList mAr = new ArrayList();
      StreamReader sr= new StreamReader(netStream);
```

Continued

Listing 24-3: *(continued)*

```
// loop from 1 (the number of the first message) to
// the number of messages on the server
for (int i = 1; i <= count; i++){
  // the TOP command retrieves the specified number
  // of lines (in this case 10) from the message
  // number indicated (by the value of i in this
  // example). This is simply to retrieve the
  // headers for the message. You could use the RETR
  // command, but that would retrieve the entire
  // body of the message as well, so TOP is slightly
  // more efficient in this case
  writeToNetStream(ref netStream, "TOP " + i + " 10");
  // read the from the StreamReader object (which is
  // the reader for netStream, the NetworkStream
  // that contains the data retrieved from the
  // server). Loop through all the lines of the
  // value that is returned from the TOP request,
  // and add those values to the message ArrayList
  s = sr.ReadLine();
  if(s[0]!='-') {
    message = new ArrayList();
    while(s!=".") {
      message.Add(s.Trim());
      s = sr.ReadLine();
    }
  }
  // the Hashtable contains the keys id, subject,
  // from, and sent, populated by the values
  // extracted from the message ArrayList. These
  // values are extracted by way of the
  // parseMessage() private method. The values
  // Subject: , From: , and Date: are the values
  // that are part of the standard message header
  ht = new Hashtable();
  ht.Add("id", i);
  ht.Add("subject", parseMessage("Subject: ", message));
  ht.Add("from", parseMessage("From: ", message));
  ht.Add("sent", parseMessage("Date: ", message));

  // add the Hashtable for the message to the mAr
  // ArrayList that will get returned to Flash
  mAr.Add(ht);
}
netStream.Close();
tcpClient.Close();
return mAr;
}
```

```
// get the contents of a single message by id. (much
// of the code in this method is the same as in
// getMessages(), so reference that method for any
// undocumented code about which you are uncertain)
public Hashtable getMessage(String username, String password,
String host, int id) {
    TcpClient tcpClient = new TcpClient();
    NetworkStream netStream = null;
    makeConnection(ref tcpClient, ref netStream, username, password,
host);

    ArrayList message = new ArrayList();
    Hashtable ht;
    string s;
    ArrayList mAr = new ArrayList();
    StreamReader sr= new StreamReader(netStream);
    writeToNetStream(ref netStream, "RETR " + id);
    s = sr.ReadLine();
    if(s[0]!='-') {
      message = new ArrayList();
      while(s!=".") {
        message.Add(s.Trim());
        s = sr.ReadLine();
      }
    }
    ht = new Hashtable();
    ht.Add("subject", parseMessage("Subject: ", message));
    ht.Add("from", parseMessage("From: ", message));
    ht.Add("body", parseMessage("body", message));
    netStream.Close();
    tcpClient.Close();
    return ht;
}

// send an email
public void sendEmail(String to, String from, String subject,
String body, String host) {
    MailMessage mail = new MailMessage();
    mail.To = to;
    mail.From = from;
    mail.BodyFormat = MailFormat.Text;
    mail.Subject = subject;
    mail.Body = body;
    SmtpMail.SmtpServer = host;
    SmtpMail.Send(mail);
}

// this method makes the connection to the host and
// logs the user in
private void makeConnection(ref TcpClient tcpClient, ref
NetworkStream netStream, string username, string password, string
host){
```

Continued

Listing 24-3: *(continued)*

```
    try {
      // connect to the host at port 110 (The standard
      // port for POP3 servers)
      tcpClient.Connect(host, 110);
    }
    catch {}

    // make sure the connection is successful
    netStream = tcpClient.GetStream();
    if(netStream == null) {
      throw new Exception("GetStream is null");
    }
    string returnMsg = readFromNetStream(ref netStream);

    // send the username and password to the server
    writeToNetStream(ref netStream, "USER " + username);
    returnMsg = readFromNetStream(ref netStream);
    writeToNetStream(ref netStream, "PASS " + password);
    returnMsg = readFromNetStream(ref netStream);

  }

  // extract a specific portion from a message
  private string parseMessage(string part, ArrayList src){
    string val, sub;
    // loop through each element of the ArrayList that
    // contains the message contents
    for(int i = 0; i < src.Count; i++){
      val = (string)src[i];

      // if the value body has been passed to the method
      // then search for the first line that is empty,
      // and return all the remaining lines.
      // otherwise, if part is not body (ie - Subject: ,
      // From: , etc), then search until finding the
      // element that starts with that value and return
      // the remainder of the line after the part value
      if(part.Equals("body")){
        if(val.Equals("")){
          string body = "";
          for(int j = i; j < src.Count; j++){
            body += (string)src[j] + "\n";
          }
          return body;
        }
      }
      else{
        if(val.IndexOf(part) != -1){
```

```
                    sub = val.Substring(part.Length);
                    return sub;
                }
            }
        }
        return null;
    }

    // send commands over the NetworkStream
    private void writeToNetStream(ref NetworkStream netStream, string
Command) {

        string stringToSend = Command + "\r\n";

        // the command that is sent must be converted to an
        // array of Bytes
        Byte[] arrayToSend =
Encoding.ASCII.GetBytes(stringToSend.ToCharArray());

        // call the Write() method of the NetworkStream,
        // passing it the array of Bytes
        netStream.Write(arrayToSend, 0, arrayToSend.Length);
    }

    // read from the NetworkStream object
    private String readFromNetStream(ref NetworkStream netStream) {
        StringBuilder strReceived= new StringBuilder();
        StreamReader sr= new StreamReader(netStream);
        String strLine = sr.ReadLine();
        while(strLine==null || strLine.Length==0) {
            strLine = sr.ReadLine();
        }
        strReceived.Append(strLine);
        if(sr.Peek()!=-1) {
            while ((strLine=sr.ReadLine())!=null) {
                strReceived.Append(strLine);
            }
        }
        return strReceived.ToString();
    }


}
}
```

Note

At the time of this writing, the .NET framework does not offer an API specifically for retrieving e-mail messages from the server. Instead, this has to be done by manually creating a socket connection to the server and issuing commands to it over the socket connection. The example code in Listing 24-3 (FlashMail.cs) does not provide a method for deleting a message, and so that functionality will not work as it does with ColdFusion and Java.

3. Compile FlashMail.cs (or FlashMail.vb) to FlashMail.dll, and keep it in the same bin directory as the source.

Developing the FlashMail Client Interface

The third step in creating the FlashMail application is to create the Flash movie:

1. Open a new Flash document and save it as flashMail.fla.

2. Rename the default layer to form, and create a three additional layers named frame actions, actions, and labels

3. Create a new Movie Clip symbol named MessageListing. This symbol is a custom component that is used to list the messages from the inbox.

4. Edit MessageListing.

5. Rename the default layer to form, and create two additional layers named text and background.

6. On the background layer, draw a light gray rectangle with a black outline. The rectangle should be 540 pixels by 21 pixels. Position the rectangle so that the upper, left corner is at 0,0. Figure 24-1 shows what this looks like.

7. On the text layer, add three dynamic TextField objects with border turned off. Set the font size to 9 in each of them. Position them as shown in Figure 24-1, and name them (from left to right) from, subject, and sentDate.

Figure 24-1: The layout of the MessageListing symbol

8. On the actions layer, add the following code:

```
// the #initclip and #endinitclip are important because
// they ensure that the code that is between them will be
// run before the code on the Main Timeline so that the
// MessageListing class will be accessible for use from
// the Main Timeline
#initclip

// important that MessageListing must extend the
// MovieClip class
MessageListing.prototype = new MovieClip();

function MessageListing(){}

// this it the method that gets called to set the
// values within the listing
MessageListing.prototype.setData = function(o){
  this.id = o.id;
```

```
       this.subject.text = o.subject;
       this.from.text = o.from;
       this.sentDate.text = o.sent;
   }

   // register the class so that the linkage id
   // MessageListing is associated with the MessageListing
   // class
   Object.registerClass("MessageListing", MessageListing);

   #endinitclip
```

9. Edit the linkage properties for MessageListing. Check the Export for ActionScript and Export in first frame options, and set the linkage identifier to MessageListing.

10. Return to the Main Timeline.

11. On the form, frame actions, and labels layers, add new keyframes to frames 2 and 3.

12. On the actions layer, add regular (non-keyframe) frames to frames 2 and 3.

13. On the first frame of the form layer, add three input `TextField` objects with border turned on. Position them as shown in Figure 24-2. Name the instances (from top to bottom) `username`, `password`, and `host`. Set `username` and `host` to be single-line, and set `password` to be a password type.

14. Add a `PushButton` instance as shown in Figure 24-2. Name this instance `loginBtn`.

15. Add static text labels as shown in Figure 24-2.

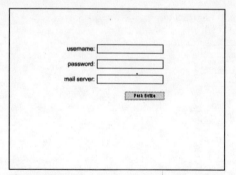

Figure 24-2: The layout of frame one of the Main Timeline

16. On frame 2 of the form layer, add two `ScrollPane` component instances. The positioning and size does not matter because ActionScript will handle it. Name the instances `inboxSp` and `messageViewer`.

17. At the bottom of the stage, place three `PushButton` instances named (from left to right) `newBtn`, `replyBtn`, and `deleteBtn`. See Figure 24-3 for the layout.

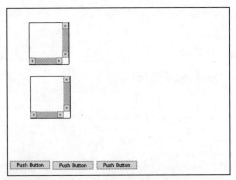

Figure 24-3: The layout of frame two of the
Main Timeline

18. On frame 3 of the form layer, add three single-line input `TextField` objects with border turned on. Position them as shown in Figure 24-4. Name these instances (from top to bottom) `from`, `to`, and `subject`.

19. Below the single-line `TextField` objects, add a multiline input `TextField` object with border turned on. Name this instance `message`, and position it as shown in Figure 24-4.

20. Drag an instance of the `ScrollBar` component onto `message` so that it snaps to it. (Snapping must be turned on for this to work).

21. Add a `PushButton` component instance at the bottom of the stage. Name the instance `sendBtn`.

22. Add static text labels as shown in Figure 24-4.

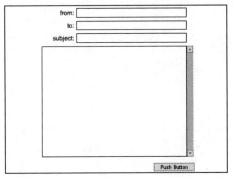

Figure 24-4: The layout of frame three of the
Main Timeline

23. On the labels layer, name frame 2 `inbox` and name frame 3 `compose`.

24. On the actions layer, add the following code:

```
#include "NetServices.as"

function init(){
  // use the correct gateway URL for your server
  var gwURL = "http://localhost/Wiley/flashgateway.aspx";
  NetServices.setDefaultGatewayURL(gwURL);
  var conn = NetServices.createGatewayConnection();
  // the service name varies slightly depending on the
  // platform:
  // CF - Wiley.chapter24.FlashMail
  // Java - wiley.chapter24.FlashMail
  // .NET - Wiley.Chapter24.FlashMail
  _root.srv = conn.getService("Wiley.Chapter24.FlashMail");
}

// this function clears all the MovieClips from _root
function clear(){
  for(var mc in _root){
    _root[mc].removeMovieClip();
  }
}

// calls getMessages() service function with the username,
// password, and host stored in a user object on _root
function getMessages(){
  var un = _root.user.un;
  var pw = _root.user.pw;
  var host = _root.user.host;
  _root.srv.getMessages(_root.getMessagesRes, un, pw, host);
}

// function called from the onResult() for both
// getMessagesRes and deleteRes
function listInbox(result){
  var i = 0;
  // create a MovieClip to hold the inbox list
  var inbox = _root.createEmptyMovieClip("inbox", 1);
  // loop through all the returned values from the server
  for(var message in result){
    // create a MessageListing component instance
    ml = inbox.attachMovie("MessageListing", "ml" + i, i);
    // position the component
    ml._y = i * 30;
    // set the data of the component to the values
    // returned for this message
    ml.setData(result[message]);
    // when the component is clicked, call the
    // getMessage() service function
    ml.onRelease = function(){
```

```
                    _root.selectedMessage = {id: this.id};
                    _root.srv.getMessage(_root.getMessageRes,
                                        _root.user.un,
                                        _root.user.pw,
                                        _root.user.host,
                                        parseInt(this.id));
            }
            i++;
        }
        // set the inboxSp scroll content to the inbox MovieClip
        _root.inboxSp.setScrollContent(inbox);
}

getMessagesRes = new Object();
getMessagesRes.onResult = listInbox;

getMessageRes = new Object();
getMessageRes.onResult = function(result){
    // store these values in selectedMessage for use with
    // the reply functionality
    _root.selectedMessage.from = result.from;
    _root.selectedMessage.subject = result.subject;
    _root.selectedMessage.body = result.body;
    // create a MovieClip called messageHolder, and a
    // TextField object in it to contain the value of the
    // message. Make the TextField 530 pixels wide
    var mh = _root.createEmptyMovieClip("messageHolder", 2);
    mh.createTextField("message", 1, 0, 0, 530, 0);
    mh.message.multiline = true;
    mh.message.wordWrap = true;
    mh.message.text = "from: " + result.from + newline;
    mh.message.text += "subject: " + result.subject + newline;
    mh.message.text += result.body;
    // set the height of the TextField to the height
    // of its contents
    mh.message._height = mh.message.textHeight + 5;
    _root.messageViewer.setScrollContent(mh);
}

// when the user sends an email, return to the inbox
// screen
sendRes = new Object();
sendRes.onResult = function(){
    _root.gotoAndStop("inbox");
}

// when the response is returned from the deleteMessage()
// service function then clear the text from the current
// message and call the getMessages() function to refresh
// the messages listed in the inbox
```

```
deleteRes = new Object();
deleteRes.onResult = function(){
  _root.messageHolder.message.text = "";
  _root.getMessages();
}
```

25. On frame 1 of the frame actions layer, add the following code:

```
stop();
if(!inited){
  inited = true;
  init();
}

loginBtn.setLabel("login");
loginBtn.onRelease = function(){
  var un = _root.username.text;
  var pw = _root.password.text;
  var host = _root.host.text;
  _root.user = {un: un, pw: pw, host: host};
  _root.gotoAndStop("inbox");
}
```

26. On frame 2 of the frame actions layer, add the following code:

```
getMessages();

inboxSp._x = 5;
inboxSp._y = 0;
inboxSp.setSize(540, 100);
messageViewer._x = 5;
messageViewer._y = 100;
messageViewer.setSize(540, 250);

newBtn.setLabel("new email");
newBtn.onRelease = function(){
  _root.clear();
  _root.gotoAndStop("compose");
}

replyBtn.setLabel("reply");
replyBtn.onRelease = function(){
  _root.clear();
  _root.action = "reply";
  _root.gotoAndStop("compose");
}

deleteBtn.setLabel("delete");
deleteBtn.onRelease = function(){
  _root.srv.deleteMessage(_root.deleteRes, _root.user.un,
_root.user.pw, _root.user.host, _root.selectedMessage.id);
}
```

27. On frame 3 of the frame actions layer, add the following code:

```
if(action == "reply"){
  to.text = selectedMessage.from;
  subject.text = "RE: " + selectedMessage.subject;
  message.text = "\n\n#########################################\n";
  message.text += "below is the content of your original email\n";
  message.text += "#########################################\n\n";
  message.text += selectedMessage.body;
  Selection.setFocus(message);
  Selection.setSelection(0, 0);
}

sendBtn.setLabel("send");
sendBtn.onRelease = function(){
  var to = _root.to.text;
  var from = _root.from.text;
  var subject = _root.subject.text;
  var message = _root.message.text;
  _root.srv.sendEmail(_root.sendRes, to, from, subject, message,
_root.user.host);
}
```

28. Test your movie. Figure 24-5 shows the login screen. Enter your username, password, and e-mail server host information, and then click the login button.

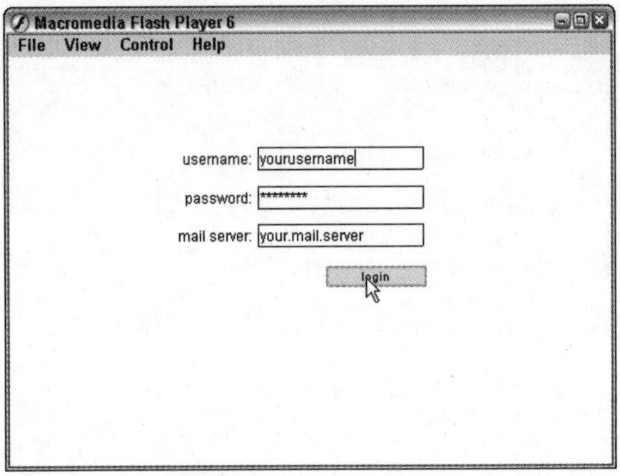

Figure 24-5: The login screen

Figure 24-6 shows the list of messages in the inbox: one from greader@somewhere.org and one from igoodie@goodie.com. By clicking on one of the messages in the list, the full e-mail message is retrieved and displayed.

Once an e-mail message is displayed, you can reply to it or delete it. In Figure 24-7, you can see that in the reply, the "to" and "subject" fields are automatically filled out, and the body of the original message is included in the response.

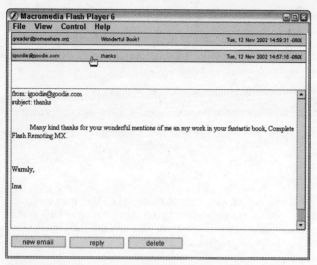

Figure 24-6: The inbox listing and the view of an e-mail message

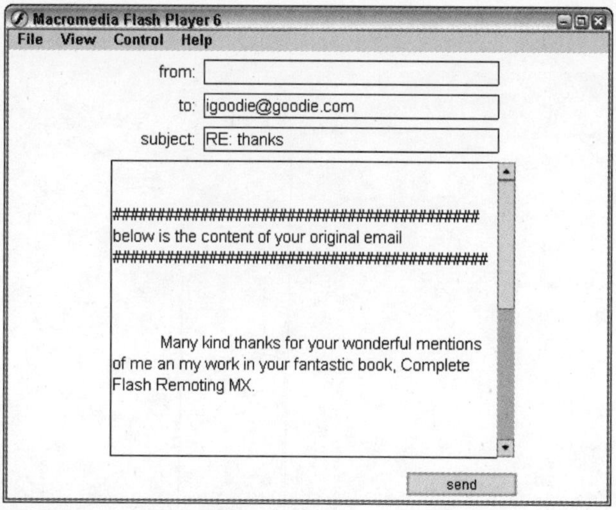

Figure 24-7: The reply to an e-mail

Extending the E-mail Client

In this chapter, you created a relatively basic e-mail client using Flash Remoting. Of course, there are many ways in which you could add further functionality to this example application. Here is a list of some ideas:

Tip   Several of these ideas would require that you add a database to the back-end of the application.

✦ Enable users to create accounts whereby they can save multiple e-mail accounts that can be retrieved through a single interface.

✦ Enable users to store contact information in an address book.

✦ Create search functionality to enable searching for messages containing certain text.

✦ Enable the user to sort the contents of the inbox according to sender, subject, or date.

Summary

In this chapter, you created a simple e-mail client that uses a Flash user interface. The e-mail client is designed so that you can retrieve e-mail messages from any POP3 mail server. You can then read, reply to, and delete those messages. Additionally, the e-mail client allows you to compose and send new e-mail messages.

✦   ✦   ✦

Index

Symbols & Numbers

& (ampersand), 21
&& (ampersand, double), 21
&= (ampersand, equals sign), 20
* (asterisk), 20
*= (asterisk, equals sign), 19
*/ (asterisk, forward slash), 13
\ (backslash), 14
\b)backspace, b), 15
^ (caret), 21
^= (caret, equals sign), 20
{} (curly braces), 26–27, 32
$ (dollar sign), 18
. (dot), 49
== (equals sign, double), 20
=== (equals sign, triple), 20, 23
! (exclamation point), 21
!== (exclamation point, double equals sign),
    20, 23
!= (exclamation point, equals sign), 20
/ (forward slash), 20
/* (forward slash, asterisk), 13
// (forward slash, double), 13
/= (forward slash, equals sign), 19
> (greater than operator), 20
>= (greater than or equal operator), 20
> (greater than operator, double), 21
>>= (greater than operator, triple with equals
    operator), 20
> (greater than sign, double), 21
>> (greater than sign, triple), 21
<= (less than, equals operators), 20
< (less than operator), 20
<< (less than operator, double), 21
- (minus sign), 20
— (minus sign, double), 20
% (percent sign), 20, 289
| (pipe symbol), 21
|| (pipe symbol, double), 21
|= (pipe symbol, equals sign), 20
+ (plus sign), 20
++ (plus sign, double), 20
+= (plus sign, equals sign), 19
(pound sign), 105, 151, 153
?: (question mark, colon), 21
" (quotation marks), 14, 153
; (semicolon), 13
_ (underscore), 18
~ (tilde), 21

A

abstractions, 35
Access (Microsoft), 80
account information, 52
Action Message Format. *See* AMF
action, operators signifying
    binary, 23–24
    ColdFusion MX, 149, 152–153
    described, 19
    listed, 20–21
    shortcut, 21–23
    strict equality, 23
ActionScript
    CFC service, example, 187
    class, defining and registering, 398
    code, examining detail, 71–73
    comments, 12–13
    conditional and looping statements, 25–29
    converting
        from ColdFusion, 155
        to ColdFusion, 154–155
        from Java, 339–342
        to Java, 342
        from .NET, 363–364
        to .NET, 363, 410
        to SSAS, 249–253
    data, 13–17
    described, 9
    event handler methods, 38–39
    expressions and operators, 19–24